Archaeology: The Historical Development of Civilizations

Second Edition

Thomas C. Patterson
Temple University

PRENTICE HALL, Englewood Cliffs, New Jersey 07632

Library of Congress Cataloging-in-Publication Data

PATTERSON, THOMAS CARL.
   Archaeology: the historical development of civilizations/Thomas
C. Patterson,—2nd ed.
      p. cm.
   Includes bibliographical references and index.
   ISBN 0-13-044298-4
   1. Civilization, Ancient. 2. Archaeology. 3. Protohistory.
I. Title.
CB311.P35 1992
930—dc20
                                              92-16556
                                                 CIP

Editorial/production supervision
  and interior design: Kari Callaghan Mazzola
Acquisitions editor: Nancy Roberts
Cover design: Maureen Eide
Prepress buyer: Kelly Behr
Manufacturing buyer: Mary Ann Gloriande

 © 1993, 1981 by Prentice-Hall, Inc.
A Simon & Schuster Company
Englewood Cliffs, New Jersey 07632

Printed in the United States of America
10 9 8 7 6 5 4 3 2 1

ISBN 0-13-044298-4

PRENTICE-HALL INTERNATIONAL (UK) LIMITED, *London*
PRENTICE-HALL OF AUSTRALIA PTY. LIMITED, *Sydney*
PRENTICE-HALL CANADA INC., *Toronto*
PRENTICE-HALL HISPANOAMERICANA, S.A., *Mexico*
PRENTICE-HALL OF INDIA PRIVATE LIMITED, *New Delhi*
PRENTICE-HALL OF JAPAN, INC., *Tokyo*
SIMON & SCHUSTER ASIA PTE. LTD., *Singapore*
EDITORA PRENTICE-HALL DO BRASIL, LTDA., *Rio de Janeiro*

Contents

Preface

A set of events, inextricably interwoven, formed a backdrop to this book. The first was a bitter, month-long faculty strike at Temple University where I teach. I actually started writing the day the strike began. I would write several hours each morning before leaving at 7 A.M. to work at strike head-quarters and walk picket lines. At the end of the day, after intense discussions of tactics and strategies, I would come home to watch the evening TV news shows which juxtaposed the strike against the other sets: the preparations and justifications for the deployment of U.S. troops to the Persian Gulf and the dissolution of centralized state power in various parts of Eastern Europe and the USSR. These too became topics of discussion and debate, part of everyday life, on the picketlines and especially in classrooms after the strike ended and I had begun to work with a peace group that was concerned with examining how and to what extent the mass media had become a propaganda office for the war department. These experiences provided insights that helped me contemplate seriously the implications of the discussions and views of individuals who were more centrally involved in the events than I was.

The fabric composed of the sets of events tells a story about how people resist in various ways and with varying degrees of success the practices of ruling classes and states that attempt to limit or cancel their capacity as actors to make their own history under circumstances not of their own choosing. The constraints imposed by states are never complete or total. The story also relates how rulers and the states they erect are bullies. While their power to police may seem and may actually be enormous, their authority ultimately rests on fragile foundations, because they must continually reproduce conditions for their being or create new ones in the never-ending, unequal struggle to maintain their position in the existing social order. These actions ultimately produce new crises and provide new opportunities for actors to remake that social order. As we have so vividly seen in the last decade, even states with apparently well-developed repressive apparatuses can be toppled quickly when people correctly access the contradictions that exist and are able to turn them to their own advantage.

The archaeological evidence examined in this book tells a similar story. The early civilizations—those class-structured, state-based societies that originally arose out of kin-organized communities and turned their members into taxpayers—were also fragile. They crystallized at different times and places and disintegrated as subject populations resisted their exactions, claims of legitimacy, and attempts to transform custom into laws that benefited rulers who continually tried to separate themselves from kin and neighbors.

Archaeology is a historical social science concerned with power and historical origins. In a very real sense, it is about how the present incorporates and understands the past. Since I teach courses that reflect on historical and philosophical issues and that stress critical thinking, I have had to struggle to make the materials my students and I discuss relevant for their goals without losing sight of how the social relations of past societies interpenetrate our own. It has meant broadening the focus of my own thought to show how the materials I teach are related to what is happening in the world today and to critical currents taught in other disciplines. In this milieu, I no longer have the burden of teaching archaeology as if it were insulated, or hermetically sealed, from what has happened and is happening outside the classroom, the university, or even the United States. This has been one of the two or three truly liberating and growth-producing experiences of my life.

Numerous people have helped me clarify my thoughts while I was writing or preparing to write this book. I especially want to thank Elizabeth Brumfiel of Albion College and Robert Paynter of the University of Massachusetts, who provided instantaneous and constructive criticism of the manuscript; needless to say, I have followed some but not all of their advice. I also want to express my gratitude to Talal Asad, Barbara Bender, Martin Bernal, Richard Burger, Carole Crumley, Stanley Diamond, Terrence Epperson, Christine Gailey, John Gledhill, Peter Gran, Lotte Hedeager, Tim Kaiser, Phil Kohl, Kristian Kristiansen, Mogens Larsen, Richard Lee, Mark Leone, Janet Levy, William Marquardt, Michael Moseley, Viana Muller, Don Nonini, Richard Pearson, Lucy Salazar, Karen Brodkin Sacks, Peter Schmidt, Karen Spalding, Maurizio Tosi, Bruce Trigger, and Martin Wobst, who have shared thoughts, criticisms, and insights. I am grateful to Jennifer Alvey, Ananth Aiyer, Nancy Roberts, and Kari Callaghan Mazzola, who helped with the final preparation of the manuscript and illustrations. Most importantly, I want to thank my students who have asked hard questions over the years and required me to think more clearly and in new ways.

Tom Patterson
Philadelphia, PA

chapter 1

Archaeology

You can't forget the past any more than you can change it. (Jake Gittes, The Two Jakes)

This story is about you. (Karl Marx, Capital)

Archaeology, according to some popular images, involves lost civilizations, unsolved mysteries about our past, the discovery of inscriptions or ancient cities in some remote part of the world, and the excavation of amazing treasures from the tomb of a long-dead ruler. Such views typically suggest that archaeologists spend all their time tramping through jungles or across deserts in search of lost tombs, cities, or civilizations and that they usually stumble accidentally across significant information. Let us reflect on the following story for a moment.

Nearly a century ago, Sir Leonard Woolley and his colleague MacIver had been excavating at an ancient town in the Sudan for nearly two months. They had searched in vain for the cemetery, which they thought would provide them with invaluable information about how the townspeople had treated their dead. They thought this knowledge would give them a glimpse of everyday life in the town—a presupposition based on the experiences of archaeologists who had previously conducted excavations at other localities.

One evening, after working all day, they walked to the top of a hill near the town to watch the sun set over the Nile Valley. Suddenly they both noticed that the plain below them was dotted with dark circles. Woolley ran down the hill, and as he approached the flat plain the circles began to disappear. MacIver called out from above, directing him to each of the patches in turn, in the middle of which Woolley made a small pile of earth. The next morning they began excavating at those piles. At every one they found the entrance to a stone-lined tomb that had been made by the ancient residents of the town. The dark patches—visible from the hilltop for only a few moments each day, when the sun's rays struck them at just the right angle—were produced by little splinters of stone chipped from the bedrock that the townspeople had dug into when they made the tombs and covered them over with the dirt and rock from the holes they had made.

This story might lead us to suspect that Woolley and MacIver were incredibly lucky—blessed with exceptional good fortune. Although there is an element of truth in this view, it is not the whole story. Archaeologists are continually on the lookout for those minute deviations from the natural—the subtle clues used by detectives—that indicate that some sort of human activity had occurred in one locality and not in another. If Woolley and MacIver had not been curious about the location of the cemetery and the information it might contain, they might never have recognized the significance of those dark patches of earth that dotted the Nile Valley plain.

ARCHAEOLOGY IS HISTORICAL SOCIAL SCIENCE

The task of archaeology is bringing the past back to life. Archaeologists want to know what everyday life was like at different times and places in the past as well as how it has developed through time. To find out, they might excavate the remains found in a 2-million-year-old site in East Africa; they might study a series of 5,000- to 8,000-year-old villages and dumps on the central coast of Peru to examine the impact the adoption of agriculture and food storage had on the inhabitants of that region; or they might examine the ruins of a Roman villa and those of nearby contemporary settlements to learn about the structure of provincial society in the days of the Roman Empire.

Archaeologists describe what they do in different ways. For most, archaeology is a historical science whose objective is to reconstruct past forms of society and their development and to study the processes of their transformation up to their union with modern societies. It involves the recovery of information about past societies through various techniques, including most notably excavation and systematic reconnaissance. More important, it involves analyzing that information to answer certain questions or to solve particular problems.

Although most archaeologists claim their major goals are the recovery, reconstruction, and recuperation of past societies, some also argue variously that they study the archaeological record for itself, that they examine the material remains of ancient societies to explain the cultural similarities and differences that existed at various times and places and how these developed historically, or that they are concerned with the interpretive practices and theories they use to relate the past to the present. This diversity of aims subtly reflects the historical development of archaeology itself. Let us briefly consider the history of archaeology and the roles it has played in societies that are undergoing profound political-economic, social, and cultural transformations.

In *Hippias Maior*, Plato (429–347 B.C.) wrote a dialogue that reputedly had taken place about a century earlier between a traveling teacher, or sophist, named Hippias and the noted philosopher, Socrates. In the dialogue, Hippias—that is, Plato—used the classical Greek word *archaiologia* to refer to inquiries into the ancestral traditions and customs of peoples and city-states, stories about the origins and ancient histories of cities, genealogies of heroes and men, and lists of archons or rulers. In the early fourth century B.C., the stem *arche* meant both "beginning" and "power"; as a result, it is the root of words that refer to origins, like *archaeology*, and of other words that involve the idea of power, for example, *monarch* ("ruler") and *hierarchy* ("belonging to a ranked order"). When Plato wrote, the two meanings were connected. Powerful individuals and city-states and pervasive customs and practices were those with historical roots.

People used accounts of the origins of cities or customs to legitimate and explain the existing social order or the changes that occurred when the positions and power relations of different states were transformed. Thus,

(a)

(b)

Archaeologists locate sites in various ways. (a) Remains, like those of a local lord's palace at San Juan de Pariache near Lima, Peru, are often exposed on the surface. (b) Remains, like this portion of an ancient platform mound at Ancón, Peru, are frequently exposed by construction or archaeological excavation.

archaiologia, the study of beginnings and power, potentially involved something more than the mere pursuit of antiquarian knowledge. The word *archaiologia* continued to be used into the first century A.D. Flavius Josephus wrote a book about the history of the Jewish people from their origins to the present with the word in its title, and Dionysius of Halicarnassus wrote another archaeology book that dealt with the archaic history of Rome. Their accounts were based on oral traditions and legends as well as classical and biblical texts.

However, the sophist practitioners of archaeology were not the only individuals in the ancient Greek world who wrote about power and the past. For example, Herodotus's (484–420 B.C.) *History* describes wars and revolts that occurred a generation before he was born as well as contemporary barbarians—that is, non-Greek-speaking foreigners—who lived in Egypt, Babylonia, and around the Black Sea. The *History of the Peloponnesian War*, written by the aristocratic Thucydides, relates details of a series of military expeditions that occurred during his lifetime and emphasizes the roles of individuals in the events, power politics, and imperialism of the period between 431 and 404 B.C. The emphasis Herodotus and Thucydides placed on current events or those of the recent past distinguished their writings from those of the archaeologists, who dealt with the more remote or distant past.

There was a resurgence of archaeological and historical scholarship on both sides of the Mediterranean during the fourteenth and fifteenth centuries. It coincided with a massive reorganization of commerce in the Mediterranean world, which was accompanied by important shifts in the distribution of wealth and political power throughout the region. These changes left the inhabitants of Mediterranean North Africa and Europe with the problem of having to explain what had happened to the traditional social order of their world. In the *Muqaddimah*, Ibn Khaldun (A.D. 1337–1406)—the great North African diplomat, historian, and social theorist—tied the social and cultural transformation of his world to changes in mercantile trade and the structures of everyday life.

The practice of archaeology gained renewed vigor in Florence and the other city-states of northern Italy during the fifteenth century, as intellectuals attempted to provide new accounts of their place in a changing world. They borrowed heavily from earlier writers; they constructed new worldviews that incorporated elements of the classical and Judeo-Christian perspectives that were already familiar or that they had discovered buried away in the copyists' archives of some medieval monastery. From their standpoint, the new social order was dynamic, constantly in flux. For many, especially the philosophers and writers called humanists, man could regain the freedom lost during the Middle Ages by retrieving and developing the capacities possessed by the peoples of classical antiquity. Thus, ancient Rome became a standard of excellence and, hence, an object worthy of investigation.

Fifteenth-century Renaissance humanists began to identify and examine various kinds of objects or monuments that had survived from antiquity for information about the past societies of the Mediterranean world and beyond.

They and their successors combined these studies with information derived from historical texts, inscriptions, traditions, genealogies, and place names—a combination of sources that constituted a well-established domain or discipline of knowledge, called antiquarianism, which thrived from the fifteenth to the nineteenth centuries.

In the waning years of the seventeenth century, Jacob Spon (1647–1685) coined the Latin word *archaeologia* to refer to what antiquarians did when they studied objects and monuments rather than the other sources of information about the past. Spon was distinguishing these practices of the antiquarians from those activities they pursued when they focused on the other kinds of information. This distinction became even more firmly rooted after the middle of the eighteenth century. Archaeologists studied ancient remains, whereas antiquarians concerned themselves with legends, place names, topographies, curiosities, relics, and even natural histories.

Spon's distinction took place against the backdrop of the scientific revolution of the late seventeenth and eighteenth centuries, which incorporated the influences of the commercial revolution (clocks, astronomy, and navigation), gave primacy to mathematics as both a basis for truth and a method of inquiry, adopted a worldview that incorporated a mechanistic philosophy (nature consists of inert matter that is in motion and can be understood in terms of the mathematical relationships governing that motion) and ideas about the destruction of nature, and embraced the concept of natural laws. In the new intellectual climate created by the scientific revolution, archaeology came to be viewed as a set of practices or techniques that could be used to gather information about the past. Conceptualizing archaeology in this fashion made it possible to focus exclusively on objects and to study them independently from the people who manufactured and used them.

Archaeology, as we know it today, has its roots in the turbulent, interconnected events of the late eighteenth century—the Industrial Revolution, the formation of capitalist social relations, the rise of modern nationalism, and Enlightenment thought. Cutting trees for fuel and to clear new lands for farming as well as the construction of railroads and canals in Europe exposed and destroyed many archaeological sites, tombs, and caches of objects before and after 1800. In Denmark, the state claimed these objects as state property and opened the first museum of archaeology in 1807 to preserve and stimulate interest in the grandeurs of the nation's past. Mining activities for coal and building materials provided new information and understandings about geology, stratigraphy, the age of the earth, and the processes involved in its formation, as well as the existence of worlds that had very different kinds of plants and animals than the modern one.

Enlightenment writers, like Adam Smith and his contemporaries in Scotland and France, began to conceptualize the development of human society as a progression through a series of stages characterized by different modes of subsistence. In their view, in the earliest stage of human society, people hunted and fished, lived in small communities, were satisfied with their circumstances, and had neither property nor viable forms of government. This era was followed by barbarism—a stage or stages in which people farmed or herded, exhibited diverse forms of government, and had communal notions about property. Civilized society, the highest stage of social development, had a number of characteristics that distinguished it from savagery and barbarism: cities; social classes; state institutions and practices; commerce; money; writing; continuous wars; and most important, private property. Thus, the highest stage of social development resembled the kind of society that was emerging in the rapidly industrializing regions of Europe, whereas the earlier stages invoked images of various native peoples in the Americas, the South Sea Islands, Asia, and Africa.

Christian Thomsen, the son of a wealthy Copenhagen merchant and the first director of the Danish National Museum, gave material expression to this framework when he organized the museum's exhibits in terms of the "Three Age System." Many of the inquiries that were conducted in Europe and North America at this time were concerned with equating archaeological remains with particular peoples, usually the earliest mentioned inhabitants of a region, or with identifying their stage of development.

Individuals—like Thomas Jefferson—who conducted these inquiries or who made observations relevant to archaeology were not, of course, archaeologists. They were not technicians who earned their livelihood through the practice of archaeology, regardless of how finely honed their technical skills might have been. The technicians came later, after the field was professionalized, after the anonymous antiquities markets emerged, and after the demand for certain kinds of information about the past was already established and routinized. Thomsen, Jefferson, and their contemporaries and immediate successors were traditional or organic intellectuals who gave voice, respectively, to the sentiments and views of already existing or emerging social classes in a social order that had not yet established itself on firm ground. They used a wide variety of information, including incorporated archaeological evidence, viewed through the lenses afforded by the various strands of Enlightenment social thought, to shed light on the important issues of the day.

History and archaeology were concerned with practical issues; their goal was not to reconstruct the past as it had been in order to satisfy some antiquarian curiosity but rather to illuminate the constant and universal principles of human nature. In the United States, the archaeology of classical antiquity, the Holy Land and the Bible, and America's past were examined for different reasons by nineteenth-century writers. Classical antiquity represented civilization, a set of images that could be and was appropriated for the emerging nation state—for example, the Roman eagle, the Senate, classical styles of architecture, and place names like Rome or Athens. Biblical history and archaeology were important because they linked missionary activity and the adoption of Christianity as necessary features of the process of becoming civilized. Archaeological evidence from the Americas was deployed by settler-colonists in arguments that sought to deny or limit the property rights of native peoples, whose everyday lives were being transformed by

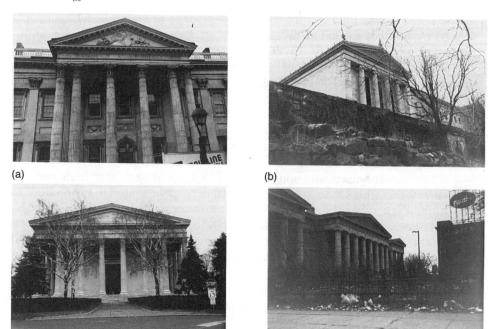

(a)

(b)

(c)

(d)

Ruling classes and states appropriate the symbolism and imagery associated with historical monuments to create heritages that legitimize existing or emerging social relations. Examples of such archaisms are (a) The First Bank of the United States, built in Philadelphia in 1824–1826; (b) Girard College, built between 1833 and 1848—its original charter was to educate orphaned Caucasian boys in Philadelphia; (c) The Philadelphia Museum of Art, built between 1926 and 1929; and (d) The Ridgeway Branch of the Library Company built in the 1870s, sold to the Free Library of Philadelphia in 1944, closed in 1955.

civilizing processes such as commerce, dispossession from their homelands, destruction of their customary institutions and practices, genocide, and resistance.

Archaeology became professionalized in a number of countries during the 1870s and 1880s. Up to that time, the practitioners of archaeology were devotees of the discipline, who earned their livelihood from other pursuits. Thus small numbers of individuals were employed as technicians either by museums or by governments. As a result, the activities of the newly professionalized archaeologists were shaped in significant ways by the interests and aims of the social classes and governments that paid their wages and supported their research, both at home and abroad.

Several countries with professional archaeologists—the United States, England, France, and Germany—consolidated their national boundaries or colonial empires during the age of imperialism, the years between about 1870 and 1914. Archaeology investigations in the new territories provided not only information about their past and present inhabitants but also explanations about how they were connected to the colonial powers. Archaeologists employed by imperial states with significant numbers of settlers in their newly acquired colonies—for example, England and Germany—seem to have favored explanations claiming that civilization arose only once or, at best, a few times and that it was carried from these centers of development to peripheral areas whose inhabitants displayed lower levels of social development. In other countries—for example, the United States—professional archaeologists tended to advocate social Darwinist or developmentalist arguments, which separated the original inhabitants from the more recent immigrants. In still other countries—like France during the Third Republic—they adopted an explicitly scientific materialist perspective, which they combined with their studies of cultural and biological evolution to discredit the antievolutionary scientific establishment of the Second Empire; the Catholic clergy; and their politically, socially, and culturally conservative contemporaries.

The professionalization of archaeology transformed discussions about the past. The arena where such discussions occurred was gradually shifted from one that was open to the devotee or nonspecialist to one in which participation was increasingly limited to properly certified professionals. As the amateurs were gradually squeezed out of the arena and they were usurped by the technician, their word no longer carried the same weight as that of the professional archaeologist. As the views of the professionals became increasingly privileged, they introduced an elaborated technical language that involved new concepts—for example, stratigraphy, associations, and gravelots—and more detailed descriptions of objects and sites. The new language eliminated any claims and assertions that were justified by references to the claimants' social position rather than their professional competence. Arguments grounded in the new linguistic code became increasingly important as buttresses that refuted or sustained positions taken in wider intellectual debates; these broader claims were typically couched in political-economic or cultural terms rather than in the narrower technical language of archaeology.

Nationalism became a pressing concern, once again, for archaeologists during the interwar years, following the social revolutions, political unrest, boundary changes, and loss of colonies that occurred at the end of World War I. For example, Julio Tello (1880–1947), a Peruvian archaeologist and senator, used archaeological remains from different localities in Peru to argue that the development of Peruvian civilization was autochthonous rather than derived from sources originating outside the country. The investigations and arguments of Gustav Kossina (1858–1931), a German archaeologist who equated different ethnic groups with particular material cultures, were used to support the expansionist policies of Nazi Germany in the 1930s. Those archaeologists who addressed the issue of nationalism spoke and wrote in the same technical language as professional colleagues who opposed their claims.

V. Gordon Childe (1892–1957), the Australian archaeologist who remained in England after World War I and the collapse of the Labor government in his own country, undertook a massive synthesis of European archaeology in the 1920s. This effort brought him into conflict with Kossina's nationalism and led him to a more refined, critical appreciation of the diffusionist arguments that were then in vogue. In the 1930s, he reasserted the importance of developmental stages, both as a fact of human history and as a method for organizing archaeological evidence. By the late 1940s, the developmental scaffolding he had proposed had been adopted, with relatively minor modifications, by archaeologists working in various parts of the world. This quickly secured his position as the most influential archaeological theorist of the first half of the twentieth century. It also provided his contemporaries with the conceptual tools they needed to discuss political-economic growth at a time when the reindustrialization of Europe and Japan and the forging of new kinds of linkages with the colonies and former colonies of the Third World were arguably the major issues of the day.

There was a significant increase in the number of archaeologists employed in many countries after World War II—for example, Poland, the United States, Mexico, and the USSR. This was particularly true in the 1960s, as various economic development and modernization programs came to fruition. In some countries—England and the United States, for instance—the profession's center of gravity shifted away from government and university employment to the private sector during and after the mid-1970s. In the United States, this shift was accompanied by a reconceptualization of history as a cultural resource that should be conserved and by increased levels of expenditure by and for enterprises that seek to define and preserve this heritage during a period experienced by the vast majority of its inhabitants as one of decline, discontent, and potential unrest.

Thus, in the last decade or so, a significant number of archaeologists became part of a "heritage industry," which seeks to construct images of the past, filtering out unpleasant aspects of past realities, of ourselves, or of everyday life in the present. Thus, the construction of a heritage is not the same as true recall of the everyday life and history of a past society. It is concerned instead with the reconfiguration of national identities rather than with history itself. What is at issue, as Robert Hewison (1987) remarked in *The Heritage Industry: Britain in an Age of Decline*, "is not whether or not we should preserve the past, but what kind of past we have chosen to preserve, and what this has done to our present."

The past is a contested terrain, over which archaeologists among others struggle. How the past is conceptualized shapes not only our understanding of the present but also our perceptions of what is possible in the future. The multiple dimensions of this struggle underlie many of the current debates within the discipline itself.

What I have suggested in the preceding pages is that archaeology—the business of bringing the past back to life—is about the beginnings of power. Consequently, it is an integral aspect of the processes of class and state formation—the rise of civilization—and of resistance or opposition to these processes. Thus archaeology is not merely the study of the processes them-

(b)

(a)

(c)

In the late 16th century, (a) John White portrayed Native Americans in poses derived from Classical Antiquity. After returning to England, he used these drawings as bases for representations of the early inhabitants of the British Isles: (b) "A Native Briton," and (c) "A Pict."

selves but also a critical feature of those processes. Viewing the discipline both as an aspect of the civilizing process and as resistance to class and state formation means that the practice of archaeology, or something resembling it, was not limited to recent times, to the West, or to industrialized nations. It allows us to contextualize and understand more fully the profound interest in the past exhibited by the archaisms in ancient Egyptian art and architecture during periods of unrest, the rewriting of history by Ssu-ma Qien after the consolidation of the first imperial state in China toward the end of the third century B.C., the collection of antiquities by the Japanese ruling classes during a major recomposition of the state in the seventh century A.D., or the construction of new heritages in Europe and the United States during the late twentieth century.

THE DIFFERENCES BETWEEN ARCHAEOLOGY AND HISTORY: A TECHNICAL DIVISION OF LABOR

Archaeologists and historians study past societies and their historical development for diverse reasons. Some want to learn how to predict human behavior. Others want to determine whether there are laws of social development that have already shaped the direction of history and will plot its course in the future. Still others want to learn about our own societies and, hence, our place in the modern world. By studying other societies and history, they gain a more comprehensive understanding of what it means to be human.

Archaeologists and historians imply that past societies and history are linked to everyday life in the present. The past interpenetrates the present, and the social relations that characterize the modern world ultimately have their roots in those of previous societies. The historical past has shaped the present; it has precluded certain courses of social development and permitted others. What is controversial or at issue here is the extent to which current structures of social relations have been shaped or determined by earlier social forms. Some archaeologists, those who advocate particularly determinist views, claim that individuals or groups are virtual prisoners of past social structures and history, almost powerless to alter the existing patterns of social relations as they continue to unfold. Other archaeologists, who subscribe to less deterministic or fatalistic views of society, argue that although people make their own history, each cohort enters into a preexisting set of social relationships that simultaneously constrains their actions and allows them to work out their own destinies, using and developing the range of cultural forms available to them.

Archaeologists are not the only people who are trying to understand and explain what happened in the past. Historians also try to do that. Clearly, the goals of the archaeologist and the historian are similar. However, it is also clear that today most archaeologists are not historians and most historians are not archaeologists. Since their goals are similar and they have the same object of inquiry—that is, past societies—what distinguishes them from each other? Many distinctions have been suggested, but the only one that stands up under close scrutiny is based on the kinds of evidence they examine and the techniques they have developed for analyzing the information they study.

Historians deal almost exclusively with written records and reconstruct the everyday life of past societies on the basis of what those documents say. Written evidence often presents a distorted view of what happened in the past. For example, until recently in some parts of the world, and even today in others, only a small segment of the population was literate, and our understanding of what that society was like is based on the views and biases of its literate class, which was usually its politically dominant class as well. As a result, historians have developed a number of techniques for checking the accuracy of their statements.

In reconstructing the past, archaeologists rely primarily on evidence that was not left intentionally—for example, food scraps in a garbage dump, a child buried in a pit scooped out of the earth, or the remains of an abandoned building. Since they use the remains for very different purposes from those of the people who left them, archaeologists are not so immediately concerned at this level about the views ancient peoples had about themselves or about others. However, they do have to worry about whether the evidence they found accurately reflects what took place and, if not, what factors—natural, human, or both—are distorting the archaeological record.

Both archaeologists and historians investigate the remains of the past that have survived to the present. They recuperate or reconstruct everyday life, history, and change from these residues. Their work is an active intellectual exercise that designates which of the shreds and scraps have historical significance and what is important about them.

Another way of saying that archaeology and history rely on different kinds of evidence and use different techniques to retrieve the past is to point out that they have different epistemologies and methodologies. Archaeology and history are complementary, in spite of their epistemological and methodological diversity, because they have the same object of inquiry: past societies and their historical development. Most archaeologists and historians believe that there is only one historically constituted material world and that it is possible to obtain knowledge about it. Thus they are talking about the same world, and their object of inquiry constitutes what philosophers of science call an ontological unity. Although there is only one world, there are diverse epistemologies—that is, ways of understanding what has happened and what is going on in that world. Under different circumstances, one epistemology or set of methodological practices may be more appropriate or informative than another. For example, in those periods before the invention of writing systems or in the absence of written testimony, archaeological evidence and practices become more important and perhaps even the only source of detailed or reliable information about everyday life and historical change.

THE ARCHAEOLOGICAL RECORD
AND ARCHAEOLOGICAL EVIDENCE

Various scholars concerned with human history or natural history—archaeologists as well as historians, geologists, and paleontologists—use the metaphor of a *record* to present and discuss, to model, what it is they investigate. The metaphor is rich since the word has multiple meanings that shade subtly and abruptly from one to the next. As a noun, *record* can refer to a performance in a track meet, any kind of written list or report, book, photographic record that assembles visual images, or phonograph record that tells a story or sings a song from beginning to end. As a verb, its meanings include "to register," "to transcribe," "to itemize," and "to preserve."

The archaeological record consists of multiple, interconnected levels, each of which is inscribed with its own distinctive kind of information. At one level, the archaeological record is analogous to the fossil record; it consists of physical objects and spatial relations that register information about past societies. However, these material remains may have been stripped from the original contexts of manufacture and use. Their modification and even their very preservation through time have been affected by the interplay of diverse physical, natural, and human processes. At another level, the archaeological record is understood as a text—the pages of a book, a photographic record, a magnetic tape, or a compact disc—that holds the story of everyday life and history at different places and times in the past. This view recognizes that the residues of past societies—for instance, their architecture, graves, food debris, and the spatial relations of these remains—also give expression to systems of social relations and meanings, both observable and unobservable, that structured everyday life and history in those social realities.

At the first level, the archaeological record consists of objects and associations that are found at places where people did something in the past—such as burying their dead, quarrying rocks to make tools or buildings, or even growing grapes to make wine. These activities involved modifying the natural environment, and the changes they wrought provide clues about what they did. The range of human activities, traces of which are found at archaeological sites, are almost as infinite as the range of human behavior itself. The size of archaeological sites also varies. At one extreme are sites with surface areas of a few square yards that were formed when someone dropped a pot or made a stone tool. At the other extreme are ancient cities like Teotihuacán, Mexico, which covered more than 9 square miles in A.D. 500 and witnessed the daily activities of more than 100,000 people.

At the second level, the archaeological record consists of the social relations and cultural meanings that are manifested in material remains and their spatial associations. It is not concerned primarily with the objects and associations themselves or with the circumstances that led to their preservation or modification. It focuses instead on the meanings inscribed in material remains. That is, it is concerned with the concrete conditions, political-economic and social relations, historical processes, and cultural creativity that underlie their production and use and that are expressed in the phenomena and events of everyday life and history. For example, it poses questions about how the members of a particular society, or of different communities and social classes in that society, understood a mural depicting a large man with a plumed headdress standing on the bodies of naked individuals whose hands are tied behind their backs. In investigating this level of the record, archaeologists have to confront the fact that superficially similar objects and associations from different social realities may have been created under diverse conditions and as a consequence of quite different social relations.

Since the various levels of the archaeological record are interconnected and intertwined—that is, they interpenetrate one another in historically contingent ways—it is necessary to move back and forth between these dimensions to gain a more complete, refined, and textured understanding and appreciation of the whole. Thus the practice of archaeology, which begins with the acquisition of evidence through survey and excavation, involves going beyond perceptions of the separateness and uniqueness of objects and their associations. It entails arranging and interrogating them in ways that permit the recuperation and reconstruction of the social reality that produced them. It necessitates a qualitative shift from ideas that are based on sensory perceptions of the material remains themselves to more abstract understandings, which are derived from generalizations and based on theoretically informed comparisons and understandings of the concrete conditions, structures, and processes that yield different kinds of society.

Objects are the things that people manufacture, modify, or move. Manufactured objects, or *artifacts* as they are usually called, can range in size and complexity from a pendant to a pyramid. They tell us a great deal about the artistic skills and technical achievements of ancient peoples. They reveal other things about the people as well, if we can determine how they were used. For example, we can learn about the characteristics of ancient musical instruments by playing them, which tells us something about the kind of music that existed in a particular ancient society.

Modified objects can also tell us something about the behavior of the people who altered them. At a number of sites, archaeologists have found chunks of siliceous rocks that look dramatically different from the way they look at places where they outcrop naturally. These chunks frequently have a pinkish color, are slightly glossy, and feel a little greasy. These characteristics can be duplicated experimentally by heating the rocks for sustained periods. Besides changing the rock's appearance, heating changes its crystalline structure and makes it a more desirable material for the manufacture of chipped stone tools than it would be in its natural, unmodified state.

Unmodified or natural objects that have been moved also provide information about everyday life in the past. Raw materials—metallic ores, for example—that have been moved over great distances provide information about the existence of ancient exchange networks and focus our attention on how the materials were obtained and transported and the political-economic and social relations that were involved in their circulation and exchange. Plant and animal remains are particularly useful because they help answer a number of questions about the people who used or consumed them. Did they have domesticated plants and animals? What were the ages or sexes of the animals they hunted or herded? At what times of the year were the people able to acquire and use the plants and animals they exploited? Which of the plants and animals provided food and which furnished raw materials for making useful objects? Did the people produce these materials by transforming land into a means of production, which they worked, or did they harvest nature and immediately consume the fruits of their labor? The answers to these and related questions provide both qualitative and quantitative information about certain activities of an ancient people that allows us to develop a rather detailed picture of their subsistence economy.

The Rosetta Stone, discovered in Egypt in 1799, displays three different kinds of writing.

The other kind of archaeological evidence consists of *associations*—the spatial relationships of objects with respect to one another and to features of their surroundings. Associations showing that objects or ideas were in use simultaneously are particularly important because they provide a context for viewing and interpreting remains that even the most detailed studies of the objects themselves would not yield. The famed Rosetta Stone, a basalt slab discovered in Egypt in 1799, is an example. The face of the slab comprises three panels, each containing a different kind of writing. The upper panel contains Egyptian hieroglyphics, which had been observed earlier but not understood. The middle register contains Demotic script, a previously unknown writing system that turned out to be a shorthand derived from the hieroglyphic system. The bottom panel contains an inscription written in ancient Greek—a language that was well understood when the Rosetta Stone was discovered. Priests from Memphis wrote the Greek text in 196 B.C. to extol the deeds and virtues of their king, Ptolemy Epiphanes of Egypt. Ancient rulers, like those of today, wanted their press secretaries to tell people what they had said, whether or not it was important or even comprehensible to those who spoke or read another language. Using this premise, it was reasonable to assume that the upper two panels contained the same message as the lower one. This assumption was proven twenty-three years later, when the texts of the upper two panels were finally deciphered. Besides showing that there were at least three writing systems and two languages in use in Egypt toward the end of the third century, the Rosetta Stone shows that there were extensive connections between Egypt and Greece at that time and that the use of Greek was sufficiently widespread to warrant bilingual messages.

The importance of associations for interpreting the past cannot be overemphasized. Like the Rosetta Stone, associations of contemporaneity—such as the various objects found in a tomb, the contents of a house that burned down before its occupants could remove their belongings, the refuse thrown into a garbage dump for a short period, or the remains of a settlement covered with volcanic ash—allow archaeologists to group together those objects and associations that were characteristic of the everyday life and activities of a particular ancient society at a given moment in the past. Such an array of contemporary objects and associations from a single archaeological site is called an *assemblage*. Perhaps the most famous archaeological assemblage, and one of the richest in terms of the information it can provide, comes from Pompeii, a Roman town at the foot of Mt. Vesuvius that was completely covered with ash when the volcano erupted in A.D. 79. As a result of the eruption a detailed record of the daily activities of the townspeople has been preserved. It includes such diverse pieces of information as the shape of the loaves of bread they ate, the locations of various kinds of workshops, the tools they used, and even the graffiti scratched on bathhouse walls and the directions to brothels (which were inscribed on the streets). The archaeological remains from Pompeii and its companion settlement, Herculaneum, provide more information about the daily activities of the Romans than written records from the period.

The Roman town of Herculaneum/Pompeii near Naples, Italy, which was buried by volcanic ash from the eruption of Mt. Vesuvius in A.D. 79.

Archaeologists usually have to consider assemblages from a number of sites in an area in order to reconstruct what life was like there at some time in the past. What they typically find is that contemporary assemblages from the same area contain either the same kinds of objects and associations or arrays of objects and associations that vary from one aggregate to another but ultimately overlap. For example, excavations in a series of third-millennium-B.C. villages located near Lima, Peru, revealed that settlements on the coast typically yielded hooks, net fragments, and enormous numbers of fish scales and bones, whereas the smaller ones situated inland produced broken hoes, digging stick fragments, and the remains of domesticated plants. The fishing nets were typically made from cotton, which was grown near the farming hamlets rather than near the fishing grounds. That the inland and coastal settlements were contemporary was shown by the fact that the inhabitants of both made and wore the same kind of twined cotton shirts.

Archaeologists typically examine a number of different assemblages, often from different sites in the same region, and they have to determine their chronological relationships. They must establish which assemblages are the oldest, which are the most recent, and which are contemporary before they can make any meaningful statements about how societies developed in that area and how they were similar to or different from the societies and processes of development found in other areas.

Archaeologists distinguish two kinds of time: relative and absolute. *Relative time*, or dating, places the various assemblages from an area in a chronological order from the oldest to the most recent. Relative dating tells us the sequence of the assemblages; however, it does not tell us the age of a particular assemblage or how long it lasted. To answer these questions, archaeologists must rely on *absolute dates*, which are typically expressed by some unit of time—years, centuries, or millennia—usually correlated with the Christian calendar. Thus, when archaeologists say a particular assemblage is 5,000 years old, they mean that it existed about 3000 B.C. Relative and absolute dates express different things, and they are obtained in different ways.

Archaeologists can establish the relative sequence of a series of assemblages by using one or both of two different methods: *stratigraphy* and *seriation*. What underlies both is the fact that objects and associations change through time. If this were not so, archaeologists could not distinguish a million-year-old assemblage from one that was 200 years old.

There are two principles of stratigraphy. The first is the *law of superposition*, which states that an assemblage found at the bottom of an undisturbed pile of assemblages is older than those found on top of it. The superposition of assemblages can occur in various ways; for example, people make a tomb by digging a hole in the ground; later they build a house on top of the tomb; still later, they erect a pyramid on top of the house; and finally, refuse and windblown sand pile up against the side of the pyramid and eventually cover the structure.

The second principle of stratigraphy has been called the *law of strata identified by their contents* by some archaeologists and the *law of faunal similarity* by paleontologists. It says that the various assemblages found in a region can be distinguished by differences in the kinds of objects and associations they contain and in the proportions in which they occur. That is, if the assemblages from two different sites contain the same materials in the same proportions, they are contemporary since no differences can be discerned between them. If the contents of two assemblages are different, the differences may reflect either different activities or differences in their relative ages.

The most important thing about stratigraphy is that it allows archaeologists to distinguish things that belong to different periods; however, they have to apply both principles of stratigraphy to establish a relative chronology. Superposition allows them to determine the sequence in which the assemblages occur. However, unless they notice the contrasts in the contents of the various assemblages, they have to treat them as if they were contemporary, even if there is superpositional evidence showing that one assemblage is more recent or older than another. These contrasts can involve seemingly insignificant details—how people decorate their pottery or the kinds of grills they put on the front of their automobiles—or items of fundamental importance, such as how they organize themselves to satisfy basic human needs.

Seriation involves arranging assemblages from the same region in a sequence by some technique other than superposition. The premise underlying all seriation arguments, regardless of whether they involve particular kinds of objects or associations or entire assemblages reflecting the total array

The stratigraphy revealed by archaeological excavations at the Temple of Pachacamac near Lima Peru.

of human activity, is that change is often a gradual process. As a result, those objects, associations, or assemblages that are most similar to one another in content will probably be closer together in the sequence and in age than those that are less similar to one another and, consequently, further apart in time.

Relative dating provides information about the succession of assemblages through time; however, it does not tell us how old they are or how long they lasted. To answer these questions, archaeologists rely on one or more absolute dating techniques. The absolute ages of assemblages and their durations in time can be determined in various ways. Perhaps the simplest is direct historical information about the site. For example, there are historical statements indicating that Pompeii and Herculaneum were covered by volcanic ash in A.D. 79. Another relatively simple technique can be used when objects of a known historical age appear in an assemblage. For instance, the Spaniards introduced blue glass beads into the Americas shortly after A.D. 1492; consequently, any archaeological assemblage in the New World that contains such beads cannot be older than that date, though it may be more recent. If this assemblage is followed by another that contains an object dated to A.D. 1550, we also know the upper age of the assemblage with the beads. It cannot be more recent than A.D. 1550. In other words, the duration or time span represented by the assemblage with the beads can be no more than fifty-eight years; it dates to a period that began no earlier than 1492 and ended no later than 1550.

Where there were ancient calendrical systems with recorded inscriptions—for example, in Egypt, Mesopotamia, China, or the Maya region of southern Mexico and Guatemala—it is possible to date archaeological assemblages containing calendrical inscriptions in terms of the calendrical system that was in use. The problem then becomes one of correlating the indigenous calendrical system with the Christian calendar. However, only a small portion of known archaeological assemblages have been dated directly by a calendrical system because of historical information about them or because they include objects of known age.

As a result, archaeologists usually rely on other techniques for absolute dating such as tree-ring counts, radiocarbon measurements, or potassium-argon dates. These and other techniques like them are called *chronometric dating methods*. They measure the rates of such natural phenomena as the growth of tree rings, the disintegration of a particular isotope of radioactive carbon, or the formation of argon gas from radioactive potassium. Consequently, they measure processes that are entirely or largely independent of human activity. The chronometric dating methods most commonly used by archaeologists are described in more detail in Appendix A.

In sum, the practice of archaeology occurs in the present. It uses residues left by past societies, which have been preserved or modified by various natural processes and human agencies, to shed light on how civilizations developed and disintegrated and how these and similar social processes and historical contingencies impinge on the world today.

FURTHER READINGS: A BRIEF GUIDE

The view that archaeology is historical social science is most clearly and forcefully expressed by the social archaeology group in Latin America, most notably Luis Lumbreras, *La Arqueología como Ciencia Social* (Lima: Ediciones PEISA, 1981); and Iraida Vargas Arenas, *Arqueología, Ciencia y Sociedad* (Caracas: Editorial Abre Brecha, 1990). This perspective is erected partly on the works of V. Gordon Childe, *Piecing Together the Past: The Interpretation of Archaeological Data* (London: Routledge & Kegan Paul, 1956), *Social Evolution* (New York: Schuman, 1951), *History* (London: Corbett Press, 1947), and *Society and Knowledge: The Growth of Human Traditions* (New York: Harper & Row, 1956).

Bruce G. Trigger, *A History of Archaeological Thought* (Cambridge: Cambridge University Press, 1990); and Jaroslav Malina and Zdenek Vasícek, *Archaeology Yesterday and Today* (Cambridge: Cambridge University Press, 1990), provide comprehensive discussions of the historical development of archaeology and its linkages with broader intellectual currents in the sciences and humanities. Agnes Heller, *Renaissance Man* (London: Routledge & Kegan Paul, 1978); George Makdisi, *The Rise of Humanism in Classical Islam and the Christian West* (Edinburgh: Edinburgh University Press, 1990); and John H. Rowe, "The Renaissance Foundations of Anthropology," *American Anthropologist*, vol. 67 (1965), 1–20, contain informative discussions of how the analytical categories of past societies get reworked during periods of rapid social transformation. The appropriations and contributions of archaeology to current, wider debates are considered in Robert Hewison, *The Heritage Industry: Britain in an Age of Decline* (London: Methuen, 1987); Isabel McBryde, ed., *Who Owns the Past?* (Melbourne: Oxford University Press, 1985); Peter Gathercole and David Lowenthal, eds., *The Politics of the Past* (London: Unwin Hyman, 1990); and Stephen Shennan, ed., *Archaeological Approaches to Cultural Identity* (London: Unwin Hyman, 1990).

Brian Fagan, *In the Beginning: An Introduction to Archaeology* (Boston: Scott, Foresman, 1988), is a comprehensive survey of the practice of archaeology. Linda Patrik, "Is There an Archaeological Record?" in *Advances in Archaeological Method and Theory*, ed. Michael B. Schiffer, vol. 8 (New York: Academic Press, 1985), pp. 27–82, examines the notion of the archaeological record. The linkages of practice and theory are examined by Thomas C. Patterson, *The Theory and Practice of Archaeology: A Workbook* (Englewood Cliffs, NJ: Prentice Hall, 1983).

chapter 2

The Theory and Practice of Archaeology

Facts are theory-laden; theories are value-laden; values are story-laden. (Donna J. Haraway, "Primates Is Politics by Other Means")

Too many of us work on the basis of unformulated and unexamined assumptions, (Karen Spalding, Frequent Complaint)

One does not defend reason by refusing to speak of the unreasonable; neither does one defend it by refusing to speak of reason. (Stanley Rosen, Nihilism: A Philosophical Essay)

Don't underestimate the power of theory. (Sarah Diamond, The Match)

Imagine a community of fifty or so men, women, and children who camp throughout the year in a canyon overlooking the ocean. They live in semi-subterranean pithouses with thatched walls and roofs. The twelve households are the basic units of production and consumption. Several times each week, adult men and boys over the ages of seven or eight go to the ocean to fish and to dive in the cold waters for mussels and clams; women and their daughters trap birds and small animals and gather edible plants and fuel in the canyon and nearby river valley habitats. The old men and women weave mats and baskets from canes and other plants they collect from the marshy area around a nearby spring or along the banks of a stream located over the ridge behind the village. They roast food in hearths outside the entrances to their homes; they dry fish during the summer months and store it in mat-lined pits near the hearth.

Because their numbers are so small, young men and women typically search for mates outside the village. They marry men or women from other settlements or from bands that move between temporary, seasonal campsites. Some go to live with their new spouses whereas others bring their new mates to the canyon, where they set up residence in an empty house or one that is built by kinfolk to accommodate them. When their newborn infants die, something that happens too often, they carefully wrap them in mats along with a small pendant, a quartz crystal, or a pretty pebble and bury them beneath the floors of their houses. When children or adults die, they too are wrapped in mats and interred in the windblown sand and refuse that have accumulated behind their houses.

After many generations, the members of the community leave the canyon. It is too far from plots of land where they can grow gourds and the cotton they use to make nets and tunics, and the mussels and clams consumed by their ancestors are no longer as plentiful as they had been. Some of the domestic groups move into the river valley with rich soils, whereas others resettle along the coast near rich fishing grounds.

(a)

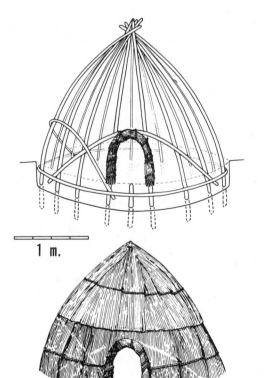

1 m.

(b)

A large area was excavated at (a) Chilca, Peru—a village that was contemporary with the nearby settlement in the canyon site. It revealed a series of dwellings resembling those found in the canyon. (b) The reconstruction of a 4th millennium B.C. dwelling at Chilca.

The people have gone. One after another, the houses collapse and are slowly covered by windblown sand. The heavy fogs that move off the ocean during the winter months soak the soil. Patches of exposed refuse absorb its moisture and gradually become more alkaline or acidic, depending on their contents. These subtle changes slowly destroy or modify the artifacts, scraps of food, and other debris that had been thrown away by the villagers. Owls that typically avoid places where people live begin to burrow into the old garbage dumps. The partially cemented refuse provides an ideal place for a nest; in the process, they move objects from one layer to another and bring twigs, prey, and other objects into their burrows.

The dispersal of the community changes the ways in which its members acquire or produce the goods they need. The two parts of the community are no longer self-sufficient, for each now depends on the other for certain essentials. For instance, the residents of the farming hamlets rely on the inhabitants of the coastal villages for fish, which they catch with nets and lines made from cotton grown by the farmers. The division of labor has also changed. The adolescent and adult males and females of the coastal villages fish and dive in the cold waters, whereas their counterparts in the inland hamlets grow cotton and gourds and then an increasingly greater variety and quantity of foodstuffs, gather edible plants, and hunt or trap birds and game. The old men and women in both kinds of settlements continue to weave mats and baskets from canes collected along the rivers and nets and tunics from the cotton grown in the river valleys. People frequently walk two or three hours—bearing food, finished goods, and raw materials—to visit and to exchange news with friends and kin who reside in another habitat.

In some settlements, the residents erect platform mounds. They heap rocks and other kinds of debris and enclose them with stone walls. They frequently plaster the retaining walls with painted adobe reliefs, depicting giant spiders, hands, or open mouths. At first, the platform mounds are small enough that the residents of a single settlement can complete them by working a few months each year for a decade or so. However, some of them become so large, involving millions of person-days of labor, that people from a number of neighboring settlements must cooperate in their construction. Eventually, many of these settlements, like the campsite in the canyon, are also abandoned. Centuries later, people bury their dead in the platform mounds; more recently, they build houses on them.

Around 1900, archaeologists began to visit the canyon and its environs, which are actually located on the central coast of Peru. They began to find first one and then another of the ancient settlements; this process continues to the present day. The archaeologists came with questions about how the ancient inhabitants had gained their livelihood, questions that were shaped by debates between groups with different theoretical perspectives about subsistence economies, foraging societies, social change, the creation of culture, and their interconnections. Their activities at the sites were informed by these debates as they uncovered and interrogated the archaeological record, decided which objects and bits of information were relevant to their aims, and formulated and modified hypotheses that would enhance their understanding of what they were finding. Their activities, their hypotheses, and even what they defined as relevant data were ladened with theoretical considerations. Since theory informed their practice, how they recuperated and reconstructed the everyday lives and history of the people who lived in the canyon and the neighboring area reflected and refracted the presuppositions they made about the formation and development of society.

The practice of archaeology is shaped by theoretical concerns that exist at distinct, interconnected levels. At one level, archaeologists focus on what some have called middle range theory—that is, the formation of the archaeological record itself and whether or not it contains direct information about human behavior and culture. Another level, which we will explore in this chapter, concentrates on how archaeologists understand the development of human society or the rise of civilization—that is, the formation of class structures, states, and the struggles they engender. How do archaeologists conceptualize and deploy analytical categories—like society, economy, change, development, or culture—to organize and convey their awareness, grasp, and appreciation of everyday life and history, both now and in the past?

THE INTERPRETATION OF THE ARCHAEOLOGICAL RECORD, EVERYDAY LIFE, AND SOCIAL THEORY

Keeping in mind that archaeology neither developed nor exists in an intellectual vacuum, let us consider how archaeologists have used and deployed various theories of society and history to interpret the forms of everyday life and events revealed in the ancient settlements of coastal Peru and to understand their significance. The theories they employ derive from or resonate with worldviews that give voice to the sensibilities and understandings of historically constituted blocs of classes, strata, and regionally based groupings that have different relations to power in modern, class-stratified societies. These worldviews crystallized during the crises provoked by the dissolution of the European city-states and the feudal social order they represented, by the events surrounding the industrial and political revolutions of the eighteenth century, and by the development of mass movements, democratic and socialist, in the nineteenth and twentieth centuries.

These views about society and history were formulated in ongoing debates, ultimately about class formation and its consequences, by organic intellectuals who found solutions to problems, justified them, and situated them within systems of beliefs to which the members' particular classes or communities could subscribe. Over the years, they reworked these worldviews to incorporate new understandings, to clarify ambiguities, and to respond to the difficulties pointed out by competing perspectives. In the process, the traditional views of earlier times were often disassembled, reconstituted, and embraced not only as sources of inspiration but also as buttresses for new arguments. Thus, the historical development of the discourse about the rise of human society and civilization is a complex, richly textured dialogue rather than a simple linear sequence in which new perspectives overcome and replace the old.

Imperialist/Colonialist Liberalism

Max Uhle (1856–1944), the leading figure in Peruvian archaeology between 1895 and 1910, was the first professional archaeologist to comment on the significance of these early settlements. Uhle came from a middle-class family with close ties to the agrarian and nonindustrial sectors and to the state bureaucracy of Saxony. Members of this class in southern Germany saw agriculture, not industry or commerce, as the fundamental precondition for the development of civilization. In this view, which was widely shared by many middle class emigrants from central Europe, cultured or civilized peoples derived their livelihoods from agriculture, whereas groups with less refined manners and behavior, which also exhibited less social order, engaged in economic activities like industry, commerce, or foraging. Thus, the early fishing and foraging community of the canyon was more primitive than the later populations, which in his view had adopted the agricultural practices of civilized immigrants, most recently from Central America and more remotely from China.

Uhle's views coincided with those of the social class that employed him: the wealthy exporting farmers who controlled the government and the dynamic sector of Peruvian economy around the turn of the century. Most of the agrarian capitalists at the time were also relatively recent immigrants who maintained close economic and cultural ties with their European homelands; they saw themselves as the true bearers of culture, civilization, and progress in what they often perceived as an otherwise backward land.

Uhle's theories of society and history, and those of his employers, combined elements of liberal and romantic worldviews. He adopted five elements from liberal social thought: (1) Outside of civil society is a state of nature, (2) economic activity distinguishes human beings from other species, (3) social institutions and practices are mutable, (4) changes in the form of economic activity are motors for social change and progress, and (5) new economic practices are typically introduced into a region by more polished or developed immigrants. He also took up several tenets of romanticism: (6) The real human values of a society, as opposed to its material ones, were cultivated by farmers, who by virtue of tilling the soil, had a closer organic connection with nature than individuals who followed mechanical or commercial pursuits; and (7) an adequate account of an ancient community is necessarily a historical explanation since the social is always constituted by and subordinate to history.

Romantic/Liberal Nationalism

Julio C. Tello (1880–1947) became Peru's leading authority on archaeology after 1912. Tello came from a peasant family that began to acquire individual parcels of land in the highlands immediately east of Lima, the capital city. Sent to Lima at the age of thirteen, he worked as a household servant while he completed his secondary education. He entered the university in 1901 and supported himself with a job at the National Library, whose director was one of the leading intellectuals of the day. Thus, Tello was raised and attended the university when the country was dominated politically by the agrarian capitalists of the coast. Nationalist sentiments and concern over the plight of the Indian, Peru's rural poor, became increasingly important political issues during this period.

Tello allied himself with the local representatives of foreign-owned extractive mining and petroleum industries and financial firms. He came to prominence in 1912, shortly after that faction had seized political power from the coastal elite and he had returned from three years of study at Harvard, London, and Berlin. He quickly became senator, university professor, and museum director. One consequence of this shift in power was that Uhle's job at the Museum of National History was not renewed, and he left the country for a new position in Chile.

Tello disagreed with Uhle's interpretation of Peruvian history and provided an alternative to it. He conceptualized it in terms of an Archaic Andean culture, which precipitated first in the north highlands and spread over the entire highland area and then to the coast. The platform mounds erected by the descendants of the canyon community marked the crystallization of Archaic Andean culture in the coastal region. Cultural development was autochthonous to Peru, not imported; its early center of development was in the highlands—the homelands of Peru's Indian population, the true bearers of authentic values and beliefs—rather than on the coast, where capitalist agricultural development depersonalized human beings by transforming them into instruments of production.

Tello's conceptualizations of culture, history, and society combined romantic and liberal thought. In his view, culture was an organic tradition, analogous to a living creature, that developed and transformed itself through time. Each culture had its own preestablished laws of development and its own character or spirit that directed the energies of individuals and led them to participate in the common tasks of the community. The enhancement of human capabilities, the formation and development of genius, could occur only in the context of the community. In the Archaic Andean culture, art and architecture with religious significance were visual expressions of the creative genius of an artistic and intellectual elite who performed rituals and gave direction and meaning to the productive and reproductive activities of the community. These mental workers, who provided the ideological glue that held the community together, were supported by surplus production and labor of direct producers and constituted a ruling class.

During the 1920s and 1930s, when Tello was the foremost archaeologist in Peru and one of its leading organic intellectuals, archaeologists in the United States and Europe who were concerned with the development of ancient Andean civilizations tried to reconcile his views with those of Uhle. This task was complicated after 1930, when the power bloc Tello was associated with was overthrown and he found himself with neither a job nor support for his research for a number of years. In 1937, Tello was able to make contact with Nelson Rockefeller; forge new alliances with archaeologists in the United States; and reassert his position as Peru's leading, but not only, archaeological spokesman.

Cultural Evolutionism: Economic Development and Progress

Tello's view of the historical development of ancient Peruvian societies was challenged in the late 1930s and early 1940s by Rafael Larco Hoyle, an influential agrarian capitalist and a very knowledgeable *aficionado* of north coast archaeology. During this period Larco read the writings of the Australian archaeologist V. Gordon Childe, who lectured to trade unionists in England and Scotland about the evolution and progress of human society. Although Larco despised unions, he recognized the utility of Childe's arguments, and appropriated and modified them to fit the historical specificity of Andean social development. His cultural evolutionary perspective became hegemonic after Tello's death and after it was adopted by influential archaeologists in the United States.

Larco, and Childe before him, emphasized the importance of agricultural production as the foundation for the development of civilization. The development of agricultural productive forces provided the basis for surplus accumulation, increased technical and social divisions of labor, exchange and commerce, and new forms of social and political organization. This, of course, was what Childe had called the "Neolithic" or "food-producing revolution." This view was especially popular among the Peruvian agrarian capitalists, who regained power from the nationalist, interventionist government they toppled in a coup d'état in 1948. In the years that followed, economic growth was led by the exporting agriculture sector; cotton and sugar production soared by more than 50 percent as the state revived and financed the expansion of irrigation systems on the north coast, increasing the amount of arable land there by more than 20 percent.

Larco and the North American archaeologists who adopted this cultural evolutionary perspective worked in a milieu that was obsessed with rebuilding the industrialized economies of Europe and Japan, which were destroyed during World War II, and with bringing economic development or progress to the Third World. Cultural evolutionism became the dominant paradigm from the late 1940s through the 1970s. The evolutionists argued that economic and social development occurred through a succession of stages, each of which was characterized by a particular subsistence economy and by economic relationships that shaped functionally associated forms of political institutions and practices, social organization, and ideas. Development occurred when innovative or modern elements spread from advanced centers to backward regions and displaced traditional elements.

The cultural evolutionists viewed communities like that found in the canyon as hunting and foraging bands whose productive forces were barely developed. More recent communities were understood to be characterized by the rapid spread and assimilation of various crafts and by the growth of food production, especially after irrigation was developed or introduced into several regions. Religion provided the ideology that joined villages into larger, more inclusive communities. Many of these communities had temple mounds that were the political-religious centers for the inhabitants of the region. Although the religious ideas emanated from a common source, they were manipulated independently at each center. These autonomous regional groupings occasionally raided one another; however, their organization and small size prevented them from carrying on wars of conquest. As the villagers cooperated in the construction of irrigation works, their populations became larger and more settled, and they gradually amalgamated into states under theocratic rulers. Eventually, the states began to compete with one another, and an era of cyclical conquests ensued in which different states sought to extract tribute from their neighbors; when the efforts of one state collapsed, they were replaced by those of another.

Like Adam Smith and other classical political economists, the cultural evolutionists viewed civilization, or civil society, as an autonomous, self-regulating economy isolated from the political sphere. Civil society was capable of progressing through a succession of stages characterized by particular modes of subsistence. The role of the state was to ensure that social order was maintained. The cultural evolutionists were functionalists who accepted the distinction between synchronic and diachronic forms of analysis. Their perspective was regional and comparative rather than particular or universal. To achieve their aim, they separated the study of cultural or social growth from the study of history. They were concerned with *evolutionary* changes, not *historical* ones. Evolutionary changes, they wrote, reflected the natural growth or unfolding of the potential inherent in a particular cultural or social type, the gradual and continuous accumulation of small incremental shifts. When the potential of the stage was exhausted, a new, qualitatively different social type with its own distinctive economic, political, and social arrangements had developed out of it. Historical changes, in contrast, were unique events, accidents that impinged on the normal growth and development of culture and society, two categories that were never clearly differentiated.

The cultural evolutionists reintroduced a comparative perspective, which examined cross-cultural regularities of development in different cultural traditions rather than their unique or divergent features. Their methodology, in the words of Julian Steward (1955:88) was ". . . avowedly scientific and generalizing rather than historical and particularizing." They proposed to use science, the methodology of logical positivism, to replace or update historical knowledge formulated in terms of the empiricist perspective that had dominated archaeological thought before the war. During the 1950s, these archaeologists produced detailed accounts of the rise of archaic civilizations in various parts of the world. Their investigations supported an elaborate conception of world history: In the areas they studied, identical developmental processes and the succession of stages led to the formation of archaic civilizations and culminated, ultimately, in their domination by the West.

Three criticisms of cultural evolutionism appeared in the late 1950s. The first questioned its functionalist assumptions, especially the presumed association of given technologies with particular forms of social organization and ideas. The second demanded greater specification of the relationship between the economic and political spheres characteristic of particular cultural stages. The third attacked the separation of the study of cultural processes from that of history and advocated, instead, studies that synthesized and explained, in a convincing fashion, the historical detail of the real sequences. The cultural evolutionists had failed to come to grips with the real events and transformations of the historical record; they were unable to deal with the mechanisms that produced the conditions and balance of forces characteristic of particular societies.

Processual Archaeology

The hegemony of the cultural evolutionist perspective began to wane in the late 1950s, partly as a result of changing political-economic conditions and the consequent demands for new kinds of explanations and partly in response to the internal development of archaeological discourse itself. With regard to the former, the institutions and practices of the states loomed large. This was as true elsewhere as it was in Peru and the United States. The purpose of state apparatuses in capitalist countries was to regulate the economy and ensure that any economic development was capitalist rather than socialist. Whereas the cultural evolutionists had located the engine of development in the economy, their successors in the late 1950s and 1960s situated it in the political realm. The claim that politics rather than economics ultimately shaped the structure and movement of society challenged the economic determinism of the cultural evolutionists.

Archaeologists responded in three ways to the geopolitical conditions that appeared in the late 1950s and to the internal critiques of cultural evolutionism. One response, which can be called modernization or neo-evolutionist theory, retained the layer-cake model of society but substituted political or ideational determination for the economic determinism of the cultural evolutionists. In these perspectives, the motors driving social evolution were respectively the unfolding of the state, viewed the highest form of social development, or the formation of increasing levels of social complexity. A second response denied that culture or society developed through a fixed succession of economically determined stages. Advocates of this view, like John Rowe, argued that the study of cultural process and the study of history were inseparable since there was no essential difference between them; however, history was, above all else, political history and, ultimately, involved studying the rise and fall of states and empires—that is, changes in prestige and power of particular groups, which were the motors of change.

There was a curious convergence in the kinds of questions asked by the proponents of these views in spite of the profound differences in their presuppositions about society and its historical development. Both groups of archaeologists asked questions about the kinds of social relations that existed within and among the coastal communities described earlier. Both groups perceived the settlement in the canyon as one inhabited by a community that lacked significant social stratification. Both groups of archaeologists saw the later communities, especially those that built large platform mounds, as manifesting different kinds of social relations. Those who presumed that large buildings require full-time architects or supervisors viewed them as class-stratified, state-based societies; others saw them as a distinctively organized intermediate society that could be situated on a continuum between kin-organized communities, on the one hand, and class-stratified states, on the other.

A third response replaced the classical political-economic model of society, used by the modernization theorists and cultural evolutionists, with one that was rooted in neoclassical economics. Implicit in this response was the idea that society should not be viewed as a community but rather as an aggregate of undifferentiated individuals, who behave as if they were buying and selling their goods in a market in order to attain some goal. This set of responses ultimately shifted attention away from a concern with culturally constituted meanings and actions toward a focus on behavior rooted in an ahistorical, asocial human nature. For instance, they provided a medium in which Malthusian and neo-Malthusian population pressure models, with their Hobbesian presuppositions about the insatiable appetites of human beings and the absence of intentionality, or "economic man" models could flourish.

During the 1960s, the advocates of this view began increasingly to view culture in narrowly utilitarian terms and to appropriate and use concepts derived from ecology. In this context, phrases such as Leslie White's remark (1959:9) in *The Evolution of Culture* that culture is the "organization of the extrasomatic ways and means employed by [humanity] . . . in the struggle for survival and existence" acquired nuanced meanings. The harnessing and transforming of the energy of nature came to be viewed in terms of adaptation—that is, groups exploiting the raw materials, or energy resources, of various ecological habitats.

In the 1960s, Edward Lanning, among others, investigated the archaeological sites described at the beginning of the chapter. He pursued two lines of inquiry. The first derived from the cultural evolutionists' concern with the development of agricultural economies and the appearance of settlements that were inhabited continuously throughout the year. The second was concerned with the territorial organization of work. These inquiries showed that the relationship between the appearance of agricultural production and permanently occupied villages was more complicated than previously assumed. In coastal Peru, the richness of the marine resources afforded opportunities for year-round settlement in certain areas of the coast before the development of agricultural production. This view was argued in narrow utilitarian terms, a perspective that ultimately derived from the neoclassical economics models incorporated into ecology, demography, and ecological anthropology, which tended to blur the difference between nature and culture. Lanning claimed that people lived in close proximity to the resources they used in order to minimize unproductive travel time, and he attempted to delimit those factors—environment, demographics, economics, settlement patterns, trade and commerce, specialization, and stratification—that were involved in the rise of Andean civilization and to assess their relative significance.

Although Lanning's presuppositions were different from those of the cultural evolutionists, neo-evolutionists, and cultural historians, his conclusions about the coastal Peruvian communities were similar in many respects. The canyon community was viewed as a nonstratified hunting and foraging band that relied extensively on marine resources; and the later settlements with large platform mounds and agrarian sectors in their subsistence economies, were seen as the centers of small states, which developed in response to the organizational needs of the society.

A number of the neo-evolutionist or processual archaeologists began to inquire about the processes that promoted or induced certain kinds of changes that eventually brought particular kinds of society into existence. Some of them conceptualized the process as brief periods of rapid and/or profound cultural change followed by longer periods of relative stability, and they formulated it in terms of the relationships between a society and its environment. Change occurred, they argued, when cultures could harness energy resources more efficiently. This view focused attention on what was happening on the boundary between the human and natural worlds. Archaeologists came to understand these connections through the concept of adaptation, the processes by which equilibrium or balance is maintained, or disrupted, between societies and their environments.

The processual archaeologists generally accepted the distinction between synchrony and diachrony, and by conceptualizing cultural systems in terms of adaptation, they tacitly assigned logical priority to the former. Thus, their theory of change was, in fact, a theory of how social order was disturbed or disrupted. It was necessary for them to establish how the system functioned before the forces or pressures impinging on it, the mechanisms they set in motion, and the changes they produced could be explained. By formulating adaptation in terms of the continually changing ways the system maintained harmony with its social and physical environment, they postulated, in effect, that systemic change was gradual and continuous, an internal response to the stresses produced by outside pressures, which were often seen as deriving from population growth. As a result, processual archaeologists also removed the culture/nature opposition by uniting elements of both into an ecosystem, where patterned interchanges of energy occurred. The cultural system was atomized: Particular productive forces and relations were stripped of their social and political contexts. The effect was that the cultural system, its structures and institutions, was viewed as reflecting the optimal or best-compromise solutions at any given moment to the problems produced by its environment.

The various strands of processual archaeology were firmly grounded in functionalism. Most advocates viewed culture as a system of functionally interrelated components, often conceptualized as technological, political, or ideological subsystems that were linked together by energy or information exchanges. A majority viewed these components as being hierarchically organized. The concept of hierarchy focused attention on how the system as a whole was managed or controlled. Was its overall stability determined ultimately by the economic base? Or was system management the function of another component? A number of the processual archaeologists rejected determination by the economic base, relocating it instead in the political superstructure, which they conceptualized as a regulator that controlled the flow of information among the lower-order components of the system.

Many processual archaeologists believed that cultural systems became increasingly more complex—that is, structurally differentiated—as they passed from one stage to the next. In other words, later systems had more components and more hierarchical levels than earlier ones. Differentiation increased the stability and efficiency of that organization and, hence, of the system as a whole. The question was how did this differentiation or fragmentation along socially beneficial and adaptive lines occur? Their answers typically invoked capacities, conditions, processes, or mechanisms that were not assigned to the system or that operated at a more fundamental level than that of the system itself.

The theoretical weaknesses of processual archaeology began to emerge by the mid-1970s, when criticisms, largely internal to the approach, appeared. Three features came under scrutiny: (1) whether covering law or systems theory explanations provided more refined understanding of cultural process; (2) the equilibrium and gradualist assumptions inherent in the notion of adaptation and functionalist theories of change; and (3) the inability of functionalist theories of change to deal with structural differentiation, the sudden appearance of new forms of organization in situations in which the continual accumulation of small, incremental changes suddenly gave way to rapid, qualitative transformations.

Archaeology and Marxist Social Theory

Marxist writers have long referred to the civilizations of ancient Peru and to the egalitarian communities that preceeded them or existed on their margins. Karl Marx, himself, wrote briefly and insightfully about the structure of Inca society; and in the 1890s, Heinrich Cunow, the general secretary of the Second International, produced several works about the organization of Andean communities during the Inca regime. Marxist social theory has long provided a consistent, if at times muted, perspective about the Andean past, especially during the periods of civil war from 1959 to 1965 and again in the 1980s and at the time of the anti-imperialist governments from the late 1960s to the mid-1970s. For example, in 1973, Luis Lumbreras—director of Peru's National Museum of Archaeology and Anthropology and an important figure in university curriculum reform at the time—published a book-length explication of Marxist social thought, *Archaeology as Social Science* (1974), and how it could be applied to the study of archaeological remains and ancient societies.

For Marxists, the world is constituted by socially organized groups of people who satisfy their physical and created needs through labor and understand their productive activity through language. Their labor and productive activity is social and takes place within particular culturally defined sets of property relations. These relations grant powers of decision making, of control, and thus of the appropriation and distribution of the goods and services that are produced. Each generation enters into a preexisting set of socially defined property relations and practices.

Class and exploitation are central concepts in a Marxist theoretical framework concerned with civilized societies. The two categories are, in fact, interrelated, as Geoffrey de Ste. Croix (1984) points out. Class is a relationship among groups of people in a community, who are identified by their position in the system of social production and by the degree of control they have over the conditions of their production, their labor power, and the goods they produce. Social classes never exist alone but always in structured relationships with one another; such class structures are the social expression of exploitation—in which the members of one group appropriate part of the product or labor of another group. The most distinctive feature of any society, then, is how the dominant classes, which control the means of production, ensure the extraction of labor power and goods that makes their own existence and reproduction possible.

The relations among the various classes of a class-stratified society are antagonistic and often violent. Thus class struggle or conflict is fundamental. The antagonism is inherent in the class structures and practices that organize social relations. The antagonism is constant; it is expressed in the open and hidden fights that structure everyday life in class-stratified societies. The settings in which the members of subject classes conduct their lives are never wholly of their own creation; however, they are never totally without some degree of power or control over their own lives. Everyday forms of passive resistance by subject communities, which avoid either open defiance of authority or direct confrontation with it, have been more typical than open rebellion or revolution. At various times and places, the weapons of passive resistance have included avoidance, laziness, deception, noncompliance, evasion, desertion, theft, and sabotage. Weapons such as these have limited or thwarted the aspirations of many dominant classes; they have been used to mitigate or deny the claims made by dominant classes, including those in the United States, where more than 20 percent of the economy is currently either informal (nontaxable) or illegal, and to advance claims against them.

In this view, power is the relationship among historically constituted social groups of actors rather than human beings understood as ahistorical, asocial individuals. It is always exercised in historically constituted social contexts. It is a relationship of force, an instrument of repression, rather than a relationship among equals, a function of consent, or a transfer or renunciation of rights. It is a form of unspoken warfare that is perpetually reinscribed in the economic inequalities, social institutions, and languages of everyday life in class-stratified, state-based societies. Unlike violence, power does not act directly or immediately on individuals; rather, it modifies their present and future actions, understandings, and perceptions. Power relations are activated in diverse forms in different places, on different occasions, or under different circumstances. Such activations may be regular and predictable occurrences or seemingly haphazard events.

Culture provides the medium in which power relations and power actions occur. Consequently, culture and politics are intimately connected. The linkage presupposes that historically constituted individuals are, in fact, social agents—who can set goals, enter into agreements, or accept responsibility for their actions—and that their capacities and sensibilities develop within concrete cultural contexts. Cultures shape social agents by assigning meaning to their experiences and to the familiar activities and events of everyday life and by providing reasons why they should act one way rather than another. However, the identities, capacities, and understandings of these social agents cannot be taken for granted because cultures change. As cultures decompose and dissolve, the identities of social agents, as well as their capacities for self-understanding, are deformed, undermined, and potentially eroded. Culture allows social actors to maintain a perspective distance from the experiential reality of their lives while simultaneously engaging in it.

Archaeologists have viewed the record left by civilizations and by the ancient Peruvian communities described earlier through the lens provided by Marxist social theory. In the latter, they have focused attention on (1) the nonexploitative, technical division of labor based on age and gender differences that structured social relations in the earliest community; (2) how this age- and gender-based division of labor was transformed as agricultural production became more important and as it was incorporated into a regionally organized, nonexploitative division of labor that emphasized community-level social relations and the circulation of raw materials and finished goods among economically specialized settlements; and (3) the elaboration of community-level social relations for purposes of large-scale construction projects that benefited the community as a whole. They have argued that the early agricultural societies with large platform mounds were relatively undifferentiated communities, whose members were bound to one another by shared interests and practices rather than exploitation and resistance. They claim that class and state formation had not occurred. Everyday life had not been disrupted because one part of the population began to pursue its own interests rather than the consensual ones of the community as a whole, in the context of the continuing institutions and practices of the theretofore classless, kin-organized community. The traditional social relations of the community had not been distorted and reorganized to accommodate the private interests of a dominant class.

They argue that the suppression of a classless, kin-organized form of everyday life occurred much later in coastal Peru, when the community-level relations of production collapsed. This development was accompanied by other changes: the construction of fortified hilltop villages; burials with headless individuals or persons entombed with additional human skulls; stone-headed maces; and individuals with depressed skull fractures; and the sudden appearance of tombs with different arrays and quantities of grave goods. Taken together these features indicate that raiding was rampant and that class and state formation occurred quickly in some regions in a context characterized by the elaboration of craft specialization, the restricted circulation of certain kinds of goods, and the use of cultural elements, like art styles, to mark the boundaries between communities that participated in different production-consumption systems. As Stanley Diamond (1974:1) observed in *In Search of the Primitive*, the appearance of class-stratified, state-based societies, the rise of civilization, began with "conquest abroad and repression at home."

The Postprocessual Archaeologies: Theoretical Countercurrents of the 1980s and 1990s

Archaeologists have variously used elements from liberal, romantic, and Marxist worldviews in their reconstructions of the historical development of human society. Some archaeologists adhered rather closely to the outlines of a particular worldview, whereas others combined features from several to inform their understandings. Critiques of the methodological underpinnings of processual archaeology have underwritten the consolidation and appearance of a number of postprocessual archaeologies since the late 1970s and 1980s. Some romanticized the past, implicitly rejecting the present. Others retained the processual archaeologists' debt to the Enlightenment's analytical categories and the notion of modernity, which privileges the present and the future over the past and treats the latter as an embryonic, less differentiated, or even less well-adapted version of the contemporary world. In the 1980s the proponents of the various postprocessual perspectives have been much clearer not only about the social and political-economic milieu in which they practice archaeology but also about their sources of intellectual inspiration. They have a growing awareness and appreciation of how the pieces of particular theoretical frameworks can be articulated and of how worldviews and frameworks differ from one another. They are becoming cognizant of the dangers inherent in uncritical appropriations of ideas or in eclectic combinations, which draw inspiration and unwanted baggage from different sources.

For the most part, the postprocessual archaeologies have adopted broader conceptualizations of history and culture than the cultural evolutionists and the processual archaeologists, who viewed culture as adaptation, utilitarian, or ideology and comprehended history as narration and a succession of unique events flowing unidirectionally through a container called time. For some postprocessual archaeologists, culture is related to everyday life and the material conditions for maintaining or changing it in particular societies; they do not view it as reducible to something that exists outside itself. History, for some, is also more than a narrative or chronicle of unique events; it is created by clashes in the realities of everyday life in particular societies, which disrupt the regular and replicable rhythms of social action and threaten to replace them with new patterns. They see culture and history as interpenetrating and interconnected.

Archaeologists are beginning to examine the development and contours of ancient civilizations in terms of the concepts of world systems or social totality. At issue perhaps is whether civilizations and their historical development are more usefully understood as relatively similar, cluster- or peer-polity interactions or distinct, unevenly developed social totalities. Also at issue is whether the state represents the highest form of social development, as the processualists imply, rather than a transitory entity that consolidates and disintegrates in contexts shaped by continually shifting relations of political domination and configurations of power. Such perspectives challenge notions about the unidirectionality of history by indicating that the processes of class and state formation and the kinds of social and cultural changes they engender are actually two-way streets. They require us to examine not only the movement from nonstates to states but also state to nonstate transitions. They demand that we explore the spatial dimensions of social development, power relations, and resistance to their implementation.

FURTHER READINGS: A BRIEF GUIDE

The formation of the archaeological record is discussed by Michael B. Schiffer, *Formation Processes of the Archaeological Record* (Albuquerque: University of New Mexico Press, 1987); and by Lewis R. Binford, *Working at Archaeology* (New York: Academic Press, 1983), and *Debating Archaeology* (San Diego: Academic Press, 1989). Mark L. Raab and Albert C. Goodyear, "Middle Range Theory in Archaeology: A Critical Review of Origins," *American Antiquity*, vol. 49 (1984), 255–268, assess middle range theory. Thomas C. Patterson,

The Theory and Practice of Archaeology: A Workbook (Englewood Cliffs, NJ: Prentice Hall, 1983), examines the interrelations of theory and practice.

Useful general overviews of theories of society and human nature are provided by Tom Campbell, *Seven Theories of Human Society* (Oxford: Clarendon Press, 1981); Leslie Stevenson, *Seven Theories of Human Nature* (New York: Oxford University Press, 1974); Roger Trigg, *Ideas of Human Nature: An Historical Introduction* (Oxford: Basil Blackwell, 1988); and Raymond Williams, *Keywords: A Vocabulary of Culture and Society* (New York: Oxford University Press, 1983). John Gray, *Liberalism* (Minneapolis: University of Minnesota Press, 1986); and Ronald L. Meek, *Social Science and the Ignoble Savage* (Cambridge: Cambridge University Press, 1976), provide constructive discussions of the historical development and distinctive features of the various strands of liberal thought. The romantic viewpoint is examined by Carl Schmitt, *Political Romanticism* (Cambridge, MA: MIT Press, 1986); Raymond Williams, *Culture and Society: 1780–1950* (New York: Columbia University Press, 1983); and Andrew Cunningham and Nicholas Jardine, eds., *Romanticism and the Sciences* (Cambridge: Cambridge University Press, 1990). Informative accounts of Marxist theories of history and society are R. S. Neale, *Writing Marxist History: British Society, Economy, and Culture since 1700* (Oxford: Basil Blackwell, 1985); Gavin Kitching, *Karl Marx and the Philosophy of Praxis* (London: Routledge, 1988); Terrell Carver, *Marx's Social Theory* (Oxford: Oxford University Press, 1981); and Georg Lukács, *History and Class Consciousness: Studies in Marxist Dialectics* (Cambridge, MA: MIT Press, 1971).

The interrelations of social theory, science, politics, and social-class structures are examined by Donna J. Haraway, "Primatology Is Politics by Other Means," in *Feminist Approaches in Science*, ed. Ruth Bleier (New York: Pergamon, 1986), pp. 77–118, *Primate Visions: Gender, Race, and Nature in the World of Modern Science* (New York: Routledge, 1989), and *Simians, Cyborgs, and Women: The Reinvention of Nature* (New York: Routledge, 1991); Sandra Harding, *The Science Question in Feminism* (Ithaca, NY: Cornell University Press, 1986), and *Whose Science? Whose Knowledge? Thinking from Women's Lives* (Ithaca, NY: Cornell University Press, 1991); and Sandra Harding and Merill B. Hintikka, eds., *Discovering Reality: Feminist Perspectives on Epistemology, Metaphysics, Methodology, and Philosophy of Science* (Dordrecht, Neth.: D. Reidel, 1983).

Thomas C. Patterson, "Political Economy and a Discourse Called 'Peruvian Archaeology,'" *Culture and History*, no. 4 (1989), 35–64, examines the historical development of archaeological interpretation in Peru. Constructive and informative discussions and/or critiques of culture history and cultural evolutionism are furnished by Kenneth Bock, "Evolution, Function, and Change," *American Sociological Review*, vol. 28 (1963), 229–237; Julian H. Steward, *Theory of Culture Change* (Urbana: University of Illinois Press, 1955); Robert McC. Adams, "Some Hypotheses on the Development of Early Civilizations," *American Antiquity*, vol. 21 (1956), 227–232, and *The Evolution of Urban Society* (Chicago: Aldine, 1966); John H. Rowe, "Stages and Periods in Archaeological Interpretation," *Southwestern Journal of Anthropology*, vol. 18

(1962), 40–54; and Thomas C. Patterson, "Development, Ecology, and Marginal Utility in Anthropology," *Dialectical Anthropology*, vol. 12, no. 1 (1987), 15–32.

The underpinnings of the various strands of processual archaeology are discussed in Mark Leone, ed., *Contemporary Archaeology: A Guide to Theory and Contributions* (Carbondale: Southern Illinois University Press, 1972); Kent Flannery, "The Cultural Evolution of Civilizations," *Annual Review of Ecology and Systematics*, vol. 3 (1972), 399–426; Stephen Athens, "Theory Building and the Study of Evolutionary Process in Complex Societies," in *For Theory Building in Archaeology: Essays on Faunal Remains, Aquatic Resources, Spatial Analysis, and Systemic Modeling*, ed. Lewis R. Binford (New York: Academic Press, 1977), pp. 353–384; and Colin Renfrew, "Systems Collapse as Social Transformation: Catastrophe and Anastrophe in Early State Societies," in *Transformations: Mathematical Approaches to Culture Change*, ed. Colin Renfrew and Kenneth L. Cooke (New York: Academic Press, 1979), 481–506.

The development of processual archaeology, its response to critiques, and its interplay with alternative approaches are examined by Matthew Spriggs, ed., *Marxist Approaches in Archaeology* (Cambridge: Cambridge University Press, 1984); Philip L. Kohl, "Materialist Approaches in Prehistory," *Annual Review of Anthropology*, vol. 10 (1981), 89–118, and "The Use and Abuse of World Systems Theory: The Case of the 'Pristine' West Asian State," in *Archaeological Thought in America*, ed. C. C. Lamberg-Karlovsky (Cambridge: Cambridge University Press, 1989), pp. 218–240; Valerie Pinsky and Alison Wylie, *Critical Traditions in Contemporary Archaeology* (Cambridge: Cambridge University Press, 1990); and Thomas C. Patterson, "History and Post-Processual Archaeologies," *Man*, vol. 24 (1989), 555–566.

chapter 3

Becoming Human

What distinguishes human existence is shared potentiality, or the capacity to learn to be concretely human. . . . We are incomplete or unfinished animals who complete or finish ourselves through culture. (Richard Lichtman, "The Production of Human Nature by Means of Human Nature")

The all-round character of human beings in any setting is what it is because of the nature of the prevailing social relations. (Norman Geras, Marx and Human Nature*)*

[One] must first deal with human nature in general, and then with [human] nature as it is modified in each historical epoch (Karl Marx, Capital*)*

Human beings are primates. The modern ones are anatomically unique. They walk on their hind legs and have long, narrow feet that are very well suited to striding. They have curved spines with large heads balanced on top; their faces are short, and their teeth are arranged in parabola-shaped arcs. They have large, opposable thumbs that give them both power and precision in grasping and manipulating objects. They have large brains with well-developed frontal and temporal areas that house centers associated with memory, handling objects, and speech. Much of what is unique about their behavior depends on labor, the use of tools, cooperation, and language as the primary means of communicating information about the world.

Between 10 and 5 million years ago, East Africa was inhabited by a hominoid species composed of arboreal quadrupeds that fed on leaves, shoots, and fruits. Its members spent large amounts of time climbing, feeding, and sleeping in trees. They were also sexually dimorphic: The adult males were much larger than the adult females.

About 5 million years ago, the local populations of this species split into two lineages, which diverged and ultimately became reproductively isolated. One line gave rise to modern chimpanzees, the other to hominids—that is, modern human beings, their fossil ancestors, and australopithecines. The protochimpanzees remained sexually dimorphic, quadrupedal forest and woodland dwellers that moved on the ground from tree to tree as they fed on arboreal foods. The earliest species in the hominid lineage were also sexually dimorphic. Local populations resided in the wooded savannas and more open habitats that were developing in eastern and southern Africa. Their members were omnivores that spent increasing amounts of time on the ground, foraging for edible seeds, roots, and tubers to supplement and eventually replace the frugivorous diet of their ancestors. They became increasingly bipedal in the process, even though they continued to climb trees to browse, to escape predators, and perhaps even to sleep.

Speciation occurred again among the African hominids about 2.5 to 3.0

million years ago and yielded two lineages. One consisted of the australo-pithecines, which perpetuated many of the anatomical and behavioral features found in the ancestral species: sexual dimorphism, relatively small brain volumes, and omnivorous diets that included large quantities of hard and abrasive objects (roots and seeds) that wore down the enamel on their enormous cheek teeth. The latest species in the lineage became extinct about a million years ago, possibly as a result of competition with terrestrial monkeys, which became common in the fossil records of eastern and southern Africa about that time.

The other lineage consisted of modern human beings and their immediate fossil ancestors of the last 2.5 million years. Human evolution during this period was a mosaic involving a number of trends and features. Males and females became larger, and sexual dimorphism was less pronounced in the long run; cheek teeth and the supporting jaw and muscular structures diminished in size; brains were reorganized and increased in volume. About 2 million years ago, these omnivores scavenged carcasses of dead animals abandoned by predators; later they began to hunt.

We now know a good deal about the physical appearance of the hominids and their descendants because of the skeletal parts and associations preserved in the fossil records of East and South Africa and later in Eurasia. The details of this account and the underlying biological processes involved are reasonably well known and summarized in Appendix 2. However, it is only part of the story of how we became human.

HUMAN NATURE AND HUMAN ORIGINS

In 1876, Frederick Engels wrote an essay, "The Part Played by Labour in the Transition from Ape to Man," in which he argued that labor was a distinctly human attribute and attempted to show the role it played in the development of humanity. Labor in its developed form was, for Engels, the process by which human beings interact with nature, appropriating its raw materials and transforming them with the use of tools to satisfy needs. He believed that labor created humanity itself. As the early hominids slowly became bipedal, their hands were increasingly freed to manipulate objects and, ultimately, to use and make tools. This development led, in turn, to new selection pressures on different parts of the body: to changes in the structure of the pelvis and the hand; manual dexterity; the organization of the brain; and language, which developed alongside these tool-related activities. As Charles Woolfson (1982:7) noted, the earliest humans "became *humanised* through labour."

What distinguishes early humans from the rest of the animal kingdom is their creative intelligence: Their productive techniques were extended and refined through time. This is not true of other animal species. Other animals occasionally use tools; for example, sea otters will place rocks on their stomachs and smash clamshells on them to get at the meat, and chimpanzees will lick a stick and then put it down a termite nest to harvest insects. Spiders weave webs, and bees build elaborate nests; however, what distinguishes these activities from those of humans is that people create structures in their mind before they build them in reality. Although other species change nature by virtue of their presence, human beings have ultimately transformed it to serve their needs. In the process, they have also remade themselves.

The "humanization" process was slow; it proceeded by what appear to be steplike increments because of the current limitations of the fossil record. Fossilized bones from East Africa indicate that hominids were already bipedal 4.5 million years ago. *Australopithecus afarensis*, which roamed through the park savannas from 4.5 to 2.8 million years ago and was the earliest species now known to be part of the human lineage, walked upright and showed some signs of cerebral reorganization; however, it still retained certain anatomical features, like brain size or the structure of its digits, that resembled its hominoid ancestors and, presumably, its protochimpanzee contemporaries.

The fossil remains of *Homo habilis*, the tropical African species that lived between 2.5 and 1.5 million years ago, indicate that its members had a human rather than an ape pattern of tooth eruption. This information implies that these early humans matured more slowly and, consequently, that dependency was prolonged. Their brains were about 25 percent to 50 percent larger than those of their australopithecine ancestors and contemporaries, and exhibited signs of further cerebral reorganization, suggesting hemispheric specialization and handedness, among other things. An indentation on the interior surface of a skull, known as KNM-ER 1470, shows the development of both lateral asymmetry and new convolutions on the brain's surface, corresponding to the expansion of that part of the parietal known as Broca's area, a center currently involved in the production of words and word sequences.

The archaeological record indicates that around 2.5 million years ago, *H. habilis* had begun to make and use simple stone tools to cut meat and tendons from animal carcasses and to smash long bones with hammerstones to extract marrow. They had figuratively moved into a scavenging niche in the forested habitats along the margins of lakes and streams, which hyenas, dogs, and the other scavengers tended to avoid. They may well have employed a "sneak strategy" to obtain bits of meat: Individuals surveyed the area to ensure that no carnivores were present; they rushed to the carcass and quickly cut off meat scraps from the bones before retreating to nearby trees to eat their prize. Sneak scavenging, given the nature of the activity, was probably done by an individual or two as their group mates watched. Individuals may have consumed and even shared meat with other members of their social group. Close examinations of their teeth with scanning electron microscopes suggest that meat was only one of the foods they consumed; their diet also consisted of grubs, tubers, seeds, and fruits.

These toolmakers used hand-sized cobbles made of dense materials, like granite, to strike large chips or flakes from the surface of finer-grained

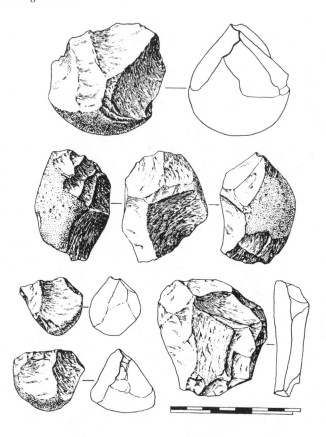

Stone tools from Koobi Fora tools, east of Lake Turkana in
northern Kenya. (a–d) cobble choppers; (e) flake struck
from a cobble chopper to resharpen its edge.

stones, like chert or obsidian. The cobbles were tools employed to make
other tools, flakes in this instance, that were then used to acquire food or
satisfy other needs. The flakes had sharp edges, which the individuals used
to strip flesh from bones and to cut animal hides, woody stems or branches,
and softer vegetable materials. They also used the hammerstones or the
sharp-edged pebble cores from which they had struck flakes to smash long
bones for their marrow.

Modern chimpanzees also make simple tools. They will strip the bark
from a plant stem to fish for termites or they will use crumbled, saliva-
soaked leaves to sponge up water. The tools they fashion are made from
objects that can be modified with their fingers, lips, or teeth. This process
contrasts with the foresight and purposiveness exhibited by *H. habilis* when
they manufactured stone tools and transformed a seemingly unyielding raw
material with an object other than their own body parts into tools that had
quite different shapes than the original substance.

In some instances, early hominids transported raw materials from one place to another. Excavations at Koobi Fora Site 50, a 1.5-million-year-old locality in northern Kenya, yielded more than 1,500 pieces of worked stone and several thousand bone fragments. The evidence suggests that the tool-makers had carried nodules of lava and chert from sources located as far away as 9 miles to the site, where there was no naturally occurring stone larger than a pea; they made tools on the spot in order to butcher a hippo-potamus that had died from natural causes or to scavenge one that been killed and abandoned by predators.

In these regards, the tool-using, toolmaking, and tool-transporting ca-pacities of the early hominids far outstripped those of nonhuman primates in the wild. Human tool use and manufacture were imitated, transmitted, and elaborated through time. These capabilities were cumulative and progressive activities for human beings. They were not cumulative and progressive among apes.

Language is a second distinctly human attribute. The communication systems of nonhuman primates are empathic and nonverbal; they are also multimodal in the sense that they involve expressions, gestures, and a lim-ited array of vocalizations that convey information about the emotions that are being felt by the members of a group and by changes in those emotional states; they convey little information about the physical environment itself. Human speech and language increase the capacity for empathic communica-tion and for conveying information about the environment.

Language is verbal thought, the medium through which the members of a human group achieve understanding and cooperation. Spoken language, as opposed to the vocalizations of nonhuman primates, allow human beings to uncouple stimulus and response and to share information about what oc-curred at times and places that are removed from the situation in which a communicative act is taking place. It expedites the communication of practical ideas and facilitates new kinds of activity among the individuals of a group. Language, according to L. Noiré (1917), who wrote about its origins, is "the voice of the community."

Two issues are involved in the origins of language: One focuses on the connections between speech and language, and the other on the form of the first language and its connections with the communication systems of nonhu-man primates.

It is clear that human speech and language originated sometime during the last 5 million years, after the hominids separated from the protochimpan-zees. In mammals, vocalizations are produced in the supralaryngeal tract, whose main functions are connected with eating, drinking, and breathing. In most mammalian species, including all of the nonhuman primates as well as the australopithecines, the larynx, or vocal chords, is situated high in the neck, which allows their members to breathe and swallow at the same time. This is also true of modern human infants; however, when they are about two years old, the larynx begins to descend down the neck, radically chang-ing the way young children eat, swallow, and make sounds. The position of

N = nasal cavity, S = soft palate,
T = tongue, P = pharynx, L = larynx,
E = epiglottis, V = vocal fold

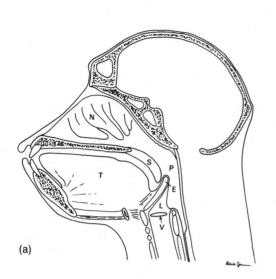

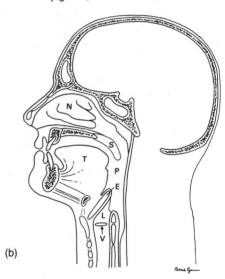

(a)

(b)

Comparison of the vocal chamber of (a) a chimpanzee and (b) modern human being.

the larynx is related to the location and shape of the bottom of the cranium, the basicranium. The basicranium-larynx configuration found in modern human beings is also linked with the adoption of upright posture. The lower position of the larynx increases the volume of the pharyngeal chamber, the voice box, where sounds emitted from the vocal chords are modified. The enlarged pharynx is the key to the production of the wide range of sounds found in modern human speech.

Fossils of *Homo erectus*, which lived from 1.6 million to 300,000 years ago, exhibit the first examples of a flexed basicranium that resembles the modern human configuration and differs from the flat, essentially apelike structures found in the australopithecines. This statement implies that the larynx of *H. erectus* had begun to descend into the neck, increasing the area and volume available to modify laryngeal sounds. It also implies that *H. erectus* could produce a greater array of sounds than its *H. habilis* ancestors. This does not mean, however, that *H. habilis* lacked control of its vocalizations. The development of language did not have to wait for the development of a vocal tract that could produce a wide range of sounds. Since speech is the sole beneficiary of the new basicranium-larnyx configuration, some kind of speech was already present and being selected for. This inference agrees with the evidence provided by the endocast of KNM-ER 1470, which indicates that *H. habilis* already possessed the beginnings of a speech production center, even though it could not produce the whole inventory of sounds achieved by its descendants.

The implication is that *H. habilis* had language or at least protolanguage skills. Language is simultaneously a representational system that divides the world into a series of analytical categories and a communication system. The function of a sign or a spoken word, which is merely an arbitrary sequence of sounds, is to replace the complexities of a representation or an analytical category with a symbol "that can be manipulated, along with other such counters, either in thought or speech" (Bickerton 1990:145). Communication made such representation systems usable. Advantages accrued to those communities whose members shared even a small vocabulary since it enhanced their problem-solving capabilities, their knowledge of their environment, and hence their ability to survive in a changing world.

Derek Bickerton (1990) has suggested that *H. habilis* possessed protolanguage. That is, the members of local populations of this species had already begun to attach arbitrary names or vocalizations to a few of the preexisting concepts in their representational system. What developed next were elements for linking words and mechanisms for expanding utterances, which ultimately permitted individuals to communicate verbally and to share increasingly diverse kinds of information with other members of their groups.

Language is the means by which reflection and the elaboration of experience take place. It is simultaneously a highly individual and a highly social process. Language is indeed the voice of a community. Questions we must now consider involve the composition, social relations, and activity patterns of the early hominid communities and how these evolved through time.

THE DIVISION OF LABOR

This discussion draws heavily on the analyses of the late Lila Leibowitz (1986) and on assessments of her work by Christine Gailey (1985, 1988). Leibowitz pointed out that writers who otherwise portray the composition and social relations of early hominid societies in quite different ways tend to agree on one thing: There was a division of labor. That is, not all of the individuals in these populations produced the same array of goods; as a result, one individual exchanged a portion of its goods in return for some of the items necessary for life that were produced by other individuals.

Biodeterminists, typically drawing on liberal social theory, root the division of labor in biology. In their view, exchange occurred because of the biological differences between males and females, which yield different dispositions and/or activity profiles. Thus, females, whose mobility is periodically constrained by the burden of infant care, remained in close proximity to home bases, foraging for vegetable foods, while the larger, more aggressive and dominant males hunted for meat, which was essential for survival. The males shared this prize with their own females and offspring. Following the logic of this perspective, the stereotypical nuclear family of mid-twentieth-century U.S. society and the subordination of women are not only rooted in biology but also projected nearly 2 million years back in time.

In contrast to the essentialist arguments of the biodeterminists, more sociologically oriented writers, drawing explicitly or implicitly on Marxist social thought, constructed a different sequence of events. In their view, the females and the males of these early groups engaged in the same subsistence activities and produced similar ranges of goods. They began to share what they did not consume with others around them, typically individuals of the opposite sex. However, there are certain problems with this formulation as well; for example, it does not adequately explain how individuals of both sexes transformed themselves from self-feeders into producers who produced different arrays of goods.

Leibowitz was suggesting that *H. habilis* and perhaps the earliest *H. erectus* populations did not have a sexual division of labor apart from biological reproduction. This view implies that since both sexes were self-feeders, the male dominance and patriarchal social relations found in some later societies are not rooted in biology but rather in specific socially and historically constituted circumstances. Also it does not imply that these early hominids were non- or protohuman, because they lacked a division of labor but rather that sex differences were not linked with production during the early stages of human social development.

Early hominid populations were sexually dimorphic; adult males were larger than adult females, but the size differences were not as great as those found in other nonhuman primate species, like chimpanzees. Leibowitz did not assume, as did many of the early researchers in primate social behavior studies, that sexual dimorphism was associated with the dominance of males or that males maintained order within groups and protected their females and young. She reexamined information about sexually dimorphic nonhuman primates and found that the larger size of the males was related to reproductive and foraging advantages, not to dominance and sex roles.

The males and females of sexually dimorphic species have roughly similar growth rates until puberty; however, the males continue to grow for several years after reaching this stage, whereas the females stop. The smaller, more compact body frames of females are correlated with more efficient storage of the fats required for fertility and for energy conservation during pregnancy, birth, and lactation. The larger body sizes of adult males are correlated with either solitary existence (orangutans) or transient group membership (chimpanzees and gorillas). Thus, larger body size gives solitary males a greater chance for survival outside a social group. Leibowitz's (1986:85) first conclusion was that sexual dimorphism "allows both males and females to engage in the *same* foraging activities, only in different geographical ranges."

Leibowitz also observed that the more sexually dimorphic primate species exhibit a great deal of variability in male roles and the relations between sexes within social groups. Chimpanzees, the apes most closely related to humans, show the greatest flexibility and diversity of relations. The core members of chimpanzee social groups are adult females and their juvenile and younger offspring. Adult males join these core groups temporarily for greater or lesser periods of time, before wandering off to forage alone or in all-male groups in different localities. Self-feeding is the rule in both the core and all-male groups, except on those rare occasions when meat is acquired and occasionally shared with individuals who are foraging nearby.

Demographic studies of the australopithecine fossil remains from South Africa, examined by Leibowitz, indicate that these species exhibited an essentially human rather than ape pattern of maturation. They reached reproductive age at about the same rate as modern humans. The paleodemographic studies also indicate that infant and juvenile mortality was high, that about half of the individuals born either died or were killed before they reached reproductive age, and that the average life span of the survivors was about twenty years. Assuming that females had their first infants shortly after reaching puberty, when they were twelve or thirteen years old, and that they did not ovulate for the three years or so they were lactating and nursing, their second offspring would have been born when they were fifteen or sixteen years old and their third when they were eighteen or nineteen years old.

Such a demographic profile has several implications. First, few, if any, females were alive when their offspring reached puberty. Second, most of the members of a social group were prepubescent individuals who had not yet reached reproductive age. Third, many of the juveniles were orphans who had to forage for themselves in order to survive. Fourth, they were exposed to a prolonged learning period in a group that was made up largely of other prepubescent individuals—a group that was large enough to ensure their safety. The thirteen *A. afarensis* individuals who were caught in a flash flood in the Hadar region of Ethiopia—five adults, four infants, and four juveniles—provide some indication of the size of one early hominid group during a part of its developmental cycle. The conclusion Leibowitz drew from the paleodemographic evidence was that age or stage of maturation, which ultimately is a culturally defined category, may have been more important than sex in structuring social relations in early human populations.

Her observations and arguments suggest a model of early hominid society. The social groups were small and composed mainly of individuals who had not yet reached reproductive age. Within these groups prepubescent males and females of the same age were roughly similar in size; they foraged from a young age for themselves, gathering various plant foods, scavenging the remains of carcasses, and perhaps even killing small or incapacitated animals when such opportunities appeared. They shared food with other individuals, when there was more than any one of them could consume. In the process of growing up in a small group, they learned to use and make simple wooden and stone tools from their peers. They shared information about the world around them through language or protolanguage. Their understandings of this world were gained through the practical activities and experiences, the successes and failures, of everyday life. They purposefully transformed their environments through tool use in production, through a rudimentary age-based division of labor, and through a propensity to share food and information.

Food sharing, whatever its nature, involved a degree of cooperation that does not exist among contemporary nonhuman primates and presumably did not exist among their ancestors. It is a distinctly human attribute that involves cooperation among individuals and new levels of trust and confidence in the motivations of others. These populations survived but did not grow rapidly. Cultural understandings and ways of doing things changed slowly. There were so few individuals in these early groups that new ways of seeing and understanding the world or of making new tools that improved their chances for survival often were not validated because of the absence of an appreciative audience.

If early human populations lacked a division of labor, when did one appear? Leibowitz argued that there are signs of its existence in later *H. erectus* populations, those that existed between about 700,000 and 400,000 years ago. Until this period, the core social groups of human populations, in her view, were made up mainly of juveniles with a few adult females and their infants and transient adult males. The adult males were loosely affiliated with the core groups; they moved in and out of these social units several times each year and spent the remainder of the time foraging alone or with other adult males. The division of labor, to the extent it existed, was structured by age rather than sexual distinctions.

Leibowitz argued that the reduced sexual dimorphism exhibited by the generally larger, later *H. erectus* individuals indicates that adult males had been incorporated into the juvenile and adult female and infant groups on a full-time basis. Their integration into these social units occurred about the same time and in conjunction with two other changes that facilitated the development of a more elaborate division of labor: the increased importance of systematic hunting and, consequently, of meat in the daily diet, and the appearance of spatially organized, hunting and hearth-centered activities that were carried out simultaneously in different places.

The changes in the productive forces that accompanied these developments occurred about the same time that human populations began to move out of the tropics and inhabit the temperate environments of Eurasia for the first time on a permanent basis. This event occurred between about 1 million and 700,000 years ago. The earliest dated artifacts in Europe—some stone flakes, scrapers, and choppers—have been found under a layer of volcanic origin at Isernia La Pineta, southeast of Rome, that was deposited around 730,000 years ago. The earliest evidence that people had tamed fire to provide heat and light; to cook food; to fire-harden the tips of spears, digging sticks, or probes; and to protect themselves from predators also dates to the period between 1 million and 700,000 years ago; it comes from the temperate region of north China.

The increased body size of *H. erectus*—some adults were about 5 feet tall and weighed between 90 and 100 pounds—indicates that their energy demands surpassed those of their smaller ancestors. According to Leibowitz, the meat they acquired by scavenging and increasingly by hunting satisfied their growing demand for additional food resources. The increased consumption of animal meat and fats not only enhanced the fertility of females but also improved infant and juvenile survival rates. This development suggested that life expectancy may have increased slightly and that the young became dependent on adults for a longer period. As a result, sharing became more common, and age began to play a more important role in structuring interpersonal relations within the group.

Increased meat consumption provided the members of these communities with the energy they needed to forage and hunt over wider areas. Sharing allowed them to separate for brief periods and to carry out different or specialized subsistence activities at roughly the same time in the various parts of the territory through which they roamed. Leibowitz distinguished between hunting and hearth-centered activities; she assumed that the adult males hunted and that nursing females or those in the later stages of pregnancy engaged in hearth-centered activities, like toolmaking or plant foraging. Thus, in her view, sexual differences became a second important dimension along which intragroup social relations were structured. More important, however, the increasingly complex technology that was appearing might have spawned specialization in teaching and learning that extended beyond age factors.

The movement of human populations out of the tropics between 1 million and 700,000 years ago coincided with a series of climatic changes, described in Appendix C, which alternately transformed the Sahara of northern Africa from a grassland to a desert and then back to a savanna. Human populations moved, along with other plants and animals from tropical Africa, into the Sahara when wetter conditions prevailed and retreated from the area when its vegetation and other resources withered during the drier climatic regimes. Some human populations, squeezed out of the Sahara by the onset of drier conditions, moved around the Mediterranean basin and entered the Eurasian landmass as glaciers were beginning to form in its mountain ranges and at higher latitudes. During such periods, some of the temperate Eurasian environments were already inhabited by herd animals, which would have provided the human immigrants with a variety of relatively accessible energy resources if they settled in those regions and adopted a mobile lifeway that would allow them to respond quickly to the movement of game.

The movement of human beings into temperate environments may have created other conditions as well. For instance, it may have promoted more permanent coresidence of adult males with core groups, especially during the winter months, when cold weather would have forced creatures without fur to make clothing and seek shelter in caves or hide-covered structures that were warmed and lit with fires in the hearths.

Leibowitz's analyses emphasize the role played by the unique capacity of human beings to create symbols and culture, to communicate with language, and to transform their environment and their own social and reproductive arrangements by making subsistence dependent on toolmaking. Although her inquiries support Engels's general conclusion, they direct attention away from the empirical weakness and linear causation of his argument toward the dialectic of using and changing a world that is experienced in cultural terms.

TOOLS AND TECHNOLOGY

Stone tools and their associations are a major source of information about human behavior from about 2.5 million to 300,000 years ago. Although hominids may have used sticks, cobbles, and simple, unworked stone flakes for a variety of purposes before 2.5 million years ago, the earliest recognizable stone tools are those of the Oldowan tradition, which have been found in archaeological contexts that date between 2.5 and 1.5 million years ago. The Oldowan stoneworking technology is simple but efficient. The toolmakers understood the fracture characteristics of lava and other rocks; they struck them with cobble hammerstones to remove flakes with sharp edges that they then used to butcher and cut meat, to saw and scrape wood, and to cut softer plant parts. That they often removed a sequence of flakes from a core to obtain one with a particular shape or size indicates that they conceptualized the characteristics of the tool they wanted before they actually began to transform the raw material from which it was made.

The earliest standardized stone tools appeared about 1.5 million years ago and belong to the Acheulean tradition. Acheulean tool kits have high proportions of bifacially chipped stone tools, the best known and most distinctive of which are hand axes and cleavers with well-defined long axes and standardized shapes. Although the size of these implements varies, their proportions are relatively uniform. Thus, many toolmakers, working over tens of thousands of years, shared the same, culturally transmitted sense of proportion concerning the appearance of stone tools.

They made these implements on large flakes or cobbles by removing flakes from two directions along a portion of their circumference to produce a flat, sharp working edge. This chipping often extends far back from the edges of the tool and frequently covers all of the two opposed surfaces. Usually, one end of a hand axe is pointed and the other rounded. These tools are probably elaborations of the "protobifaces" found in some of the later Oldowan assembles. Unlike the hand axes that come to a point, the cleavers have relatively straight cutting edges oriented perpendicular to their long axes. The hand axes may have been thrown or used as mattocks, and the cleavers may have been used for chopping; scraping meat from bones; or cutting through ligaments, tendons, and bone. The flake removed in the course of making these tools may also have been made into other kinds of tools, such as scrapers or knives, which were also used to cut meat, scrape hides, or sharpen sticks.

The Acheulean tradition of making tools changed over time. About 300,000 years ago, the makers of stone tools began to use a variety of prepared-core techniques; that is, they chipped the surface of a suitable rock or cobble in such a way that the shape and size of the last flake to be removed from the core were predetermined by the preparatory work. These prepared-core techniques—of which the best known is called the Levallois, or tortoise-core technique—were widespread in Europe, North Africa, and the Near East. Assemblages with prepared cores have also been found at various localities in sub-Saharan Africa and eastern and south Asia from India to northern China and through the Malay Peninsula and Indochina to Java.

EVERYDAY LIFE 300,000 YEARS AGO

Early archaeological sites in which the associations of tools, bones, and other remains are the result of human activity rather than mechanical or natural processes are less common than archaeologists assumed ten or twenty years ago. Various sites—whose archaeological associations were thought to display high degrees of integrity; that is, they were the products of human rather than mechanical activity—have been restudied, and the integrity of the associations may be lower than originally claimed.

Several archaeological sites that date between about 250,000 and 500,000 years ago have yielded information about the daily lives of our distant ancestors. The archaeological remains at these localities were left by humans belonging to the species *Homo erectus*.

One of the sites is Terra Amata, located in Nice on the French Riviera in beach deposits that are roughly half a million years old. When the site was occupied, the climate was somewhat cooler and more humid than it is now. The people lived on a sandy beach strewn with cobbles and on a sand dune behind it that overlooked a small cove. The camp was sheltered from the winds that blew almost continuously from the north and west. Saltwater plants grew along the edge of the cove, and a small freshwater stream that flowed by the campsite was covered with water lilies during the spring. Pine and oak trees grew on the coastal areas and foothills behind the dunes. Farther up the hills fir and Norway pine were abundant. Small herds of elephants, oxen, and rhinoceroses browsed on the trees and bushes of the coastal lowlands. Red deer also browsed in the lowlands and on the tree-covered slopes beyond. Wild boars and ibex were found in the forested areas at higher elevations.

Henry de Lumley, who excavated Terra Amata, thought that the people who camped there lived in oval huts that ranged from 26 to 49 feet in length and from 13 to 20 feet in width. The walls of these flimsy structures were formed by wooden stakes about 3 inches in diameter that were driven into the sand and held in place by rocks and boulders piled against them. Inside each hut were several posts about a foot in diameter that probably supported a ridge pole, which in turn supported the stakes and branches that formed

WORK SPACE

WORK SPACE

HEARTH

WORK SPACE

Reconstruction by Henry de Lumley of an oval hut found at Terra Amata on the French Riviera. (*From Henry de Lumley, "A Paleolithic Camp at Nice." Copyright © 1969 by Scientific American, Inc. All rights reserved*.)

the sides of the huts. Traces of eleven living floors superimposed almost exactly on top of one another and separated by thin lenses of windblown sand led de Lumley to suggest that the site was occupied for eleven consecutive years, presumably by the same group of people. However, a later study by Paola Villa showed that the integrity of the stratigraphic units was not as high as de Lumley had assumed since stone flakes from various living floors could be fitted together to reform the cores from which they had been struck; consequently, there was no way to distinguish the activities found on one floor from those found on the others. This finding also raises questions about the huts. Was there just one hut on the sand dune? Were huts rebuilt on the same spot several years in a row and other materials reused from one year to the next? Or were there no huts at all?

The people carried out various activities at Terra Amata. A toolmaker sat on an animal skin amid chips and other debris produced by making stone tools. A spherical wooden bowl with a rough bottom was filled with something that dried into a nondescript whitish substance. Lumps of red ocher, a natural red pigment, had been rubbed and worn through use into pencil-like objects. Meat was cooked over open fires in the hearths. Human feces found outside one of the huts contained the pollen of plants that flower in the late spring and early summer, which suggests that people came to Terra Amata around late April and remained there until June. One of the stone tools found at the campsite was made from rock that outcrops more than 30 miles away, indicating not only that they moved around during the year but also that they carried certain tools with them for future use; these prized implements were repaired and maintained before they were finally abandoned.

The people of Terra Amata ate turtles, birds, and a variety of mammals. Although they hunted small animals, like rabbits, they seem to have preferred larger animals, especially red deer. They also butchered elephants, wild boars, ibex, rhinoceroses, and oxen; they probably avoided healthy adult animals and preyed instead on very young, very old, and sick or injured animals because they were easier to kill. They may also have eaten mussels, limpets, and oysters gathered along the shore of the cove and scavenged fish that washed up on the beach.

Torralba, an open site in north-central Spain, provides additional information about the subsistence activities of our mid-Pleistocene ancestors. When it was used, either 200,000 or 400,000 years ago, the climate of the area was about 5° to 10° F. cooler than it is today. Torralba lies in a small, steep-sided valley. Pine trees grew on the plateau above the cliffs forming the edge of the valley and gradually merged with the steppe grasslands found at higher elevations. A river flowed slowly across the valley floor through ponds and marshes choked with reeds and sedges. Areas covered with low grasses bordered these seasonal swamps. Game was probably more abundant in the valley-floor grasslands than in the pine parklands and steppe grasslands that covered the plateau, especially during the spring and autumn, when elephants, horses, wild cattle, and other large herbivores moved though the valley.

Judging from the virtual absence of small-animal and bird remains, the human inhabitants of the Torralba apparently were interested principally in large animals, some of which had strayed too close to the edge of the swamp and had become stuck in the muddy ground. In some instances, they may have set grass fires on the valley floor to drive animals into swampy or muddy areas, where they would become mired. Fires may have been built near the dead animals, presumably to keep away insects and to smoke the meat that was being removed from the carcasses. The humans skinned animals with small, sharp flakes, which were discarded when they became dull, and they butchered the various kinds of animals in different ways. For example, they frequently removed the limbs of smaller animals such as horses or red deer; consequently, the skeletal remains of these species are generally incomplete and scattered over the site. Larger animals, like elephants, were usually butchered on the spot and slabs of meat were carried away; as a result, the skeletons of the large species are usually fairly complete but disarticulated.

Torralba and the nearby site of Ambrona were located on game trails that herd animals used during the spring and autumn as they moved between summer and winter pastures. Thus, human groups established seasonal campsites in the valley around Torralba in the spring and fall months,

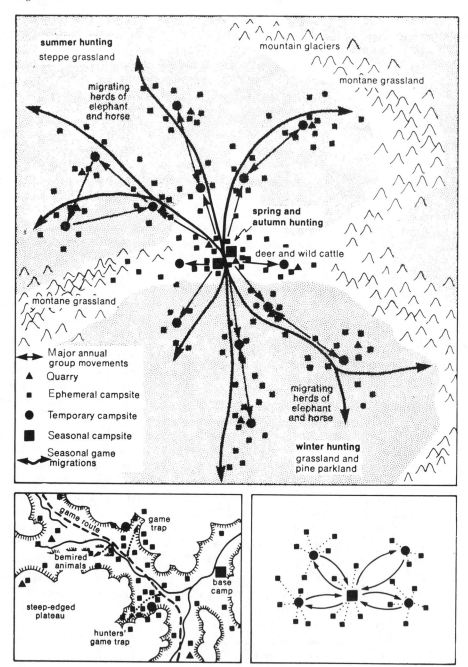

The seasonal movements of human groups dwelling and hunting around Torralba, Spain.

when game was especially abundant. As the annual migrations drew to a close, the groups dispersed and followed the herds into the steppe grasslands during the summers and the pine parklands in the winter months.

Zhoukoudian (Choukoutien) Cave—a half-million-year-old site located southwest of Beijing, China—has yielded, over the past sixty years, the remains of at least forty *H. erectus* individuals, several thousand stone flakes used as implements, and a wide variety of animal species: giant beavers, horses, water buffalo, and deer, to name some of the more common ones. Some of the animal bones were burned, suggesting that they had been cooked over fires. This raised questions about how the hominid remains, many of which had been broken open, got into the cave. Was this a sign of human cannibalism, as some popular writers suggested, and thus support for the argument that humans are innately aggressive? Or was it the product of other causes?

It now appears that the early hominids were not the only occupants of the cave. They alternated residence or use of the cave with packs of scavenging, giant hyenas, who used it as a den. It is highly unlikely that the two species used the cave at the same time. The hyenas dragged animal parts into the den, consumed the meat, broke and chewed the bones, and defecated in the cave. This practice suggests that the remains of the forty human beings found in the cave, about half of whom were children who died before the age of fourteen, were introduced and consumed by carnivorous scavengers during the 50,000 years or so in which the cave deposits accumulated. Based on these figures, hyenas consumed one human being every 1,250 years, which suggests that human flesh was not one of their major protein sources. The data provide no support at all for claims that the human beings who sporadically occupied Zhoukoudian Cave killed and cannibalized other members of their species for meat.

The processes of humanization began about 5 million years ago with the emergence of hominids—terrestrial bipeds whose brains already exhibited some signs of cerebral reorganization. By 2 million years ago, they were culture-bearing, social creatures who foraged and scavenged, who made tools, who used language for thought and verbal communication, and who occasionally shared the products of their labor with other members of their social groups. These skills, along with a continually expanding capacity for cooperation, enhanced the survival of the species, not only in the tropics but also after human groups moved into the temperate areas of Eurasia around 750,000 years ago.

FURTHER READINGS: A BRIEF GUIDE

Frederick Engels's essay, "The Part Played by Labor in the Transition from Ape to Man," is reprinted in his *The Origin of the Family, Private Property and the State*, ed. Eleanor B. Leacock (New York: International Publishers, 1972), pp. 251–264. The implications of the essay, in light of research studies, is examined by Charles Woolfson, *The Labour Theory of Culture: A Reexamination of Engels's Theory of Human Origins* (London: Routledge & Kegan Paul, 1982); Bruce G. Trigger, "Engels on the Part Played by Labor in the Transition from Ape to Man: An Anticipation of Contemporary Anthropological Theory," *Canadian Review of Sociology and Anthropology*, vol. 4, no. 3 (1966), 165–176; and Sherwood L. Washburn and Ruth Moore, *Ape into Man* (Boston: Little, Brown, 1987).

Paul Heyer, *Nature, Human Nature, and Society: Marx, Darwin, Biology, and the Human Sciences* (Westport, CT: Greenwood Press, 1982); John Lewis, *The Uniqueness of Man* (London: Lawrence & Wishart, 1974); Richard Lichtman, "The Production of Human Nature by Human Nature," *Culture, Nature, Socialism*, no. 4 (1990), 13–51; Leslie Stevenson, *Seven Theories of Human Nature* (Oxford: Oxford University Press, 1987); Roger Trigg, *Ideas of Human Nature: An Historical Introduction* (Oxford: Basil Blackwell, 1988); and Norman Geras, *Marx and Human Nature: Refutation of a Legend* (London: Verso, 1983), discuss theories of human nature, including those that see it rooted in biology and those that view it as historically constituted in the concrete social relations of given societies.

For discussions of scavenging by early hominid populations, see Robert J. Blumenshine, "Characteristics of an Early Hominid Scavenging Niche," *Current Anthropology*, vol. 28, no. 3 (1987), 383–406; and Pat Shipman, "Scavenging or Hunting in Early Hominids: Theoretical Framework and Tests," *American Anthropologist*, vol. 88, no. 1 (1986), 27–43.

Fossil evidence for the evolution of the human brain is examined and assessed by Ralph L. Holloway, "Cerebral Brain Endocast Pattern of *Australopithecus afarensis*," *Nature*, vol. 303, no. 5916 (1981), 420–422; Ralph L. Holloway and Marie C. de la Coste-Lareymonde, "Brain Endocast Asymmetry in Pongids and Hominids: Some Preliminary Findings on the Paleontology of Cerebral Dominance," *American Journal of Physical Anthropology*, vol. 58, no. 1 (1982), 101–110; and Ralph L. Holloway, "Human Brain Evolution: A Search for Units, Models and Synthesis," *Canadian Journal of Anthropology*, vol. 3, no. 2 (1983), 215–232.

The development of language and human speech are discussed by Derek Bickerton, *Language and Species* (Chicago: University of Chicago Press, 1990); Jeffrey T. Laitman, "The Anatomy of Human Speech," *Natural History*, vol. 93, no. 8 (1984), 20–27; and L. Noiré, *The Origin and Philosophy of Language* (Chicago: Open Court Publishing, 1917). Nonhuman primate communication systems are examined by Jane B. Lancaster, "Primate Communication Systems and the Emergence of Human Language," in *Primates: Studies in Adaptation and Variability*, ed. Phyllis Jay (New York: Holt, Rinehart & Winston, 1968), pp. 439–457; and Peter Marler, "Communication in Monkeys and Apes," in *Primate Behavior*, ed. Irven B. DeVore (New York: Holt, Rinehart & Winston, 1964), pp. 544–584.

For thought-provoking analyses of the composition and social relations of early hominid society, see Lila Leibowitz, "In the Beginning . . .: The Origins of the Sexual Division of Labour and the Development of the First

Human Societies," in *Women's Work, Men's Property: The Origins of Gender and Class*, ed. Stephanie Coontz and Peta Henderson (London: Verso, 1986), pp. 43–75. Christine W. Gailey, "Sex and Gender in Human Origins: Lila Leibowitz on Early *Homo* Populations," paper presented at the annual meeting of the American Ethnological Society, Toronto, 1985, and "Evolutionary Perspectives on Gender Hierarchy," in *Analyzing Gender: A Handbook of Social Science Research*, ed. Beth B. Hess and Myra M. Ferree, (London: Sage Publications, 1988), pp. 32–67, offers a critical assessment of her work.

Evidence for the conservation and use of fire is summarized by J. Desmond Clark and F. W. K. Harris, "Fire and Its Roles in Early Hominid Lifeways," *African Archaeological Review*, vol. 3, no. 1 (1986), 3–28; and Stephen R. James, "Hominid Use of Fire in the Lower and Middle Pleistocene: A Review of the Evidence," *Current Anthropology*, vol. 30, no. 1 (1989), 1–26.

Recent discussions of the movement of human populations out of the tropics into temperate regions are Elizabeth S. Vrba, "Ecological and Adaptive Changes Associated with Early Hominid Evolution," in *Ancestors: The Hard Evidence*, ed. Eric Delson (New York: Alan R. Liss, 1985), pp. 63–71; Clive Gamble, "Man the Shoveler: Alternative Models for Middle Pleistocene Colonization and Occupation in Northern Latitudes, in *The Pleistocene Old World: Regional Perspectives*, ed. Olga Soffer (New York: Plenum Press, 1987), pp. 79–98, and *The Paleolithic Settlement of Europe* (Cambridge: Cambridge University Press, 1986); Neil Roberts, "Pleistocene Environments in Time and Space," in *Hominid Evolution and Community Ecology*, ed. Robert Foley (New York: Academic Press, 1984), pp. 25–54; Chris B. Stringer, "The Origin of Early Modern Humans: A Comparison of the European and non-European Evidence," and Robert Foley, "The Ecological Conditions of Speciation: A Comparative Approach to the Origins of Anatomically-Modern Humans," both in *The Human Revolution: Behavioural and Biological Perspectives on the Origins of Modern Humans*, ed. Paul Mellars and Chris Stringer (Princeton, NJ: Princeton University Press, 1989), pp. 232–244 and 298–320.

Olduvai Gorge, Koobi Fora, and other early sites in East Africa are discussed by Glynn L. Isaac, "The Archaeology of Human Origins: Studies of the Lower Pleistocene in East Africa 1971–1981," in *Advances in World Archaeology*, ed. Fred Wendorf and Angela E. Close, vol. 3 (Orlando, FL: Academic Press, 1984), pp. 1–87.

Terra Amata is described and discussed by Henry de Lumley, "A Paleolithic Cap at Nice," *Scientific American*, vol. 218, no. 5 (1969), 42–50; and Paola Villa, *Terra Amata and the Middle Pleistocene Archaeological Record of Southern France* (Berkeley: University of California Press, 1983).

Torralba is examined by Leslie G. Freeman, "Acheulean Sites and Stratigraphy in Iberia and the Maghreb," in *After the Australopithecines*, ed. Karl W. Butzer and and Glenn L. Isaacs (The Hague: Mouton Publishers, 1975), pp. 661–743, and "The Analysis of Some Occupation Floor Distributions from Earlier and Middle Paleolithic Sites in Spain," in *Views of the Past*, ed. Leslie G. Freeman (The Hague: Mouton Publishers, 1978), pp. 57–116; Karl W.

Butzer, *Archaeology as Human Ecology: Method and Theory for a Contextual Approach* (Cambridge: Cambridge University Press, 1982); and Pat Shipman and Jennie Rose, "Evidence of Butchery and Hominid Activity at Torralba and Ambrona: An Evaluation Using Microscopic Techniques," *Journal of Archaeological Science*, vol. 10, no. 3 (1983), 465–474.

Zhoukoudian is considered by Lewis R. Binford and Chuan Kun Ho, "Taphonomy at a Distance: Zhoukoudian, 'The Cave Home' of Beijing Man?" *Current Anthropology*, vol. 26, no. 4 (1985), 413–442; and Lewis R. Binford and Nancy Stone, "Zhoukoudian: A Closer Look," *Current Anthropology*, vol. 27, no. 5 (1986), 453–476.

chapter 4

Human Society and Modern Human Beings

[A] mode of production based on a division of labor between the sexes, a form of primitive communism, developed out of a prior mode or protomode. . . . [Communities manifesting such a division of labor] are presumed to have been foraging groups in which each individual collected the total range of foods . . . and sharing took place at times between those who foraged together. (Janet Siskind, "Kinship and Mode of Production")

Foraging peoples have played an important role in human history. They represent the original condition of humankind, the system of production that prevailed during virtually 99 percent of human history. (Eleanor Leacock and Richard Lee, Politics and History in Band Societies)

The transition from ancient to fully modern human beings occurred between 300,000 and 40,000 years ago. We know relatively little about what happened during its early stages, the period that lasted from about 300,000 to 70,000 years ago. There are only a few human fossils from this time, and these are fragmentary and incomplete. However, given what we know about the appearance of ancient and fully modern human beings, we can be quite certain that the major anatomical changes that occurred during the early stages were confined largely to the shape of the head and reflect the expansion of the parietal and temporal lobes of the brain. These changes were adaptive responses to a social milieu in which increased memory, capacity for speech, and facility at integrating and associating sensory information were advantageous.

Human behavior changed slowly during the transition, at least by today's standards; however, it was changing many times more rapidly than it had at any previous time in human history. The early archaic *Homo sapiens* continued to do many things the same way their mid-Pleistocene ancestors did them. For example, they continued to use Acheulean tools that were only slightly different in shape from those used by their remote ancestors half a million years earlier; however, some of them also made tools in a new way, called the Levallois technique, which made more efficient use of raw materials than earlier stoneworking methods.

The reason human behavior changed so slowly up to this time was that human groups were small; they probably numbered between ten and twenty individuals until about 300,000 years ago. This fact was important because new behavior and perceptions of the world usually originate among individuals who have not yet learned the culturally accepted ways of doing things or of viewing what is around them. These individuals were, and still are, concentrated among the younger rather than the older members of a group. When their numbers were small, innovative behavior and perceptions were validated less often. Thus, many innovative ideas were stillborn, and others perished without a trace for lack of an audience that was responsive and supportive. The outcome of this situation was that old patterns of behavior and ways of looking at the world were perpetuated.

By itself, the number of individuals in a group is a neutral factor in the process leading to technological, social, and cultural change. If concentrations of individuals occur within a group and the processes of imitation, collaboration, and validation are encouraged, there is a greater certainty that innovative ideas and behavior will emerge—particularly when these interactions take place in a social milieu that anticipates that change will take place and actively encourages it. Frequently, the members of a group limit their expectation of change to certain aspects of culture. For example, in our own society we expect fairly rapid changes in commodities produced for sale in the market, like computers or clothing fashions, and little or no change in other aspects, such as language or values.

The productive forces of these early societies were not well developed. Their resource base was small, their tools were simple, the labor power available to wield these implements in order to appropriate raw materials was minimal, and the productivity of the labor power was low. Yet people were able to produce more than just what was necessary to meet their needs and to ensure the continuation of their community into the future. That is, they carried out work activities above and beyond the labor necessary to sustain the group. The ability to perform surplus labor, regardless of the amount, was absolutely essential for demographic replacement, for the reproduction of the social relations that constituted the community, and for the further development of its productive forces. The effects of surplus labor were most noticeable when technological innovations were adopted and the productivity of labor, and in some instances the size of the group as well, increased. Without the time to try new ways of doing things, there would have been no innovations or they would have occurred much less frequently. The time to experiment was provided by the surplus labor of the group.

THE STRUCTURE OF HUMAN SOCIETY: 100,000 TO 40,000 YEARS AGO

Seventy thousand years ago, our ancestors lived in a social milieu that was fundamentally different from anything we are familiar with today. There were no social classes, and there was no state to promote the welfare of individuals or to prevent them from satisfying their needs. People lived in small groups. For days, perhaps even months, they saw only people they knew. The appearance of a stranger in their midst must have been a notable event, one that was both exciting and perhaps slightly frightening. People were totally dependent on one another for survival in a way that is very difficult for us to understand.

The most distinctive features of such societies were (1) the collective possession of and use-rights to food and other raw materials; (2) cooperation and sharing; and (3) the absence of a social division of labor, that is, exploitation, in which the members of one group permanently appropriated or extorted labor or goods from other members. Eleanor Leacock (1982) has argued that there was no exploitation in these early (primitive) communal societies because of the unity of the production process and the direct participation of all members in the production, distribution, circulation, and consumption of socially produced goods. Thus each individual was dependent on the group as a whole, and there were no structural differences between producers and nonproducers. Such a distinction existed only at a particular instant in time and only from the perspective of a given individual who was too young for, too old for, or not a participant in a particular labor process. The distinction disappeared when the focus was extended beyond the particular moment, the particular individual, and the particular work activity. It was inverted as a participant, a direct producer, in one work activity became a consumer in the next.

At this time, the main technical divisions of labor in these communities may have been more structured by age differences than by gender. If so, we can distinguish three groups, each of which played a different economic role at any given moment. The adults, both men and women, made up the group that must have been largely responsible for the acquisition of food and the production of other goods. A second group contained infants and children—individuals who were too young to be engaged more than marginally in the productive process. The third group consisted of individuals who were either too old or had ailments, like arthritis, that made it difficult for them to forage or hunt but perhaps did not prevent them from carrying out other work activities, like hide preparation or sewing.

Some subsistence activities, such as collecting wild plants, could have been carried out by a number of individuals working independently. Other subsistence activities, such as driving animals over the cliffs at La Quina, were complex tasks that required the cooperation of a number of individuals. An important question is this: How were these cooperative work groups organized? In a social setting where community membership and size were not completely stable because of sporadic or periodic fragmentation, cooperative production units were organized to carry out particular tasks. Although it is unlikely that any single individual participated in every cooperative work activity, it is likely, given the age structure and size of the communities, that they cooperated repeatedly with one another over time.

It is clear that these hunters and gatherers shared the products of their labor with infants and children, on the one hand, and with old or ailing individuals, on the other. For example, they cared for a fifty-year-old man from La Chapelle-aux-Saints who had relatively few teeth and a severe case of spinal arthritis for several years before he died. On at least two different occasions they cared for the man from Shanidar Cave whose arm had been amputated—once after he lost his limb and, later, as he recuperated from a severe head injury. By sharing with and caring for the infants and children, the adults in the group were ensuring the continued existence of the group itself over a period that encompassed more than one generation. This process is called *social reproduction*.

Richard Lee (1990:227–228) points out that social reproduction is a complicated process. It involves (1) those activities—for instance, the provisioning of food, tools, and emotional support—that occur on a daily and generational basis and restore an individual's capacity for work; (2) the biological reproduction of life and demographic replacement; and (3) the reproduction or modification of the necessary conditions and social relations that allow the members of a community to persist through time.

The relationship between older and younger generations may well have been enmeshed in the division of labor between men and women. Many archaeologists assume that there was a sexual division of labor in early human societies. If they are correct, the men in these social units pursued one set of productive activities while the women carried out another. Furthermore, each sex had access to a portion of the goods produced by the other. This allowed the members of the group to undertake some risky productive activities, such as long-range hunting, whose outcome was uncertain; they knew they would still have access to the more certain production—say, plant foods—of the other sex. The relationship between the sexes, in short, was one of sharing, which involves both rights and obligations.

It is not economics that provides the motivation for men and women to share with one another and with the members of other generations in their social unit. The driving forces are social and cultural—those that can be couched in terms of relationships with the supernatural or ties of kinship among different members of the group. These social relations—sets of rules that define from whom an individual can claim labor and goods and to whom he or she must give them—may reflect the existence of kinship systems during this period. The presence of burials among the Neanderthal populations of western Europe and their contemporaries elsewhere in the Near East during this period suggests that people may already have begun to define their social relationships in terms of kinship and descent. What is also clear, however, is that kinship systems—which occasionally coincide with our notions of biological or genealogical relations—were not essential for the maintenance and functioning of human societies at this stage in their development.

By 100,000 years ago, human beings had already resided in Africa, Eurasia, and the Indonesian archipelago for many millennia. Archaeological sites in western Europe, the Ukraine, the Near East, and South Africa have been analyzed, described, and discussed in considerable detail. These reports provide the basis for sketching a picture of certain aspects of everyday life at that time.

Southwestern France

Archaic *Homo sapiens*, including the classic Neanderthals and their ancestors, inhabited the well-watered valleys of western Europe between

120,000 and about 40,000 years ago. They lived in caves in the limestone cliffs that formed the edges of these valleys. The Périgord region of southwestern France is one area where archaeologists have found abundant traces of their activities.

The climate of the Périgord deteriorated rapidly shortly before the onset of the last major glacial cycle about 70,000 years ago. It became both drier and colder. Temperatures were 20° F lower in July and more than 40° F lower in January than they are now. Thus the summers averaged in the low 50s and the average winter temperatures were less than 10° F. The mixed forests that had covered the region were replaced by tundra and steppe at low elevations and by cold-adapted alpine plant formations at higher elevations. Scattered stands of pines, dwarf birch, and alders probably grew along the riverbanks. The fauna consisted of both tundra and alpine species. Gigantic herds of reindeer must have grazed in the area, as well as musk oxen, mammoths, giant elks, and horses. Cave bears and ibex lived in the limestone uplands.

The inhabitants of the Périgord region occupied more than thirty caves during the first part of the last glacial cycle. This works out to about one cave every thousand years. However, radiocarbon measurements indicate that some of the caves were probably occupied simultaneously, suggesting that the population of the region increased in the period between 70,000 and 40,000 years ago.

The cave sites ranged in length from about 45 to 75 feet and were about 30 feet wide. Stakes 2 to 3 inches in diameter were driven into the ground around the entrances of the caves or in front of the large, open rock shelters. These stakes probably supported a wooden framework covered with animal hides and branches that served as a windbreak and kept out the cold during the winter months. These wooden frameworks were undoubtedly convenient for other things as well—a place to hang up game for butchering or to suspend pieces of meat so they could dry in the sun.

Anthropologists have compiled information from different societies to establish a rough correlation between house size and the number of residents: 20 square feet per person for the first six inhabitants and 100 square feet for each additional individual was typical. This method of approximation suggests that the human groups living in the Périgord caves ranged from eighteen to twenty-seven individuals and that La Quina, the largest cave, would have housed thirty-six persons at most. Another method of estimating population size, based on the quantity of animal remains, suggests that fewer than forty people camped at Saltgitter-Lebenstadt in northern Germany for a few weeks during the summers about 55,000 years ago.

The skeletons of thirty-nine Neanderthal individuals in western Europe provide information about the population structure of these groups. Almost 40 percent of the individuals died in infancy or early childhood; another 10 percent died before their twentieth year. Fifteen percent of the survivors died between the ages of twenty-one and thirty, and 25 percent between thirty-one and forty. Thus, half of the individuals died before reaching adulthood.

Most women died before their thirtieth year, which suggests that the majority of the individuals who lived longer than thirty years were men. Because of differential mortality, there were more men than women in these communities; the ratio may have been about twelve men to ten women. In a group of thirty individuals, five would have been women of childbearing age.

The increased size of these groups is undoubtedly part of the reason human behavior began to change more rapidly. Larger communities meant that more individuals were available to validate new ideas and behavior and transmit them to other members of the group. Also, there may have been more than one community inhabiting the same general area. Given the size of a region like the Périgord, these groups must have interacted with one another on a face-to-face basis at least occasionally during the year. Even minimal contacts among groups would have facilitated communication and the spread of new ideas and behavior from the members of one social unit to those of another. This process—however infrequent, brief, and low-key the contacts may have been—created larger audiences, which means that original ideas and behavior had a better chance of being validated. It also provided a larger group af people who could adopt innovations and introduce them into other social units.

The inhabitants of the Périgord region were particularly fond of reindeer; however, they hunted and consumed a wide variety of other large herbivorous mammals as well. Mammoths, woolly rhinoceroses, red deer, horses, oxen, boars, ibex, and roe and fallow deer are only a few of the other large species found in their camp dumps. If we assume that each member of these communities ate about 2 pounds of meat a day, a group of thirty would have needed about 1,800 pounds of meat each month. This meant they had to kill about fourteen reindeer, which weigh roughly 250 pounds each and provide about 125 pounds of usable food. Smaller mammals like hares and foxes were trapped and furnished additional food and/or raw materials needed by the group. During the summers, the group that camped at Saltgitter-Lebenstadt also hunted swans and ducks and fished for perch and pike in the stream that flowed by their campsite. Undoubtedly the inhabitants of Europe also ate plant foods during this period, but the archaeological record is not clear about the kinds of plants they consumed and used.

The people of the Périgord used Mousterian tools, which were made on stone flakes removed from prepared cores. The toolmakers struck small chips off the edges of a flint nodule to create a striking platform; they then struck flakes with predetermined shapes from the core. This stoneworking technique is called the Levallois technique, and tools made in this fashion have been found from the Atlantic Ocean to the area north of the Black Sea and from England to South Africa. Mousterian assemblages contain many different kinds of tools: awls for piercing hides and wood, scrapers for removing meat, spear points for killing game, denticulates for sawing and shredding, and various kinds of knives for cutting.

The inhabitants of the Périgord region used different tool kits to per-

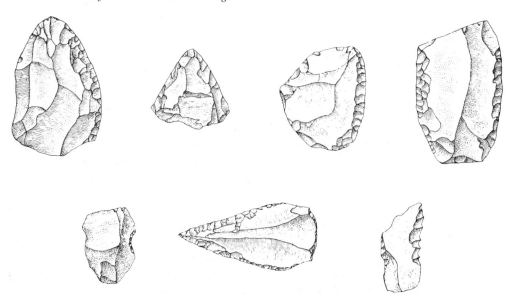

A Mousterian toolkit. (a–d) Side scrapers; (e) notched tool; (f) point; (g) denticulate. (*From Richard G. Klein, "Ice-Age Hunters of the Ukraine." Copyright © 1974 by Scientific American, Inc. All rights reserved.*)

form different tasks. For example, one tool kit contained two kinds of borers; a beak-shaped engraver; and some other tools that probably were used to make objects from wood and bone—spear shafts, handles, or pegs—and cordage from animal hides. Another kit contained several kinds of spear points and a wide variety of scrapers; these tools were probably used to kill and butcher animals. A third kit contained knives and sharp flakes that may have been used for cutting and preparing meat. Another contained denticulates and scrapers that presumably were used for shredding, sawing, and smoothing wood and other plant materials. A fifth kit contained spear points and various kinds of scrapers, including one that looked like a push plane. These tools were probably used for killing and butchering but may have been employed in more specialized activities as well.

The tools used to process foods—denticulates, scrapers, and knives—were frequently made of flint obtained in the immediate vicinity. The hunting tools—spear points and certain types of scrapers—were often made from raw materials found a mile or more from the base camp, suggesting that the inhabitants of the Périgord region used whatever raw materials were at hand when they made stone tools. What they may have carried with them were hammerstones and other implements used to make stone tools. They probably valued these much the way that today's artisans value their tools. Primary tools were probably much more important to the toolmakers than the implements they fashioned with them.

The toolmakers seem to have used the Levallois technique most frequently to manufacture tools for hunting. The hunting implements—spear points, knives, and scrapers—were much more uniform or standardized in appearance than the denticulates and other tools associated with domestic or maintenance activities. The hunting tools were made on flakes of a predetermined size and shape, whereas those used for other purposes were often made on flakes of various sizes and shapes.

Death was ever-present among these people. Many died in infancy and childhood, and most were dead by their fortieth year. In a group of thirty, two or three individuals died each year. In some instances we can determine what caused them to die. For example, a middle-aged individual from Monte Circeo, near Rome, died from a blow to the temple. An individual from Shanidar Cave in Iraq was stabbed and died with a stone spear point embedded in his thorax. Another individual from Shanidar died accidentally when the roof of the cave collapsed on him. He had already survived having his arm amputated below the elbow and was recovering from head injuries inflicted by a sharp object.

Disease was the other major cause of death among ancient populations. The people in these groups were susceptible to diseases, such as trichinosis, that are acquired by eating raw animal foods. They were also susceptible to zoonoses, infections of other animals that are transmitted by biting insects; among these are anthrax and botulism. Internal parasites, such as hookworms or amoebas, that are found in fecal matter were probably present as well. Tetanus, which is found in dirt, must have taken a heavy toll. Infectious diseases like mumps, measles, or smallpox were not important; germs could not perpetuate themselves because of the small size of the groups.

The first deliberate burials occurred during the early part of the last glacial cycle. The inhabitants of Le Moustier, a site in the Périgord region, buried an eighteen-year-old with considerable care and tenderness. The individual was placed on his or her side, legs bent, and head resting on the right arm as if asleep; meat and stone tools were placed in the grave. A group living around La Ferrassie, another site in southern France, buried two adults and four children on the floor of the cave, aligning the bodies in an east-west direction. Child burials were often quite elaborate. For example, a child from the site of Teshik-Tash in southern Russia was surrounded by half a dozen goat frontlets whose horns had been pushed into the ground. A young child was placed on a bed of wildflowers in Shanidar Cave before being covered with earth.

The Ukrainian Steppe

The Ukrainian steppe north of the Black Sea was already inhabited more than 45,000 years ago, when periglacial steppe covered the permanently frozen ground of the area. The winters were long, relatively snowless, and cold with average temperatures hovering around 0° F. The summers were

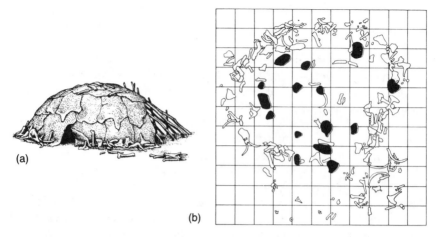

(a)

(b)

Shelter at Moldova, Ukraine. (a) Reconstruction of the shelter; (b) Plan of the shelter; each square in the grid is one meter on a side. (*From Richard G. Klein, "Ice-Age Hunters of the Ukraine." Copyright © 1974 by Scientific American, Inc. All rights reserved.*)

short but warm enough for the growth of a variety of hardy grasses, which provided food for more than a dozen species of herbivores. During the summers, the inhabitants followed migratory herds of reindeer, horse, and bison across the steppe grasslands. In the north, people hunted reindeer and horses, whereas their neighbors in the south pursued bison.

The people, and the animals, moved into river valleys during the winters as fierce winds swept across the steppe and the rivers froze. One winter campsite was at Moldova, which lies in the Dneister River valley about 200 miles northwest of the Black Sea. The people lived in tents: wooden frames covered with animal skins that were held in place by heavy mammoth-bone anchors piled around and on top of the structures to prevent them from blowing away. Particularly heavy bones—skulls, tusks, shoulder blades, and pelvises—were collected especially for this purpose. One hut was oval-shaped, about 33 feet long and 25 feet wide. Fifteen hearths provided light and warmth for its dozen or so residents. Its occupants probably dressed in fox and wolf hides when they ventured outside in search of game.

Coastal South Africa

About 130,000 years ago, some of the inhabitants of southern Africa camped in caves and rock shelters. One is located on the coast at the mouth of the Klasies River, overlooking the Indian Ocean. The 60-foot-deep cave was formed when the sea level was higher than it is today and waves crashed against the cliffs, eroding the softer rocks and sediments. Its first inhabitants moved into the cave after the level of the sea receded, and their refuse and other traces of their activities began to accumulate on the cave floor. The cave provided protection against the cool westerly winds that swept over the coastal plain. The people lived there intermittently on several different occasions between 120,000 and 70,000 years ago.

The cave's residents used a variety of raw materials and foods. Their stone tools, called Middle Stone Age, resembled the Mousterian assemblages of North Africa and Eurasia. With stone-tipped spears, they hunted several species of antelope and young buffalo in the mixed forest and grassland habitats near the cave. They clubbed or speared Cape fur seals and sea birds—like penguins, cormorants, and gulls—that lived on nearby beaches. They scavenged the dolphins and large fish that occasionally washed up on the shore, and they supplemented their diet with mussels, limpets, and other shellfish, which they collected with a little wading in the intertidal zone at low tide. On at least five occasions, human beings died, and fragments of their skeletons—mostly mandibles and teeth—were incorporated into the refuse accumulating in or around the cave.

EVERYDAY LIFE IN THE LATE PLEISTOCENE: 40,000 TO 10,000 YEARS AGO

Between 30,000 and 40,000 years ago, human beings, who were fully modern in appearance, once again moved into previously uninhabited lands. They crossed the open water that separated Australia and New Guinea from the Indonesian archipelago and mainland Asia and began to live in the diverse environments of that enormous island continent. They crossed the Japan Sea, presumably from Korea, and occupied the Japanese archipelago for the first time. And they moved out of Siberia across the Bering Straits into the American Arctic; from there, they moved rapidly into areas south of the continental ice sheets that covered much of Canada.

Various archaeologists suggest that an important transition occurred about 40,000 years ago. Some link the transition to the appearance of fully modern human beings; they are concerned with which of the three models discussed toward the end of Appendix C most fully explains what occurred. Others view the transition primarily in terms of technological changes: The Levallois technique of removing flakes from a prepared core was modified, or refined, so that all of the flakes were removed by blows struck from the same direction. Thus even a relatively unskilled toolmaker could produce flakes that were quite uniform in size; moreover, cores worked in this fashion would yield not only many more flakes but also a much greater amount of cutting edge than the earlier Levallois technique. Flakes or blades were then fashioned into a variety of tools, which were hafted or cemented to wooden or bone handles.

Still other archaeologists conceptualize the transition in social or cultural terms—for example, the crystallization of regional stone toolmaking traditions; the restructuring of social relations within particular regional communities; or the constitution and elaboration of spatially and temporally organized, technical divisions of labor. The discovery at St. Césaire in south-western France of a human being with Neanderthaloid features in a 32,000-year-old deposit that also contained Châtelperronian tools made with the new stoneworking techniques indicates that the technological and organizational changes of the Upper Paleolithic were not causally connected either with genetic changes in human populations or with the purported replacement of one kind of human being by another. In other words, correlations based on contemporaneity do not always or necessarily imply causal relations.

It is clear, however, that the number of human beings in the world had increased. There were more human populations, communities in some regions had more members than their predecessors, and there was undoubtedly more contact among communities residing in the same area. Larger communities—some with thirty or forty residents and a few with seventy or more inhabitants at certain times of the year—promoted the survival and well-being of their constituents over extended periods. In a larger group, individuals had more opportunities to satisfy their needs and more opportunities to expand their capacities by recognizing and meeting the needs of others. There were also significantly more opportunities for new kinds of behavior and ways of viewing the world to be validated and adopted by other members of the social unit. Spoken language facilitated all these developments by allowing the members of a community to share information about the world they lived in.

Larger groups meant that the members of a community had to acquire more food to maintain a particular standard of living. In a sense, every human group sets an upper limit on its size by defining what elements of the natural environment constitute resources and by developing the means—tools, techniques, and knowledge—to exploit those raw materials. When materials necessary for life are inadequate to sustain a group at a particular standard of living, the members have only a limited number of ways to deal with the situation. They can redefine what elements of the environment constitute resources so that more raw materials are available; or they can reduce the number of individuals relying on the resources of a given area through some method of population control, such as splitting the group into two or more segments and having some of the segments move out of the area. They can also increase the productivity of their labor through some technological or organizational innovation.

The increased number and extent of archaeological sites dating from this period suggest that human groups fragmented, moved into new territories or created them, and grew in size, repeating the process several times. Thus the individuals organized themselves in such a way that group size was flexible, and the group was able to split into two or more fragments fairly easily. The process of division might have been a seasonal one that reflected the cyclical availability of food resources. It might have been a temporary one that occurred for short periods, perhaps when food was scarce or when the members of the group were feeling antagonistic toward one another. Or it might have been a permanent division that occurred when one segment moved into a new territory and the rest of the group remained behind in the old one.

Southwestern France

The Périgord region underwent a series of severe climatic changes between 35,000 and 10,000 years ago. At the beginning of this period the climate of the area was much like that today; the well-watered valleys were covered with grassy meadows and woodlands of oak, elm, and pine. After about 30,000 years it became colder and drier. The winters were longer; the woodlands became smaller and almost disappeared from the area altogether; the lush grasses of the meadows were replaced by hardy bunch grasses, which could grow in soils that were frozen most of the year, and by lichens that fastened themselves to rocks. The height of this cold, dry period occurred about 19,000 to 20,000 years ago. Around 17,000 years ago the climate became warmer and more humid, and stands of evergreens began to reappear in the river valleys. Later, as the climate ameliorated even further, deciduous trees like oak and elm began to reappear.

The toolmakers used a new technique for making stone implements called the punch blade technique. The stoneworkers prepared a roughly cylindrical core about 4 to 6 inches in length. Then they placed a bone or antler punch on the top edge of the core and struck it with a hammer. A long, narrow blade was removed from the side of the core. The toolmakers continued to remove blades from the core in this fashion until the core became too small to work efficiently. A small core weighing about 2 or 3 pounds would yield enough blades to make about 75 feet of cutting edge; this is roughly ten times as much cutting edge as could be obtained with earlier stoneworking techniques.

Stone tools made with these blades came in a much wider variety of shapes and forms than anything that had been used in the region before. Many of the tools had no antecedents in the earlier stone tool kits of the Périgord. The toolmakers of this period were highly original. They devised entirely new kinds of tools for particular purposes. This process occurred not just once or twice but repeatedly throughout the time from 35,000 to 10,000 years ago. The result was a series of tool assemblages, each with its own characteristic set of tools and tool shapes. The earliest of these are the Châtelperronian assemblages, which date from between about 37,000 and 30,000 years ago. They were followed by Aurignacian (30,000 to 24,000 years ago), Upper Perigordian (24,000 to 20,000 years ago), Solutrean (20,000 to 17,000 years ago), and Magdalenian (17,000 to 12,000 years ago) assemblages.

A three- to fourfold increase in the number of caves and rock shelters occupied between 30,000 and 24,000 years ago suggests that the population of the region had increased substantially. The number of habitation sites in the region and, by implication, the size of its population stabilized until about 17,000 B.P. (years before the present). Both began to increase again;

Upper Paleolithic cave site in Southwestern France.

roughly twice as many sites have yielded Magdalenian tools as Aurignacian or Solutrean assemblages, suggesting that population growth in the Périgord was not continuous but rather increased dramatically on two different occasions—once during the time of the Aurignacian and again during the Magdalenian.

Furthermore, the later occupation layers in the Périgord are consistently larger than earlier ones. Three rock shelters, occupied between 30,000 and 24,000 B.P., were more than 150 feet long and 30 feet wide and could have housed about 50 individuals, assuming 20 square feet for each of the first six inhabitants and 100 square feet for each additional one. Laugerie Haute—a cave occupied between 24,000 and 20,000 B.P.—is nearly 500 feet long and 100 feet wide. A more conservative method for estimating population size—the logarithm of the surface area in square meters—suggests that Laugerie Haute had about 70 residents. La Magdaleine, a site that extended from the river to the back of the cave, also covered more than an acre and would have had a population of 65 individuals, using the second method of estimating population numbers. About 20 miles down the Dordogne River from La Magdaleine was a series of rock shelters that housed 50 to 70 persons. According to this method, about 130 persons lived in tents at Solvieux between 17,000 and 12,000 B.P. This suggests that the Périgord region as a whole was probably inhabited by 500 to 1,000 persons for much of the time between 30,000 and 12,000 B.P.

Many of the larger sites were occupied continuously throughout the year, judging from the ages of the animal remains found in their refuse deposits. Some of the smaller sites may have been camps that were inhabited for brief intervals—a week or less—by work parties of six to eight individuals who had left the main campsite. Other sites, intermediate in size be-tween the main settlements and the temporary hunting and collecting camps, were probably occupied by households of a dozen or more individuals, per-haps on a more or less permanent basis; these production-consumption units were clearly not nuclear families, given the age structure, life expectancy, and other demographic characteristics of Middle and Upper Paleolithic popula-tions.

Some communities modified the appearance of the caves and rock shel-ters in which they lived. They dug out ancient deposits to produce roomier, more regular living areas. Sometimes they carried cobbles from nearby streams and carefully paved parts of the floor. In some caves, they built stone walls along the edges of the living areas to support wooden frame-works that were covered with animal skins to keep out the wind and cold. In the cave of Arcy-sur-Cure, located outside of the Périgord about 100 miles southeast of Paris, the residents put up a tent inside the cave and used mammoth tusks as stakes to support the skin covering. At Pincevent, a Magdalenian site southeast of Paris, one tent-covered living floor had three separate sleeping areas, each with its own hearth to provide light and warmth during the summer and early fall evenings when the camp was occupied.

During much of the Upper Paleolithic, the inhabitants of the Périgord region hunted reindeer almost to the exclusion of all other terrestrial her-bivores. Although the remains of other species do occur, they are exception-ally rare. However, communities outside the Périgord hunted other game. For instance, the inhabitants of the Pyrenees relied extensively on mammoths and the community at La Solutre consumed enormous numbers of wild horses.

The communities of southwestern France had more effective hunting weapons than their ancestors. They used spear throwers—sticks about 2 feet long with a handle at one end and a hook at the other to hold the butt end of the spear. The spear thrower is an extension of the hunter's arm and gives the weapon both greater range and more striking power. With spear throw-ers, hunters could heave spears over 400 feet and kill at ranges of about 100 feet. Thus they no longer had to get as close to their prey as their ancestors did. In addition, many archaeologists believe that the inhabitants of the Périgord region also had bows and arrows, even though the evidence is slim. The oldest known bows come from Denmark and are about 8,000 years old; some stone-tipped wooden arrow shafts have been found in 10,000-year-old reindeer hunter camps in northern Germany; and small stones with represen-tations of feathered projectiles scratched on them have been found in 20,000-year-old archaeological deposits at La Colombière in France.

Animal drives were a very effective means of acquiring food and other raw materials. Teams of individuals—presumably men, women, and even older children—collaborated to stampede herds or individual animals over cliffs or into pitfalls. At Predmost in Czechoslovakia hunters drove more than 1,000 mammoths into pits dug especially for that purpose. Beneath the cliffs

Reconstructed hunt in which animals are driven over the edge of a hill into a corral or trap, where they are subsequently killed and butchered.

at Solutre are the skeletons of more than 100,000 horses killed by the inhabitants of that area about 20,000 years ago. Of course, not all of the horses were killed at the same time. The accumulation of skeletons represents animal drives that were carried out sporadically over a period of perhaps 1,000 years.

The inhabitants of southwestern France dramatically expanded their food supply about 11,000 years ago when they developed fishing equipment and techniques for catching fish in large numbers. Fishing became particularly important during the late Magdalenian, when many of the settlements were located on the riverbanks. Most of the fish bones identified are salmon, which spawned in the Dordogne and Vézère rivers and their tributaries during the fall.

Clearly, some tasks involved in acquiring food—such as large-scale animal drives or intensive fishing along the rivers when the salmon were running—required the cooperation of a number of people. This work consisted of a series of overlapping tasks that required the collaboration of several production units working sequentially and independently to achieve a particular goal. The animal drives or intensive fishing did not take a lot of time—perhaps no more than a few weeks. However, in all likelihood they were performed every year, and so the people involved had to organize themselves in such a way that they could muster enough individuals to do the work that needed to be done at those particular times. Furthermore, when work projects were carried out on this scale by a number of people, it is impossible to determine who owns the final product because it belongs to everyone in general and to no one in particular. Therefore the people of the Périgord must have had a set of rules governing the redistribution of these communally produced goods to all the members of the group.

Subsistence activities frequently involved temporally and spatially organized, technical divisions of labor. During the fall months, for example, reindeer herds were migrating through the valleys to winter pastures at about the same time that salmon were moving up the rivers to spawn. Thus, two important sources of food were available at the same time, and there were conflicting demands for the time and labor of the group. Such conflicts could be resolved in various ways. For example, some production units could hunt while others fished; they could hunt one day and fish the next; or production units residing in one place could hunt, while those living in another fished. Technical divisions of labor also imply that these communities had ways of circulating and distributing food resources and other raw materials among their members.

The increased productivity of the communities in the Périgord region allowed their members to extend and refine activities and practices that were not directly involved with the acquisition of food and other necessities of life. For example, one toolmaker fashioned elaborate stone knives or spear points that were too large and thin ever to be used for work; one of their functions must have been to display his or her workmanship. At the same time, the inhabitants of southwestern France and southern Germany were beginning to make personal ornaments—necklaces of perforated animal teeth and carved shells that had been brought from places 200 or 300 miles distant. They carved beads and pendants out of bone, antler, and ivory, and both men and women must have worn them with pride. They also carved small figurines out of soft stone and painted slabs of rock with a wide variety of animals and figures: Some were used to decorate their homes, and others were painted on walls and ceilings far back in the caves. The latter could be seen only with the aid of lamps—stone bowls filled with animal fat and a burning wick.

Czechoslovakia

Dolni Vestonice was a small settlement located next to a stream that flowed swiftly out of the Pollau Mountains of central Czechoslovakia into the marshy bottomlands of the Thaya Valley. People lived there about 25,000 years ago. The settlement was built on a peninsula that jutted out into the marsh, so its houses were surrounded on three sides by swamp. The area was not glaciated then; the edge of the ice sheet was several hundred miles to the north. It was intensely cold, however. The winters were long and the summers short and cool. Pine and willow trees grew in the sheltered valleys, and tundra grasses, mosses, and lichens covered the open plains during the short summers. Mammoths, reindeer, bison, wolves, and hares—all cold-adapted animals—abounded in the area.

The settlement consisted of four huts built inside a compound. Piles of mammoth bones stood near the huts; more bones were strewn along the banks of the stream and in it. Tusks and other large bones formed parts of the wall and were laid against the skin tents to keep them from blowing away. The huts were oval; the largest was 45 feet by 27 feet and had five hearths to light and heat the inside. A fifth, slightly more recent, hut was located about 250 feet uphill from the rest of the settlement; it was circular, semisubterranean, and about 18 feet in diameter. There was a clay oven in the center of the hut; several thousand pieces of clay—some shapeless and others representing parts of animals—were scattered on the floor. No one lived there; it was a place where small clay figurines were made.

The settlement at Dolni Vestonice and the lifeways of its inhabitants, which focused on the seasonal movement of the mammoths, provide some clues to the social and economic organization of central European communities about 25,000 years ago. That the structures of the winter camp were surrounded by a wall suggests that their residents formed a small community, divided into four living groups, each occupying a separate hut and consisting of about fifteen individuals. Both the living groups and the larger group they formed had their own social and economic realities. For certain activities—say, hunting mammoths during the summer months, when the animals were dispersed—the real unit of appropriation may have been the domestic group, which followed the animals across the grasslands of central Europe. As fall approached, the groups came together once again with old acquaintances—individuals they had known since childhood. Now, with the animals coming together and the size of the herds increasing daily, the basic unit of appropriation may have been the community as a whole rather than the constituent households.

The Central Russian Plains

About 25,000 years ago, a number of communities lived in small settlements in the tundra-steppe grasslands that covered the plains of central Russia, 300 to 400 miles below the thick, glacial ice sheets that blanketed the north. During the frigid winter, these communities of thirty to sixty individuals each moved onto the sparsely wooded floodplains of the frozen rivers. In the late spring, as the rivers thawed and the floodplains turned to marshes, they returned to the higher ground of the plain and spent the

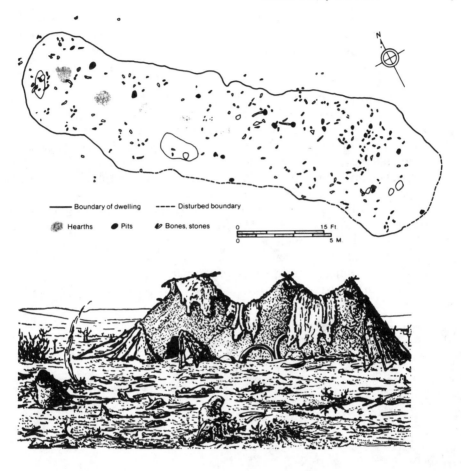

Boundary of dwelling   ---- Disturbed boundary

Hearths   Pits   Bones, stones

Reconstruction of a skin-covered IV long house at Kostenki IV.

Reconstruction of a house built from bones at Mezhirich in the Ukraine.

short, cool summers there, hunting mammoths, reindeer, horses, and other large animals and trapping foxes and hares for their pelts. Some of the game they killed was consumed immediately, and other parts of their prize were stored in pits to be used during the cold months when they were near the frozen rivers.

Several of the winter camps were elaborate, consisting of houses built from mammoth bones that had been collected and brought to the site. For example, at Mezhirich, one dwelling had retaining walls made from mammoth skulls, one of which was painted, and mandibles arranged in a chin-down herringbone pattern; another house was made of alternating rows of chin-down and chin-up mandibles; and a third consisted primarily of long bones. Olga Soffer (1987:379) estimates that depending on its size, a mammoth-bone dwelling took between 54 and 176 person-days of labor to complete. Besides the art embodied in the houses, their inhabitants also carved bone objects, made jewelry of amber, bone, and shell; and decorated garments with fox and hare pelts.

Some domestic groups were clearly able to produce or accumulate more of these art objects than others, and access to these goods was often

A middle-aged woman buried at Sungir near Moscow. The tomb is about 25,000 years old. More than 3500 mammoth ivory and bone beads were sewn to a pullover shirt made of animal hide or fur; these beads took more than 1000 hours to carve and were sewn in place at the time she was buried. In addition to the shirt, she wore trousers, a cape, mocassins, and a cap with drilled fox teeth and beads sewn to it. On each of her arms she wore 25 ivory bracelets interspersed with beaded bracelets. An enormous amount of labor was invested in preparing the dead woman's clothing.

ascribed—a result of membership in one of these highly productive units—rather than achieved. Some of this labor power seems to have been used to express differences in wealth, or access to labor. For example, there are three burials at Sungir, each of which was interred with a variety of objects, including tunics decorated with more than 3,000 beads. The burial goods involved large investments of labor; it took at least fifteen minutes to manufacture each of the nearly 10,000 beads on the tunic of the sixty-year-old man, the eight-year-old girl, and the eleven-year-old boy interred at the site. The uniformity of the beads suggests that they were manufactured by only a few individuals. The labor associated with the burials, like that involved in building the mammoth-bone houses, involved activities, practices, and sentiments that were not directly related to the survival needs of the group.

Wealth differentials, reflecting access to labor power, clearly existed on the Russian plain about 24,000 B.P. Presumably, large domestic units, with access to the labor power of more individuals, had the capacity to produce goods beyond their immediate subsistence needs; such items may have not only marked their status within the settlement but also been circulated to the members of other communities on the Russian plains. After 20,000 B.P., social relations within the communities were transformed, and the members of large domestic units no longer invested large amounts of labor in burial practices.

The Levant

About 18,000 years ago a new way of life began to emerge among the inhabitants of the coastal plain of Israel and the hills beyond. Hippopotamuses and warthogs were the largest residents of the marshes that covered much of the plain; birds were undoubtedly varied and plentiful in these habitats. Deer, gazelles, goats, and wild cattle grazed on the grass-covered hills overlooking the swamps. Small streams rose in highlands and flowed into the Mediterranean during the January to March rainy season. The eastern slopes of the hills overlooked the Jordan Valley, which was covered with stands of grass interspersed with oak and pine trees and low shrubs that were well adapted to the long, dry summers.

Animal bones found at campsites on the sand dunes and in the oak forests overlooking the coastal plain indicate that their occupants were exploiting a much greater range of animal resources than earlier inhabitants in the area. Large animals—gazelles, goats, and deer—still provided the bulk of the meat, although small animals like rodents, tortoises, snails, and birds were also consumed. However, the animal remains from a few campsites indicate that their inhabitants were primarily concerned with a single species. For example, 80 percent of the animal bones recovered at Wadi Madamagh near Petra are from goats; more than 75 percent of those from Nahal Oren near Haifa are from gazelles. It is unlikely that the occupants of these sites were specialized hunters since the vegetation of the areas immediately surrounding the camps could not have supported large numbers of these animals.

The residents of these and similar sites apparently rounded up as many goats or gazelles as they could catch, particularly females and young, and began herding them. This practice assured the human population of a reliable supply of meat throughout the year. It also meant, however, that the people could stay in one place only as long as pasture was available. When the animals had depleted the wild grasses, the group had to move to a locality where fresh pasture was available. One area they moved into, probably during the late spring, was the Jordan Valley, with its broad grasslands and scattered stands of trees.

At Ain Gev, a small site on the shores of Lake Tiberias in the Jordan Valley, archaeologists found a number of round houses that date from this period. Inside one of them were grinding slabs, a mortar, and small stone blades with a silica sheen. This sheen was produced when grass was cut with the chipped-stone implements, indicating that the inhabitants of the camp were using the wild grasses that grew in the area. Two grasses that must have been particularly abundant there in late April, after the rain stopped, are wild wheat and barley. With very primitive stone tools a group of three or four individuals could harvest enough wild grain in an hour to feed themselves for several weeks.

These groups may have kept their small herds away from stands of wild cereals that they could use, ensuring them a supply of grain, while their animals could graze on plants that lacked economic importance. As wheat and barley became less plentiful in the valley and the animals began to deplete their pasture, the herders may have moved up into the limestone hills to the west, where the cereals were just beginning to open and fresh pasture was available. This combination provides the environmental base for the later development of pastoral and agrarian economies, which we will consider in more detail in subsequent chapters.

FURTHER READINGS: A BRIEF GUIDE

Changing conceptions about the lifeways of our fossil ancestors who lived between c. 50,000 and 400,000 years ago are discussed by Lewis R. Binford, "Human Ancestors: Changing Views of Their Behavior," *Journal of Anthropological Archaeology*, vol. 4, no. 4 (1985), 292–327; and Alexander Marshack, "Evolution of the Human Capacity: The Symbolic Evidence," *Yearbook of Physical Anthropology*, vol. 31 (1989), 1–34.

The mode of production concept and the mode of production variously called primitive communism, kin-based, or the primitive communal form are discussed by Janet Siskind, "Kinship and Modes of Production," *American Anthropologist*, vol. 80, no. 4 (1978), 860–872; Eleanor Leacock and Richard Lee, eds., *Politics and History in Band Societies* (Cambridge: Cambridge University Press, 1982); Claude Meillassoux, "On the Mode of Production of the

Hunting Band," in *French Perspectives in African Studies*, ed. Pierre Alexandre (London: Oxford University Press, 1973), pp. 187–203; and Thomas C. Patterson, "La creación de cultura en las formaciones sociales pre-estatales y no-estatales," *Boletín de Anthropología Americana*, no. 14 (Mexico, 1986), pp. 53–61.

The concept of social reproduction is examined by Richard Lee, "Primitive Communism and Inequality," in *The Evolution of Political Systems: Sociopolitics in Small-scale Sedentary Societies*, ed. Steadman Upham (Cambridge: Cambridge University Press, 1990), pp. 225–247; Olivia Harris and Kate Young, "Engendered Structures: Some Problems in the Analysis of Reproduction," in *The Anthropology of Pre-capitalist Societies*, ed. Joel S. Kahn and Josep R. Llobera, (London: Macmillan, 1981), pp. 109–147; and Veronika Bennholdt-Thomsen, "Subsistence Production and Extended Reproduction," in *Of Marriage and the Market*, ed. Kate Young, Carol Wolkowitz, and Roslyn McCullagh (London: Routledge & Kegan Paul, 1984), pp. 41–54.

Southwestern France and its archaeology are surveyed by Clive Gamble, *The Palaeolithic Settlement of Europe* (Cambridge: Cambridge University Press, 1986). More detailed discussions of everyday life are provided by Philip G. Chase, "How Different Was Middle Paleolithic Subsistence? A Zooarchaeological Perspective on the Middle to Upper Palaeolithic Transition," in *The Human Revolution: Behavioural and Biological Perspectives on the Origins of Modern Humans*, ed. Paul Mellars and Chris Stringer (Princeton, NJ: Princeton University Press, 1989), pp. 321–337, and *The Hunters of Combe Grenal: Approaches to Middle Paleolithic Subsistence in Europe*, British Archaeological Reports, International Series S286 (Oxford, 1986); and Eric Trinkhaus, ed., *The Mousterian Legacy: Human Biocultural Change in the Upper Pleistocene*, British Archaeological Reports, International Series S164 (Oxford, 1983). Sally Binford and Lewis Binford, "A Preliminary Analysis of Functional Variability in the Mousterian of Levallois Facies," *American Anthropologist, Special Publication*, vol. 68, no. 2, pt. 2 (1966), 238–295; and Paul Mellars, "The Character of the Middle-Upper Palaeolithic of Southwestern France," in *The Explanation of Culture Change*, ed. Colin Renfrew (London: Gerald Duckworth, 1973), pp. 255–276, present alternative interpretations of the variability of Mousterian tool assemblages; the former argue that they reflect the activities being carried out, whereas the latter views it in terms of technological change over time. The evidence for Middle Paleolithic burial practices is discussed by Robert H. Gargett, "Grave Shortcomings: The Evidence for Neanderthal Burial," *Current Anthropology*, vol. 30, no. 2 (1989), pp. 157–190; L.P. Louwe Kooijmans, Yuri Smirnov, Ralph S. Solecki, Paola Villa, Thomas Weber, and Robert H. Gargett, "On the Evidence for Neanderthal Burial," *Current Anthropology*, vol. 30, no. 3 (1989), 322–330; and Eric Trinhaus, *The Shanidar Neanderthals* (New York: Academic Press, 1983). The human populations of this period are examined by Chris Stringer, *The Neanderthals* (London: Thames & Hudson, 1988).

Moldova and other sites in the Ukraine are examined by Richard Klein, *Ice-Age Hunters of the Ukraine* (Chicago: University of Chicago Press, 1973).

Klasies River Cave, its history, and its contents are described and discussed by Ronald Singer and John Wymer, *The Middle Stone Age at Klasies River Mouth in South Africa* (Chicago: University of Chicago Press, 1982); Richard Klein, "Biological and Behavioural Perspectives on Modern Human Origins in Southern Africa," and H. J. Deacon, "Late Pleistocene Paleoecology and Archaeology in the Southern Cape, South Africa," both in *The Human Revolution: Behavioural and Biological Perspectives on the Origins of Modern Humans*, ed. Paul Mellars and Chris Stringer (Princeton, NJ: Princeton University Press, 1989), pp. 529–546, and   547–565. Lewis R. Binford, *Faunal Remains from Klasies River Mouth* (Orlando, FL: Academic Press, 1984), argues that the earliest inhabitants of the cave were scavengers, not hunters, who used stone tools to extract marrow from the desiccated long bones of dead animals.

Brian Fagan, *The Journey from Eden: The Peopling of Our World* (London: Thames & Hudson, 1990), is a readable account of the transition from the Middle to the Upper Paleolithic about 40,000 years ago. More detailed accounts are Randall White, "Rethinking the Middle/Upper Paleolithic Transition," *Current Anthropology*, vol. 23, no. 2 (1982), 169–192; Antonio Gilman, "Explaining the Upper Palaeolithic Revolution," in *Marxist Perspectives in Archaeology*, ed.   Matthew Spriggs (Cambridge: Cambridge University Press, 1984), pp. 115–126; Anthony Marks, "The Middle to Upper Paleolithic Transition in the Levant," in *Advances in World Archaeology*, ed. Fred Wendorf and Angela Close, vol. 2 (New York: Academic Press, 1983), pp. 51–98; Paul Mellars, "The Character of the Middle-Upper Palaeolithic in Southwestern France," in *The Explanation of Culture Change*, ed. Colin Renfrew (London: Gerald Duckworth, 1973), pp. 255–276; and Martin Wobst, "Locational Relationships in Paleolithic Society," *Journal of Human Evolution*, vol. 5, no. 1 (1976) 49–58.

For brief overviews of southwestern France, see Paul Mellars, "The Ecological Basis of Social Complexity in the Upper Palaeolithic of Southwestern France," in *Complexity among Prehistoric Hunter-Gatherers: The Emergence of Cultural Complexity*, ed. T. Douglas Price and James Brown (Orlando, FL: Academic Press, 1985), pp. 271–297; and Clive Gamble, "Culture and Society in the Upper Paleolithic of Europe," in *Hunter-Gatherer Economy in Prehistory: A European Perspective*, ed. Geoff Bailey (Cambridge: Cambridge University Press, 1983), pp. 201–211.

The remains found at Dolni Vestonice are summarized by Walter Fairservis, *The Threshold of Civilization: An Experiment in Prehistory* (New York: Scribners, 1975).

For the central Russian plain, see Olga Soffer, "Patterns of Intensification as Seen from the Upper Paleolithic of the Central Russian Plain," in *Complexity among Prehistoric Hunter-Gatherers: The Emergence of Cultural Complexity*, ed. T. Douglas Price and James A. Brown (Orlando, FL: Academic Press, 1985), pp. 235–270, *The Upper Paleolithic of the Central Russian Plain* (Orlando, FL: Academic Press, 1987), and "Upper Paleolithic Connubia, Refugia, and the Archaeological Record from Eastern Europe," in *The Pleistocene*

Old World: Regional Perspectives, ed. Olga Soffer (New York: Plenum Press, 1987), pp. 333–348. See also Alexander Marshack, "Upper Paleolithic Symbol Systems of the Russian Plain: Cognitive and Comparative Analysis," *Current Anthropology,* vol. 20, no. 2 (1979), 271–311.

The Levant and the archaeological evidence on which this summary is based are discussed by Joy McCorriston and Frank Hole, "The Ecology of Seasonal Stress and the Origins of Agriculture in the Near East," *American Anthropologist,* vol. 93, no. 1 (1991), 46–69; Andrew M. T. Moore, "The Transition from Foraging to Farming in Southwest Asia: Present Problems and Future Directions," in *Foraging and Farming: The Evolution of Plant Exploitation,* ed. David R. Harris and Gordon C. Hillman (London: Unwin Hyman, 1989), pp. 620–631; and Carlo Viti-Finzi and Eric S. Higgs, "Prehistoric Economy in the Mount Carmel Area of Palestine. Site Catchment Analysis," *Proceedings of the Prehistoric Society,* vol. XXXVI, (Cambridge, 1970), pp. 1–37.

chapter 5

Beyond Progress: Power Relations and Multiple Histories

Neutrality is a defence mechanism, a symptom of being colonized without admitting it. It is a familiar trick of neurosis. (Guillermo Cohen-Degovia, "A Little Hiroshima in Panama")

Before discussing several of the big questions asked by archaeologists—for example, the development of food production, sedentism, and the rise of civilization—it is necessary to consider a historical and theoretical issue and the problems it poses. For the last two centuries, archaeologists have participated, consciously or not, in polemics that emerged during the Enlightenment. These disputes were concerned with the interconnections of diverse spheres of everyday life in western Europe: knowledge and science, material productivity, political-economic and social institutions, human welfare, morality, and aesthetic creativity.

The polemics were provoked by change: the development of new kinds of everyday life, the establishment of settler-colonies by Europeans, the development of industrial capitalism in western Europe and the United States, imperialism, colonialism, and the emergence of states as both consumers and regulators of economic production. Archaeologists contributed to the debates by describing and explaining the antecedents and the historical development of the new lifeways that were emerging at the time and why they appeared in some areas and not in others. Their inquiries buttressed arguments about the linkages of increased knowledge, technological innovation, increased productivity, and the transformation of political-economic and social institutions. They framed both their questions and answers largely in terms of the analytical categories and presuppositions of Enlightenment social thought.

The idea of progress was one of the most influential doctrines of the Enlightenment among both popular and intellectual circles. It was virtually an article of faith in the nineteenth century and a dominant belief for many during much of the twentieth century. It was condoned by groups with diverse worldviews. Liberals and Marxists accepted its claims but drew different conclusions from them. Conservatives bemoaned the fact that change had occurred at all, and romantics lamented the consequences of progress and the rise of civilization.

The idea of progress is a theory of history. It claims that historical change is inevitable and directional and that human intervention can only accelerate or impede the rate at which nations make nature serve their purposes, increase their welfare, or improve their institutions. In this view, contemporary civilization originated in and advanced from earlier, more primitive forms that existed in the past; they are advancing now because new scientific and technological knowledge has increased their control over nature; and they will continue to move in a desirable direction in the foreseeable future. The idea of progress also claims that progress and civilization are universal and that the industrializing countries of western Europe and the United States are the bearers of both. Thus, history, when viewed through the lens furnished by the doctrine of progress, becomes identical with the development of the Western industrial, capitalist states. By virtue of their vanguard role, so the theory goes, they are continually in the forefront of history and more advanced than other societies. They lead, and other societies follow.

In other words, the idea of progress proclaims the primacy and uniqueness of the West; the developmental trajectories of societies in other parts of world will eventually recapitulate the various historical epochs through which the West has already passed. In the same breath, the advocates of the idea of progress simultaneously proclaim and deny differences between Western and non-Western societies. They homogenize the latter, reducing their variability to a few stereotypes, and then portray them as either invisible or different—inferior, damaged, or immature versions of what has already occurred in the West. They write the history of non-Western societies from the standpoint of the all-knowing and powerful; they then attempt to impose or inscribe their stereotypes of society and history on the less powerful. This Eurocentric view of the world is ethnocentric; it is a political act, a form of oppression.

Non-Western intellectuals, who have first-hand experience with the underside of progress in their own countries, have often expressed their ambivalence and even challenged its authenticity. Since the 1960s, they, and a few writers in the West, have increasingly begun to explore their histories and cultures from a different standpoint—that of less powerful or marginalized communities. The advocates of progress have typically dismissed such efforts as irrational plunges into relativism; they have claimed instead that progress is a rational process that is also fragile and easily threatened or disrupted by moments or forces of irrationality, such as World War I, the Russian Revolution of 1917, and the political instability resulting from decolonization and the activities of the emergent and non-aligned states of the Third World after World War II. In short, progress is disrupted by any event, force, or condition that disturbs the unfettered development of Western capitalism.

It is necessary to put politics and power relations back into our discussions. We can no longer afford to disguise or deny the complexity of history and the linkages among diverse societies, both past and present, by using abstract, often rhetorical images—like savages, barbarians, or formative villagers—to represent them. We must pay attention to community and locality, to the resistance emanating from place and region, and to social movements; at the same time, we must begin to appreciate cultural differences and develop an understanding of their significance in the inherently unstable circumstances constituted by unevenly distributed power and by the contradictions it engenders.

REALISM, TOTALITY, AND SOCIAL FORMATION

Some processual and postprocessual archaeologists, as well as some Marxists, have adopted a realist standpoint to grapple with these issues. There are diverse strands of realism, and a minimal list of realist assertions would include the following: (1) that there is an objective, material world, which exists independently of consciousness and which is knowable by consciousness; (2) that the senses give us only a world of appearances and that these appearances conceal another level of reality; and (3) that everyday life in the world of appearances is generated by and partially reveals the existence of the unobservable relations and processes that constitute that concealed level of reality.

Realism incorporates an ontological notion of system or totality, in which the whole is more than the sum of the interconnected parts. A totality, like the civilizations studied by archaeologists, is a structured and historically determined complex that exists through the diverse ways in which its parts are linked to one another in and through a continually shifting and changing set of interrelationships. Systemically, a totality comprises the entities that are subordinate to it, and at the same time, it is subject to multiple sources of determination by more complex totalities. Historically, the systemic character of a totality is relative in the sense that it changes and is always confined to a specific historical period.

A social totality has two levels: the phenomenal world of appearances—that is, everyday life—and the level of the unobservable processes and relations that are simultaneously revealed in the everyday as well as concealed by it. At the level of appearances, a civilization is a historically constituted, internally differentiated set of communities that are linked together and organized by the institutions and practices of class and state structures, on the one hand, and by resistance to them, on the other. The communities themselves are organized groups of individuals, units of production and management, with relatively homogeneous systems of values. Men and women are born into a community, whose organizational patterns and ethic shape how they live and how their lives are replicated or modified through time. The cultures of the various communities are often diverse and refract in complex ways differences in their relations to power.

The basic forms of everyday life in a civilization made up of a number of distinct communities are not homogeneous. In fact, they are typically at odds with one another since civilizations are class-stratified, state-based societies whose rulers extract labor and goods from the members of subordinated communities and groups. Civilizations are unities of interacting contradictions, which maintain or even foster limited forms of diversity under conditions of exploitation at the same time as they attempt to homogenize the parts or at least domesticate the heterogeneity of the constituent communities. Their class and state structures crosscut and intersect those of the encapsulated communities even as they arrange the subordinated groups into various hierarchies. By virtue of occupying different places in structures of power, the various classes, communities, or groups of a civilization typically have alternative understandings of the totality.

This is why peasant communities have been depicted as part societies with part cultures. It is the source for W. E. B. DuBois's recognition of the dialectic of multiculturalism and multiple consciousness described in *The Souls of Black Folk*. It is the basis for the complex stratification of language into genres and sociolects, in which distinctive social groups—defined by age, gender, kinship, social position, and so on and by relation to power—define abstract speech communities and themselves in different ways.

The men and women of communities create culture in the course of everyday life. Culture gives meaning to their social activities and to the concrete, material conditions in which they take place. Since the various communities that make up a civilization have different, often contradictory positions and relations to power, the culture created through praxis within the framework of existing social relations is shaped by those contradictions as they are perceived and experienced by the men and women of the various communities.

The unobservable level of a totality is the domain of modes of production—economic bases, property relations, and the corresponding forms of social consciousness—that structure and give meaning to everyday life and history in particular, historically concrete civilizations. The world of everyday life is not an epiphenomenon of the unobservable level. The various spheres of human activity are not simply built on some economic reality but rather actively organize economic reality through their own relatively autonomous, complex institutions and practices. That is, the social relations that structure production and reproduction do not exist independently of those spheres. The relations or linkages of the two are better described by terms like overdetermination, semiautonomy, reciprocal interaction, or uneven development.

Thus, in instances of class formation, the true nature of the economy is obscured since the emergent hierarchies of social categories—for example, castes or estates—cannot be reduced directly to economic-class relations. These hierarchies of noneconomic social categories disguise both the real economic-class relations and the real contradictions that emerge from them. In such instances, the hierarchically organized social categories, rather than economic-class structures, appear as "natural" groups or relations.

In this view, everyday life and history are intertwined. Everyday life is the raw material of history, the stage on which it is enacted. History is the derailment or disruption of the everyday, phenomenal world; it is change rather than the replication or reproduction of the framework of social relations that shape everyday life. The connection has also been portrayed in terms of the interpenetration of residual, dominant, and emergent elements of culture and modes of production. The linkages have the capacity to generate new understandings and practices for actors who occupy different places in power structures and whose routine conduct and perceptions are contingent on, but not completely determined by, their positions within the existing frameworks of social relations. Whether the existing institutions and practices are reproduced or new ones are constituted rests on the abilities of groups of actors to overcome the constraints and contradictions that exist at particular moments. From time to time, history does present real alternatives, where the actions of groups occupying particular places in structures of power do make a difference and can result in emancipatory changes.

Adopting the concept of totality—viewing civilization as a continually shifting patchwork of internally differentiated communities bound together by interacting contradictions and mediations—has several methodological consequences for any comparative study of their formation and development. It juxtaposes studies of the similarities and differences of the constituent communities of a civilization and their linkages with an analysis of the particular sociocultural and historical circumstances in which the various communities were constituted and to which they were responses. Such a comparative approach allows us to address systematically and historically the issues of uneven development, the formation of class and state structures, resistance, ethnogenesis, and fragmentation.

COMMUNAL MODES OF PRODUCTION

The relations of production and reproduction, which shaped everyday life in societies manifesting communal modes of production, operated at different levels, both conceptually and in reality. In many kin-based communities, the real appropriation of nature seems to have occurred at the level of the domestic unit, represented by households; these were the basic units of production and consumption that procured the foodstuffs and many of the raw materials that were transformed into useful items by the men, women, and children in the units.

Although individual domestic groups were clearly capable of acquiring food and other necessities for life, they were not able to ensure either demographic replacement or the reproduction of the social conditions necessary for life. The latter were also not carried out by the 50 or 100 individuals who resided together in many early settlements. Local populations of this magnitude were simply too small to have been autonomous, independent demographic entities. Consequently, there must have been matrimonial mobility among different local groups, involving the movement of men, women, or more likely both among settlements of varying sizes. The resulting social composition of the different local groups would mirror this practice. If only men moved, settlements were probably made up of women with kin ties, their children, and husbands from the outside; if only women moved, settlements would have consisted of men who were related to one another, their offspring, and women from other local communities.

Although the real appropriation of nature and production occurred at the level of domestic groups and local communities, demographic replacement and the social reproduction of the domestic groups and the communities themselves were underwritten by their participation in more inclusive social networks that included other, structurally similar groups. The demographic necessities for mating and maintaining stable population sizes suggest that the communities defined by these networks could not have been much smaller than five hundred individuals. These wider communities, largely invisible or unrecognized in the archaeological record, provided the resources and the ideological cement required for demographic and social reproduction.

Collective control over production and consumption also meant that no member of the community ate well while others starved and that decisions affecting everyday life were consensual rather than imposed. Various practices and values—leveling devices, as Richard Lee (1988, 1989) has called them—promoted an adherence to egalitarianism and inhibited the formation of any long-standing or hereditary differences in status and wealth. These egalitarian relations of distribution ensured that the community members had what they needed to subsist and to raise their children, the next generation; they ensured that the conditions for both demographic and social production were perpetuated; and they constrained the development of individual ownership or possession of the major means of production. As a result of the leveling mechanisms, the members of these communities did not accumulate goods on any significant scale. Exchange—more concerned with creating and reaffirming friendships than with procuring raw materials or finished goods—also ensured the reproduction of these communities. It established a pool of friends that individuals could turn to in times of need, an intercommunity network that enabled people to deal with fluctuations of resources by visiting friends in other areas when food, water, or other necessities were scarce in their own lands. Cooperation was valued, and little weight was placed on whether or not help was given unselfishly; there were undoubtedly sanctions that made it difficult or impossible to avoid such obligations. It is also necessary to keep in mind that communalism and cooperation were probably achieved at some cost to the quality of interpersonal relations, that these communities were not perfect systems of equality, and that interpersonal relations within and between communities were not necessarily tranquil and harmonious.

Communities at levels of development similar to those described in Chapters 3 and 4 are frequently portrayed in terms of two overlapping images. The first is that they lived in harmony with nature and did not alter the balance of forces by introducing destructive changes into the areas where they lived. The second image is concerned with how they lived: One version states that they lived a miserable, semistarvation existence and were engaged in an eternal quest for food; the other says that they were the original affluent societies and their members worked only a few hours a day to get what they needed. Both were probably true at different times and places.

A moment's reflection suggests that the members of ancient communities often changed their environments through various social and economic means: They killed game and may even have facilitated the extinction of some of Pleistocene species; they engaged in a number of activities—for example, cutting down trees, clearing vegetation, and dropping seeds—that altered both the configuration and composition of local plant communities. They were flexible enough to deal regularly with local, seasonal, and even annual fluctuations in the availability of different foods in the diverse environments they inhabited.

By the eighth millennium B.C., the inhabitants of some regions were already harvesting the returns of seeds they had planted around springs, along the banks of rivers, or in rich alluvial soils on the edges of valleys. They were increasing the density and availability of certain economically important species in localities near their campsites. They were modifying not only the spatial distribution of these species but also the composition of larger plant communities. More important, they were slowly transforming land from an object of labor, provisioned by nature and yielding immediate returns, to an instrument of labor—a means of production—that would yield returns only after considerable labor investments over an extended period of time. The productivity of the initial attempts at plant cultivation was low, judging by the paucity of cultivated plant remains in archaeological deposits. The cultivation of wild plants and then domesticated species was merely one of a number of economic practices; it could be pursued because the labor demands were initially quite low and the productivity of other subsistence activities was sufficiently high and reliable to permit individuals to engage in a few practices that were characterized by delayed consumption.

FOOD PRODUCTION AND THE TRANSFORMATION OF THE PRODUCTIVE FORCES

Much of the post-World War II research on early food-producing societies was provoked by the theories of V. Gordon Childe, the Australian archaeologist and social theorist, who projected a materialist conception of history back in time to the period before there was writing. Childe portrayed the history of human society in terms of a series of revolutionary transformations of the productive forces that provoked massive reorderings of the social relations shaping everyday life. The first transformation, the Neolithic revolution, was part of the technological watershed that occurred when people began to produce more than enough food to satisfy their subsistence and reproductive needs. As their ability to produce food surpluses grew, they became increasingly self-sufficient and were able to extend and support technical divisions of labor that involved a few craftspersons and other specialists who were not engaged in full-time food production. This development opened up new opportunities for exchange and other kinds of relations with neighboring communities. Some archaeologists also linked the development of food production with the appearance of sedentary farming villages, although Childe himself argued that the two were not directly related.

The various attempts to clarify, elaborate, modify, and even replace Childe's thesis have significantly added to our understanding of certain aspects of the development of food production in various parts of the world. Much of this research has been descriptive, or carried out and reported in terms of an ecological-functionalist theoretical framework that has stressed interactions between environment and technology and the constraints they are presumed to place on social relations. As a result, we know a great deal about certain aspects of the transition to food production and less about others.

First, communities in many areas utilized a variety of plant and animal species to gain their livelihoods. Some of the resources occurred in one or only a few habitats, whereas others—like wild cereals and other grasses—were widespread and could be found in a number of different habitats. As a result, groups living in nearby areas may have exploited many of the same resources; however, in certain seasons, they may have consumed very different foodstuffs because of the ecological peculiarities of areas where they lived. One model for the development of plant cultivation suggests that communities began to sow the seeds of economically important plants to increase their abundance and availability near their campsites. This practice ensured that at least some seeds and fruits might be harvested in years when favorable conditions prevailed. Once cultivation proved productive when conditions were favorable, the people began to plant seeds when conditions were less favorable and foodstuffs, on the whole, were not as abundant.

Second, the way land was transformed into a means of production, as well as the rate at which it occurred, apparently varied significantly from one area to another and from region to region in the same area. In the highlands of southern Mexico, for example, the shift was a slow, unsteady movement that took place over period of several millennia. In some of the coastal areas, like Veracruz, the shift from a foraging to an agrarian economy seems to have been more rapid, as relatively sedentary groups adopted cultivation practices developed and honed in other regions. When they adopted the practices they also acquired plants that were already domesticated and had been consumed for centuries or even millennia elsewhere in Mesoamerica.

Third, cultivation and the move toward agricultural production occurred in the context of a network of social relations that linked domestic groups into local bands and bands into larger communities. These relations involved alliances, exchange, distribution, and reciprocity. They ensured the demographic and social reproduction of everyday life at different levels of the larger communities—domestic units, microbands, and macrobands. Since domestic groups, following diverse hunting and foraging routines, were already constituents of larger communities, it is informative to consider why some of them chose to intensify subsistence production—to produce or acquire more foodstuffs in the same amount of time—and the consequences their actions might had on the larger communities to which they belonged. Barbara Bender (1978, 1981) sees the intensification of subsistence activities, the changes people make in their daily and seasonal routines, as attempts to resolve conflicts between escalating social demands on production and an inadequate production base.

The social demands on production were probably episodic rather than steady or uniform. From this perspective, the important question is not whether there was sociocultural variability—that is, some groups were cultivators and others hunted and foraged—but rather under what conditions the new forms of production were added to the subsistence activities of communities. On the one hand, cultivation, as a form of intensified production, may have been dropped from the daily and seasonal routines of local groups during lean years, when fewer kinds of food resources were available. On the other hand, cultivation and other forms of intensified production may have become less important in the routines of everyday life when social demands, arising at the level of the larger community and involving debts incurred as a consequence of delayed reciprocity, were ultimately resolved.

Finally, the successful and unsuccessful transitions to food production in various parts of the world resonate with two broader theoretical debates concerned with the locus of technological change. The first examines the question of whether or not groups of individual producers act rationally and strive to upgrade their skills and means of production so the burden of labor will lie less heavily on them. If agriculture is ultimately more productive than other, nonagricultural subsistence activities in the long run, why did some of the presumably utility-maximizing communities end up pursuing suboptimal subsistence strategies? That this practice actually occurred in different areas challenges the usefulness of rational action theories, which argue that individuals or collectivities always pursue cost-effective strategies to achieve desired, utility-maximizing ends. Evidence from Mesoamerica and elsewhere suggests instead that the new forms of activity and social relations were the unintended consequences of rational actions that were supposed to reproduce existing structures or practices.

The other debate is concerned with whether or not the productive forces develop autonomously, or independently of social structure, because they are rooted in the material facts of human nature and the human situation. This has been called the primacy of the productive forces thesis. It claims that the level of development of the productive forces determines the relations of production and that human history, before the Industrial Revolution, was characterized by a slight tendency toward technological progress. It locates the motor for progress in the human condition, which is viewed as one of scarcity, but sees this process operating on and through the existing social relations, which control the productive forces. Thus, whereas the level of development of the productive forces determines the relations of production, it is the relations of production that determine how those forces will be deployed and how the objects produced will circulate, be distributed, and consumed. The relations of production establish what cannot happen; however, beyond these constraints, they do not shape the form of what can occur in historically specific societies. This form is shaped by people making their own history, given the opportunities for and limitations on social action that are imposed by the already existing social relations. This statement implies that the dynamics of social relations are independent of the specifics of the subsistence economy—that is, they do not reflect the constraints of the productive forces in some simple, unmediated manner.

EARLY SEDENTARY COMMUNITIES

In many parts of the world, communities abandoned the mobile lifeways of their ancestors and began to reside in villages they occupied on a year-round basis. This greater stability of residence was marked by the appearance of more durable dwellings and by the fact that the villagers did not fragment into smaller units and disperse during part of the year. This development meant that they had been able to store enough food to satisfy their subsistence needs during the seasons of the year when food was scarce. Their subsistence economies had shifted from those that involved the immediate consumption of a variety of foodstuffs to ones that involved the storage and consumption of large quantities of particular foods. Certain conditions are necessary for the development of food-storing subsistence economies: abundant quantities of a suitable, seasonally available resource; the existence of efficient harvesting techniques; and the ability to preserve and store large quantities of foodstuffs—like wheat, acorns, maize, and smoked or dried fish—that could be eaten during those times of the year when food was not especially plentiful. By storing large quantities of food, the people did not have to move as the seasonal or local availability of particular foodstuffs in the wild declined.

Sedentarism, as Alain Testart (1982) has observed, is related to the development of food storage. In many parts of the world, the appearance of sedentary villages was closely associated with the storage of agricultural produce and, hence, with the development of food-producing subsistence economies. What distinguished the village farmers from their foraging ancestors, who occasionally planted seeds and harvested those that ripened, was the role intensive food storage played in their economic calculations. The shift involved new forces of production; land was transformed from an object of labor that yielded immediate returns to a major means of production that generated delayed returns only after considerable inputs of labor. Such a shift entailed new attitudes toward nature, time, and work. These food-storing farmers had become more dependent on the results of work they had performed over a period of time in the past—cultivating, harvesting, preserving, and storing plant foods—than they were on the bounty that nature offered them at the present.

What conditions might lead or compel a kin-based community to develop and rely more intensively or even exclusively on stored foods than on the acquisition and immediate consumption of foodstuffs taken from the wild? Such practices may have less to do with creating a surplus than with intensifying production or increasing productivity to satisfy some immediate, short-term, socially constructed need. In other words, the development of both food storage and food production are embedded in the social relations that characterize everyday life in highly varied, kin-based communities.

Archaeologists working in coastal Peru have argued that the appearance of sedentary villages was linked with the development of net fishing, food-preservation techniques, and the construction of storage facilities. Parts of these communities resided in permanent fishing villages, and the remainder foraged or lived in small farming hamlets. The appearance of sedentary village life may have set the stage for population growth. It also marked the emergence of new social relations of production that did not replicate the earlier technical divisions of labor. Although the real units of appropriation and consumption continued to be domestic groups, community-level social relations, based ultimately on cooperation, were extended and involved in the regular acquisition of raw materials from distant localities, the appearance of a spatially organized division of labor involving economically specialized settlements, and public construction and storage. The community-level relations constituted the conditions for the reproduction of the community.

John Clark and Michael Blake (1989), archaeologists who work on the Pacific coast of southern Mexico, have argued that the appearance of early sedentary villages was linked with development of social differentiation among previously egalitarian and largely self-sufficient households during the early second millennium B.C. Both were the result of bigmanships that emerged under conditions of increased exchange, especially of exotic goods. Bigmen manipulated social relations to create personal followings, to gain control over the production of others, and to siphon off goods to enhance their own prestige and that of their followers. They redistributed the exotic goods they obtained at village feasts, supported part-time craft specialists around their households, and buried their dead with different arrays and quantities of grave goods.

The two arguments are intriguing. The first claims that social and economic development were manifestations of the elaboration of community-level relations of production—that is, of those systems of customary rights and obligations moored in kin relations. The second asserts that the dynamics involved the appearance of bigmen, who drew followers who were not kin and who lacked the kind of authority that derives from participation in traditional or customary production relations of the community; consequently, their positions were inherently unstable because they were always faced with the possibility that their followers would align themselves with other, competing bigmen and that they would be unable to re-create the conditions that sustained their support—that is, the public redistribution of goods. Although the two interpretations differ in a number of ways, they agree that the communities in both areas manifested the communal mode of production. However, they claim that the communities were constituted on the basis of different variants or forms of this mode of production.

CLASS AND STATE FORMATION

For most of human history, the social relations were structured by kinship, residence, and crosscutting technical divisions of labor based on age and gender that created, initially at least, complementary spheres of men's and women's activities. The small size of many settlements meant that there was matrimonial mobility and that some individuals did not reside in their natal villages or hamlets. However, larger villages were often made up of a number of descent groups whose members resided in spatially distinct wards; this diminished and, in some instances, eliminated altogether the necessity for intervillage matrimonial mobility.

Customary authority in such settlements and their hinterlands, according to Pierre Clastres (1987:189–215), was minimally constituted by intersecting and interdependent principles reflecting kinship and residence. That is, authority was divided and had multiple foundations. This meant, in practice, that there were some individuals whose authority was based on their places in networks of kin relations and others who derived their importance from the roles they played in the affairs of these spatially organized communities.

The tension created by the cleavages based on kinship and residence were the motors of history and change in these communities. On the one hand, kindreds expressed and sought to maintain their identities by appropriating the labor power and products of their own members; this was a centrifugal force that had the potential to fragment the village community. On the other hand, individuals whose authority derived from their place of residence rather than their membership in a kin group sought to integrate the disparate elements of the community into a totality through requests for labor to undertake projects, like the construction of public buildings, that benefited the community as a whole and by acting as peacemakers to resolve the inevitable conflicts that erupted among individuals, families, and groups within those communities. This is the tension between the relations of production and the relations of reproduction. The former operate at the level of the kin-based groups, the real units of appropriation and consumption; the latter function at the level of the community and re-create the conditions necessary for its maintenance.

Class and state formation involve the simultaneous dissolution of the old community-level relations of reproduction and their reconstitution along new lines that facilitate the extortion of labor and/or goods by the members of one group from those of another. Exploitative social relationships never emerge alone, isolated from other changes in the society. The appearance of class structures and the social division of labor they represent are rooted in social processes that involve violence, repression, and conquest. The constitution of social classes is connected with the formation of the state. The various institutions, practices, and legal codes of the state represent the interests of the dominant class. The state ensures that bodies are counted for taxation and conscription, that taxes and tribute are collected, that internal dissent is suppressed or deflected outward toward other communities, that bureaucrats and overseers are selected, that stationary or moving capitals are established, that production is reorganized to satisfy new patterns of distribution and exchange, and occasionally even that distinctions are created between town dwellers and their rural kinfolk. Customary authority, exercised in the context of these processes, is often transformed into the exploitative exercise of power.

At issue is whether customary authority was converted or transformed into coercive power that enabled its holders to extort labor and/or goods from their kin and neighbors. If so, how were the individuals possessing it able to constitute themselves as a class? How were they able to transform themselves from members of kin and residential groupings into masters able to dominate their kin and neighbors and appropriate their services and goods? How were the interpersonal relations and perceptions of both the rulers and the ruled affected by the fact that as they attempted to extend their domination, the masters became increasingly dependent on the work performed by their subordinated kin and neighbors and on their continued submission, when at the same time they were forced to deny increasingly what their subjects viewed as evil in them, the bases of their own domination and oppression?

Some descriptions of kin-based communities stress that experience and inventiveness are pooled. When crises or tasks requiring organization and supervision appeared, the community selected organizers and persuaded them to serve. The authority of the leaders was ad hoc and provisional. Tendencies toward class and state formation occurred when these temporary and provisional leaders were not inclined to relinquish their authority—that is, when they attempted to transform it into power. Such efforts necessarily required the support of others in the community. If and when they succeeded in seizing authority and transforming it into power, a class structure was formed and the state was born. If these would-be rulers were unable to establish and assert their claims, neither class structures nor state apparatuses were created; class and state formation had failed. In this sense, both class and state formation are historically contingent. They are one lane of a two-way street; the other lane involves the dissolution of class structures and the centralized institutions and practices of the state—what Marc Abèlés (1981:12–13) has called the state/nonstate transition.

Many accounts of the nonstate/state transition focus on the concentration of political power—that is, legislative, administrative, and judicial—in as few hands as possible. They examine how authority, granted for limited periods of time by the community, was usurped. Some analyses situate the original extortion of the community and the impetus for class and state formation in the political realm; they emphasize the potential ability of charismatic war chiefs or leaders in times of crisis to seize authority and convert their retinues and/or close kin into a ruling class supported by the labor and goods of direct producers. Other analyses situate the original extortion and the impetus for class and state formation in the domain of ritual personages, the custodians of ancestors' shrines, who appropriated for their own use gifts that were formerly consumed by the community that offered them and who successfully exploited their position to add political dimensions to their ritual offices and to crystallize class differences between themselves and the larger community.

Evidence from different civilizations indicates that the locus or loci of power shifted on more than one occasion during the history of these states. For example, in Teotihuacán state, which controlled a significant part of central Mexico during the first millennium A.D., the locus of power, which had consolidated originally around a military leader, was seized by a faction of ritual and political actors, who were subsequently displaced by a reemergent or new faction of the military in the years immediately preceding the local revolt that destroyed the new ruling class and buildings identified with the state. What is not entirely clear at this time are the particular sociohistorical conditions and circumstances that made these changes possible and the specific struggles that accompanied their emergence and development at different periods in the state's history. What is clear, however, is that there were multiple centers of power inside and outside the state, and that there were struggles both within the ruling class and between its members and the direct producers who grew the food, built the palaces, and made the objects that underwrote the state apparatus and the leisured existence of certain layers of the ruling class.

Imperial states, like Teotihuacán, often attempted to extend their political hegemony to adjoining territories and populations and to incorporate or articulate their political economies with their own. Although the extension of power is often understood as conquest, the process of expansion was never an indiscriminate one that involved merely the encapsulation of weaker neighboring communities and polities. Since the extension of power or conquest always has underlying motives, the political economy of expansion plays a determinate role in structuring the relations between the metropolitan state and the peoples on its margins.

Distinctive kinds of institutions and practices develop in areas that have been linked with or incorporated into the state for different reasons. When the state incorporates peoples and their lands to extend its own subsistence production, it requires tax assessors, collectors, and overseers to ensure that the subject populations provide the labor, food, and other goods it demands. When the state attempts to control commerce, it must establish control over the groups engaged in production and exchange, over the routes on which the merchants and their goods travel, and over the markets where these items are exchanged. Populations that possess little of interest to the state and its ruling class are frequently encapsulated but not particularly bothered as long as they acknowledge the sovereignty of the metropolis. Thus, imperial states, like Teotihuacán, exhibit a range of differentiated political-economic and social relations between the metropolis and its peripheries; each of these potentially yields a distinctive cultural formation that gives meaning to the uniquely constituted aspects of everyday life in different parts of the domain.

STATE FORMATION AND UNEVEN DEVELOPMENT

Jean-Jacques Rousseau (1964:141), in his *Discourse on the Origin and Founda-tions of Inequality among Men*, written in 1754, was one of the first to conclude that class stratification and state formation began with theft:

> The first person who, having fenced off a plot of ground, took it into his head to say *this is mine* and found people simple enough to believe him, was the true founder of civil society. What crimes, wars, murders, what miseries and horrors would the human race have been spared by someone who, uprooting the stakes or filling in the ditch, had shouted to his fellow men: Beware of listening to this impostor; you are lost if you forget that the fruits belong to all and the earth to no one!

Rousseau believed that there was nothing intrinsic in the human com-munity that implied that it would necessarily transform itself into civilization. This was also true of the kin-based communities with extended community-level relations of production and reproduction that thrived in coastal Peru, Mesoamerica, and other parts of the world now and at various times in the past. There is nothing inherent in their political-economic and social struc-tures that imply that they will transform themselves into class-stratified, state-organized societies. They contain no latent potential waiting to unfold as soon as the right conditions appear. Class and state formation are, instead, historically contingent processes that occur in the context of both societal and regional structures that shape and constrain the potential for human action. Even in kin-based communities, these structures are characterized by contra-dictions, by competing, often unequal tendencies that develop along moving lines of force and through time, and between which any equilibrium is inherently unstable. The contradictions are continually reconstituted on new grounds and under ever-changing conditions. The historical development of these contradictions is not steered by some teleological motor that ultimately creates the conditions for their resolution. What class and state formation do when these processes occur, is eliminate some of the ambiguities that charac-terize everyday life in kin-based communities.

Class and state formation are clearly regional processes that simultane-ously affect a number of societies. They create uneven development, and the state-based societies that emerge are unstable. They promote kin-civil con-flicts at home when they resolve the contradictions and ambiguities of every-day life in ways that favor one group over another. They create new tensions along their margins, both when they succeed in encapsulating neighboring communities and when these groups successfully resist subordination, annex-ation, or conquest.

This perspective is an alternative to positions that view class stratifica-tion and state institutions and practices as the necessary consequence or outcome of evolutionary processes driven by elaborations of the productive forces, demographic or ecological pressures, or the appearance of market economies. It situates class and state formation in the ambiguities and contradictions of everyday life and argues that such events and changes cannot be divorced from history. It also recognizes that groups with different relations to power in such circumstances typically have different sensibilities and understandings of those conditions and the events that occurred.

FURTHER READINGS: A BRIEF GUIDE

The idea of progress as a product of the scientific revolution is examined by Edgar Zilsel, "The Genesis of the Concept of Scientific Progress," *Journal of the History of Ideas*, vol. VI, no. 4 (1945), 325–349, and "Physics and the Problem of Historico-sociological Laws," *Philosophy of Science*, vol. 8, no. 4 (1941), 567–579. The extension of the idea to the realm of human society is discussed by Hans Baron, "The *querelle* of the Ancients and the Moderns as a Problem for Renaissance Scholarship," *Journal of the History of Ideas*, vol. XX, no. 1 (1959), 3–22; Richard F. Jones, *Ancient and Moderns: A Study of the Rise of the Scientific Movement in Seventeenth-century England*, 2nd ed. (Berkeley: University of California Press, 1961); Frederick J. Teggart, *The Idea of Progress* (Berkeley: University of California Press, 1929); Ernest L. Tuveson, *Millennium and Utopia: A Study in the Background of the Idea of Progress* (Berkeley: University of California Press, 1949); and Gabriel A. Almond, Marvin Chodorow, and Roy Harvey Pearce eds., *Progress and Its Discontents* (Berkeley: University of California Press, 1982). Ronald L. Meek, *Social Science and the Ignoble Savage* (Cambridge: Cambridge University Press, 1976), discusses the background and development of the "four stages theory" of progress, which emphasizes the role played by modes of subsistence in the development of political economy, both as an object and a field of inquiry.

Although non-Western and ancient societies are mentioned by social theorists, critics, and writers as diverse as Michel de Montaigne, Francois de Voltaire, and Karl Marx, their involvement in the development of Western social thought since the sixteenth century has often been indirect, implied, and unacknowledged. The extent of their influence is explored by Talal Asad, ed., *Anthropology and the Colonial Encounter* (Atlantic Highlands, NJ: Humanities Press, 1975); Partha Chatterjee, *Nationalist Thought and the Colonial World: A Derivative Discourse?* (London: Zed Press, 1986); Edward Said, *Orientalism* (New York: Vintage, 1978); Benjamin Keen, *The Aztec Image in Western Thought* (New Brunswick, NJ: Rutgers University Press, 1971); Peter Hulme, *Colonial Encounters: Europe and the Native Caribbean, 1492–1797* (London: Methuen, 1986); and Martin Bernal, *Black Athena: The Afroasiatic Roots of Classical Civilization*, 2 vols. (London: Free Association Books, 1987–1991). The controversies over the representation of non-Western peoples by themselves and others are addressed by Samir Amin, *Eurocentrism* (New York: Monthly Review Press, 1989); Robert Young, *White Mythologies: Writing History and the West* (London: Routledge, 1990); Francis Barker, Peter Hulme, Margaret Iversen, and Diana

Loxley eds., *Europe and Its Others*, 2 vols. (Essex, Eng.: University of Essex, 1984); and Homi K. Bhakha, ed., *Nation and Narration* (London: Routledge, 1991).

Roy Bhaskar, *Scientific Realism and Human Emancipation* (London: Verso, 1986), and *Reclaiming Reality: A Critical Introduction to Contemporary Philosophy* (London: Verso, 1989); Jarrett Leplin, "Introduction," in his *Scientific Realism* (Berkeley: University of California Press, 1984), pp. 1–7; and Sean Sayers, *Reality and Reason: Dialectics and the Theory of Knowledge* (Oxford: Basil Blackwell, 1985), provide clear discussions of realism and its implications. The concept of totality is examined by Martin Jay, *Marxism and Totality: The Adventures of a Concept from Lukács to Habermas* (Berkeley: University of California Press, 1984). Archaeologists who have advocated realist standpoints include Kent Flannery, "Culture History v. Culture Process: A Debate in American Archaeology," *Scientific American*, vol. 217, no. 2 (1967), 119–122; Guy Gibbon, *Explanation in Archaeology* (Oxford: Basil Blackwell, 1989); Colin Renfrew, "Comments on Archaeology into the 1990s," *Norwegian Archaeological Review*, vol. 22, no. 1 (1989), 33–41; Michael Shanks and Christopher Tilley, *Reconstructing Archaeology: Theory and Practice* (Cambridge: Cambridge University Press, 1987); and Thomas C. Patterson, "Archaeology, History, and the Concept of Totality," paper presented at the annual meeting of the American Anthropological Association, New Orleans, 1990.

The primitive, kin-based, or communal mode of production has been discussed by a number of writers, including Eleanor B. Leacock, "Relations of Production in Band Society," in *Politics and History in Band Societies*, ed. Eleanor B. Leacock and Richard B. Lee (Cambridge: Cambridge University Press, 1986), pp. 159–170; Richard B. Lee, "Reflections on Primitive Communism," in *Hunters and Gatherers: History, Evolution, and Social Change*, ed. Tim Ingold, D. Riches, and James Woodburn (Oxford: Berg Publishers, 1988), pp. 252–268, and "Primitive Communism and the Origin of Social Inequality," in *The Evolution of Political Systems: Sociopolitics in Small-scale Sedentary Societies*, ed. Stedman Upham (Cambridge: Cambridge University Press, 1989), pp. 225–246; Pierre Clastres, *Society Against the State: Essays in Political Anthropology* (New York: Zone Books, 1987); and Thomas C. Patterson, "La creación de cultura en las formaciones sociales pre-estatales y non-estatales," *Boletía de Antropología Americana*, no. 14 (Mexico, 1986), pp. 53–61.

V. Gordon Childe's *Man Makes Himself* (New York: New American Library, [1936] 1983) was a seminal work. The significance of his writings are discussed by Linda Manzanilla, ed., *Studies in the Neolithic and Urban Revolutions: The V. Gordon Childe Colloquium, Mexico, 1986*, British Archaeological Reports, International Series 349 (Oxford, 1987); and Bruce G. Trigger, *Gordon Childe: Revolutions in Archaeology* (New York: Columbia University Press, 1980). David Rindos, *The Origins of Agriculture: An Evolutionary Perspective* (Orlando, FL: Academic Press, 1984), pp. 1–36, is a useful, critical survey of theories dealing with the origins of agricultural food production.

The consequences of the intensification of production are examined by Barbara Bender, "Gatherer-Hunter to Farmer: A Social Perspective," *World*

Archaeology, vol. 10, no. 2 (1978), 204–222, "Gatherer-Hunter Intensification," in *Economic Archaeology: Towards an Integration of Ecological and Social Approaches*, ed. Alison Sheridan and Geoff Bailey, British Archaeological Reports, International Series 96 (Oxford, 1981), pp. 149–157, and "Prehistoric Developments in the American Midcontinent and in Brittany, Northwest France," in *Prehistoric Hunter-gatherers: The Emergence of Cultural Complexity*, ed. T. Douglas Price and James A. Brown (New York: Academic Press, 1985).

The interrelations of food storage and sedentism are explored by Alain Testart, "The Significance of Food-storage among Hunter-Gatherers: Residence Patterns, Population Densities, and Social Inequalities," *Current Anthropology*, vol. 23, no. 5 (1982), 523–537; and Barbara Bender, "The Dynamics of Nonhierarchical Societies," in *The Evolution of Political Systems: Sociopolitics in Small-scale Sedentary Societies*, ed. Stedman Upham (Cambridge: Cambridge University Press, 1989), pp. 247–263. John Clark and Michael Blake, "The Pacific Coast Early Formative Project, Chiapas, Mexico: The Implications of Recent Archaeological Research," paper presented at the Circum-Pacific Prehistory Conference, Seattle, 1989, discuss sedentism in coastal southern Mexico. The dynamics of bigmanships are examined by Robert Paynter and John W. Cole, "Ethnographic Overproduction, Tribal Political Economy and the Kapauku of Irian Jaya," in *Beyond the Myth of Culture: Essays in Cultural Materialism*, ed. Eric B. Ross (New York: Academic Press, 1980), pp. 61–99; and Martin A. van Bakel, Renée R. Hagesteijn, and Pieter van de Velde eds., *Private Politics: A Multi-disciplinary Approach to 'Bigman' Systems* (Leiden, Neth.: E. J. Brill, 1986).

The issues of class and state formation and power relations are diverse. See, for example, Jean-Jacques Rousseau, "Discourse on the Origins and Foundations of Inequality (Second Discourse)," *The First and Second Discourses*, ed. Roger D. Masters (New York: St. Martin's Press, 1964), pp. 77–181. The analytical framework used here is discussed in more detail by Christine W. Gailey and Thomas C. Patterson, "State Formation and Uneven Development," in *State and Society: The Emergence and Development of Social Hierarchy and Political Centralization*, ed. Barbara Bender, John Gledhill, and Mogens T. Larsen (London: Unwin Hyman, 1988), pp. 77–90, and "Power Relations and State Formation," in *Power Relations and State Formation*, ed. Thomas C. Patterson and Christine W. Gailey (Washington, DC: Archeology Section, American Anthropological Association, 1987), pp. 1–26. Jérôme Rousseau, "On Estates and Castes," *Dialectical Anthropology*, vol. 3, no. 1 (1978), 85–95, distinguishes different kinds of social hierarchy. The fragility of state institutions and practices are examined by Marc Abélès, " 'Sacred Kingship' and the Formation of the State," in *The Study of the State*, ed. Henri J. M. Claessen and Peter Skalník (The Hague: Mouton Publishers, 1981), pp. 1–13; Stanley Diamond, "Dahomey: A Proto-state in West Africa," Ph.D. dissertation in Anthropology, Columbia University, New York, 1951; and Thomas C. Patterson, *The Inca Empire: The Formation and Disintegration of a Precapitalist State* (Oxford: Berg Publishers, 1991).

chapter 6

Mesopotamia

Mesopotamia has been called the "cradle of civilization." (Michael Roaf, Cultural Atlas of Mesopotamia and the Ancient Near East)

Is bombing the Cradle of Civilization back into the Stone Age, the act of a civilized state or genocide? (placard, Washington, DC, January 26, 1991)

Civilization originates in conquest abroad and repression at home. Each is an aspect of the other. (Stanley Diamond, In Search of the Primitive)

It is doubtful if very many governments in human history have been considered "legitimate" by the majority of those exploited, oppressed, and maltreated by [them]. . . . Governments tend to be endured, not appreciated or admired or loved or even supported. (Immanuel Wallerstein, The Modern World-System)

Mesopotamia—the fertile stretches of land along the Tigris and Euphrates rivers and their tributaries in Iraq, Syria, and the adjacent regions of Turkey and Iran—is part of a larger area called the Near East. The Near East is encircled by the Black, Mediterranean, and Red seas on the west and by the Caspian Sea and the Persian Gulf on the east. Its diverse landscapes—the Taurus and Pontus mountain ranges in Turkey, the Zagros Mountains east of the Tigris River, and the basalt desert of Jordan—are the products of plate tectonic processes that began 200 million years ago and continue to the present day. These and subsequent processes—erosion, sedimentation, earthquakes, floods, drought, and deforestation—have combined to produce a complexly textured patchwork of environments and human habitats, characterized by different climates and vegetation.

As harsh and forbidding as the Near East can be, the diverse habitats of the landscape, the seas that encircle it, and the lakes provided the raw materials used by the ancient inhabitants to create complex forms of everyday life. By extracting raw materials for consumption or use, by converting land into pasture and arable fields, the ancient peoples transformed the landscape and its raw materials into something that had not existed earlier. The irrigation canals they dug into the desert made it bloom; sheep and goats provided wool and food; the marshes and swamps of estuary formed by the Tigris and Euphrates rivers yielded fish and birds.

The transformations that occurred were not uniform throughout the entire area. They manifested instead the subtle but significant variations that result when peoples live in diverse habitats, have complex historical pasts and varied relations with their neighbors, and emphasize different elements in the forces and relations of production. Even slight differences of emphasis in the forces of production—the raw materials taken from the environment and the implements and labor power employed to transform them into useful

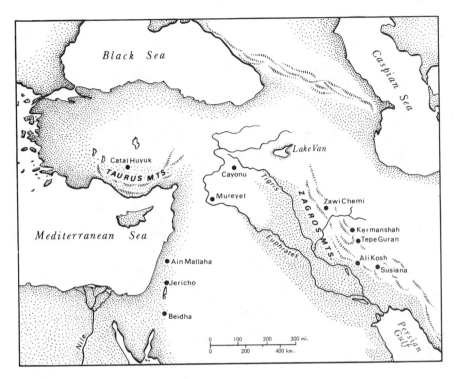

The location of early food-producing settlements in the Near East.

items—can yield significant variations in the details of the organization of labor. They affect the labor processes by introducing new forms of specialization and technical divisions of labor. Differences in the relations of production—whether the producers themselves control their means of production and labor power, or whether these are controlled by another class that extracts goods or labor from them—constitute another source of variability.

THE ADVENT OF FOOD PRODUCTION IN THE NEAR EAST AND ITS CONSEQUENCES

Archaeologists typically refer to the entire Near East when speaking about the origins of food production and to only part of the area, Mesopotamia, when dealing with the rise of civilization. Joy McCorriston and Frank Hole (1991) show that the first instances of plant domestication occurred in the Jordan Valley and its environs in the southern Levant about 10,500 years ago. The Early Neolithic (c. 8500 to 5500 B.C.) communities of the region began sowing the seeds of emmer wheat, barley, peas, and other legumes to extend the range and increase the abundance of these edible food plants and to

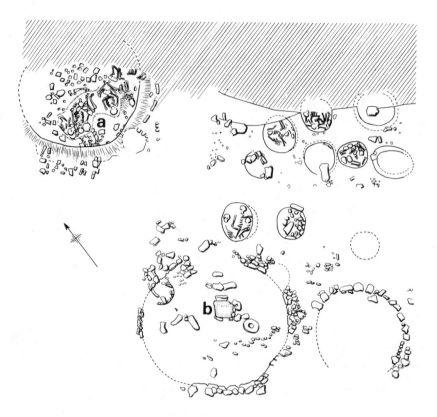

A portion of the village at Ain Mallaha showing its circular houses and storage pits, some of which were reused for burials.

supplement the game they hunted and the wild plants they collected in the vicinity of their settlements. In doing so, they modified the vegetation around their villages and transformed land into a means of production. They stored their harvests in pits and ground the seeds on mortars found in permanent villages, like Ain Mallaha near the Jordan River. A number of these villages housed several hundred individuals, who resided in semisubterranean, circular huts; Jericho, possibly the largest settlement, was surrounded by a massive stone wall and ditch and may have had as many as 1,500 residents. By 7000 B.C., the farming communities of the Levant had already added domesticated livestock—sheep and goats and pigs in some places—to their subsistence economies.

The inhabitants of these early Levantine communities buried their dead in cemeteries and beneath their houses. Two kinds of evidence shed light on the role played by the dead in everyday life. First, the presence of a genetically recessive trait in a burial population at one site, and its absence at others, suggests the biological continuity of the populations of these settlements extended over a number of successive generations. Second, archaeolo-

Human skull covered with plaster from Jericho.

gists have found a number of headless individuals buried at Jericho, Beidha, and other settlements in the Jordan Valley that were occupied more than 9,000 years ago. Typically the head was buried separately or kept in a room. The facial features of the skulls were often restored with plaster and paint, and fragments of life-sized plaster heads found at Jericho seemingly served as substitutes for real ones. These portrait skulls may well be material representations of ancestor cults, which defined not only membership in domestic groups and communities but also access to their means of production through descent from particular venerated ancestors. Thus, the dead defined an individual's place in the community and, consequently, his or her share of its wealth; such relationships are typically expressed in terms of kinship, with the kinds of rights and obligations that kin ties involve.

Whereas the inhabitants of the Levant farmed, their contemporaries in the Zagros Mountains, which mark the eastern edge of the Mesopotamian lowlands, were hunter-foragers who formed small bands and followed migratory game through the mountain valleys, stopping at different times and places to collect locally available plant foods: wild cereals, lentils, acorns, and pistachios. During the ninth millennium B.C., small groups camped at Zawi Chemi cave during the summers to collect wild plants and hunt sheep, goats, and red deer. By 8000 B.C., the cave's occupants were consuming large numbers of anatomically wild sheep, mostly young males, which suggests that they may already have been keeping herds of anatomically wild sheep consisting mainly of females and juveniles.

Ali Kosh, a settlement on the Deh Luran Plain in the foothills of the Zagros in east-central Iran, provides additional information about the development of food production. About 8000 B.C., some 50 to 100 individuals began to reside during the winter and spring near a semipermanent swamp that was bordered by rushes and sedges. They herded anatomically wild goats and a few sheep; hunted gazelles, other herbivores, and migratory waterfowl that visited the swamp between November and March; and fished and collected mussels and turtles. The absence of available foodstuffs and raw materials during the summer months suggests that the residents left their homes in this season and took their herds to pastures in the high mountain valleys to the east, where they encountered other communities doing the same thing. The groups exchanged information, raw materials, and finished goods—for example, stone tools made from obsidian quarried in the Lake Van region 500 miles to the north, cowrie shell beads from the Persian Gulf, copper from central Iran, or turquoise from the area around the Afghanistan border. Their goats mated with animals from other communities, and new genetic traits like medially flattened horn cores were introduced and became established in the local herds.

As time passed, the inhabitants of Ali Kosh began to grow emmer wheat and barley on the mud flats around the swamp, a practice that changed natural ground cover. The amount of land under cultivation or turned over to pasture increased, the abundance of certain economically important wild plants in close proximity to the village declined, and weeds appeared and began to compete with the crops. Although the productivity of these habitats increased, their ecological diversity and stability were diminished. Another consequence was that the villagers had to travel further afield to hunt the wild ungulates that apparently still provided much of the meat they consumed; this fact suggests that they kept sheep and goats mainly for their wool, hair, and milk rather than for their meat.

About 5500 B.C., the inhabitants of the Deh Luran Plain began to build small dams and canals to water their fields. They moved their villages from the edges of the seasonally flooded marshes to areas near the streams that flowed out of the mountains. Although farming probably continued to depend mainly on rainfall during this period, any water-control system, however simple, provided insurance against crop failures or poor harvests in years when the rains were late or inadequate. The villagers used polished stone hoes attached to wooden handles with asphalt to break up the alluvial soils of their new fields. They planted new, more productive varieties of wheat and barley and continued to grow lentils, vetch, and flax. Each of the half dozen villages at Deh Luran, as well as those on the Susiana Plain 70 miles to the southeast, was surrounded by intensively cultivated fields. As time passed, these became increasingly alkaline as the irrigation waters brought various salts to the surface, and the villagers began to grow more and more barley, which has a higher tolerance for alkaline soils than does wheat.

Subsistence economies based on food production had already appeared in Anatolia by the seventh millennium B.C. The inhabitants of Çatal Hüyük, a large village overlooking a swamp on the Konya Plain between 6500 and 5600 B.C., resided in a series of contiguous houses that resembled a pueblo in the American Southwest. They entered their single-room dwellings through a hole in the roof that also provided light and vented smoke; many of the white-plastered walls were painted with murals depicting scenes from everyday life. They grew einkorn and emmer wheat in fields near the swamp. These undoubtedly attracted deer and other animals, which enhanced the importance of hunting in their subsistence economy. They also kept small herds of domesticated cattle, which provided 90 percent of the meat they consumed as well as transport for raw materials, like wood and obsidian, brought down from the hills.

Each household at Çatal Hüyük probably consisted of 3 to 8 individuals, and the total population of the town around 6000 B.C. may have been 4,000 to 5,000 persons. The more than 400 burials uncovered during the excavations reveal that infant and childhood mortality were high; nearly 40 percent of the population died before reaching maturity. Women typically lived to about thirty, and men had a life expectancy of about thirty-four years. Some of the individuals buried there had at least one parent who had

Çatal Hüyük, Turkey. (a) Plan of the southeast quarter of the settlement. (b) reconstruction of the southeast quarter.

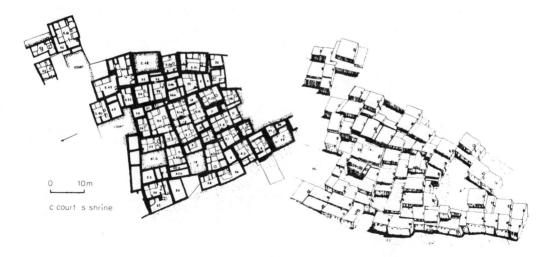

0   10m

c court s shrine

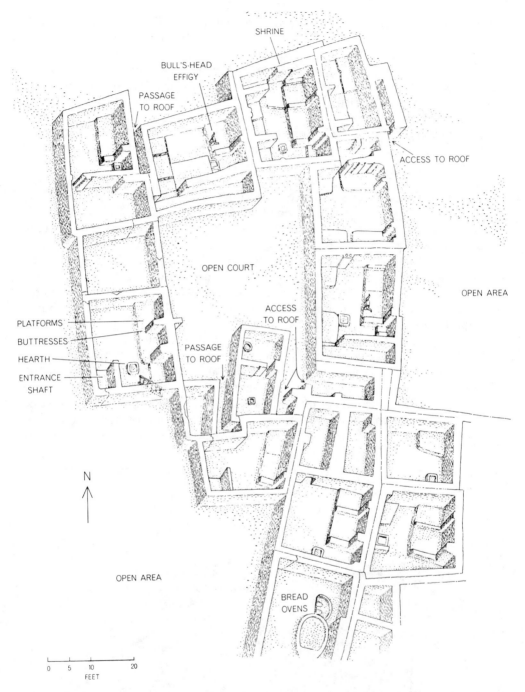

SHRINE

BULL'S-HEAD
EFFIGY

PASSAGE
TO ROOF

ACCESS TO ROOF

OPEN COURT

OPEN AREA

PLATFORMS

BUTTRESSES

HEARTH

ACCESS
TO ROOF

ENTRANCE
SHAFT

PASSAGE
TO ROOF

N

OPEN AREA

BREAD
OVENS

0   5   10   20
        FEET

The arrangement of households, shrines, and courtyards in the southeast quarter of Çatal Hüyük. (*From James Mellaart, "A Neolithic City in Turkey." Copyright © 1964 by Scientific American, Inc. All rights reserved.*)

been born elsewhere, judging by hereditary features of their teeth and skeletons. Many residents suffered from malaria, others broke bones after falling, and at least one person was gored by a bull. When individuals died, their bodies were exposed to the elements until the flesh had disappeared. The skeletons were then wrapped in cloth or animal skins and placed under houses, where they usually joined other burials. Most burials lacked grave goods, except for a few containers of food or an occasional tool or weapon. A few individuals were interred in shrines; they tended to have more grave goods, including exotic items such as daggers made from Syrian flint or jewelry fashioned from Red Sea cowrie shells.

The settlements of the earliest food-producing communities in the Near East varied in both size and appearance. They ranged from small, rural hamlets consisting of a couple of domestic groups to towns with several thousand residents. They typically occurred in clusters, separated from one another by vast uninhabited tracts. The various local groups that formed a settlement cluster presumably also constituted the community from which their members chose mates. Thus, the settlement cluster was a materialization of the community-level relations of production and reproduction. The real units of production and consumption were the domestic groups that inhabited the various residential structures; many were probably not nuclear families but rather extended kin or residential groupings that shared both work and the fruits of their labor.

After 5500 B.C., some communities fissioned; some of their members moved into the uninhabited areas, and many of their kin and former neighbors remained in the ancestral homelands. As a result, settlements continue to flourish in the established regions and also began to appear in the sparsely inhabited areas, slowly in some and suddenly in others. The distinctive pottery styles that appeared during the sixth millennium B.C. reflected regionally organized social networks. For example, settlements that used locally made Halaf pottery existed in the foothills stretching across northern Syria and Iraq, where the Tigris and Euphrates rivers and many of their tributaries rose; the villagers and townspeople residing along the lower courses of the two rivers near the estuaries used 'Ubaid pottery, whereas their contemporaries in the Samarra region near Baghdad to the north or on the Susiana Plain, 200 miles to the east, used related but distinctive local wares.

Regardless of the size of the settlements, most of the domestic groups engaged in subsistence activities: farming, herding, and the production of goods they used themselves and/or shared with neighbors. However, by the end of the seventh millennium B.C., some households produced goods, on a part-time or seasonal basis or on demand, that circulated beyond their own settlements; thus, to a limited extent, production was also spatially organized. For instance, many residents of Umm Dabaghiyah on the middle Euphrates hunted and exported onager hides, and some residents at Yarim Tepe, a contemporaneous village 70 miles to the north, smelted copper and lead or made pottery. What is not clear is how this specialized and seemingly territorially organized work was coordinated with the technical divisions of labor—structured by kinship, age, or gender—that existed in settlements, where the domestic groups engaged primarily or exclusively in subsistence production and where community-level social relations functioned mainly to ensure demographic and social reproduction.

At this time, exchange linked communities in different parts of the Near East; it transferred surplus raw materials and goods from one community to another. However, it was unintegrated and unintegrating since it did not produce the goods, conditions, or social relations the communally organized societies needed to sustain themselves. It allowed the members of different communities to engage their opposites without abandoning the places each of them held in their own societies. The consequence was that each of them occasionally acquired raw materials and goods from neighbors and less frequently from more remote sources. This statement directs attention to the kinds of social relations that were created or renewed during the exchange process: who produced the goods? How were the exchange processes organized? Who, if anyone, controlled them? And how were exotic items distributed once they arrived in the communities?

VILLAGE COMMUNITIES, INTENSIFICATION, AND THE FORMATION OF CITY-STATES

During the later half of the sixth millennium B.C., the inhabitants of the foothill settlements along the upper reaches of the Tigris and Euphrates rivers and their tributaries—from Lake Urmia in the east almost to the Mediterranean Sea in the west—began to use pottery whose forms and designs were derived not from the Halaf style that was indigenous to the region but rather from 'Ubaid vessels that were made and used along the lower reaches of the two rivers. Moreover, after 4800 B.C., pottery vessels manufactured in 'Ubaid villages located near fields, palm groves, and marshes of the estuaries were carried to more than fifty campsites located along the eastern shore of the Persian Gulf in Saudi Arabia, Bahrain, Qatar, and the United Arab Emirates. These were inhabited by local foraging and fishing peoples.

Another feature of everyday life in southern Mesopotamia and on the Susiana Plain during the late fifth and early fourth millennia B.C. was the elaboration of community-level relations of production, manifested in the construction of water-control systems and public buildings—platform mounds surmounted by small shrines. Structures of this kind, like the one at Susa, required at least 60,000 to 80,000 person-days of labor to build. Labor demands of this magnitude were clearly beyond the capacity of single domestic groups and, therefore, must have involved individuals from a number of households in the town or the wider community.

By the first half of the fourth millennium B.C., the landscape was dotted with a number of independent towns surrounded by villages, hamlets, and perhaps even isolated farmsteads. These included Susa on the Susiana Plain as well as Uruk, Nippur, Kish, and other towns that stretched like beads along the banks and floodplains of the Euphrates River. Robert Adams (1981) views these towns as places and populations that concentrated the demand for finished goods; that organized expeditions to procure metals, wood, and other raw materials from distant areas; that received labor, foodstuffs, and manufactured goods from residents of the surrounding countryside; and that provided the peasants with finished goods, raw materials, and items from distant lands.

The connections of the towns to their hinterlands and to one another shifted continuously during this period. What happened on the Susiana Plain is representative of the kinds of shifting configurations of relations that existed elsewhere. Around 4000 B.C., Susa, located on the western edge of the plain, was the largest population center; however, villages and hamlets were spread across the entire plain. By about 3700 B.C., three villages were nearly as large as Susa itself. Two centuries later, Susa reestablished itself as the major town; however, there were two other towns almost as large: one to the south and the other on the eastern edge of the plain. Between 3300 and 3100 B.C., the population of the Susiana Plain declined. Some settlements, particularly those in the middle of the plain, were abandoned as their inhabitants concentrated around Susa or Choga Mish, a town on the east side of the plain, or left the area altogether. This shift was accompanied by the appearance of hostilities—military scenes on seal impressions were found in both

Early settlements on the Mesopotamian Plain.

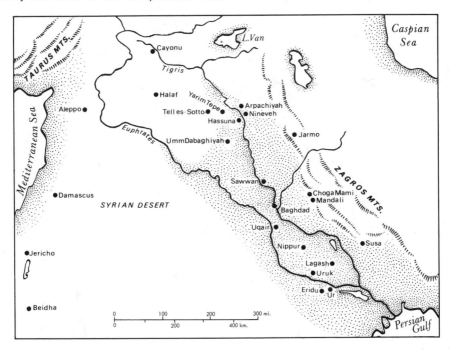

towns—and by events taking place around Uruk to the west. The Susiana
Plain became virtually uninhabited for several centuries after about 3100 B.C.

In the early part of the fourth millennium B.C., Uruk was the center of
one of a number of settlement clusters along the Euphrates. It was neither
the largest town nor the center of the most populous cluster; other towns—
Nippur, Tell Diehim, or Tell al-Hayyad to the north—were as large or larger,
and the settlement cluster that formed around them had a population estimated at nearly 40,000—twice the number that resided in Uruk or the farmlands, date groves, and marshes that surrounded it. Around 3300 B.C., the
population of the Nippur cluster declined to about 20,000, whereas that of
Uruk and the growing number of villages and hamlets that formed around it
swelled to more than 40,000. Two centuries later, Uruk covered nearly 200
acres and may have had 10,000 residents. By 2900 B.C., it was a walled city
that covered more than 1,000 acres; the population of the region had swelled

A plan of the walled city of Uruk, Iraq.

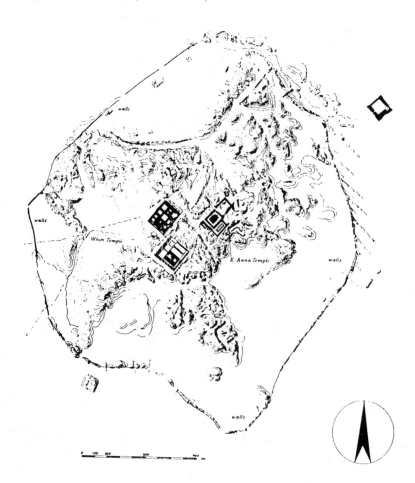

to more than 80,000 individuals, the majority of whom lived in the city. At that moment, Uruk was many times larger and more populous than any other settlement in Mesopotamia.

The obvious question is, what happened? What provoked the explosive growth of Uruk and its environs in the later half of the fourth millennium? Robert Adams (1981:87–88) has speculated that the engine for growth appeared when a continuously increasing proportion of Uruk's own population began to engage in secondary or tertiary economic activities—for example, craft work, commerce, or services—that were not directly related to subsistence food production. This development created a pull, a magnet that at-

The White Temple at Uruk during the 4th millennium B.C. (a) reconstruction of the structure showing the sanctuary on the temple platform; (b) reconstruction of the structure from ground level.

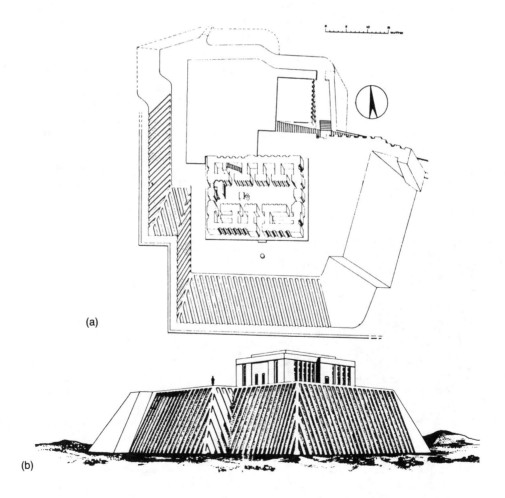

(a)

(b)

tracted the inhabitants of other regions, like Nippur or Susiana, who came to the Uruk countryside as agricultural laborers and construction workers.

An enormous amount of labor was required to complete the public construction that occurred at Uruk between 3300 and 3000 B.C. Minimally, the building projects included the high wall enclosing the city and two temple complexes, the Anu Ziggurat and the Eanna Precinct. The former—a large platform surmounted by a structure called the White Temple—was the last of a series of shrines erected on the same site; the shrine—probably dedicated to An, the principal god of the city—required an estimated 7,500 person-years of labor to complete. The Eanna Precinct was even more extensive, and the labor demands probably rivaled those for the White Temple; it was an immense complex of courtyards, structures, and terraces built around the second temple platform, which was dedicated to Inanna, who was simultaneously the goddess of Uruk, the wife of Eanna, a deity associated with the ripening of crops, and the patroness of the communal storehouse.

Each of the Mesopotamian towns apparently had a principal deity that reflected the economic realities of its environs. In the south, the gods were heroic men and women who hunted and fished in the marshes; along the lower Euphrates, the deities were cowherds and orchard keepers; further north, around Uruk and beyond, they were portrayed as shepherds and farmers who were linked with fertility, weather, and particular agricultural implements. The deities had human appetites; they courted, married, died, and returned. They were portrayed as the members of a family, whose head resided at Nippur. The connections among the various deities were continually re-created by the caretakers of temples that were established in different communities.

The first writing system appeared at Uruk, Kish, and other centers in Mesopotamia around 3300 B.C. The texts indicate that the temples were more

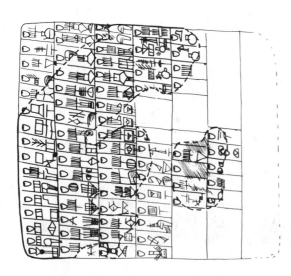

An early cuneiform tablet from Uruk that lists standard professions.

than sanctuaries dedicated to particular deities. They were also major economic units that structured both production and consumption. Igor Diakonoff (1972) argues that the original aim of the temple economies was to create goods that could be exchanged with other communities and to accumulate stores that could be used by the community in emergencies. For example, the Eanna Precinct in Uruk was involved in agriculture, animal husbandry, craft production, commerce, the acquisition and delivery of raw materials, and the provision of rations. About 90 percent of the 4,000 texts from the Eanna temple were clerical records listing allotments, sacrifices, the partition of fields and herds, and the organization of textile production and metalworking. The remainder were mainly the practice exercises of students learning the 700 written characters used by scribes trained to record economic transactions, poetry, and literature.

The various temple communities were headed by individuals called *en*; at that time, the term referred to a political-religious office concerned with successful management. Thus, in a city like Uruk, with more than one temple, there were several *en* wielding authority at any given moment. Thorkild Jacobsen (1957) suggests that authority and power were concentrated in the hands of a "council of elders," which presumably included the *en* as well as the heads of prominent kin and local groups in and around the city. In times of crisis, these councils made grants of extraordinary administrative, legislative, and judicial authority to individuals called *lugal*, who were supposed to serve for a specified period of time. On some occasions, the *lugal* apparently refused to relinquish the authority granted to them. When they usurped this authority and attempted to transform it into political power, they established conditions necessary for state formation. The *lugal*, and their supporters or retainers, were attempting to pursue their own interests in the context of the continuing institutions and practices of the old, communally organized society. Whereas some scholars locate the original extortion of the community and the impetus for state formation in the political realm, others have situated it in the realm of ritual; they imply that the *en*, the custodians of the shrines, received additional authority during times of crisis and, in some instances, consolidated it into differences of rank and privilege that distinguished them from the rest of the community.

The basic institutions of these communities were kin and locally organized corporate groups that dispersed authority among their members. Although there were individuals in the communities—the *en*, the council of elders, and later the *lugal*—who had real authority, their positions and authority were enmeshed in webs of relations defined by kinship and residence. The autonomy of these groups—their control over the labor of the members, the goods they produced, and their capacity to reproduce themselves—was challenged when authority was usurped and transformed into power relations, that is, during those moments when institutions and practices that could sustain exploitation crystallized. In the process, the institutions and practices of the communally organized society were transformed as the structures and relations of the old communal mode of production were distorted, deformed, dissolved, and reconstituted with the appearance of the state and civil society.

The rapid expansion of Uruk after 3300 B.C. marked an instance when state formation succeeded in southern Mesopotamia. Evidence about the particulars of the process and the conditions in which it occurred is obscure. However, given that wealth differences or differential access to particular goods was poorly developed in Uruk and neighboring towns, it seems likely that the major cleavages in southern Mesopotamia were territorial ones that distinguished the various kin and local communities that constituted Uruk from those located outside this web of social relations. The various kin and local groups of Uruk retained considerable control over both their members and their means of production; as a result, the usurpers and their allies were not able to extract either the labor or goods they desired on any predictable or regular basis from their commoner kin and neighbors. Consequently, the would-be rulers or Uruk forged alliances with these nonruling groups. The allies attempted to extract labor and goods from communities on the margins of the city and its hinterlands; the alliance entailed encapsulating communities outside Uruk and enmeshing them in a web of tributary relations.

The threat posed by Uruk—boatloads of armed individuals moving along the network of river channels in southern Mesopotamia or the sudden appearance of outposts and trading enclaves in northern Mesopotamia, on the upper reaches of the Euphrates, in the Zagros Mountains, or on the central plateau of Iran—provoked various responses among the communities on its margins. Some—like those at Nippur and Kish to the north or Lagash and Ur—responded to the crisis by building palisades around their settlements and by granting extraordinary powers to particular officials, thereby establishing conditions that could potentially precipitate additional episodes of state formation. The residents of the villages and hamlets left their homes to seek protection in the fortified towns. Others retained varying degrees of control over their lives by forging pacts with Uruk that specifie . the nature of the tributary relations, that is, the amounts and kinds of exactions; although these agreements limited the impact of the tribute payments, they also altered social relations within the communities. Other groups on the periphery fragmented. Some members retained their autonomy by fleeing and becoming nomadic peoples in remote, inaccessible mountainous areas or in the desert; the emerging state was unable to tax or extract labor from these peoples since it could neither find nor count them. The remaining members became subject populations of the emerging state.

The historically contingent process of state formation in southern Mesopotamia produced uneven development—a continually shifting mosaic of city-states; semiautonomous, kin-organized communities; and nomadic peoples that moved in areas beyond their control. Uneven development, rather than the simultaneous appearance of a number of city-states with diverse forms, was perhaps the most obvious consequence of state formation.

The exploitation of tribute-based states created unstable conditions; it provoked contradictions between the needs of the locally organized communities of direct producers and the demands of the states and their rulers. These contradictions were manifested in varied, continually shifting acts of resistance, compliance, conflict, and occasionally even open revolt. The traditional leaders of the local communities were usually the ones who had to deal with the problem: They had to retain the support of their kin and neighbors in order to ensure that they provided the labor and goods demanded by the state. If their requests were excessive, the community might refuse them; if the demands were not met, the state might step in. There were also other contradictions besides the one between the state and communities—for example, between factions within the emerging ruling class of the state, between the state and subject populations, or even between traditional leaders and others who had potential claims to their positions. The contradictions created by state formation also created possibilities for class struggle and for different kinds of alliances. Together they constitute the historical contingency of state formation, the nonstate/state transition, and the dissolution of state institutions and practices, the state/nonstate transition.

State formation and the struggles it provoked precipitated a unending succession of crises during the third millennium B.C. Uruk's fate was sealed relatively early, when the Euphrates shifted to a new channel and left the city stranded in the desert with a rapidly diminishing supply of water. However, crises or periods of unrest, which had been haphazard, contingent events before the advent of states, became institutionalized, permanent conditions after their appearance. They created the conditions for their own reproduction. For instance, the inhabitants of Lagash and Umma fought a destructive war lasting five generations over a few plots of arable land; as a result of the struggle, war leaders in both towns were given extraordinary powers, which they attempted to retain and make hereditary. The power of the various city-states, relative to one another and to the communities on their margins, ebbed and flowed continuously as the latter were alternately enveloped in their webs and successfully extricated themselves from the burdens they imposed.

KIN COMMUNITIES, CLASS, AND GENDER IN THE CITY-STATES AND EARLY EMPIRES

The impetus for state formation in Mesopotamia came from economic and religious leaders who made themselves rulers; acquired private estates; and were sustained by the toil of their kin and neighbors, of refugees, and of various categories of unfree laborers, mostly women, who had either been sold or given to public institutions to pay off debts or who had been captured or purchased abroad. Everyday life in the Mesopotamian city-states was structured, according to Allen Zagarell (1986) and others, by the intersection of the social relations of the three economic sectors during the Early Dynastic period (2900 to 2350 B.C.): the landholdings of the kin communities, the private estates of temple and state officials, and the public estates of the temples and palaces themselves. Thus, corporately and privately held lands already existed alongside the temple and palace estates by the early third millennium B.C., and possibly even earlier as well. The relative importance of each sector varied through time and from one city-state to another.

Localized kin communities made up of domestic groups claiming descent from the same ancestor frequently owned a number of agricultural fields in the same area that were worked by the men and women of the various households. Men and women shared agricultural work and herding; women were cooks, weavers, and midwives, and men maintained the irrigation canals or worked as carpenters and smiths. Thus, the division of labor based on gender differences was not elaborately developed among the direct producers in the kin communities. The labor of the men and women in the community was occasionally supplemented with that of female slaves, who were either acquired abroad or obtained locally as debt payments. The authority of the community leaders derived from their age, life experience, and kin relations; they were its managers and representatives, the individuals who organized work, adjudicated disputes, bought and sold fields or houses, and occasionally even put kinsmen and kinswomen into slavery to pay off debts.

The leaders, the representatives, of these communities were also frequently public officials in the temple and palace corporations who used their positions to expand their power. Some purchased private estates and used their kin and unfree labor from the corporations and/or their communities to work their lands and to produce the goods they consumed or sold. Many also placed their sons in the corporations as scribes or cloistered their daughters as priestesses in the temples.

The temples and palaces were large, the self-sufficient households of the gods and of kings and queens. Their staffs included free individuals; officials, who often had private estates of their own; overseers with use-rights to fields and other means of production; dependent workers with households and use-rights to land; and individuals who received rations because they were either slaves or from families with labor obligations. To some extent, an individual's state of servitude determined the kind of work that he or she performed. Dependent and servile men performed agricultural and manual labor, and some male officials were scribes. In the temple corporations, the sisters and daughters of kin leaders were often priestesses; the women sustained by rations, especially in the temples, mass-produced textiles and other goods that were used by the temple corporation, stored for use by the communities in times of emergency, and redistributed. Occasionally, goods that were left over were sold to individuals or merchants. The labor forces of the temple and palace corporations were not recruited or reproduced under the conditions that prevailed in the kin communities but rather under circumstances that were more directly controlled by the state.

The class structures that developed in the Early Dynastic city-states crosscut the socially constituted units that appeared to be natural ones: the kin communities and the temple and palace corporations. There was a class that owned the means of production and derived its income from the labor of direct producers; it included the leaders of kin communities and high officials in the temple and palace corporations, many of whom had acquired landed estates of their own. There was a class of freemen and freewomen who had use-rights to the land and other means of production of the various kin communities by virtue of their membership in those groups and participation in their activities. There was a class of dependent and servile individuals who did not own their means of production and were forced by extra-economic means to toil as direct producers, mainly in the corporations and on the private estates of officials and, to a lesser extent, in the kin communities. The composition of the various classes was not stable.

High palace officials were, at times, deposed, murdered, or enslaved; the direct producers of kin communities were occasionally donated to one of the corporations or put into slavery; dependent and servile individuals, whose freedom was purchased or whose debts were forgiven, became freemen and freewomen, who returned to the safety of their own kin communities whenever possible or were forced to exist on the margins of society without access to major means of production.

Men and women lose autonomy during and after the formation of states; however, they lose it differently since gender as well as class shapes their experience of the transformation and determines their identities. That is, the experiences and identities of ruling-class women were different from those of servile women or those whose lives were embedded in the social relations of the kin communities. Dependent and servile women, employed in the corporations, probably confronted a marked, gender-based division of labor as they made textiles and other forms of wealth for the corporations, their officials, and the kin communities that ultimately supported these public institutions. Technical divisions of labor based on gender distinctions were less pronounced in the kin communities, where both men and women toiled at many of the same tasks to produce foodstuffs and finished goods that were consumed or used by their own and other domestic groups in the larger social unit.

Ruling-class women often exerted a great deal of power, both in concert with and independent of their fathers, husbands, or brothers. For instance, two of the rulers of Kish were women; some but not all of the wives of kings were queens who controlled lands and administered the activities of their own estates; and elite women often exercised power as priestesses in the god cults and occasionally as *en* or *lugal*. In some instances, male rulers arranged marriages for their sisters, daughters, and sons to cement political alliances with the ruling elites of other city-states. They also occasionally appointed their sisters and daughters as priestesses in the temples, where the sequestered women were forbidden to bear children. Their aim may have been to pacify local authorities who opposed them. However, their sisters and daughters retained control of both personal and real property, which they typically willed to the temple corporations, administered and controlled by their ruling-class sisters rather than their male kin.

Supralocal states, or empires, were relatively rare in the history of Mesopotamian society. They were absent during the first half of the third millennium B.C., when the kin communities retained much of their autonomy and voice in local affairs. However, the authority of the kin communities waned as their means of production were gradually sold and domestic groups were slowly but steadily alienated from their ancestral communities. Their property increasingly fell into the hands of individual families or the temple or palace corporations. The assault on the structures of the kin communities significantly diminished their ability to resist the exactions of the state at the same time as it made the alienated domestic groups more dependent on the institutions and practices of the city-states' palaces and temples. Another feature that mitigated against the formation of supralocal states was that the patron gods and goddesses of particular city-states were typically partial to their own citizens in conflicts with other polities and favored solutions that benefited them. Processes that strengthened local political institutions at the expense of regional ones made it difficult for empires to crystallize and ensured that they would be unstable and short-lived.

Mogens Larsen (1979) indicates that empires flourished during six relatively brief phases of Mesopotamian history: (1) the Akkadian Empire of Sargon (2350 to 2200 B.C.); (2) the Ur III dynasty (2100 to 2000 B.C.); (3) the Old Babylian Empire of Hammurabi in the eighteenth century; (4) the Middle Assyrian Empire (1350 to 1200 B.C.); (5) the Neo-Assyrian Empire from the ninth to seventh centuries B.C.; and (6) the Neo-Babylonian Empire that was destroyed by the Persians in 539 B.C. Let us briefly consider certain aspects of the earlier empires, their implications, and the conditions under which they developed.

The Akkadians were the driving force behind the formation of the first imperial state in Mesopotamia. Its founder and first ruler was Sargon, who according to an Akkadian legend, was the son of a priestess at the temple of Ishtar and a nomad. His mother bore him in secret and set him adrift in a basket on the Euphrates, where he was found and raised by a palm gardener. He subsequently served as a cupbearer to the king of Kish and then acquired political power of his own, presumably through the intervention of two temple corporations. He became a rival to the rulers of Kish and built his capital at Akkad. He and his forces subjugated the city-states in southern Mesopotamia; they then established garrisons and outpost in the north and finally in the cedar forests of Lebanon and the silver mountains of southern Anatolia. Sargon removed some local leaders—for example, those in Uruk, Umma, and Lagash—and replaced them with retainers who spoke and wrote Akkadian rather than Sumerian. Sargon also appointed his daughter, Enkheduanna, a devotee of the Inanna cult, as priestess of the Moon God temple in Ur and the An Temple in Uruk. Her poetry and hymns survive and tell us how the ruler of Ur drove her from the city after her father died and as her brother, Rimish, struggled to lay claim to Sargon's legacy.

Both Rimish and his brother, who succeeded him, were confronted with rebellions when they ascended to the throne of Akkad; both were murdered

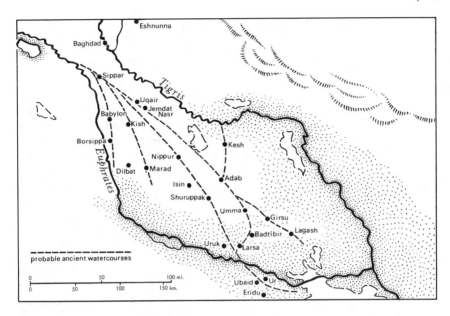

The cities of Sumer and Akkad.

in palace conspiracies. They were followed to the throne by Naram-Sin, Sargon's grandson and Rimish's nephew, who attempted to portray himself as divine and who appointed his daughter as the high priestess at Ur. Although this practice continued for several centuries, the Akkadian Empire did not. It ended suddenly as a result of disputes over succession; the invasion of nomads; a series of military defeats; and the reluctance of provincial administrators to forward the raw materials, finished goods, and gold the king needed to finance wars, build buildings, and pay officials. Balkanization accompanied the collapse of the imperial state.

In 2112 B.C., Ur-Nammu, the governor of Ur, became king of the city-state and founder of the Ur III dynasty. His forces then subjugated Uruk, Lagash, Eridu, and other city-states in southern Mesopotamia and in the mountainous areas to the east. By eliminating Lagash, the overseas trade from Oman, Bahrain, and the Indus Valley moved through Ur. Like the last Akkadian kings, Ur-Nammu and his successors claimed divine honors. Ur-Nammu extended Ur's hegemony by appointing his daughter as a priestess of the Nanna cult in Ur and a son as *en*-priest of the Inanna temple at Uruk. He further expanded its sphere of influence through diplomacy, intimidation, and an arranged marriage between another son and the royal family of Mari, a city-state located 400 miles up the Euphrates. In addition, he ordered large-scale public works—ziggurats, palatial residences, city walls, and canals in the Ur, Nippur, and various provincial cities—which were completed during and after his reign.

The Ur III Empire was a centralized state with a highly organized and efficient bureaucracy, whose powers derived from the king. The state comprised forty provinces, each of which was ruled by a governor who was appointed by the king and rotated on a regular basis from one province to another. Although these officials had broad administrative and judicial powers, they lacked autonomy; they could not enter into alliances or wage war without the king's permission. The legal code Ur-Nammu promulgated is not well known; however, several of the parts that are known dealt with issues of control: adultery by married women, divorce, sexually intimacy of a man with another person's female slave, and slaves who have fled from their owners.

The powerful Ur III Dynasty collapsed rapidly about 2100 B.C. as a result of a famine; rivalries within the ruling family; the elimination of officials in the north, followed by wars of liberation in various regions on the periphery; and the destruction of Ur by the city-state of Elam and its tribal allies from the Zagros and beyond. The last king of the dynasty was captured and presumably killed by the Elamites. The collapse of the Ur III Empire was followed by a period of political fragmentation and decentralization, during which various local rulers attempted to imitate Ur and various kin and tribal groups attempted to reassert their autonomy.

Archives uncovered at Larsa contain a large number of private contracts. The situation they typically describe involves an individual who gets a loan of silver or barley to pay a creditor. The interest rates, usually 20 to 30 percent, increased if the loan was not repaid on time. When individuals failed to repay the loan, they might be imprisoned, their lands might be sold, they or their children might be sold into slavery, or the products of their labor were mortgaged until the debt and the interest were paid in full. The archives also contain records of privately managed households and enterprises, of merchants traveling on their own behalf and at their own risk, and of numerous land sales.

Production was atomized and the autonomy of the kin communities was severely limited by the beginning of the Old Babylonian Empire in 1792 B.C.—a state that barely outlived Hammurabi, its founder and only successful ruler. Hammurabi ensured his reputation for posterity by having a set of laws, the Code of Hammurabi, carved on a stela in Babylon. This code contained 280 judgments on civil and criminal matters, including statements about corruption; theft; looting; murder; kidnapping; runaway slaves; rents; the legal position of women; dowries; the property of married women; divorce; and the legal position of certain kinds of priestesses and prostitutes, neither of whom were subject to the patriarchal authority of their fathers, husbands, or brothers. It appears that the autonomy of women in general, and ruling-class women in particular, was more restricted than it had been earlier, a direct consequence of the disruption of the kin communities.

FURTHER READINGS: A BRIEF GUIDE

An informative, lavishly illustrated introduction to the area is Michael Roaf, *Cultural Atlas of Mesopotamia and the Ancient Near East* (Oxford: Equinox, 1990). The chapter-opening epigrams are from Stanley Diamond, *In Search of the Primitive: A Critique of Civilization* (New Brunswick, NJ: Transaction Books, 1974); and Immanuel Wallerstein, *The Modern World-System: Capitalist Agriculture and the Origins of the European World-Economy in the Sixteenth Century* (New York: Academic Press, 1974).

The development of food-producing economies in the ancient Near East is discussed by Joy McCorriston and Frank Hole, "The Ecology of Seasonal Stress and the Origins of Agriculture in the Near East," *American Anthropologist*, vol. 93, no. 1 (1991), 46–69; Andrew M. T. Moore, "The Development of Neolithic Societies in the Near East," in *Advances in World Archaeology*, ed. Fred Wendorf and Angela Close, vol. 4 (Orlando, FL: Academic Press, 1985), pp. 8–70; Donald O. Henry, *From Foraging to Agriculture: The Levant at the End of the Ice Age* (Philadelphia: University of Pennsylvania Press, 1989); Frank Hole, Kent V. Flannery, and James A. Neely, *Prehistory and Human Ecology of the Deh Luran Plain*, Memoirs of the Museum of Anthropology, University of Michigan, no. 1 (Ann Arbor, 1969); James Mellaart, *The Neolithic of the Near East* (New York: Scribner 1975); and David R. Harris and Gordon C. Hillman, *Foraging and Farming: The Evolution of Plant Exploitation* (London: Unwin Hyman, 1989).

The social significance of Çatal Hüyük is examined by Philip Kohl and Rita Wright, "Stateless Cities: The Differentiation of Societies in the Near Eastern Neolithic," *Dialectical Anthropology*, vol. 2, no. 3 (1977); 271–308; and J. Lawrence Angel, "Early Neolithic Skeletons from Çatal Hüyük," *Anatolian Studies*, vol. XXI (1971), 77–98. Frank Hole, "Settlement and Society in the Village Period," in *The Archaeology of Western Iran: Settlement and Society from Prehistory to the Islamic Conquest*, ed. Frank Hole (Washington, DC: Smithsonian Institution Press, 1987), pp. 79–105, discusses and assigns to periods the changes in everyday life that occurred between 8000 and 3500 B.C. 'Ubaid society is examined by various writers in Elizabeth F. Henrickson and Ingolf Thuesen, *Upon This Foundation: The 'Ubaid Reconsidered*, CNI Publications 10 (Copenhagen: Carsten Niebuhr Institute of Ancient Near Eastern Studies, University of Copenhagen, 1989); and Sabah A. Jasim, *The Ubaid Period in Iraq*, British Archaeological Reports, International Series 267 (Oxford, 1985). The archaeology of the eastern Arabian Peninsula is discussed by Maurizio Tosi, "The Emerging Picture of Prehistoric Arabia," *Annual Review of Anthropology*, vol. 15 (1986), 461–490.

The intensification of social relations in the fourth millennium B.C. is discussed by Robert McC. Adams, *Heartland of Cities: Surveys of Ancient Settlement and Land Use on the Central Floodplain of the Euphrates* (Chicago: University of Chicago Press, 1981); Hans J. Nissen, *The Early History of the Ancient*

Near East, 9000–2000 B.C. (Chicago: University of Chicago Press, 1988), esp. pp. 65–128; Henry T. Wright, "The Susiana Hinterlands during the Era of Primary State Formation," and Gregory A. Johnson, "The Changing Organization of Uruk Administration on the Susiana Plain," both in *The Archaeology of Western Iran: Settlement and Society from Prehistory to the Islamic Conquest*, ed. Frank Hole (Washington, DC: Smithsonian Institution Press, 1987), 141–155 and 107–139; and Frank Hole, "Symbols of Religion and Social Organization at Susa," in *The Hilly Flanks and Beyond: Essays on the Prehistory of Southwestern Asia. . .* , Studies in Ancient Oriental Civilization, ed. T. Cuyler Young, Jr., Philip E. Smith, and Peder Mortensen, no. 36 (Chicago: Oriental Institute of the University of Chicago, 1983), pp. 315–333.

The social formation of the early city-states is discussed by Igor M. Diakonoff, "Socio-economic Classes in Babylonia and the Babylonian Conception of Social Stratification," in *Gesellschaftsklassen im Alten Zweistromland und in den angrenzenden Gebieten*, XVIII. Recontre Assyriologique Internationale, ed. Dietz O. Edzard (Munich: Bayerische Akademie der Wissenschaften, 1972), pp. 41–49, and "The Rural Community in the Ancient Near East," *Journal of the Economic and Social History of the Orient*, vol. XVIII, pt. II (1975), 121–133; Thorkild Jacobsen, "Early Political Developments in Mesopotamia," *Zeitschrift für Assyriologie und vorderasiatische Archäologie*, Band 52 (1957), 91–140, and *The Treasures of Darkness: A History of Mesopotamian Religion* (New Haven, CT: Yale University Press, 1976); and Ignace J. Gelb, "On the Alleged Temple and State Economies in Ancient Mesopotamia," *Studi in onore di Edoardo Volterra*, tomo VI. Publicazioni della Facoltà di Giurisprudenza dell'Università di Roma 45 (Milan: A Guiffrè, 1969), pp. 137–154.

Class and state formation are discussed by Christine W. Gailey and Thomas C. Patterson, "State Formation and Uneven Development," in *State and Society: The Emergence and Development of Social Hierarchy and Political Centralization*, ed. John Gledhill, Barbara Bender, and Mogens T. Larsen (London: Unwin Hyman, 1988), pp. 77–90; Allen Zagarell, "Structural Discontinuity— A Critical Factor in the Emergence of Primary and Secondary States," *Dialectical Anthropology*, vol. 10, nos. 3 and 4 (1986), 155–178, and "Pastoralism and the Early State in Greater Mesopotamia," in *Archaeological Thought in America*, ed. C. C. Lamberg-Karlovsky, (Cambridge: Cambridge University Press, 1989), pp. 280–291.

Allen Zagarell, "Trade, Women, Class, and Society in Ancient Western Asia," *Current Anthropology*, vol. 27, no. 5 (1986), 415–430, is a perceptive summary of everyday life in the Early Dynastic period. For indications of gender and class relations, see the evidence presented, but not necessarily the conclusions drawn, by Gerda Lerner, *The Creation of Patriarchy* (New York: Oxford University Press, 1986); see also Susan Pollock, "Women in a Men's World: Images of Sumerian Women," in *Engendering Archaeology: Women and Prehistory*, ed. Joan M. Gero and Margaret W. Conkey (Oxford: Basil Blackwell, 1991), pp. 366–387; and Jean-Marie Durand ed., *La Femme dans la Proch-Orient Antique* (Paris: Editions Recherches sur les Civilisations, 1987).

The formation and disintegration of empires in Mesopotamia is introduced by the essays in Mogens T. Larsen, ed., *Power and Propaganda: A Symposium on Ancient Empires* (Copenhagen: Akademisk Forlag, 1979), pp. 75–103; and Robert McC. Adams, "Contexts of Civilizational Collapse," and "The Collapse of Ancient Mesopotamian States and Civilization," both in *The Collapse of Ancient States and Civilizations*, ed. Norman Yoffee, and George Cowgill (Tucson: University of Arizona Press, 1988), pp. 20–43 and 44–68. Mesopotamian societies of the second millennium B.C. are discussed in Igor M. Diakonoff, ed., *Ancient Mesopotamia, Socio-economic History: A Collection of Essays by Soviet Scholars* (Moscow: Nauka Publishing House, 1969); Igor M. Diakonoff, "Women in Old Babylonia Not under Patriarchal Authority," *Journal of the Economic and Social History of the Orient*, vol. XXIX, pt. III (1986), 225–238; and Elizabeth C. Stone, "The Social Role of the Naditu Women in Old Babylonian Nippur," *Journal of the Economic and Social History of the Orient*, vol. XXV, pt. I (1982), 50–70.

chapter 7

Central and South Asia beyond the Iranian Plateau

Overproductive systems are only incidentally constrained by social factors and produce, rather, in relation to the material requirements of those in control of the means of production. Similarly, overproductive systems are unconstrained by the natural limits of their environment. Instead overproductive systems by definition cannot reproduce themselves within a limited set of resources. Such systems seek continuously to expand their resource base, either internally or by expanding into the environments of other systems. (Robert Briglio, "Recasting the Mode of Production")

Merchants had a certain latitude to accumulate capital, even though they were in the last analysis at the mercy of the ruling apparatus that often "borrowed" their capital, with no necessary requirement to repay, or imposed heavy forced "contributions" to the public coffers when the state faced economic difficulties. (Janet L. Abu-Lughod, Before European Hegemony)

East of Mesopotamia lies the Iranian Plateau, a vast desert that stretches one-third of the way across Asia, separating the Tigris and Euphrates rivers from the Indus Valley and the lands beyond. The plateau resembles an enormous raised block surrounded on three sides by broad ranges of mountains. The northern rim of the plateau is less well defined between the Caspian Sea and the Hindu Kush Mountains, where it dips and merges with the vast plains and deserts of central Asia. The summers are hot and dry on the Iranian Plateau; rain and snow fall in the mountains during the winters and feed small rivers that flow onto the plateau before disappearing into sinks and marshes. The moisture supports a variety of plant formations through the foothills and along the river channels, habitats favored by the plateau's inhabitants for at least the last 40,000 years.

Caravan routes crossed the Iranian Plateau in historic times; these were the ancient roads that connected the peoples of the plateau and beyond with those of Mesopotamia. The northern route passed along the Elburz Mountains and brought the peoples of Iran and Mesopotamia into contact with the inhabitants of the steppes and deserts of central Asia. It passed through Afghanistan and divided in the Hindu Kush Mountains. One branch continued eastward into the high plateaus of Sinkiang and beyond; the other crossed the Khyber Pass and followed the Indus River southward through the high valleys and gorges of Pakistan. The southern route led from the head of the Persian Gulf through Khuzistan along the Fars and opened into the hills of Baluchistan, which overlook the Indus Valley.

Caravan and foot travel were never easy from the plains of Mesopotamia and the Indus and Ganges rivers into the largely landlocked regions lying between them and to the north. Travelers faced real dangers as they crossed mountain ranges and deserts, yet cross them they did, increasingly from the third millennium B.C. onward, as states expanded to incorporate

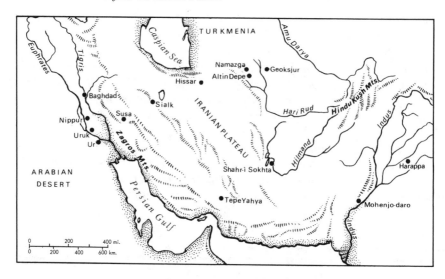

Ancient settlements on the Indo-Iranian frontier.

areas from which they obtained essential resources. The area discussed in this chapter consists of a series of overlapping regions, whose boundaries appeared and dissolved as a consequence of historical events or the formation and disintegration of political entities and exchange relations.

THE CULTURAL DIVERSITY OF THE EARLY FOOD-PRODUCING, KIN-BASED COMMUNITIES

During the sixth millennium B.C., small groups, camped in caves on the eastern shore of the Caspian Sea, hunted onagers and gazelles and fished for carp and sturgeon. Further east, the Kelteminar peoples—hunting and foraging groups—lived in open settlements along the Amu Darya River, which flows out of the Hindu Kush Mountains east of Tashkent and opens into the Aral Sea. Their settlements usually consisted of a single large house built on a framework of wooden posts covered with wood, reeds, and earth. A fire burned in a large, permanent hearth near the center of the house, and temporary fires, perhaps for domestic use, were built around its edge. It appears that an entire Kelteminar community—perhaps an extended kin group of twenty-five to thirty individuals—lived together in a single house, one of which covered more than 2,400 square feet.

The earliest food-producing communities of Turkmenistan also date from the sixth millennium B.C. Their inhabitants established sedentary villages on small alluvial fans in the piedmont areas at the foot of the Iranian Plateau. Since the streams on which they depended for water often changed course, the villagers moved frequently in order to be close to the new river

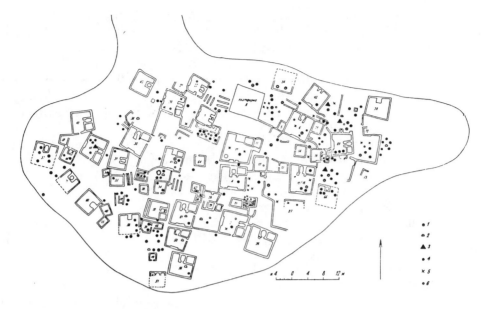

The early settlement of Dzejtun in southern Turkmenia.

channels. Dzejtun is one of the earliest of these settlements. It was probably occupied between 5800 and 5300 B.C. During this time it had a population of about 120 to 180 individuals, who lived in 30 households, each of which had 5 or 6 members. Sometimes 2 or 3 houses shared a common courtyard, where various domestic activities were carried out. After the settlement had been occupied for several centuries, its residents built a clubhouse or shrine near the center of the village; the building was twice as large as the houses and had colorful geometric and zoomorphic designs painted on its walls.

The residents of Dzejtun and their contemporaries in other villages in the area may have used dogs to herd the domesticated sheep and goats that provided dairy products and the bulk of the meat they consumed. They hunted gazelles, onagers, and wild pigs for food and foxes and wolves for fur. The villagers grew barley as well as dwarf and bread wheat in agricultural fields located on the stream banks.

Chakmakli Tepe and at least a dozen other villages in the piedmont region southwest of Dzejtun were occupied around 5000 B.C. These were small settlements, whose inhabitants grew wheat and barley and raised sheep, goats, and cattle, which provided more than 60 percent of the meat they consumed. They also wove woolen textiles, and the pottery vessels they used resembled those that were being made by potters in various settlements on the Iranian Plateau near the Caspian Sea. The inhabitants of Chakmakli Tepe also used copper tools—awls, piercers, and knives. Since copper deposits are unknown in Turkmenistan, they must have obtained either the implements or the ore from peoples living on the plateau in northern Iran.

The layout of Chakmakli Tepe differed from those of the earlier settlements. There were two blocks of buildings separated from each other by a street that ran down the middle of the village. Each block consisted of several households or apartments with their own kitchens, living areas, and workrooms. In each building complex there was also a a large common room or shrine with red-painted walls and floors. The layout of the community suggests that it may have been divided into two distinct groups, each composed of several households.

Fourth-millennium B.C. settlements in the same foothill region of Turkmenistan had a different layout than their predecessors. The inhabitants of some twenty small villages lived in individual households with their own courtyards; the twenty or so houses in each village were placed around a larger building that was a gathering place for the community. However, two of the settlements dating to this period were much larger. Kara Tepe covered more than 35 acres and may have had a population of 2,500. The other large settlement developed in the Geoksyur Oasis, north of the piedmont; it was surrounded by a number of small villages, several of which had palisades or fortification walls. The inhabitants of these communities still acquired copper tools or ore from the Iranian Plateau; they were also getting semiprecious minerals, like turquoise or carnelian, from the same region.

Village farming life was already established in South Asia by the seventh millennium B.C. Early food-producing settlements were found in the piedmont and mountain valleys of Pakistan and Afghanistan—for example, Kili Ghul Mohammad in the Quetta Valley of Baluchistan. Mehrgarh on the Kachi Plain at the foot of the Bolan Pass currently provides the greatest insights into this period of South Asian history. Its earliest inhabitants grew domesticated wheat and barley and harvested wild barley, dates, and jujube. They hunted a variety of large wild animals—gazelles, water buffalo, sheep, goats, cattle, pigs, deer, and elephants—that lived on the plains and in the piedmont habitats near Mehrgarh. By about 5500 B.C., the population relied almost exclusively on domesticated animals: cattle, goats, and sheep. The village residents lived in multiroomed households and used the open spaces between the structures for domestic purposes and burials. The grave goods in the brick-lined tombs indicate that they were already obtaining seashells from the coast, turquoise and lapis lazuli beads from the Afghanistan borderlands, and copper beads possibly from the Iranian Plateau.

The cultural and organizational diversity evident in the early food-producing communities in the Near East also existed in those of Soviet central Asia and along the margins of the Indus drainage. These kin-based, communally organized societies undoubtedly exhibited matrimonial mobility; poorly defined technical divisions of labor that were incompletely organized by age, gender, and kin ties; and the kinds of interpersonal and social relations that simultaneously grant autonomy to individuals and have the potential for ambiguous or multiple understandings and representations. Subsequent episodes of class and state formation and disintegration in central and south Asia, and elsewhere, reduced both the diversity and ambiguities that were typical of these kin-organized, primitive communities.

STATE FORMATION ON THE IRANIAN PLATEAU
AND CENTRAL ASIA DURING THE THIRD MILLENNIUM B.C.

Complex political and economic developments occurred on the Iranian Plateau during the third millennium B.C. Communities in the Zagros Mountains and the south-central portion of the plateau were linked culturally with those of the Mesopotamian plain between about 3300 and 2800 B.C.—that is, the period when Uruk was hegemonic. Some of the highland and desert settlements have yielded tablets and seals with inscriptions written in Proto-Elamite—a different language from Sumerian, the one used in southern Mesopotamia.

One of the settlements was Tepe Yahya, which is located 500 miles southeast of Susa in a valley near the Arabian Sea. It was first occupied more than 6,500 years ago by people who grew domesticated cereals and herded cattle, sheep, and goats. Camel bones were also present in the refuse deposits; however, it is not clear whether these animals were domesticated. The inhabitants used steatite, a soft green stone that outcrops in the area, to make carved bowls. By 3000 B.C., a number of residents toiled regularly in workshops to produce steatite bowls. One workshop contained more than 1,200 fragments of vessels in various stages of manufacture; some were undecorated, and others bore design motifs that appeared on steatite bowls found in Mesopotamian settlements dating to this period. It probably took a stoneworker a day to hollow out a couple of bowls and carve the standardized design motifs on their exteriors, using bronzelike chisels, awls, and pins. At first these tools were made from copper ores that contained a lot of arsenic; later their copper tools contained tin impurities. However, since copper ores with arsenic and tin impurities do not outcrop near Tepe Yahya, its inhabitants must have imported copper ores or ingots, or even the tools themselves, from other localities on the Iranian Plateau.

Lapidaries in various settlements to the west—for example, Susa or Mari—also made steatite bowls that were decorated in the same style as those produced at Tepe Yahya; however, X-ray diffraction studies indicate that they obtained the steatite from several different sources that were distinct from the one used by the Tepe Yahya stoneworkers. The evidence from Tepe Yahya focuses attention on two issues: How was production organized within the community itself? And how did exchange distort and/or transform the social relations of production? Philip Kohl (1978) has argued that trading activities significantly altered the productive activities of villages like Tepe Yahya and, consequently, that they also transformed the existing social relations of these kin-based communities by enmeshing them in wider networks. Since there is little evidence that Tepe Yahya itself was a ranked or socially stratified community, the question becomes whether the production relations were modified at the level of the individual domestic production-consumption units or at the level of the village community. It seems that some of the nonstratified communities, whose members resided in villages and hamlets in western and southern Iran, were apparently border peoples linked by developing and shifting exchange and/or tribute relations to the city-states that had crystallized on the Mesopotamian plains.

At the same time, peoples residing north and east of the desert in the central part of the Iranian Plateau had connections with contemporary communities in Turkmenistan and neighboring areas in central Asia but not with those in Mesopotamia or south Asia. Thus, the communities on the eastern side of the plateau and its northern piedmont constituted a semiautonomous region characterized by its own distinctive patterns of political and economic development during the third millennium B.C. Maurizio Tosi (1977, 1979) has referred to the area as Turan; it encompassed a number of environmentally and culturally diverse regions that were linked together by the formation and disintegration of various class and state structures after about 3000 B.C.

Shahr-i Sokhta, the largest settlement on the eastern plateau, grew steadily during the first half of the third millennium B.C. and had a population of more than 10,000 between 2300 and 2100 B.C. None of the thirty villages around it had more than 100 to 150 inhabitants. Although subsistence production—agriculture, herding, and the manufacture of objects for local use and consumption—must have dominated everyday life, the inhabitants of Shahr-i Sokhta also manufactured objects made of steatite and lapis lazuli, the brilliant blue mineral found high in the Hindu Kush Mountains. Chunks of limestone containing lapis lazuli were quarried or mined in the mountains located more than 500 miles northeast and brought by camel caravans to the workshops in the large town, where archaeologists have found beads and other objects made of the blue stone in various stages of manufacture.

Some of the differences between Shahr-i Sokhta and the villages around it were marked. The absence of lapidaries and metalsmiths in the smaller settlements suggests that production was centralized and concentrated in the town, which means that the technical division of labor was organized both spatially and at the regional level. The workshops were segregated within the town, both before and after the spatial arrangement and relations of the buildings became more regular, around 2500 B.C. Grave goods buried with craftworkers attests to their importance in the local economy; the tombs of a lapidary, jeweler, and potter contained numerous and diverse items, including lambs that were sacrificed at the time of the burial.

The marked differences in burial practices, as well as the quantities and varieties of goods placed in the tombs, suggest that social differentiation and ranking were features of the community dominated by Shahr-i Sokhta. For example, a small number of tombs contained two or more individuals who were interred at the same time; two graves contained a pile of long bones surrounded by human skulls, four in one tomb and eight in the other. Nine of the twelve individuals buried with seals were women, mostly in their late twenties. Four of the women buried with seals were interred in a grave that contained six skeletons. Some of the individuals in the more lavishly furnished tombs may also have resided in the large, multiroomed dwellings concentrated in one part of the town.

Settlement in the piedmont of Turkmenistan reached its greatest extent between 3000 and 2500 B.C. The inhabitants of the villages and small towns that dotted the area lived in apartment complexes with interconnecting rooms that had various uses: sleeping, domestic activities, living, and storage. Several of the larger settlements—for example, Altyn Depe—were fortified and had multiroom houses with their own courtyards, in addition to the apartment complexes similar to those found in the villages. Some degree of craft specialization became apparent during this period as well. Pottery kilns were found in one village, slag deposits associated with copper smelting were found on the outskirts of another, and jewelers and metalsmiths had workshops in the towns. This finding indicates that some aspects of production were organized on a regional scale and that there was some elaboration of the community-level relations of production.

In some villages, the dead were interred in crypts. There were twenty-seven vaults at Parkhai II, which contained a total of 450 individuals. Each crypt had a single articulated skeleton, the most recently interred individual, surrounded by piles of bones that had been pushed to the side when the tomb was opened to receive its newest occupant. Descent may well have determined the burial vault in which an individual was interred. Besides human bones, the crypts also yielded an array of objects: turquoise and lapis lazuli beads, bronze jewelry, and bronze weapons.

Social differentiation became quite pronounced in the Turkmenistan piedmont between 2500 and 2200 B.C. More than half the villages and hamlets occupied earlier were abandoned as their inhabitants moved to Namazga Depe and Altyn Depe—the region's only two cities, each of which may have had a population of 5,000 to 10,000 persons.

Altyn Depe was located at the confluence of two streams in an elm-covered area of the piedmont. This walled city, which spread over 125 acres, contained three kinds of residential structures: large multiroom apartment complexes that were probably occupied by kin groups or extended families, small houses with courtyards that were occupied by single domestic groups, and multiroom elite residences located in close proximity to public and ritual buildings. At the center of the public and ritual complex was a 180-foot-long stepped platform with a 50-foot-high tower on the uppermost, fourth tier. A multiroomed burial vault located next to the stepped platform contained the remains of forty individuals; sixteen women, twelve men, and three children over the age of six years can be identified in the piles of human bones found in the different rooms. The crypt was also filled with a number of objects: stone weights; seals made from turquoise, lapis lazuli, ivory, agate, carnelian, and gold; bull and wolf heads made from gold; bone gaming sticks; and a plaque. Other residents of the elite center were typically interred alone or, in a few instances, with another person. The most lavishly furnished grave of this type was that of a women in her mid-thirties who was buried with a silver mirror, a double stone vessel, bronze and silver objects, beads made from various precious metals and stones, and an ivory rod. Another richly furnished tomb was that of an adult woman buried with a teenager, two female figurines, gold rings, and a beaded necklace made of gold and various precious stones. These tombs were found in the elite residential areas of the city.

Craftworkers lived in the apartment complexes away from the public and ritual buildings. Potters lived in the northwest; jewelers and metalworkers, in the south; and the individuals who made milling stones, in the west. More than 500 individuals were recovered in the 200 graves found in these neighborhoods. Many tombs contained single individuals with no or only a few grave goods; there were also a few crypts, one of which contained the remains of at least thirty-eight individuals.

The fortification walls of the city, the bronze weapons found in some tombs, differences in domestic architecture, and the diversity of burial practices suggest that Altyn Depe was part of a class-stratified, state-based society. Craft specialization—that is, technical divisions of labor presumably organized around domestic and/or kin groups—and economic centralization and concentration in the city point to a marked urban-rural dichotomy in the wider society. About the same time that the two cities began to grow explosively, a number of regionally distinct styles suddenly appeared in central Asia; these marked the limits of production-consumption spheres that were independent of those centered in Namazga Depe and Altyn Depe. They may also mark the boundaries of polities and communities that crystallized on the margins of the city-states that appeared in southern Turkmenistan toward the middle of the third millennium B.C.

Like all state-based societies, the one that developed in Turkmenistan was inherently unstable and disintegrated within a few centuries. The two cities were virtually or completely abandoned as the power of their ruling classes waned and disappeared altogether. The habitats around the cities had been degraded, possibly as a consequence of overurbanization; many of their residents may have resettled in Bactria on the plains of the Surkhandarya River, a major tributary of the Amu Darya River in northwest Afghanistan and southern Uzbekistan. A state-related cultural tradition crystallized in this region at the close of the second millennium B.C.

Rectangular forts or fortified palaces are distinctive features of several Bactrian sites that were occupied around 2000 B.C. They were typically surrounded by domestic structures, which some archaeologists believe were occupied by elite or retainer populations that retreated to the fortresses during times of crisis. The fortresses were used for both residential and economic purposes. The one at Sapalli Depe had living quarters, sleeping rooms, and a bakery with four ovens and grinding implements. After the fortress at Sapalli Depe was abandoned, it was used as a cemetery. One hundred thirty-eight graves were dug into the walls and floors of the settlement; these included 125 individual and 13 collective burials. Males were typically buried lying on their right sides and women on their left sides. The richest grave contained a women interred with more than fifty objects, including thirty pottery vessels. Two sheep lying on their left sides were also entombed at Sapalli Depe, one with eighteen vessels and the other with eleven pots. Animal burials have also been found at other sites in the region.

The burial practices at Sapalli Depe and other sites in Bactria suggest a society that was certainly structured by age; gender; and to a lesser extent, wealth. Four individuals buried at Sapalli Depe had silk garments, which indicate contact with the Far East. Other sites in the region—for example, Shortugai—may have housed enclaves from the Indus Valley to the south. There was some craft specialization, organized at the domestic level. The evidence concerning Bactria around 2000 B.C. shows that political power was decentralized and wielded at the local level by an elite class of warlords, whose consumption patterns were, in important ways, not strikingly different from those of their subjects in this area of uneven social and political development.

HARAPPAN SOCIETY: CLASS-STRATIFIED OR KIN-BASED?

The earliest known food-producing villages in the Indus Valley appeared somewhat later than those in the nearby piedmont and mountain basins. Their inhabitants grew millet and other grains; kept herds of humped cattle and smaller numbers of donkeys, goats, and sheep; hunted locally available wild game; and used two-wheeled carts. Nearly 250 settlements, dating between 3200 and 2600 B.C., were located in various parts of the valley. The villages, known as Early or Pre-Urban Harappan, were found along the Indus River and its major tributaries. The settlements varied in size from less than an acre to about 50 acres. Seventy percent of them were smaller than 10 acres, and only three covered areas of about 50 acres. Virtually all of the architectural remains were domestic or communal buildings; two settlements—Kot Diji in the lower reaches of the Indus River and Kohtrash in the Sind—may have had fortification walls.

Amri was a middle-sized Early Harappan settlement that covered about 20 acres and may have had a thousand or so residents. It was located on the edge of arable land overlooking the floodplain of the Indus River. Its residents lived in rectangular houses, about 20 feet long and 10 feet wide, with flat roofs and mud floors. After the settlement had been occupied for a while, the inhabitants built a large mud-brick platform toward the edge of town; postholes on the summit of the platform indicate that a wooden building stood there.

Referring to the sites as Early Harappan carries the connotation of uniformity. This is unfortunate since subtle distinctions in the shapes and decoration of pottery vessels—material representations of spheres of production, exchange, and use—existed during the early part of the third millennium B.C.

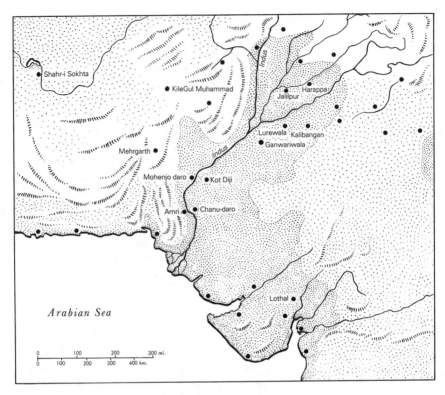

Harappan settlements in the Indus Valley.

and indicate the presence of several regionally based social groupings with semiautonomous cultural patterns. That the residents of different settlements in the same grouping were minimally linked to one another by the circulation of goods suggests that the community-level relations of production and reproduction were elaborate; however, there is no evidence that social relations within these wider communities themselves were ranked or stratified, nor is there evidence of village-level craft specialization to indicate that the production relations of the regional communities were spatially organized in significant ways.

A number of pervasive and apparently contemporaneous social changes occurred over vast portions of the Indus Valley during a relatively brief period of time, perhaps a century or two at the most; these marked the beginning of Mature or Urban Harappan society (2600 to 2000 B.C.). The transition was abrupt. Various communities adopted a relatively standardized system of weights and measures and a writing system that shared many signs with the Sumerian and Proto-Elamite scripts used in Mesopotamia and coastal regions of the Persian Gulf and Arabian Sea. Some of the communities built massive brick platforms and drainage systems and organized these and other constructions in accordance with a grid system.

The transformation began around Kalibangan on an old channel of the central Indus. According to Jim Shaffer and Diane Lichtenstein (1989), it involved the encapsulation of those semiautonomous cultural groupings from Gujarat and the Narbada River in the south to Baluchistan, Pakistan, and the Punjab in the north and their incorporation into a wider social and cultural entity; the Harappan regional grouping was the largest if not the hegemonic ethnic unit in the complex cultural mosaic called Mature Harappan society. The conditions that precipitated the changes, or were associated with them, included new forms of social and economic organization that facilitated the expansion of craft specialization and trade or that allowed groups in the region either to gain or retain access to land and raw materials. Shaffer (1982) does not believe that Mature Harappan society had a centralized political structure.

Gregory Possehl (1990) sees the transformation as marking the appearance of civilization—that is, urban and state-based societies—in the Indus Valley toward the middle of the third millennium B.C. His understanding is based on an analysis of settlement patterns; the development of public architecture; evidence for social stratification and differentiation; and the appearance of subtle regional variations in the uniformity of Mature Harappan culture, which contrast with the regional style zones that prevailed earlier. He suggests that trade relations, presumably along the Arabian Sea and Persian Gulf, with Mesopotamia and with central Asia probably played a significant role in the development of new social relations, occupational specialization, population agglomeration, and social stratification in the Indus Valley.

Almost 1,000 Mature Harappan settlements are known in the Indus Valley and its environs. The vast majority were small, a few acres in extent with populations of a hundred or so; however, 5 were cities that were significantly larger and had greater populations than the next largest tier of settlements. Each of the 5 cities—Mohenjo-daro, Ganwariwala, Harappa, Lurewala, and Rahhi Shahpur—covered more than 200 acres and had 10,000 to 20,000 residents. Ganwariwala was located on an extinct channel of the river, about 250 miles upstream from Mohenjo-daro and about 250 miles southwest of Harappa, which lay on another tributary of the Indus. Lurewala was located approximately midway between Ganwariwala and Harappa. Although these cities are often viewed as the major regional administrative and commercial centers of Mature Harappan society, it is necessary to keep in mind that the vast majority of the population lived in rural villages or small towns. They produced their own food and many of the finished goods they used or consumed; they acquired the rest of the items they needed—for example, metal tools—from craft specialists who worked part time and resided in other settlements.

Three of the five cities had impressive public architecture that required enormous amounts of labor for construction. The immense mud-brick platforms, called citadels, were built on the western edges of both Harappa and Mohenjo-daro. The Harappa platform, the smaller of the two, was 50 feet

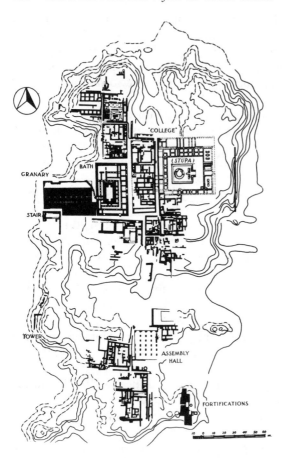

The citadel—the large man-made rectangular platform—at Mohenjo-Daro.

high and covered an area about 1,400 feet by 650 feet. The citadels in both urban centers were covered with various kinds of buildings: storehouses; assembly halls; and at Mohenjo-daro, a bath or pool fed by well water. The residential districts of the two cities were located east of the citadels and separated from them by open areas. The houses opened onto streets or narrow alleys that followed a grid pattern. In many of the houses at Mohenjo-daro, pottery pipes led from latrines to open drains that flowed in the streets outside. In large towns, like Lothal and Chanhu-daro, the residential districts were also separated from workshop areas.

Mature Harappan society was structured in such a way that enormous amounts of labor could be recruited for construction projects; craft production could be organized at least partially on a regional basis; and some objects, notably stamp seals, which may have been badges of marriage, were not available to everyone. Most of the seals and metal objects were found in habitation areas, which suggests that they were not wealth objects or status markers. Thus, there is very little evidence indicating marked rank or class differences in Mature Harappan society. Analyses of human skeletons dating

The residential area at Mohenjo-Daro.

to this period confirm the idea that there were not marked differences in consumption; 350 skeletons showed little evidence of stress and no proof that some individuals were significantly better nourished than others.

The data suggest two possibilities. On the one hand, Mature Harappan society manifested some form of the communal mode of production in which the community-level relations of production and reproduction were extended in ways that facilitated the mobilization of labor; these relations may also have been distorted or deformed by exchange relations with peoples residing outside the area. On the other hand, Mature Harappan society may have consisted of a series of city-states in which cross-class alliances based on residence mitigated against the formation of significant wealth differentials within the various communities; in this instance, political power was undoubtedly decentralized.

In either case, urban life, which reached its apex around 2200 B.C., was inherently unstable; the cities were completely abandoned or inhabited only by a few squatters during the waning years of the third millennium B.C. Furthermore, a number of villages and small towns in the Sind were also abandoned at this time, possibly as a result of changes in the course of the Indus River or because rural peoples left their homesteads to avoid tribute exactions by the city dwellers. At the same time that the population of the Indus Valley was declining, there were significant increases in the number of

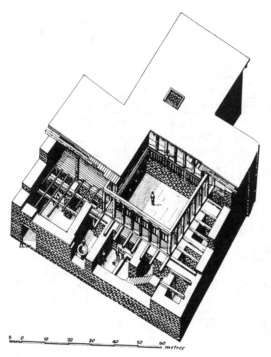

Reconstruction of a residential structure at Mohenjo-Daro.

settlements and residents of Gujarat to the south, and there was a veritable population explosion in eastern Punjab near the upper reaches of the Ganges River. This population shift was accompanied by a decline in craft specialization and in the long-distance trade of luxury items. Most of the new settlements were small: agricultural villages covering a few acres or campsites used by pastoral peoples, which states have always found notoriously difficult to count and tax.

STATE FORMATION IN THE INDO-GANGETIC WATERSHED AND WESTERN GANGES VALLEY DURING THE FIRST MILLENNIUM B.C.

The dramatic social changes that occurred in the Indus Valley during the Late Harappan phase (2000 to 1300 B.C.) were not uniform in every region within the river basin. They were also accompanied by significant organizational changes in other parts of the Indian subcontinent, most notably the Indo-Gangetic watershed and the Ganges Valley to the east. Thus, subsequent historical developments in India cannot be completely disentangled or separated from the events that surrounded the collapse of the Indus cities around 2000 B.C. and the social conditions that emerged in their wake. The watershed and upper reaches of the Ganges Valley were a major refuge for peoples leaving the Indus in the second millennium B.C. Class and state formation occurred in the western Ganges toward the middle of the first millennium B.C. However, as Romila Thapar (1984) points out, the fact that state formation took place does not mean that all of the region's inhabitants were uniformly affected by the consequences. State formation produces, and is the product of, uneven social development; it creates diverse social and cultural conditions that impede or stymie the ongoing processes of class and state formation in some instances and facilitate them in others. The crystallization of states is often limited initially to small nuclei, like islands in a vast sea, that either ignore or actively resist their precipitation and subsequent consolidation.

The inhabitants of the upper and middle reaches of the Ganges Valley, both the original occupants and the refugees who arrived there in the second millennium B.C., had mixed economies that combined cattle herding and grain agriculture. For many communities, cattle pastoralism was the dominant economic sector, the activities of which shaped the rhythm of everyday life: continually moving herds from one pasture to another in search of fresh grass and water and the daily milking of cows, to name only two. Cattle were the major means of production, simultaneously the source and the symbol of wealth. The communities that lived in the area during the early part of the first millennium B.C. were kin-organized, corporate, landholding groups that bestowed their names on the territories they claimed as grazing and agricultural land. Rights to land, which was also a means of production, was critical for the herders since it ensured the success and reproduction of their herds, the creation of wealth; however, herds were also enlarged by stealing cattle from neighboring communities. In Vedic society, the pilfered animals were then redistributed at community assemblies, major portions of the spoils going to chiefs and brahmanic ritual leaders, whose practices and interventions with the gods ensured the success of the cattle raids. Thus, an individual's wealth could be measured by the number of cattle he or she owned.

Agriculture became increasingly important in the Ganges Valley after about 1000 B.C., and its seasonally organized activities imposed a different tempo on everyday life. In this economic regime, land itself became a source of wealth and provided community leaders with a new power base. The concept of territory that was available for all members of the community to use was transformed into the notion of arable fields that were distributed by the chiefs for particular individuals or families to till. In this situation, community leaders, whose authority and power had formerly derived from their ability to protect herds and pastures, appropriated the authority to distribute agricultural lands. This practice created a peasant economy in which the household production units of the peasantry had specific rights and obligations vis-à-vis the chiefs and ritual leaders, who guaranteed the fecundity of their fields and their prosperity. Their gifts ensured divine intervention, protection, and good harvests.

Peasant households could attempt to increase their wealth and the size of their gifts by intensifying the productivity of the fields they were already working or by bringing new fields under cultivation. In such circumstances, they probably attempted to exercise greater control over the productive and reproductive activities of their members, especially women, who are, after all, not only the direct producers of goods but also the ones who reproduce the labor power of the domestic group. The social relations of the peasant production units became increasingly patriarchal as they were enveloped in class and state formative processes—that is, the transformation of gifts into tribute exactions. Attempts to turn gifts into tribute were often challenged in the Ganges Valley and elewhere. The peasant households could resist the exactions of the chiefs through deceit, or they could attempt to free themselves altogether from the extortions by fleeing to areas where the traditional leaders had neither authority nor power.

In the Indo-Gangetic watershed, the peasant households successfully asserted their control over land and labor; they prevented the chiefs and ritual leaders from transforming themselves into a ruling class that lived through the efforts of others and that ensured the reproduction of their lifestyle with retainers who armed themselves with bows and iron-tipped arrows. In the middle Ganges Valley, the peasant domestic groups were less fortunate. The chiefs and priests succeeded in transforming gifts into tribute and in reducing some of their kin into subject populations. The ruling elites that emerged in the region retreated toward the middle of the first millennium B.C. to fortified palaces, where different factions often quarreled with one another over how they should divide the tribute, stolen cattle, and slaves they received. The tensions that developed within the ruling groups added to the instability that had already been created by their antagonistic relations with the subject peasant populations of the countryside and with neighboring communities in frontier areas and borderlands.

The rise of cities in the Ganges Valley, such as Kausambi, which was twice as large as any of the Mature Harappan urban centers, marked the appearance of various commercial groups and professions connected with trade, systems of weights and measures, and money—the universal exchange value that facilitated the exchange of one item for another. The cities were political centers that added commerce. They appeared in those regions where the role of the ritual leaders had been weakened, either through the efforts of the chiefs who had proclaimed themselves divine or because the peasant households, merchants, and artisans followed the Jaina or Buddhist sects, which withheld the gifts their predecessors and contemporaries had given to the traditional priests of Vedic society.

Jainism and Buddhism are oppositional religions, which provide alternative understandings and explanations of the existing social relations. Both were closely linked with the development of urban centers. Jainism spread rapidly among the moneylenders and merchants who trafficked in finished goods. Buddhism, which in fact rejects brahmanic representations of the social world, appealed mainly to merchants, artisans, and cultivators, all of whom had low status in the traditional society. These formerly marginalized, subordinated households were able to use the wealth they produced in new ways. Wealth—regardless of whether it was measured in grain, cattle, or currency—was distributed differently. Banking and moneylending, along with commerce and trade, became increasingly prestigious and important pursuits.

One of the most notable technological changes that occurred during the early part of the first millennium B.C. was the increasing use of iron, mostly for weapons at first and then for tools. This development meant that smiths had located sources of iron ore, that they could mine the deposits, and that they could make and sustain fires hot enough to melt the minerals in order to obtain the pure metal. The blacksmiths were a highly suspect, low-status group of itinerant craftsmen, who possessed these special skills to process and forge weapons, tools, and other goods. They moved from village to village, exchanging their services or finished goods for food, money, or other forms of wealth. The relative scarcity of iron ores and the secrecy surrounding their craft impeded or prevented the development of self-sufficient peasant and elite households.

Evidence for the acquisition of these skills is provided not only by the iron implements themselves but also by the appearance of a particular kind of pottery, known as Northern Black Polished Ware, which was widely used in the area and required firing temperatures as high as those needed for smelting iron. These vessels were used to carry salt mined in Punjab and grains to farflung political and commercial centers, such as Taxila, on the margins of the Achaemenid Empire to the northwest; Gujarat, with its maritime connections to the Persian Gulf; and Yamuna, which lay astride trade routes to central India, where iron ores and other raw materials were found.

The human landscape of the Ganges Valley became a mosaic during the first millennium B.C. The lands and pastures of corporate, kin-based communities coexisted side by side and interspersed with chiefdoms, petty monarchies, commercial and craft centers, and peasant villages. They were linked together by class struggle, matrimonial mobility, religious cults that appealed to different sectors of the local populations, and itinerant craftsworkers, and traders. Petty states that attempted to count people and tax their activities quickly discovered that the practices they used to appropriate labor and goods from sedentary peasant communities or from pastoralists were not particularly effective ways to tax merchants, bankers, or moneylenders in the commercial centers or the traders, peddlers, and craft specialists who moved continuously from place to place.

Romila Thapar (1984) has observed that the political economy during the expansion of state control determines how the social relations among the state, its ruling class, and the subject populations are organized. Expansion into an agricultural region requires tax assessors and collectors to collect tribute and administrators to reorganize the encapsulated communities. Control over commerce and craft production demands either military control over trade routes or administrative agents to tax production and exchange at their sites. The growth of cities, and the concomitant development of artisan and merchant classes, provided states with potentially new sources of revenues; they also provided subordinated classes and communities with potentially new ways of resisting the exactions of states and their ruling classes.

The Mauryan Empire, the first imperial state in the Indian subcontinent, began to consolidate its control over the Ganges Valley in the fourth century B.C. In less than a century, it encapsulated three-fourths of the subcontinent and brought more than 100 million people under its rule. It incorporated communities and polities with highly varied political economies: tribal peoples in the interior and the borderlands, kin communities with hereditary chiefs, petty states with rural hinterlands, and city-states dominated by com-

State-based societies on the Indian subcontinent during the first millennium B.C.

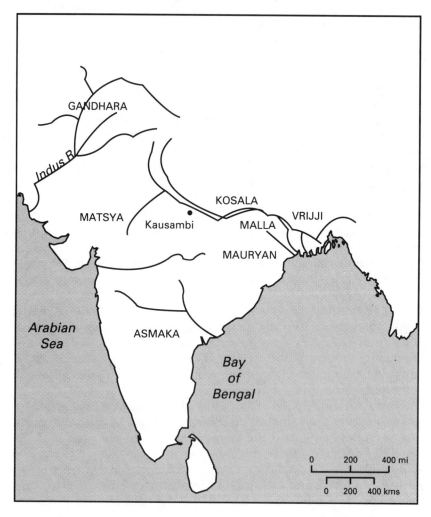

mercial activities. It succeeded in exerting control through cunning and deception; disguising new forms of revenue extraction as traditional practices. However, the success of India's first imperial state was short-lived. The Mauryan empire was already disintegrating into a series of successor states by the end of the third century B.C., its rulers unable to settle on succession to the throne, to retain the loyalty of their provincial administrators, or to maintain high levels of tribute extraction from their subject populations.

FURTHER READINGS: A BRIEF GUIDE

Philip L. Kohl, "The Use and Abuse of World Systems Theory: The Case of the Pristine West Asian State," in *Advances in Archaeological Method and Theory*, ed. Michael B. Schiffer, vol. 11, (San Diego: Academic Press, 1987), pp. 1–36, and "The Balance of Trade in Southwestern Asia in the Third Millennium B.C.," *Current Anthropology*, vol. 19, no. 3 (1978), 463–492, assesses the cultural and historical unity and diversity of the area.

The development of food-producing subsistence economies in central and south Asia is discussed by V. M. Masson, "Prehistoric Settlement Patterns in Soviet Central Asia," in *Man, Settlement and Urbanism*, ed. Peter J. Ucko, Ruth Tringham, and G. W. Dimbleby (London: Gerald Duckworth, 1972), pp. 263–278; Philip L. Kohl, *Central Asia: Palaeolithic Beginnings to the Iron Age* (Paris: Editions Recherche sur les Civilisations, 1984), esp. pp. 35–72; M. Lechevallier and G. Quivron, "The Neolithic in Baluchistan: New Evidences from Mehrgarh," in *South Asian Archaeology 1979*, ed. H. Hartel (Berlin: Dietrich Reimer, 1981), pp. 71–92; and J. F. Jarrige and Richard H. Meadow, "The Antecedents of Civilization in the Indus Valley," *Scientific American*, vol. 243, no. 2 (1980), 122–133.

Class and state formation on the Iranian Plateau and in central Asia are examined by Maurizio Tosi, "The Archaeological Evidence for Protostate Structures in Eastern Iran and Central Asia at the End of the 3rd Millennium B.C.," and Raffaele Biscione, "The Crisis of Central Asian Urbanization in II Millennium B.C. and Villages as Alternative Systems," both in Jean Deschayes, ed., *Le Plateau Iranien et l'Asie Centrale des Origines a la Conquete Islamique*, Colloques Internationaux du Centre National de la Recherche Scientifique, no. 567 (Paris, 1977), pp. 45–66 and 113–129; Philip L. Kohl, ed., *The Bronze Age Civilization of Central Asia: Recent Soviet Discoveries* (Armonk, NY: M. E. Sharpe, 1981); Philip L. Kohl, "Prehistoric 'Turan' and Southern Turkmenia: The Problem of Cultural Diversity," in *Frontiers of the Indus Civilization: Sir Mortimer Wheeler Commemoration Volume*, ed. B. B. Lal and S. P. Gupta (New Delhi: Books and Books, 1984), pp. 321–331, and "A Note on Chlorite Artefacts from Shahr-i Sokhta," *East and West*, vol. 27, no. 4 (1977), 111–127; Philip L. Kohl, "The 'World Economy' of Western Asia in the Third Millennium B.C.," Maurizio Tosi, "The Proto-urban Cultures of Eastern Iran and the Indus Civilization. Notes and Suggestions for a Spatio-temporal Frame to Study the Early Relations Between India and Iran," and Marcello

Piperno, "Socio-economic Implications from the Graveyard at Shahr-i Sokhta," all in Maurizio Taddei, ed., *South Asian Archaeology 1977*, vol. 1 (Naples: Seminario di Studi Asiatici, Istituto Universitario Orientale, 1979), pp. 55–86, 149–172, and 123–141; Muhammad A. Dandamaev and Vladimir G. Lukonin, *The Cultures and Social Institutions of Ancient Iran* (Cambridge: Cambridge University Press, 1989); Pierre Amiet, "Archaeological Discontinuity and Ethnic Duality in Elam," *Antiquity*, vol. LIII, no. 209 (1979), 195–204; and C. C. Lamberg-Karlovsky, "Mesopotamia, Central Asia, and the Indus Valley: So the Kings Were Killed," in *Archaeological Thought in America*, ed. C. C. Lamberg-Karlovsky (Cambridge: Cambridge University Press, 1989), pp. 241–267.

Overviews of south Asian archaeology are furnished by Bridget and Raymond Allchin, *The Rise of Civilization in India and Pakistan* (Cambridge: Cambridge University Press, 1982); Jerome Jacobson, ed., *Studies in the Archaeology of India and Pakistan* (Warminster, Eng.: Aris & Phillips, 1987); and Walter A. Fairservis, Jr., *The Roots of Ancient India: The Archaeology of Early Indian Civilization* (Chicago: University of Chicago Press, 1975). The formation of Indus Valley, or Harappan, society is examined by Gregory L. Possehl, "Revolution in the Urban Revolution: The Emergence of Indus Urbanization," *Annual Review of Anthropology*, vol. 19 (1990), 261–282; Jim G. Shaffer and Diane A. Lichtenstein, "Ethnicity and Change in the Indus Valley Cultural Tradition," in *Old Problems and New Perspectives in the Archaeology of South Asia*, Archaeological Reports 2, ed. J. Mark Kenoyer, (Madison, WI: University of Wisconsin, 1989) pp. 117–126; Jim G. Shaffer, "Harappan Culture: A Reconsideration," in *Harappan Civilization: A Contemporary Perspective*, ed. Gregory L. Possehl (New Delhi: Oxford and IBH Publishing, 1982), pp. 41–50, and "Reurbanization: The Eastern Punjab and Beyond," manuscript, 1988; Walter A. Fairservis, Jr., "An Epigenetic View of Harappan Culture," in *Archaeological Thought in America*, ed. C. C. Lamberg-Karlovsky, (Cambridge: Cambridge University Press, 1989), pp. 205–217; and Daniel Miller, "Ideology and the Harappan Civilization," *Journal of Anthropological Archaeology*, vol. 4, no. 1 (1985), 34–71.

Class and state formation in south Asia are examined by Romila Thapar, "State Formation in Early India," *International Social Science Journal*, vol. XXXII, no. 4 (1980), 655–669, "The State as Empire," in *The Study of the State*, ed. Henri J. Claessen and Peter Skalník (The Hague: Mouton Publishers, 1981), pp. 409–426, and *From Lineage to State: Social Formations in the Mid-First Millennium B.C. in the Ganga Valley* (Bombay: Oxford University Press, 1984); Sudharshan Seneviratne, "The Mauryan State," in *The Early State*, ed. Henri J. Claessen and Peter Skalník (The Hague: Mouton Publishers, 1978), pp. 381–402, and "Kalinga and Andhra: The Process of Secondary State Formation in India," in *The Study of the State*, ed. Henri J. Claessen and Peter Skalník (The Hague: Mouton Publishers, 1981), pp. 317–338; R. S. Sharma, "Class Formation and Its Material Basis in the Upper Gangetic Basin (*c.* 1000–500 B.C.)," *Indian Historical Review*, vol. II, no. 1 (1975), 1–13; Aparajita Chakraborty, "The Social Formation of Indus Society," *Economic and Political Weekly*, vol. XVIII, no. 50 (1983), 2132–2138; and D. P. Agrawal, "The Indian Bronze Age Cultures and Their Metal Technology," in *Advances in World Archaeology*, ed. Fred Wendorf and Angela Close, vol. 1 (New York: Academic Press, 1982), 213–265.

chapter 8

The Far East

Nationalism appears as the uncritical, and hence manipulable, identification with power. Its ideal end is national unity or the subordination of contested social differences. (Sheldon Wolin, The Nation*)*

Patriots identify themselves with the fortunes of their states. Except among aristocrats, the breed hardly existed before nationalism elbowed its way into Western societies and spread cancerously from there. Ergo, there is no patriotism outside the national state system. (Leslie Dunbar, The Nation*)*

Can patriotism be given a new meaning? Perhaps, by replacing uncritical subordination to class hierarchy with democracy in the workplace and in the wider society. (Seymour Melman, The Nation*)*

The Far East is an immense area. It stretches from the Gobi Desert of Inner Mongolia southward through China, Indochina, and Malaysia into Indonesia and New Guinea and eastward from the Himalayas and the Tibetan Plateau to Japan, Taiwan, and the Philippines. It covers more than 10 million square miles and includes virtually every kind of ecological habitat found in the world today. There are tropical jungles and grasslands in the south, arid deserts and steppes reaching from Chinese Turkistan to Mongolia, subarctic tundras in Manchuria and Tibet, large temperate valleys carved by the rivers that flow out of the mountains to the west and empty into the China Sea, and landscapes in coastal China, Cambodia, and New Guinea that were built by their inhabitants.

People first lived in parts of the Far East more than half a million years ago. Archaeologists have found human remains dating that far back in Java and more recent ones at various localities in China, including Zhoukoudian (Choukoutien) Cave outside Beijing. In those days, the peoples of the inhabited areas of the Far East hunted game and used various food plants. Around 12,000 years ago, the inhabitants of the dunes and oases of the Gobi Desert hunted ostriches and other animals in the steppe and desert. Their contemporaries in the forests around Beijing hunted deer, bears, and other mammals in the wooded areas and gazelles in the nearby grasslands; one group had marine shells, which suggests they traded or moved seasonally between the foothills of the Mongolian Plateau and the Yellow Sea. The Jomon communities that lived around lakes and rivers and in the coastal regions of central Japan hunted, foraged, and fished; their diets included various kinds of mollusks and fish, including deep-water species like bonito and tuna. Below the Tsinling Mountains—that is, the tropical forests and grasslands of South China, Indochina, Indonesia, and the Philippines—communities used simple stone tools and had diverse subsistence economies that reflected local or regional differences in the availability of foodstuffs and raw materials; the

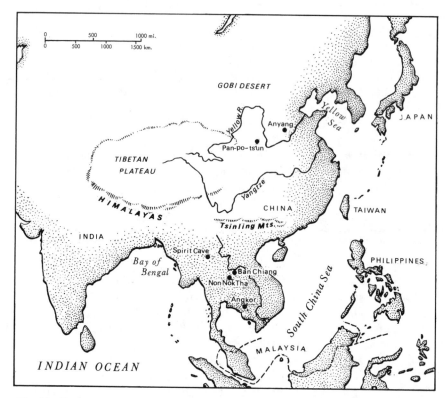

The Far East.

coastal peoples of southern China and Indochina fished and collected shell-fish in the estuaries and littoral, and their inland contemporaries hunted a variety of mammals and collected a wide range of plant foods and raw materials.

EARLY FOOD-PRODUCING COMMUNITIES

People first lived at Spirit Cave in the tropical forests of northern Thailand about 11,000 years ago. Spirit Cave is one of the more thoroughly investigated sites in the Far East that date to this period. Its occupants used simple Hoabhinian stone tools to make more specialized tools from raw materials found along the stream that passed by their campsite or in the nearby forest. They hunted a variety of animals in the forests and along the stream: deer, pigs, antelopes, monkeys, and dugongs, to name only a few. They fished and collected mollusks and crustaceans from the stream and gathered cucumbers, betel nuts, almonds, broad beans, water chestnuts, pepper, and gourds in the forest and grew them in gardens near the cave; all of these plants were subsequently domesticated, but it is not clear that they were domesticated at the time Spirit Cave was occupied. A typical meal at the camp was a stew made from small pieces of meat mixed with vegetables and spices and cooked in a bamboo container over an open fire.

Forest clearing, a significant feature of gardening and farming, appeared in several of the heavily forested regions of the Far East about the time Spirit Cave was occupied. A pollen core from central Taiwan shows, about 12,000 years ago, that secondary forests began to grow near Sun-Moon Lake and that fragments of charred trees were already accumulating in the sediments of the lake bottom. About 9,000 years ago, the inhabitants of the Kuk Basin in southeastern New Guinea diverted a stream to irrigate taro or yam gardens; pollen evidence indicates that extensive forest clearing had already taken place in the basin by 4000 B.C. Their contemporaries who camped at the Kiowa rock shelter in the south-central highlands of New Guinea were already eating domesticated pigs by 4500 B.C.

Rice was one of the earliest plants domesticated in the Far East. Wild species flourished from the foothills of the Himalayas overlooking the Ganges Valley through the wet forests and plains of northern Indochina and southern China below the Tsinling Mountains. The domestication process proceeded from grain gathering through cultivation and transplantation into habitats where the plant had not thrived earlier; domestication occurred when annual seeding by the people was necessary for the propagation of the plants. Domestication probably took place in a number of localities in swampy areas along the Ganges River and its tributaries in northeast India and northern Thailand and along the Yangtze River in south China. Rice cultivation was already well established in Thailand by 5000 B.C., judging by rice grains found at the site of Kon Phanom Di; the appearance of slate knives, similar to those used to harvest rice, at Spirit Cave around 7000 B.C. suggests that rice cultivation may have begun several millennia earlier.

Plant cultivation appeared on the plains of the Yellow River and its tributaries in northern China during the sixth millennium B.C. The earliest cultivators settled in small villages on ridges overlooking the marshes and wetlands of the alluvial floodplains, where they grew foxtail and broom-corn millets. The residents of these communities kept domesticated pigs, dogs, and chickens; hunted deer throughout the year; and harvested walnuts, hazelnuts, and acorns in nearby deciduous forests. They lived in circular, semi-subterranean pithouses, stored the food they had harvested in nearby pits, made pottery and stone and bone implements outside their houses, buried their dead in cemeteries, and steamed their meals in coarse pots.

Regional differences in the appearance and everyday life of the early farming communities of China and Indochina were becoming evident by 5000 B.C. For example, the inhabitants of villages around the lakes and streams that emptied into the lower Yangtze River in southern and eastern China often lived in houses that were raised on wooden piles or built on artificial mounds. The plant foods they consumed were also different from those eaten by their contemporaries to the north. They grew rice, gourds, and

Reconstruction of the early farming village of Pan-p'o-ts'un near Sian, China.

water caltrop and harvested aquatic plants like water chestnuts and lotus seed; kept domesticated dogs, pigs, and water buffalo; fished; collected shellfish; and hunted birds and mammals.

Between 5000 and 2000 B.C., a number of regionally distinct cultural groupings crystallized in various parts of China and other regions of the Far East. Each comprised a cluster of villages and hamlets located in fairly close proximity to one another whose inhabitants shared certain aspects of everyday life, from the kinds of food they consumed to the ways they decorated pottery vessels, that distinguished them from the members of other clusters. The groups represented regionally organized production, exchange, and consumption units. Their existence suggests that they were interdependent rather than self-sufficient, and suggests the elaboration of community-level relations of production, matrimonial mobility, and social reproduction. They include the various temporal phases and regional variants of the Yangshao culture in the middle Yellow River Valley, the Ta-wen-k'ou culture in the Shantung highlands and seacoast of northeast China, and the Yueh culture of coastal south China and northeast Indochina, to name only a few.

At first, these regional clusters seem to have developed in relative isolation from one another, resembling islands in an archipelago. Subsequently, during the later part of the third millennium B.C., some of them began to forge linkages. This marked the beginning of an early episode of class and state formation, of uneven social development, and of conditions that possibly promoted the exodus of Austronesian-speaking populations from the south China mainland to the island worlds of the South China Sea and eventually to those of the Pacific Ocean.

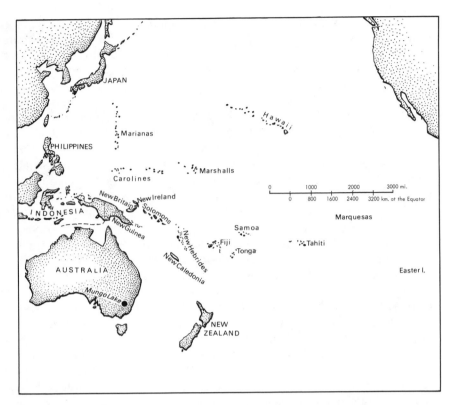

The Pacific Islands.

EARLY STATE FORMATION AND UNEVEN DEVELOPMENT IN NORTH CHINA

Class and state formation seem to have occurred in the Yellow River Valley below the confluence of the Wei and Huang tributaries in the late third millennium B.C. at Lung-shan culture sites in Shandung and Henan provinces, which have yielded the highly distinctive pedestal bowls and tripod cooking pots. The residents of Ch'eng-tzu-yai, which lies at the foot of the Shandung Mountains and overlooks the lower reaches of the Yellow River, built an enormous stamped earth fortification wall. The wall, nearly 30 feet thick and 20 feet high, enclosed a rectangular, 50-acre compound that was approximately 1,500 feet long and 1,300 feet wide. Ch'eng-tzu-yai was the largest of a number of fortified towns that were built in the area at the time. The walls were built for protection.

The evidence for the violence that accompanies state formation comes from the contemporary village of Chien-kou, which seems to have been on the margins of the Lung-shan expansion. The skulls of six individuals found in one house show that they had been struck in the head and then scalped.

The bodies of a number of males and females, both old and young, were dumped in a well; some of them had been decapitated, and others, who showed signs of struggling, were apparently buried alive. Some archaeologists speculate that the victors decapitated their vanquished foes and used their severed heads as drinking cups.

The violence abroad, evidenced by the events at Chien-kou, was accompanied by the rapid consolidation of social-class structures in the core area of the lower Yellow River Valley. The cemetery of the walled settlement of Ch'eng-tzu-yai exhibited marked differences in the quantities and kinds of objects interred with different kinds of burials. Four classes of burials can be discerned: (1) Five individuals, buried in wooden caskets, were interred with large numbers of objects; (2) six individuals, buried in caskets, had some grave goods; (3) seventeen individuals were buried in pits with a few items; and (4) fifty-four individuals buried in pits had no grave goods. Further evidence of social stratification comes from the cemetery at the large but poorly known settlement of Hsiang-fen, located upstream from Ch'eng-tzu-yai. Three classes of burials were discerned there: (1) Nine males were interred in large individual graves; cinnabar was sprinkled in their wooden coffins, and the hundred to two hundred objects placed in their tombs included crocodile-skin drums, furniture, painted wooden objects, whole sets of pottery vessels, and jade rings. Some of the large graves were flanked by shallow tombs that contained females adorned with headdresses and armlets. (2) Eighty individuals were interred with some grave goods; a few of them had been placed in coffins. (3) six hundred and ten individuals had been buried in pits without grave furnishings.

The late third millennium B.C. graves of northeast China contrasted markedly with those of earlier periods and neighboring areas, where there was little or no discernible evidence for social differentiation. Thus, class and state formation was a local affair, limited largely at the time to the lower Yellow River Valley. Differences in the kinds and quantities of goods placed in the various tombs indicate that a very small number of individuals had considerably greater access to society's wealth than the vast majority of its members, and that certain items were consumed or used only by the ruling class. The differences also indicate that class formation was a process with significant gender dimensions. Although the position and authority of women, as a group in Lung-shan society, seems to have declined, those associated with the ruling class had significantly greater control of wealth than either men or women of the lower classes, which either lacked status and wealth differentials or did not mark them in their burial practices.

Different constructions of authority, gender, and power relations occurred in communities outside the orbit of the Lung-shan state. These presumably entailed the appearance of increased control over the activities and movement of goods and members, especially younger women, in those communities struggling to avoid or limit the effects of encapsulation by the marauding or tribute-based state; such communities, although lacking class structures, might exhibit patriarchal authority patterns, in which power was vested temporarily in the elder men of the extended households and lineages. Traditional, more egalitarian authority and gender relations may have continued to persist in those communities whose members emigrated or fled to avoid the pillaging, kidnappings, slave raids, or tribute and labor exactions of the state. In other words, the expansion and encroachment of the state-based Lung-shan society precipitated various kinds of tribal social formations in the hinterlands and beyond.

The emergence of state-based societies has immediate effects on the organization and production relations of surrounding societies. The organization of those in closest proximity to the state, but independent of it, will reflect the degree of threat of the expanding state. State formation, in spatial terms, creates a ripple effect of increasing stratification and increasingly rigid forms of kinship in surrounding societies, the most militarized and most stratified being closest to the state. If the state is weak, the autonomous kin societies on the periphery will retain communal control over production and reproduction but will have more rigid forms of kin-determined use-rights and marriage arrangements. If the tribute-based state is strong, the communities on the periphery will lose control over production—production is atomized to the level of their individual households—whereas they will retain communal control certain resources, reproductive processes, and military activities. States destroy kin societies in their midst and create conditions for genocide and ethnocide. On the peripheries, resistance to state penetration may foster more rigid and repressive conditions within societies with altered forms of a communal mode of production; in the process, gender relations are often distorted and skewed in the struggle between kin-based productive and reproductive priorities and those demanded by the representatives of the state. For the encapsulated kin communities or those on the margins of the state, the conditions created in the process of state formation involve resistance on a number of political and cultural fronts.

The Lung-shan state or states, since class formation may have occurred in more than one village, in lower reaches of the Yellow River Valley were unstable. Their power withered and disintegrated within a few centuries. Successor states and dynasties, located on the margins, usurped their power and position during the early part of the second millennium B.C. These were centered around Erh-li-t'ou (Yen-shih), about 250 miles up the Yellow River Valley from the fortified Lung-shan town of Ch'eng-tzu-yai. The walled towns and palaces at Erh-li-t'ou were linked in complex ways to the formation of the Hsia state and dynasty; however, Xia (Hsia) was not the only dynastic state in north China at the time. Written records of the Shang state, which date to the middle of the second millennium B.C., list thirty-three alien states outside its domain. State formation involved opening up new lands for agricultural production and/or swallowing up small states in borderlands. By the twelfth century B.C., the number of alien states listed in the Shang annals had been reduced to eight. The three most important, historically, were Xia;

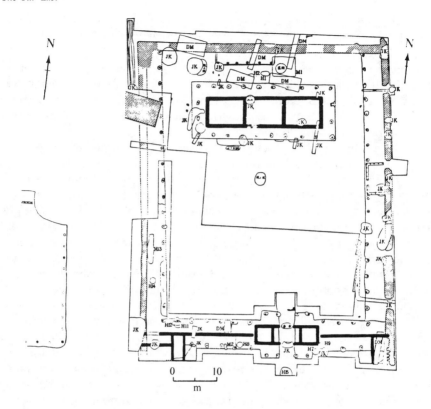

Palace foundations at Elr-li-t'ou, China.

the slightly later Shang state centered on the eastern edge of the old Xia domain in the middle Yellow River Valley; and the Western Zhou (Chou) state, which was centered further upstream in the Wei River Valley.

We know a good deal about the organization of Shang and Western Zhou societies during the later half of the second millennium B.C. As a result, we can draw some tentative conclusions about the structure of the earlier state-based societies in north China. The basic units in these state-based societies were corporate landholding groups, whose members claimed descent from a common ancestor, resided in walled towns, and had use-rights to the common lands. These groups sporadically fissioned, as cadet lineages carried the clan name into new territories. Authority was vested in experienced and charismatic individuals who claimed genealogical proximity to the clan founder; they were typically aided by councils of elders and certain ritual leaders, *kan*, who played an important role in forging marriage alliances.

Estate and class structures were superimposed on the traditional, localized kin communities in the early state-based societies. Each estate was a category of people who shared legal rights and obligations that were different from those of people in the other estates. They did not equate precisely with social classes—that is, groups of people whose members are identified by their position in the whole system of production, by the control they have over their labor power and means of production, and by their relation to other classes. There were four estates in the early state-based societies of north China: royalty; officials; commoners, who produced the goods, paid the taxes, and made up the bulk of the population; and slaves. The estate structure was not stable since commoners were both ennobled and enslaved; nobles and officials were frequently enslaved; and freed slaves became commoners or nobles.

At the top of the class structure were the kings, who claimed their positions by virtue of genealogical proximity to the clan founders, the imperial families, and the consort families. The kings traditionally married close kin to ensure succession; however, they also took consorts or concubines to forge alliances with other groups. Imperial consorts, like Fu Hao, were powerful individuals by virtue of their social position; they performed rituals, led military campaigns, held title to their own lands and walled towns, and exerted a great deal of control over their male kin. Contradictions within the ruling class must have been particularly apparent at times of succession, when any number of individuals could lay equally legitimate claims to the throne. The princes, who were potential claimants to the throne, were often granted titles to towns on the margins of the state to remove them from the happenings at the imperial court. Other members of the ruling class included the kings' meritorious and loyal companions-at-arms, who were frequently granted titles to land and labor, and the clan leaders of the walled towns, who received gifts in return for the foodstuffs, goods, and labor provided by their commoner kin and slaves—the two classes of direct producers in the traditional landholding communities. The class structures of the early states were also unstable; the kings of alien states were occasionally captured, enslaved, sacrificed, and replaced by officials whose positions reflected their loyalty to the victorious ruler.

The class structure of Shang society was apparent in how the dead were buried. More than 1,200 tombs were found at Anyang, a late Shang capital. All but 11 were the graves of commoners; each contained a single skeleton and a few pottery vessels as offerings. The other 11 were royal tombs, each of which housed structures that took more than 7,000 person-days of labor to complete. One royal tomb contained a central coffin surrounded by the bodies of many individuals who were sacrificed and interred at the same time. Some had their own coffins; some had been decapitated. Each of the royal tombs also contained an enormous array and quantity of objects—for example, chariots; bronze and pottery vessels; and various kinds of jade, stone, and metal jewelry.

Many of the later Shang kings established their own capitals. These were typically large, dispersed settlements, such as Anyang, which covered 10 to 15 square miles. The center of the town was the administrative and ceremonial precinct for the surrounding villages. In one capital, this precinct was enclosed by a 4.5 mile-long earthwork that was 70 feet thick and 40 feet

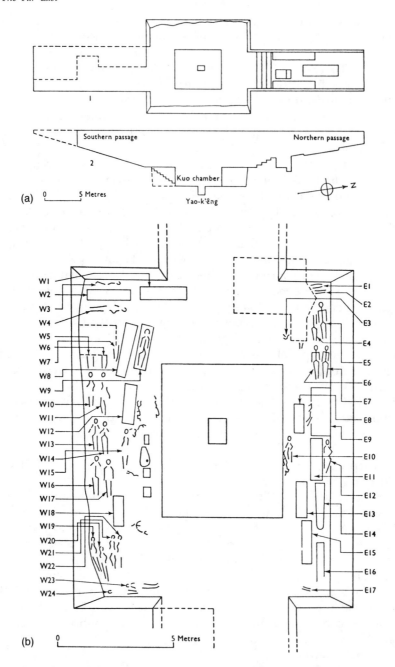

One of the Shang royal tombs found at Anyang, China. (a) Plan and cross-section.
(b) The arrangement of human victims on the raised platform of the tomb. One hundred
thirty-one victims, including eighty-nine human beings, were placed in the tomb of a
member of the Shang royal family when he was buried. (*From Kwang-chih Chang*, The
Archaeology of Ancient China. *Copyright © 1986 by Yale University Press. Reprinted by
permission.*)

high. Nearby villages contained dwellings of artisans and their workshops, where various items—carved bone, bronze, pottery, and fabrics—were produced for the palace and the state. Channels that ran among the villages drained off sewage and provided water for the agricultural fields and gardens that were scattered through the capital and dominated the landscape outside the royal precinct.

David Keightley (1983) has described the late Shang state as a continually shifting network of paths and encampments that were used by the king and his entourage as they traveled throughout the domain to bring gifts and to accept tribute and hospitality from subject populations. The king and his supporters may have spent as many as three hundred days a year away from the capital. The state was more powerful in some areas than in others because of the king's marital alliances, the success of the crops, the loyalty of local clan leaders, the presence of imperial armies, or the ability of neighboring communities to resist its advances and attempted extortions.

Thus, the Shang kings actually had political control of only a small part of the Yellow River Plain, although they and their officials and retainers exacted labor and goods from the inhabitants of a wider area. The Shang rulers must have engaged almost continuously in various diplomatic maneuvers and raids to acquire captives for labor and sacrifice and to bring new lands and peoples under their control. During the twelfth century B.C., according to traditional sources, the last Shang king was attacked and ultimately toppled by one of his own vassals, a petty lord whose territory and town were allegedly gifts of the Shang ruler himself. The vassal founded the royal house of the Western Zhou state and incorporated some Shang territories into its domain.

The political power of the Zhou rulers waned in the ninth century B.C. as regional lords and clan leaders began to ignore their obligations to the imperial court and fought with one another and with the kin-organized communities in the borderlands to the north and south; these frontier societies were variously described as non-Chinese, or barbarian. The power of the Western Zhou throne had all but evaporated by the beginning of the Spring and Autumn period (722 to 481 B.C.) as a hundred or so successor states of varying sizes and importance struggled to maintain their autonomy and position with continual diplomatic maneuvering and sporadic raids. The Spring and Autumn period was marked by the formation of a league, a confederation of small, independent states that allied themselves with the Ch'i state in Shandung to protect themselves from the threat posed by the Ch'u state, which had crystallized in the lower Yangtze River Valley. The league lasted two centuries, preserving relatively peaceful conditions and the illusion of unity under the sovereignty of the Zhou ruler.

Warfare became almost endemic and much more destructive during the Warring States period (480–221 B.C.). Most of the hundred or so smaller states and polities that had existed earlier were absorbed by one of the seven kingdoms that came to dominate political life in north China during the later half of the first millennium B.C. However, this was not the only change that

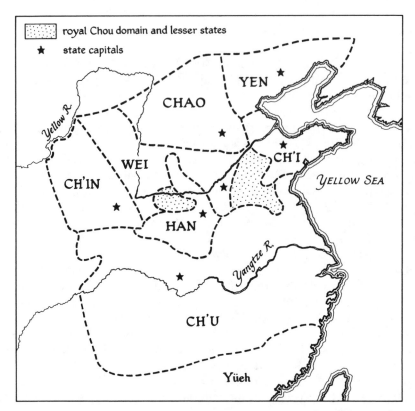

Warring States Period polities in northern China. (*From Charles O. Hucker,*
China's Imperial Past. Copyright © 1975 by Stanford University Press.
Reprinted by permission of the Board of Trustees of the Leland Stanford Junior
University.)

occurred. Rivers were channeled and canals were built to facilitate water
transportation and to increase the amount of arable land. Estate and class
structures were continually being decomposed and reconstituted to reflect the
changes in power and power relations that emerged under these circumstances.

This state of flux was also evident in the worldviews that crystallized
during this period and gave voice to the sentiments, understandings, and
aspirations of classes with different relations to power. These new perspectives on nature and society challenged the views of the established nobility,
who understood the differences between themselves and others as innate or
divinely inspired. The followers of Confucius (551–479 B.C.), many of whom
came from classes or groups that had recently lost wealth and power, typically argued that people were alike, that social differences were not innate,
and that rulers should appoint capable individuals to office to maintain the
existing social order. Mo Tzu was a former Confucian who gave voice to the

sentiments of ritual specialists and funeral directors bent on social reform during the late fifth century B.C. The Mohists believed that individuals with ability should be advanced on their merits and, hence, opposed the inherited wealth and offices of the nobility. Menicus (c. 372–289 B.C.) and his aristocratic followers argued that benevolence was a moral imperative for rulers and that if they failed to treat their subjects well, they could be deposed by anyone who would treat people fairly. The Taoists, who came largely from the disenfranchised lower nobility and commoners, drew no distinction between the natural and social worlds and saw the institutions and practices of class structures and states as interfering with the unfolding of nature. The Legalists—the Reaganites and Thatcherites of their day—were mostly upwardly mobile landlords and government officials who tied their fortunes to those of one state or another and claimed that nature and society were governed by different laws; that rituals were important because they maintained social order; and that if people worked harder, they would not be poor. They were responsible for the book burnings that occurred during the reign of Qin Xi Wangdi, the founder of the first imperial state on the north China plains.

North China was unified politically for the first time in 221 B.C., when Qin Xi Wangdi annexed the last of the six states that had struggled to gain supremacy in the third century. After proclaiming himself the First Sovereign Emperor, he took a number of steps to consolidate his power and that of the state over the old nobility, the peasants, and the merchants. He broke up the estates of the old nobility, who were forced to live in the capital city, under the watchful eye of the imperial state, far removed from their ancestral landholdings and followers. He disarmed the nobility and had their weapons melted and cast into gigantic bells and figures that were placed in the imperial palace. He stripped the nobles of most of their former privileges and placated them with honorary titles and palaces modeled after the ones they had formerly occupied.

He divided the empire into thirty-six administrative districts, or commanderies, each of which was governed by an administrator in charge of civil affairs, a military governor in charge of the troops, and an inspector who oversaw and controlled their activities. The officials were appointed and supervised by the emperor and the inner circle of imperial counselors. The new imperial bureaucracy was made up of men of wealth and merit, who attained office not by birthright but rather by demonstrated loyalty to the emperor. Their activities were buttressed by an exceedingly harsh legal code with severe penalties for even the most petty crimes. The state further promoted centralization and facilitated imperial rule by standardizing the written language, coinage, and system of weights and measures. In 213 B.C., it burned the books of poets, historians, and philosophers whom the state viewed as denigrating the present because they praised the past.

The Qin state viewed agriculture as the ultimate basis of its wealth and, consequently, attempted to control agricultural production. Its economic regulations gave peasants the right to buy, sell, and own land; however, this right did not create a class of yeoman farmers since much of the land was bought up by a few wealthy landowners, who rented it at high rates to their tenants. The peasants—both freeholder and tenant—were heavily taxed by an imperial state that conscripted labor to tear down old fortifications; to build roads, canals, palaces, and the imperial mausoleum; and to complete the construction of the Great Wall along the northern frontier. The peasantry was also liable for military conscription, land taxes paid in produce, poll taxes paid in cash, and the forced purchase of iron and salt. The exactions were twenty to thirty times greater than they had been earlier. In addition, the peasantry was confronted with avaricious and dishonest officials. As the numbers of convictions and executions increased, peasants, as well as escaped convicts and slaves, fled into the mountains and forests, where they became hermits, threw in with robber bands that preyed on unfortunate peasants and travelers, or joined rebel groups that opposed the exactions of the state and the exploitation of the newly emerging landlord class. Commerce and the activities of the merchants were also suppressed. The government monopolized the production and exchange of basic commodities: salt and iron. In 214 B.C., merchants—together with vagabonds and convicts—were deported to thinly populated commanderies in the northern frontier regions.

Qin Xi Wangdi, who survived three assassination attempts during the later years of his reign, died in 210 B.C. His death sharpened the contradictions in Qin society and sparked an intense struggle over succession. While the palace was plagued with various intrigues, plots, and assassinations, civil war erupted outside. The old nobility rose against the state in order to regain the power and influence it had lost; generals defied the authority of both the inspectors, who spied on them, and the officials of the imperial court; and various groups of peasants and commoners rebelled against the demands of the state. Within a few months of the emperor's death, there were six different rebellions, and politically motivated assassinations became commonplace. These were followed closely by the secession of frontier provinces in the south and by attacks on imperial installations and forces in the northern commanderies by Xiongnu horsemen from the steppes. In 206 B.C., one of the rebel leaders, described variously as a crude peasant or a low-level Qin official who took the name Gaozu, entered the imperial palace and proclaimed himself emperor. He spent the next eleven years getting rival groups to acknowledge his claim; this effort entailed suppressing rebellions and subordinating the eighteen kingdoms they had established during the civil war.

When corvée laborers and convicts worked to complete the Great Wall, the Qin armies dispersed the tribal peoples living near it. The nomads moved into the steppes to avoid prolonged encounters with the imperial soldiers. However, they returned as the civil war intensified, and some of the frontier commanderies claimed their independence from the remnants of the imperial state. The nomads had transformed their social organization during their years in the steppes. The son of an old chieftain consolidated his political power, and a weakly developed class structure appeared. The Xiongnu horse-

The Great Wall of China, which was completed during the Qin dynasty at the end of the 3rd century B.C.

men returned not merely to occupy their tribal lands in the Ordos but also to attack merchants traveling the caravan routes through inner Asia, to raid frontier settlements that remained loyal to the weakened Han state, and to extract tribute from its rulers. For the next fifty years, the Xiongnu posed a continual threat; they periodically invaded the northern reaches of the Han state and required its rulers to make more and more concessions to retain an uneasy peace. As part of the original peace agreement, the Xiongnu leader received a Chinese princess in marriage and annual tribute payments of silk, food, and wine; the Xiongnu paid nothing in return. To the south, a mosaic of independent kingdoms and chiefdoms arose along the southern periphery of the weakened Qin state after the collapse of imperial authority; for example, the kingdom of Nan-yueh-Kuo, which developed in the region from Canton and Kweilin in the east to Hanoi and Danang in the south, asserted its autonomy in 207 B.C., and the inhabitants of coastal Fukien were never fully incorporated into the emerging Han state.

By the time Gaozu was enthroned in 202 B.C., the power of the state was badly weakened. More than two-thirds of the old empire was divided into fiefs, and the number of commanderies that remained under state control had been reduced by more than half. Qin policies, which had forced the old nobility into the capital city, created the conditions for the formation of a new landlord class in the territories they left. The civil wars unleashed new forms of class struggle and class formation in the countryside. Some of the old nobles, who returned to reclaim their estates, were confronted by the powerful provincial landlords and the local officials they controlled or had corrupted; a few successfully reasserted their claims with the support of followers or the imperial state. Bandit leaders, often from the commoner estate, gained respect, loyalty, and influence in some areas because of their ability to maneuver successfully within the constraints imposed by the local political conditions and thereby to bring benefits to their supporters. The new emperor had to leave some of his companions-in-arms in possession of the kingdoms they had conquered and controlled; these retained a great deal of autonomy and appointed many of their own officials. Finally, the emperor ennobled favorites and meritorious individuals, granting them fiefs. Both the kingdoms and the fiefs were hereditary, passing in their entirety to the eldest son of the incumbent's principal wife.

The emergence of powerful local elites and the ennobling of the emperor's kin and companions-in-arms created two levels of government: a locally controlled one and an imperial network directed by the emperor and his close advisors. The provincial ruling classes—the kings, the large landholders, and the bandits—posed a real threat to the imperial state because they had armies or could mobilize armed resistance to the demands of the state. The advisors appointed by Gaozu and, later, some of their descendants formed the inner core of the imperial bureaucracy for more than half a century. During this period, the imperial state often found it difficult or impossible to dislodge the provincial ruling class from positions of power. However, the Gaozu and the Han emperors who followed him on the throne took steps to consolidate their rule. Given the prevailing balance of forces, there was a protracted struggle for power within the ruling class, and as a result, the imperial policies of the period have frequently been described as laissez faire.

Gaozu began the process of reasserting crown and state power by forcing the powerful families to resettle in a sparsely inhabited area, where they would be under continuous imperial surveillance. This practice was followed by each of his successors, one of whom even forbade the members of the resettled families from living in the same place. Gaozu also eliminated those kings who did not belong to the imperial family. By the time of his death in 195 B.C., only one king not affiliated with the imperial family remained. He replaced the six who had been killed or driven off their thrones with nine of his sons. However, the process was interrupted, to some extent, by the Empress Dowager Lu, who ruled through her son for several years and then, for all intents and purposes, assumed the throne herself. She used her position to strengthen the power and wealth of her kinsmen, killed several of Gaozu's sons by concubines, and placed three of her own family members on the thrones of kingdoms. This act set off a struggle between Gaozu's family and his advisors, on the one hand, and the Empress Dowager Lu's family, on the other. She was never able to consolidate her power, and her family was wiped out after she died in 180 B.C.

During the second century B.C., the princes were required to live in their kingdoms, which were not land grants but rather the right to receive roughly two-thirds of the taxes that were collected from a specified number of households. The remainder of the taxes collected were turned over as cash payments to the imperial treasury. This practice provided the emperor with revenues and removed his sons from the intrigues of the imperial palace.

However, it also re-created the problem posed by consort families: the prince's mother and her male relatives. The princes who occupied thrones in the kingdoms also had claims to the imperial throne occupied by one of their brothers; consequently, they posed a continuous threat to the emperor.

The threat manifested itself on several different occasions during the second century B.C., when one or more of the princes fomented a rebellion to overthrow the emperor. The emperors usually retaliated by dividing the kingdoms into smaller units to diminish the princes' incomes, relieving them of their administrative powers and replacing them with loyal officials. Wudi, who ascended to the imperial throne in 140 B.C. and reigned for more than fifty years initiated policies that concentrated the power of the crown. He diminished the power of the imperial family and high officials, who often came from powerful provincial families that opposed his actions, by surrounding himself with advisors he had himself ennobled; he gave appointments, usually military ones, to the members of his consorts' families. He created an imperial university and schools in the chief town of each commandery to train perspective government officials and appointed "cruel officials," who murdered the members of powerful families that remained in their natal communities instead of moving to the mausoleum towns. He broke up the old fiefs, decreeing that estates should be divided equally among all of the heirs rather than passing to the eldest son. He continued the practice of subdividing administrative units and establishing new ones through military conquest along the periphery of the state; these wars were supported by raising taxes; selling aristocratic orders to wealthy families; and creating state monopolies that controlled the production and sale of iron, salt, and alcohol.

The Qin and Han rulers believed that agriculture promoted wealth and prosperity; consequently, they periodically suppressed secondary occupations—that is, those in industry and commerce. However, there was a contradiction. Although agricultural pursuits were more prestigious, they were less remunerative than commercial and industrial activities. Consequently, the state continually struggled to get people to forsake the secondary occupations and return to the land. There were ebbs and flows in this struggle; the merchants and industrialists prospered when the state did not interfere too much, and they suffered when it attempted to control production and regulate commerce.

Merchants were commoners who enjoyed less prestige than either scholars or farmers. There were poor merchants, peddlers and shopkeepers, and there were rich ones, who were among the wealthiest families of the Qin and Han states. More than a quarter of the forty-one wealthiest individuals in the state followed one or more of the secondary occupations: cattle and pig breeding, fish raising, mining, iron smelting, manufacturing, and moneylending. A few of them acquired their wealth illegally through grave robbing, gambling, robbery, or dealing in contraband. A number were merchants who bought cheap and sold dear; their profits, regulated by law, were never less than 100 percent on each transaction. Many were moneylenders who charged usurious interest rates; for example, during the rebellion in 154 B.C., they expected and received ten times the amount of the original loans. They invested in land and followed agricultural pursuits to protect the money they had gained through other activities.

Qin Xi Wangdi limited the merchants' activities and opportunities. They were sent to the frontiers, they could not become officials, they could not own land, and they could not wear certain kinds of garments or ride horses. However, markets thrived in the frontier garrisons, and merchants, as well as the garrison soldiers, also thrived. Legal items—silk and lacquer goods— were freely exchanged; there was also traffic in contraband—iron vessels; agricultural implements; weapons; and livestock, especially female animals. Merchants caught trafficking in contraband were executed. A number of merchants, who served as soldiers and officers during a rebellion in 197 B.C., were offered rewards to secure their help in disorganizing the rebels; however, the emperor must not have been pleased with their actions, for he continued the restrictions on their activities and issued a new edict that prohibited them from bearing arms.

The secondary occupations fared better after 194 B.C. For the next sixty years, the merchants, craftworkers, and industrialists thrived because of the increased demand for their goods at the imperial court, in the kingdoms, and among the wealthy families. They associated with the dominant and subordinate factions of the ruling class and with powerful government officials; they traveled freely throughout the state and beyond. During this period, merchants' carts filled the roads, and exotic and luxurious articles were plentiful in the markets and cities. Households abandoned agriculture to pursue the secondary occupations, which increased the proportion of the population that did not grow their own food. At the same time, landownership became increasingly concentrated as wealthy families, including those that pursued secondary occupations, purchased agricultural land, especially the irrigated fields located near towns, and commanded the services of large numbers of people. The farmers, who had abandoned their fields or been dispossessed, drifted from place to place, and the poor sold their children to pay debts and taxes.

Merchants and industrialists fared less well when the state consolidated and centralized power after 154 B.C. Emperor Wudi increased their taxes and confiscated their goods to finance the costs of the rebellion and wars of conquest on the northwest frontier. He confiscated their fortunes and properties, moved them to garrison towns or areas where they could be watched, and forbade family members from living together. In 120 B.C., he reestablished state control over the minting of coins and introduced a new medium of exchange, which further diminished the assets of the wealthy families; these actions were reinforced with the death penalty for counterfeiting. The following year, merchants were forbidden to own land. At the same time, Wudi established state control over the production and sale of iron, salt, and alcohol. These monopolies were initiated and organized by two businessmen, who had been brought into the government as assistants to the minister of agriculture, who was also in charge of commerce and finance.

Commerce and industry were originally launched from the countryside. Peasant households sold some of their produce in the market because so many of their expenditures involved cash payments. Farming and textile production were intimately linked and based on a gender division of labor: Men farmed and women spun, wove, and made clothes. As a result, cottage production involved local staples, animals, and cloth. When conditions were peaceful, the peasants sold their goods in the market and purchased goods they did not produce for themselves. When the tranquility was disrupted and they were unable to buy or sell in the market, they switched some of their production efforts from goods that could be marketed to those that the household needed.

The two most important rural manufactures were iron and salt. They occurred in areas where the raw materials were plentiful. Both enterprises employed large work forces to obtain the raw materials and the fuel needed to process them. Iron foundries often had more than a thousand workers, some of whom were skilled craftsmen. One industrialist family engaged in salt production used more than a thousand refugees, who were not always under the authority of the state. This suggests that the industrialists, who produced iron and salt, employed some wage workers; these definitely included skilled artisans and may also have involved peasant farmers employed during the off-season and farmers who had permanently abandoned agricultural pursuits.

After iron smelting and salt manufacturing became state monopolies, the work forces were drawn from four sources: state-owned slaves; corvée laborers, who worked one month each year without pay; convicts; and skilled craftworkers who were paid cash wages. The working conditions must have been less than satisfactory since the workers of at least one state factory revolted. State-controlled factories survived the reign of Wudi, though on a much reduced scale. In the middle of the first century B.C., thousands of craftworkers were employed in state-controlled textile factories, and their annual wages amounted to several hundred million cash. Opponents of the state monopolies argued that they should be reduced in scale or eliminated altogether because they were too expensive and the wages paid to the workers were too high.

UNEVEN DEVELOPMENT, RESISTANCE, AND STATE FORMATION IN FRONTIER AREAS

Both the Qin and Han rulers conceptualized the world order in terms of the Five Zone theory—that is, Chinese civilization was divided into five hierarchically organized, concentric zones. The innermost was the royal domain from which the king received daily tribute. This was surrounded by the lords' zone—dependent kingdoms established by the king—from which he received monthly tribute. Immediately outside was the pacified zone, whose inhabitants paid tribute three times a year. Next were the barbarians who lived in the controlled zone and paid tribute once a year. Beyond them, in the wild zone outside the Chinese world, resided the independent barbarians who perhaps paid tribute once in a lifetime.

Later Han (A.D. 25 to 220) chroniclers distinguished class-based or estate-stratified societies, *kuo*, from nonstratified, kin-organized groups. India, the kingdom of Choson, and the hundred or so polities of Japan that had entered into communications with the Chinese government were *kuo*, as were numerous polities in southern Indochina during the middle of the third century A.D. This term did not apply to the tribes of the Tonkin Delta or the inhabitants of Fukien, which lies inland from Hong Kong. For four centuries, from c. 200 B.C. to A.D. 220, the Han state established a continually shifting web of mercantile, tributary, and political relations with various non-Han societies on its peripheries. These included contacts with the Mediterranean civilizations; the steppe nomads of Manchuria and central Asia; the agricultural communities of Korea and Japan, and the island peoples of Sumatra, Java, and Borneo.

The last half of the second century A.D. was a time of widespread disruption in the Far East. The Han state, which unified much of northern China, was regularly attacked by the steppe nomads, by the tribes, chiefdoms, and kingdoms of south China; and by the Indochinese tribal peoples, who rebelled between 154 and 165. After 168, no year was free from civil unrest. The most extensive rebellion was the Yellow Turban uprising of 184 to 189, in which peasants from two-thirds of the imperial domain revolted and gained the support of various border peoples. This Taoist-inspired rebellion proclaimed equality and the common ownership of land. In the liberated areas, the Yellow Turbans abolished Han imperial institutions and killed its officials; in other provinces, they refused to acknowledge the legitimacy and authority of imperial magistrates. The Yellow Turbans and a contemporary Taoist movement in the south marked the end of the centralized power of the Han state. For the next thirty years, local and regional leaders asserted or reasserted their autonomy, not only in China but also in Japan and Korea.

Japan

By 108 B.C., the Han state had established intermittent relations with more than thirty Japanese polities, a confederation called Wa, which acknowledged a hereditary ruler who resided in Yamatai. In A.D. 57 and again in 108, their ruler sent envoys bearing tribute payments, usually slaves and cloth, and requests to the imperial governor in Lolang, the provincial capital in northern Korea.

Between 147 and 189, a civil war raged in southern Japan, and for a number of years, there was no ruler. After the war, Wa had antagonistic relations with nearby groups and stationed an official north of its territory to oversee and intimidate people on the periphery. Wa's ruler was Pimiko, an unmarried noblewoman, who occupied herself with magic and sorcery after she ascended to the throne. She had a thousand women attendants and was served by a classificatory brother, who brought food and acted as her spokesman. She lived in a heavily guarded, fortified palace and levied taxes on neighboring communities. Between 238 and 247, she dispatched envoys on five different occasions to the kingdom of Wei, one of the powerful successor states that emerged in north China after the collapse of the Han empire. These envoys—who were received by a provincial governor residing in Taifeng near Seoul—brought tribute, acknowledged their loyalty to the Chinese, and requested his assistance in settling a dispute with their neighbors. When Pimiko, who had reigned for nearly fifty years, died, she was buried with a hundred retainers beneath a mound, perhaps similar to the keyhole-shaped burial mounds erected around Osaka in the late third and early fourth centuries A.D. during the formative years of the Yamato state. A male successor, who followed Pimiko on the throne, was soon assassinated and replaced by a young girl from Pimiko's lineage, possibly with the help of a border guard sent by the governor in Taifeng. Soon thereafter, the new ruler sent tribute—gems, textiles, and slaves—to the Wei court.

Chinese descriptions of Wa indicate that noblemen and noblewomen controlled separate but overlapping spheres of activities; war and administration were the domain of ruling-class men, whereas magic, sorcery, and communication with the supernatural world made up the sphere of elite women. The two spheres were complementary, not hierarchically organized.

Early keyhole-shaped tomb from the Kofun Period, southern Japan.

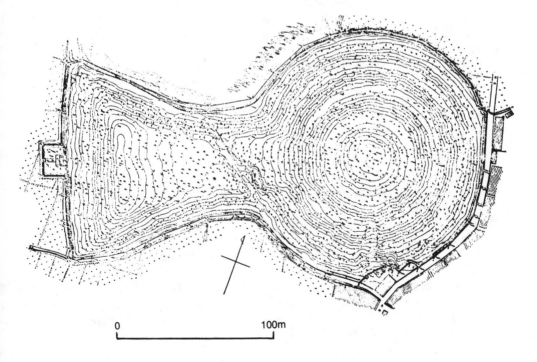

0   100m

Hypergamy—the practice in which commoner women marry elite men and thereby improve the status of their male relatives—is one practice that creates conditions that promote the development of complementary spheres of elite male and female activity. In Japan, during the third century A.D., the authority, prestige, and power of elite women grew as warfare became endemic and increasingly the domain of noblemen. Warfare, the elite's source of wealth, was also the locus of important ritual activities performed by its women, the ritual specialists who sanctified men's activities, giving them both legitimacy and power.

At the time, Yamato society was dominated by a continually shifting configuration of *uji*—landholding, bilateral kindreds—that maintained their positions by force, that extended their influence through marital and cooperative linkages with real and fictive collateral descent groups, and that rationalized their hegemony in terms of the religious power claimed by the family chieftains as a result of their descent from divine ancestors or former rulers. The *uji* controlled considerable numbers of agricultural workers and military forces. The royal family and the emperor, who claimed descent from the sun goddess, were merely first among equals. They shared state power with *uji* chieftains, who served the ruler at the same time as they struggled with one another to gain control over people's labor. Whereas the royal family, the chieftains allied with the state, and their immediate kin belonged to the ruling class, their more distant kin were poor relatives who had fallen on hard times.

During Pimiko's lifetime, gender was clearly only one consideration involved in selecting political and war leaders, and female rulers were not uncommon in either Japan or Korea in the early half of the first millennium A.D. Japanese chronicles describe the female Emperor Jinko as the descendant of a former emperor who became a royal consort in the late fourth century. She was a spirit medium capable of summoning and speaking for deities. After her husband's death, she ascended to the throne, maintained complex diplomatic and military relations with the three Korean kingdoms, and raised an army that subsequently defeated two of her dead husband's sons in a dispute over succession to the throne. Her ritual, administrative, and military powers contrast markedly with those of later noblewomen, who married kings, meddled in successional disputes, and even served as regents or corulers but lacked the capacity to sanctify political office because their ritual powers had increasingly become an integral part of the king's inheritance from his father.

Clearly, Jinko was a noblewomen with considerable ritual, administrative, and military power. However, elite women were no longer the only ritual specialists in Yamato society. One of her distant kin, the Emperor Sujin, who was the son of the emperor who also formed the basis of her claim to imperial descent, had many years earlier appointed an elite man, the descendant of a deity himself, to intercede with his divine ancestor. Thus, by the time Jinko ruled, both noblemen and noblewomen were ritual practitioners, the men as a result of their descent from a deity and the women by virtue of a perceived capacity to produce abundance and success. The male ritual specialists were, of course, the heads of local and regional *uji*, who performed ceremonies at ancestral Shinto shrines.

In mid-fifth-century Japan, kingship circulated among brothers, who competed for the throne because there was no recognized rule of succession. Potential heirs manipulated marriage and residence rules to gain allies and assembled retinues of noble warriors who supported their claims and eliminated or neutralized their rivals. This practice undermined any unifying tendencies and structure the Yamato court possessed since the various factions could and regularly did seek alliances with regional chieftains who lived on the margins of the state.

By the end of the century, the Yamato state completed its restructuring of the spheres of activity for elite men and women, creating a ritual domain for men while simultaneously diminishing the ritual roles of elite women. Although ruling-class men and women remained united against the commoners, gender relations within the ruling class had been transformed. Noblemen occupied political, administrative, and military roles that were sanctified by *uji* chieftain-priests, men who controlled ancestor worship and were part of the state apparatus. Since succession was regularized and kingship passed to the eldest surviving son, ruling-class women, especially those of the central or secondary royal lineages or the Soga clan, could become queens and the mothers of potential rulers. Thus, these women could expand their political influence as coregents.

The Emperor Keitai, a regional chieftain who claimed descent from earlier Yamato rulers, seized the throne in the early sixth century and transformed the structure of the state. He subjugated the autonomous *uji* on the margins of the state and incorporated their chieftain-priests into the state apparatus as its local representatives. He also seized agricultural estates to support the court; these were worked by peasants detached from local communities. The detached peasants, who were dependent on the state for their existence and reproduction, were supervised by special agents of the court or by the state's local representatives. The Emperor shared power with clans that provided soldiers and ritual specialists.

The *uji* that supported Keitai and his successors continued to pursue their own interests in the context of the alliance, and a dispute erupted among them in the mid-sixth century. On the surface, it concerned whether or not to accept Buddhism, but the real issue was whether to adopt Chinese and Korean institutions and practices, including Buddhism, to centralize power and strengthen the Japanese state. The Soga family, the main advocates for borrowing, were opposed by the clans that provided elite guards and Shinto ritualists for the court. The Soga defeated them in 587 and, five years later, placed a Soga niece on the throne. She reigned as female emperor until 628 and is portrayed as strong-willed and independent, on the one hand, and a puppet of her Soga kin, on the other.

A number of mainland institutions and practices were adopted or emulated during her reign. She adopted the Chinese-style title *tenno*, which means "master of the people and the whole land" and contrasts with the title *okimi*, "first among equals," used by earlier Yamato sovereigns. Her family appropriated for itself a number of the emperor's functions: praying for rain and entertaining envoys from the tribal peoples in the north. Buddhism flourished, and the Soga built a number of Buddhist temples. The emperor's brother, the crown prince, promoted a system of ministerial ranks and a written constitution and sent students to the continent to observe systems of government in T'ang China and Korea. Although the Soga family strengthened their positions, the imperial line, the Sun family, was not deprived of its powers. Its ancestress, the Sun Goddess, was elevated to the highest position in the Shinto pantheon and made ancestress to the nation.

The centralization of state power united ruling-class noblemen and noblewomen against commoners and their lower-ranking kin. It blurred the distinction between the formerly autonomous and complementary spheres of gender-related activities, which were gradually decomposed and reconstituted along new lines within the dominant class. Ruling-class noblewomen were no longer described as ritual specialists, spirit mediums, or oracles since new ritual domains had been constituted for members of the ruling class with close ties to the state. *Uji* chieftains and Shinto priests were the ritual specialists who interceded with ancestral deities, and Buddhist priests, who advocated the maintenance of social order, were increasingly influential voices of the state and the Soga family. Ruling-class women were now described as empress-consorts, the mothers and sisters of potential rulers, and even female emperors—roles that gave them considerable political influence.

In 645, a palace coup led by the Nakatomi clan destroyed the Soga family's power and influence at the imperial court. The new ruler, who claimed that kingship was the exclusive domain of the imperial family, descended from the Sun Goddess and former rulers, inaugurated a series of reforms that consolidated and strengthened the power of the imperial family and the state. The reforms were based on institutional practices adopted from mainland states and modified to meet local conditions, on various Buddhist beliefs about the necessity of maintaining social order, and on neo-Confucian concepts about the primacy of the state and administrative techniques.

The reforms attacked the privileges and power of the *uji*: the creation of a bureaucracy that was dependent on the state rather than the *uji* families, the redistribution of land to each peasant and to members of the ruling class for the offices they held and meritorious service to the emperor, and firming up distinctions between the high-ranking nobility that lived in or near the court and those that resided in the countryside. Although the reforms did not strip the *uji* chieftains of their power, they did place the state between the chieftains and their traditional bases of wealth and power. The *uji* system continued, but the activities of the chieftains were channeled in new directions since the reformers had imposed a system of land distribution and tax collection that transformed the peasants from hereditary dependents on local chieftains to state serfs who owed tributes and/or labor service directly to the central state. *Uji* society—which was based on regionally organized, bilateral kindreds—viewed labor, not land, as wealth. Wealth and power correlated with numbers of people; as a result, the wealthiest and most powerful *uji* were also the largest and, hence, the ones with the greatest capacity for extending their influence. As the Yamato rulers pushed individual rather than communal landholding into the *uji* homelands, the chieftains also began to accumulate landed property.

The reforms failed to resolve the successional disputes that had brought civil unrest to Yamato society. Conflicts erupted regularly because of the unresolved problems created by large numbers of potential heirs and the difficulties involved in getting rid of surplus claimants. The reforms also introduced other tensions. One that came to a head after the capital was moved to Heian in 784 involved the fragmentation of the *uji* communities into ruling-class segments closely linked with the imperial city and provincial gentry that continued to reside in the countryside. The number of *uji* that could participate in the affairs of state was restricted. The men who filled the highest offices of the bureaucracy were drawn from the urban, ruling-class segments, and their rural kin filled the lower-ranking positions in the provincial areas. Legal and administrative degrees that sustained the reforms called for military garrisons in provincial areas that were manned by local peasant conscripts under the leadership of local gentry. Thus, the rural chieftains, unlike their aristocratic kin in the capital, lived near their landholdings, had direct access to local labor, and were able to link the authority they derived from custom with the power that accrued to them through their hereditary state offices. In 743, the provincial officials received tax exemptions and hereditary rights to the lands that accompanied their offices. Their demand for labor increased sharply and led to corruption, local abuses, and the diminished flow of tax revenues to the higher levels of the state bureaucracy. However, when state power weakened and the garrisons were disbanded, the provincial military organizations continued to operate. Their members were drawn from the rural gentry and rich peasants, who were increasingly less constrained because of the growing impotence of the emperor and the urban-based, upper levels of the bureaucracy.

The inheritance of landed property became an important issue after land was privatized in the late seventh century. According to the legal code of 701, eldest sons inherited the residence, slaves, servants, and half the movable property of their fathers, and the remainder of the movable property was divided among his brothers. Thus women could not inherit landed property. A new legal code promulgated in 718 stipulated that land and residences were to be apportioned among the eldest son, his mother, his brothers, and his sisters in a 4:4:2:1 ratio. Thus, women of the rural gentry were able to assert their rights of inheritance, both as the daughters and the sisters of landowners and as the mothers of their eldest sons. Although women of the courtier and gentry classes could not amass landed property by holding office, they could inherit it from men. They continued to inherit and own landed estates into the fourteenth century. As a result, they had their own siphon, independent from that of their male kin, to tap the wealth of the countryside.

Southeast Asia

The tradition of sedentary, agricultural communities in Southeast Asia stretches far back into the past, long before states appeared on the plains of north China or in the Ganges River Valley. The small village communities, made up of farmers and metalsmiths, that dotted the landscapes of the interior were already exchanging goods with their contemporaries in the coastal areas by 2000 B.C. There were increasingly frequent contacts between these villages and their successors and the state-based societies of China and India during the later half of the first millennium B.C. Intensification, new products, and novel ideas were consequences of the new social relations that developed as the region became a hinterland for state-based societies to the north and west.

The Dongson communities centered in the Red River Valley of North Vietnam were the most distant of the southern barbarians encountered by Han merchants in the second century B.C. The site of Co Loa near Hanoi, established a century earlier, was surrounded by three ramparts and two moats, which were built over a period of several hundred years. The outermost rampart enclosed nearly 1,500 acres of land and reservoirs. Nearby cemeteries dating to this period indicate that there were status differences in the society. Some caches, since hardly any human bones have survived in many of the tombs, contained axes, daggers, spearheads, and large metal vessels; others yielded dugout canoes as well as bronze weapons and utensils, a few of which may have come from China. However, the bulk of the bronze objects, including a 150-pound drum, were manufactured locally by Dongson smiths, who specialized in the production of both bronze and iron objects. Similar moated villages and cultural remains, dating to this period, have also been found on the alluvial plains of the Chao Phraya River, which empties into the Gulf of Thailand below Bangkok.

The moated villages appeared suddenly and marked a significant departure from the existing pattern of small, self-sufficient communities. The construction of moats, reservoirs, and ramparts required considerable amounts of labor power and represents the intensification of community-level relations of production and increased levels of food production to support the men and women who built them. These settlements are currently viewed as centers where petty chieftains or bigmen prospered by controlling the production of metal objects and the trade in salt.

Protostates—that is, societies in which the institutions and practices of class and state have precipitated but have not yet been consolidated or reproduced—began to appear in parts of Southeast Asia around A.D. 200. The best known, and perhaps the most important, was Funan, which was centered on the lower course and delta of the Mekong River. Its capital city was Vyadhapura (Temu) located in southern Cambodia about 150 miles from the sea and its trading emporium, Oc-èo, in the lower Mekong Delta. Canals connected Oc-èo with villages that were located more than 40 miles inland. The commercial center in the delta covered more than 1,100 acres, and like earlier seats of chiefly power in the area, it was surrounded by a moat and wooden palisades. Its inhabitants lived in raised bamboo houses set on stilts or pilings and included foreign merchants among their numbers. At the center of the city was the king's two-story palace and a shrine that was tall enough to be seen from great distances in the surrounding countryside.

Traditions indicate that Funan's first male ruler was a foreigner, who married the daughter of a powerful local chieftain, and that the people of the polity subsequently chose one of their male descendants as a war leader. This war chief attacked and subjugated neighboring communities and kingdoms during the third century A.D. As a result, Funan's frontier and sphere of influence shifted almost continuously as groups variously acquiesced to its demands, allied themselves with its chieftains, resisted their attempted extortions, or rebelled. About the same time, Funan was rapidly being incorporated into maritime commercial networks that extended westward to the Malay Peninsula and the Ganges Delta, southward into the island world of Indonesia, and northeastward to coastal China and beyond. This combination of circumstances meant that the Funan chieftains or rulers had to work out practices that would simultaneously allow them to control the production of food and commodities, to regulate the activities of the merchants engaged in the overseas trade, and to mediate between the foreign merchants and the local populations.

This was not a problem during the fourth century, when the volume of commerce grew steadily and the Funan rulers derived most of their revenues from the foreign merchants, many of whom were Buddhists who had trading partners with similar class-based religious beliefs in India, the Malay Peninsula, and the islands to the south. However, it became a major problem after 450, when ships ladened with goods from India or Java avoided navigational hazards and the growing threat of piracy along the Funan coast by sailing directly to Cham's trading emporia on the east coast of Vietnam. The fortunes of Funan declined rapidly, and the inhabitants of its trading center abandoned the city.

Up to that time, the Funan rulers had demanded little from the farming communities and peasant villages that made up the agrarian sector of its economy. In the mid-fifth-century, as its need for revenues from the agrarian sector increased, the state demanded enormous amounts of labor to expand the water-management system. It concentrated labor power on irrigated lands that were controlled by the ruler and the state; it jettisoned its ties with Buddhist merchants and installed Brahman ritual specialists to assist in the administration of the increasingly agricultural domain; and it moved the capital city inland to Angkor in the agricultural belt. The attempt to reorganize the Funan state failed in the sixth century because of internal disputes,

Angkor Wat.

struggles over succession, opposition from neighboring communities, and polities. As its position declined, Cham and Khmer became the centers of civilized state-based societies, one on the coast and the other inland, the former deriving its revenues largely from commerce and the latter from the goods and corvée labor of the farmers who built the shrines and supported the temple personnel of the capital, Angkor Wat.

FURTHER READINGS: A BRIEF GUIDE

The archaeology of the Far East is typically treated geographically. For overviews of China, see Kwang-chih Chang, *The Archaeology of Ancient China* (New Haven, CT: Yale University Press, 1986); Jacques Gernet, *A History of Chinese Civilization* (Cambridge: Cambridge University Press, 1982); Henri Maspero, *China in Antiquity* (Amherst: University of Massachusetts Press, 1978); and Paul Wheatley, *The Pivot of the Four Quarters: A Preliminary Enquiry into the Origins and Character of the Ancient Chinese City* (Chicago: Aldine, 1972).

Southeast Asia and its insular extensions are surveyed by Peter Bellwood, *Prehistory of the Indo-Malaysian Archipelago* (Orlando, FL: Academic Press, 1985); Charles Higham, *The Archaeology of Mainland Southeast Asia from 10,000 B.C. to the Fall of Angkor* (Cambridge: Cambridge University Press, 1989) and "The Later Prehistory of Mainland Southeast Asia," *Journal of World Prehistory*, vol. 3, no. 3 (1989), 235–282; Donn T. Bayard, ed., *The Origins of Agriculture, Metallurgy, and the State in Mainland Southeast Asia* (Dunedin, NZ: Otago University Press, 1984); J. Peter White and James F. O'Connell, *A Prehistory of Australia, New Guinea and Sahul* (Sydney: Academic Press, 1982);

Paul Wheatley, *Nagara and Commandery*, Research Paper Nos. 207–208 (Chicago: Department of Geography, University of Chicago, 1983), and "Satyarta in Survarnadvipa: From Reciprocity to Redistribution in Ancient Southeast Asia," in *Ancient Civilizations and Trade*, ed. C. C. Lamberg-Karlovsky and Jeremy A. Sabloff (Albuquerque: University of New Mexico Press, 1975), pp. 227–284; Kenneth R. Hall, *Maritime Trade and State Development in Early Southeast Asia* (Honolulu: University of Hawaii Press, 1985); George Coedès, *The Indianized States of Southeast Asia* (Honolulu: University of Hawaii Press, 1964); G. Carter Bentley, "Indigenous States of Southeast Asia," *Annual Review of Anthropology*, vol. 15 (1986), 275–305; R. B. Smith and W. Watson, eds., *Early South East Asia* (Oxford: Oxford University Press, 1979); L. Cabot Briggs, *The Ancient Khmer Empire*, Transactions of the American Philosophical Society, no. 41 (Philadelphia, 1951); and Leonid A. Sedov, "Angkor: Society and State," in *The Early State*, ed. Henri J. Claessen and Peter Skalník (The Hague: Mouton Publishers, 1978), pp. 111–130.

Korea and Japan are surveyed by C. Melvin Aikens and Takayasu Higuchi, *Prehistory of Japan* (New York: Academic Press, 1981); Jeong-Hak Kim, *The Prehistory of Korea* (Honolulu: University of Hawaii Press, 1978); Sarah M. Nelson, "Recent Progress in Korean Archaeology," in *Advances in World Archaeology*, ed. Fred Wendorf and Angela Close, vol. 1 (New York: Academic Press, 1982), pp. 103–150; (Richard Pearson, Gina L. Barnes, and Karl L. Hutterer, eds., *Windows on the Japanese Past: Studies in Archaeology and Prehistory* (Ann Arbor: Center for Japanese Studies, University of Michigan, 1986); Richard Pearson, "Chiefly Exchange Between Kyushu and Okinawa, Japan, in the Yayoi Period," and Hiroshi Tsude, "Chiefly Lineages in Kofun-Period Japan: Political Relations Between Centre and Region," both in *Antiquity*, vol. 64, no. 245 (1990), 912–922 and 923–928; Cornelius J. Kiley, "State and Dynasty in Achaic Yamato," *Journal of Asian Studies*, vol. XXXIII, no. 1 (1973), 25–50; Thomas C. Patterson, "Gender, Class, and State Formation in Ancient Japan," (Philadelphia, 1989); and Gina L. Barnes, "*Jiehao, tonghao*: Peer Relations in East Asia," in *Peer Polity Interaction and Socio-political Change*, ed. Colin Renfrew and John F. Cherry, (Cambridge: Cambridge University Press, 1987), pp. 79–92, and "The Role of the *be* in the Formation of the Yamato State," in *Specialization, Exchange, and Complex Societies*, ed. Elizabeth M. Brumfiel and Timothy K. Earle (Cambridge: Cambridge University Press, 1987), pp. 86–101.

The archaeology and history of the inner Asian steppes are discussed by Owen Lattimore, *The Inner Asian Frontiers of China* (New York: American Geographical Society, 1940); René Grousset, *The Empire of the Steppes: A History of Central Asia* (New Brunswick, NJ: Rutgers University Press, 1970); Ildikó Lehtinen, *Traces of the Central Asian Culture in the North; Finnish-Soviet Joint Scientific Symposium Held in Hanasaari, Espoo 14–21 January 1985*, Suomalais-Ugrilaisen Seuran Toimituksia, Mémoires de la Société Finno-Ougrienne 194 (Helsinki: Suomalais-Ugrilainen Seura, 1986); and Esther Jacobsen, *Burial Ritual, Gender and Status in South Siberia in the Late Bronze-Early Iron Age*. Papers on Inner Asia, no. 7 (Bloomington, IN: Indiana University, 1987).

Useful surveys of the development of early food-producing communities in the Far East are Charles Higham and Bernard Maloney, "Coastal Adaptation, Sedentism, and Domestication: A Model for Socio-economic Intensification in Southeast Asia," Jack Golson, "The Origins and Development of New Guinea Agriculture," and Les Groube, "The Taming of the Rain Forests: A Model for Late Pleistocene Forest Exploitation in New Guinea," all in *Foraging and Farming: The Evolution of Plant Exploitation*, ed. David R. Harris and Gordon C. Hillman (London: Unwin Hyman, 1989), pp. 650–666, 678–687, and 282–304; Charles Higham, "The Ban Chiang Culture in Wider Perspective," *Proceedings of the British Academy*, vol. LXIX (London, 1983), pp. 229–261; Chester A. Gorman, "A Priori Models and Thai Prehistory: A Reconsideration of the Beginnings of Agriculture in Southeast Asia," in *Origins of Agriculture*, ed. Charles A. Reed (The Hague: Mouton Publishers, 1977), pp. 321–355; Richard Pearson and Anne Underhill, "The Chinese Neolithic: Recent Trends in Research," *American Anthropologist*, vol. 89, no. 4 (1989), 807–822; Richard Pearson, "Social Complexity in Chinese Coastal Neolithic Sites," *Science*, vol. 213 (1981), 1078–1088; Ping-ti Ho, "Loess and the Origins of Chinese Agriculture," *The American Historical Review*, vol. 75, no. 1 (1969), 1–36; Takeru Akazawa, "Cultural Change in Prehistoric Japan: Receptivity to Rice Agriculture in the Japanese Archipelago," in *Advances in World Archaeology*, ed. Fred Wendorf and Angela Close, vol. 1 (New York: Academic Press, 1982), pp. 154–212.

The settlement of the Pacific Islands is discussed by Peter Bellwood, "The Prehistory of Island Southeast Asia: A Multidisciplinary Review of Recent Research," *Journal of World Prehistory*, vol. 1, no. 2 (1987), 171–224; Patrick V. Kirch, "Advances in Polynesian Prehistory: Three Decades in Review," in *Advances in World Archaeology*, ed. Fred Wendorf and Angela Close, vol. 1, (New York: Academic Press, 1982), pp. 52–102; and Matthew Spriggs and Christopher Chippendale, eds., "Special Section: Early Settlement of Island Southeast Asia and the Western Pacific," *Antiquity*, vol. 63, no. 240 (1989), 547–626.

Evidence for Lung-shan class and state formation in north China during the third millennium B.C. is presented by Chi Li, S. Y. Liang, T. P. Tung, S. N. Fu, C. T. Wu, P. C. Kuo, and Y. H. Liu, *Ch'eng-tzu-yai*, no. 52 (New Haven, CT: Yale University Publications in Anthropology, [1934] 1956). Subsequent episodes of class and state in north China are examined by Morton H. Fried, "Tribe to State or State to Tribe in Ancient China?" Kwang-chih Chang, "Sandai Archeology and the Formation of States in Ancient China: Processual Aspects of the Origins of Chinese Civilization," and David N. Keightley, "The Late Shang State: When, Where, and What?" all in *The Origins of Chinese Civilization*, ed. David Keightley (Berkeley: University of California Press, 1983), pp. 467–494, 495–522, and 523–564; Kwang-chih Chang, *Shang Civilization* (New Haven, CT: Yale University Press, 1980); Kwang-chih Chang, ed., *Studies of Shang Archaeology* (New Haven, CT: Yale University Press, 1986); and David N. Keightley, *Sources of Shang History: The*

Oracle-Bone Inscriptions of Bronze Age China (Berkeley: University of California Press, 1978).

Subsequent episodes of class and state formation are examined by Charles O. Hucker, *China's Imperial Past: An Introduction to Chinese History and Culture* (Stanford, CA: Stanford University Press, 1975); Shouyi Bai, ed., *An Outline History of China* (Beijing: Foreign Languages Press, 1982); Cho-yun Hsu and Katheryn M. Linduff, *Western Chou Civilization* (New Haven, CT: Yale University Press, 1988); Zhongshu Wang, *Han Civilization* (New Haven, CT: Yale University Press, 1982); Denis Twitchett and Michael Loewe, eds., *The Cambridge History of China*, vol. 1, *The Ch'in and Han Empires, 221 B.C.–A.D. 220* (Cambridge: Cambridge University Press, 1986); Arthur Cotterell, *The First Emperor of China* (London: Penguin Books, 1981); and Albert E. Dien, ed., *State and Society in Early Medieval China* (Stanford, CA: Stanford University Press, 1990). The worldviews that emerged during the first millennium B.C. are surveyed by Colan A. Ronan, *The Shorter Science and Civilisation in China: An Abridgement of Joseph Needham's Original Text*, vol. 1 (Cambridge: Cambridge University Press, 1978).

Rebellion and surveillance in the Han state are discussed by Anthony F. P. Hulsewé, "Royal Rebels," *Bulletin de l'Ecole Francaise d'Etrême-orient*, tome LXIX (1981), 315–325; Rafe de Crespigny, "Inspection and Surveillance Officials under the Two Han Dynasties," in *State and Law in East Asia; Festschrift Karl Búrger*, ed. Dieter Eikmeier and Herbert Frank (Wiesbaden, Ger.: Otto Harrassowitz, 1981), pp. 40–79; and Howard S. Levy, "Yellow Turban Religion and Rebellion at the End of Han," *Journal of the American Oriental Society*, vol. 76 (1956), 214–227.

chapter 9

Africa and Egypt

Ancient Egypt was not a sudden and miraculous flower of the African genius. It was not an oasis. It was not an isolate. . . . Egypt was the node and center of a vast web linking the strands of Africa's main cultures and languages. (Ivan Van Sertima, "Race and Origin of the Egyptians.")

Through Pharaonic Egypt, Africa lays claim to being the cradle of one of the earliest and most spectacular civilizations of antiquity. (Bruce Trigger, "The Rise of Egyptian Civilization")

In reality, whatever may have been the "virtues" of Egypt's social organization, it finally created, like Greece, intolerable abuses and uprisings as virulent as the Greco-Roman revolts. (Cheikh Anta Diop, The African Origin of Civilization: Myth or Reality*)*

If Orientalist Eurocentrism has fabricated ex nihilo *the myth of the "Orient," this myth cannot be countered with a corresponding, inverted "Afro-Asianist" myth, but only with specific and concrete analyses of each of the sociocultural areas in the two continents. (Samir Amin,* Eurocentrism*)*

Africa is a gigantic plateau whose highest part is its eastern edge; it dips gradually toward the north and the west, and large rivers—the Nile, Congo, and Niger—drain much of the plateau before emptying into the Mediterranean Sea or the Atlantic Ocean. The Sahara Desert, an expanse of rock and sand more than 3,000 miles wide, now stretches across all of North Africa. Tropical forests appear beyond the Sahel grasslands that fringe the southern edge of the desert; they rim the coastline of West Africa from Nigeria to Zaire before reaching inland to the Ruwenzori Mountains. Below the rain forests lie the grasslands and deserts of Southwest Africa, which stretch from Angola and Zimbabwe to the southernmost tip of the continent. East Africa is covered with scrub forests and grasslands that reach northward into the Sudan, where they gradually merge with the Sahara.

Africa is an old continent. Two-billion-year-old rocks and sediments make up its southern part. More than 15 million years ago, a massive rift developed in East Africa. Active volcanoes appeared along the fault and spewed lava over the countryside. Lakes formed and became progressively more saline as seasonal streams dumped their waters onto the floor of the rift valley. Several million years later, waters from Lake Victoria began to flow northward and ultimately merged with the tributaries of the old Nile River, which rose in the Ethiopian highlands. The waters of these combined rivers flowed northward, plunging through narrow gorges and flowing steadily across the Sahara as they dropped from an elevation of more than 3,700 feet to sea level during the course of their 4,000-mile journey.

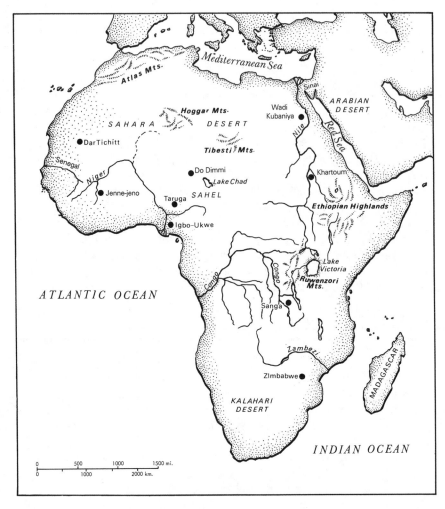

Africa.

During the last million years or so, the vegetation cover of the Sahara has alternated between desert and tropical grasslands. When glaciers formed in the upper middle latitudes of Eurasia and North America, the grasslands fringing the southern edge of the Sahara pushed northward, and the mountains in the central part of the desert—the Tibesti and the Hoggar—received more water than they do now. About 15,000 years ago, forests grew in the desert highlands, and streams flowed from them into large permanent lakes—like Lake Chad, which covered 120,000 square miles—that were scattered through the Sahel grasslands at the time. As the northern glaciers retreated, the climatic and environmental conditions of the Sahara were changing. By 8000 B.C., the margins of the desert were already expanding southward, and areas that had once been well watered were becoming progressively drier. Lake Chad shrank to less than a tenth of its former size, and some of the smaller bodies of water disappeared altogether.

THE DEVELOPMENT OF FOOD-PRODUCING ECONOMIES: FISHING, PASTORALISM, AND AGRICULTURE

Small communities have camped or settled along the margins of African lakes and rivers for millennia. One group, which spent at least part of its year near the Nile at Wadi Kubbaniya in Upper Egypt about 18,000 years ago, hunted mammals; fished and collected mollusks from the river; ground the rhizomes of sedges, rushes, and waterlilies in stone mortars; and gathered wild millets and fruits from the floodplain and nearby habitats. Judging by the infant feces found in the excavations, the inhabitants of the camp weaned young children on a finely ground plant-food mush. Their contemporaries and successors in other lacustrine and riverine environments probably pursued similar subsistence activities and consumed similar arrays of locally and seasonally available foodstuffs.

Groups lived at a number of riverside and lakeshore localities in the Rift Valley and along the broad band of lakes and streams that formed across the central and southern Sahara during wet periods. They had a relatively uniform material culture that is sometimes called Mesolithic because of the importance of aquatic resources. By the seventh millennium B.C., the inhabitants of camps from the Atlantic Ocean to the Sudan and southward to the headwaters of the Nile exploited their rich and varied aquatic faunas of lakes and rivers—mollusks, fish, hippopotamuses, and crocodiles; they fished with shell hooks and harpoons and used spears tipped with small stone points to kill large aquatic animals and antelopes, gazelles, and other mammals found in nearby grassland habitats. Many of them used pottery vessels, decorated with wavy lines, to carry and store water and grains and to cook food. As the lakes along the central and southern margins of the Sahara began to dry up, first the small and then the larger ones, the Mesolithic communities either abandoned the region or devoted more of their time and energy to other subsistence practices, notably pastoralism and plant cultivation.

Groups in the Tibesti Mountains of southern Libya and northern Chad kept small herds of domesticated cattle and other livestock as early as the seventh millennium B.C. This suggests that cattle may have been domesticated independently in North Africa at about the same time or shortly after they were domesticated in southeastern Europe and Anatolia. Cattle herding spread quite rapidly in North Africa. Groups that moved through the grassland environments of the Sudan already had herds in the sixth millennium B.C., and a thousand years later most of the meat consumed by the inhabitants of Capelletti Cave in northern Algeria came from domesticated cattle. By the fourth millennium B.C., groups across the southern Sahara from Khartoum in the Nile Valley to Niger and Mali and southward into the Rift Valley of East Africa kept domesticated cattle along with smaller numbers of goats and sheep. More than 2,000 years ago, some communities in the South African grasslands were already herding cattle and goats.

Cattle played an increasingly important role in the subsistence economies of peoples who lived in the grasslands and savannas of the Sahel and eastern and southern Africa. They were a means of production, a source of wealth that reproduced itself and multiplied, rather than a raw material that was plucked from the environment to be consumed immediately. Cattle herding was a time-consuming, labor-intensive activity. The animals had to be watered and pastured, which often required moving them over considerable distances; they had to be milked each day; and they had to be protected from predators. When the pastoralists were fortunate, their herds grew and their wealth increased.

The cattle herders of the Sahel and East Africa were fortunate. They may have been the world's wealthiest people around the beginning of the third millennium B.C. This wealth attracted the attention of the rulers of the small city-states that were crystallizing at the time in Upper Egypt. Narmer, the unifier of Upper and Lower Egypt and the founder of the Egyptian state's First Dynasty, sent an expedition into Nubia and the Sudan to establish diplomatic relations, to trade, and to pillage and plunder. A contemporary account indicates that the spoils of the campaign included 400,000 cattle, 1,422,000 goats, and 120,000 human captives. Several centuries later, Sneferu, a Fourth Dynasty ruler, stole 200,000 head of cattle and enslaved 7,000 persons on another campaign into Nubia. These were clearly not the only cattle-rustling and slave-raiding expeditions sent by the Egyptian rulers against the wealthy, kin-organized communities that lay beyond the margins of the state; in some periods, they occurred fairly frequently. The captives acquired on these forays became soldiers or field hands who expanded agricultural fields and pastures in the Nile Valley; the stolen livestock fed the growing population of the state and added materially to the wealth of its ruling class, as Richard Lobban (1988) has argued.

More than 15,000 years ago, the inhabitants of desert and grasslands environments of the Sahara and Sahel were already harvesting a variety of wild cereal grasses and grinding their seeds on stone mortars. The cultivation of some of these grasses may have begun as early as the sixth millennium B.C. Sorghum was the most widespread of the African cereals. Domesticated sorghum, the wild forms of which are indigenous to the Sahara grasslands, was already being consumed in Yemen and Arabia during the later half of the third millennium B.C., and there are reports that it was used around Khartoum in the sixth millennium B.C. Finger millet, the wild forms of which are found in the uplands of Ethiopia, Kenya, and Uganda, was being cultivated by the middle of the fifth millennium B.C. in the Ethiopian Highlands; teff and noog, two other cereal grains, were also domesticated in this region. The Niger River Delta was another center, where African rice, fonio, and yams were domesticated, possibly during the third millennium B.C., judging by the rather sudden appearance of ground stone axes in the region.

Widely scattered farming villages appeared in the Nile River Valley around 5000 B.C. Their inhabitants lived in reed huts. They planted barley and emmer wheat in the mud flats around the margins of the swamps and lakes that bordered the river, and they harvested the crops and wild grasses with small stone sickles set in wooden handles and stored them in basket-lined silos built on high ground next to the villages. They kept a few goats and sheep, fished, and hunted aquatic animals and those that came out of the savanna for water. Some villagers wore ornaments made of shells from the Mediterranean or amazonite, a mineral that comes from the Tibesti Mountains to the west.

Many of the early food-producing communities in Africa had mixed subsistence economies that combined hunting and foraging with fishing, livestock herding, and farming. In some of the earliest food-producing communities, the various activities and practices of the subsistence economy may have been organized or scheduled around line and harpoon fishing. Although fishing has continued to provide important quantities of food in some areas even to the present day, it no longer plays the dominant or pivotal role it did 8,000 or 9,000 years ago. The activities associated with cattle and livestock herding gradually became the ones that structured and scheduled the other subsistence practices of the communities with mixed economies. By the fourth millennium B.C., the pastoral sectors of mixed subsistence economies were the motors that organized society, drove food production, and created wealth in the vast grassland areas of the continent that stretch from the Atlantic coast through the Sahel to the Sudan and southward to the Cape of Good Hope. Agriculture—the cultivation of fodder and foodstuffs—which became the dominant economic sector in a few regions, like the Nile Valley, seems to have been of secondary importance and existed in symbiosis in those regions where livestock herding was vigorously pursued.

THE FORMATION AND DISINTEGRATION OF EARLY STATES IN EGYPT

During the fourth millennium B.C., village communities with mixed subsistence economies occurred mainly in two parts of the Nile River Valley in Egypt. There was a cluster of villages and hamlets at the head of the delta in Lower Egypt near Cairo; three communities—This, Naqada, and Hierakonpolis—about 400 to 500 miles upstream, dominated the cultural landscape of Upper Egypt. The intervening part of the valley was only sparsely inhabited at the time.

Early State Formation in Upper Egypt

Class and state formation occurred in the corporate, landholding communities of Upper Egypt. The processes involved at least the partial resolution of structural tensions between relations of production that operated at

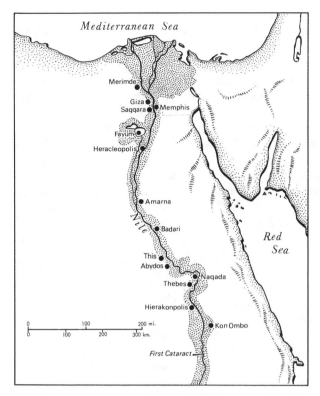

Ancient Egypt.

two different levels. This was the dilemma. Households with different numbers and mixes of men, women, elderly persons, and children were the real units of appropriation in these communities; households with many productive individuals had the capacity or potential to produce a surplus above and beyond what they needed to sustain themselves: wealth that could be passed on to the next generation. However, the households also had to participate in activities and relations that operated at the level of the community in order to retain access to the collectively held lands, means of production, and raw materials; these practices typically redistributed labor and goods horizontally, which blocked or inhibited the development of wealth differences among the various households. By 3500 B.C., the paradox was at least partially resolved, judging by the unequal accumulation of wealth among the various households of each community. However, the goods accumulated by one generation of the domestic groups were not put at the disposal of their descendants; they were placed in the tombs of the dead, where they were not supposed to be retrieved either by the members of the households themselves or by the community.

Differences between richer and poorer graves in the cemeteries of the three Upper Egyptian communities bear witness to the development of status or class differentiation. There were typically two kinds of tombs in the small village cemeteries: The majority of the individuals were interred with only a few grave goods, whereas the tombs of a few individuals in each settlement were more lavishly furnished. The more diverse burial practices and tomb types in the cemeteries near the three large towns suggest that wealth differentials and social stratification were more developed there.

The practice of removing goods from circulation stimulated subsistence production, the beginnings of craft specialization, local exchange, and grave robbery; it also intensified the acquisition of exotic materials from distant places: ivory, ebony, and other goods from the lands to the south; turquoise and copper from the Sinai; olive oil from Palestine; lapis lazuli from Afghanistan, marine shells; and manufactured items from Mesopotamia. Gold was one of the raw materials the Upper Egyptian communities introduced in these exchange networks. The materials were carried overland or by boats that traveled up and down the Nile. The community at This controlled traffic along the Nile with the villages in the delta and beyond; Naqada controlled gold mines in the eastern desert and had easy access to the Red Sea; and Hierakonpolis was the emporium for goods from Nubia and sub-Saharan Africa.

The three Upper Egyptian communities struggled with one another for control of foreign goods. Judging by changes in the kinds of tombs that were built, Naqada was the first loser in the three-way struggle for power; this event may be related in the early Upper Egyptian myth that describes how Horus, the falcon and patron deity of Hierakonpolis, defeated Seth, the god of the community centered at Naqada. A few decades later, the residents of Hierakonpolis also stopped building elaborate tombs, as This asserted its hegemony over the region. The ruling family incorporated these essentially local deities into a state pantheon and gave each of them attributes that explained and supported the existence of the new state; for example, Horus became the main deity and embodiment of kingship, and Seth became the sponsor of royal power. By doing so, the rulers simultaneously acknowledged the local communities and the cults dedicated to their patron deities and rationalized their existence. The communities incorporated into the state undoubtedly emphasized different attributes of their local gods than the ones attributed to them by the state.

Shortly before 3000 B.C., Narmer, an Upper Egyptian ruler from This, and Scorpion, one of his predecessors, attacked and defeated communities in the delta and the oases of the western desert. Narmer unified Upper and Lower Egypt and was the first ruler portrayed wearing the crowns of two regions. After asserting control over the sparsely inhabited middle portions of the Nile Valley, which were becoming a haven for refugees from the subordinated communities and disenfranchised classes, Narmer then turned his attention against the peoples and communities that lived beyond the frontier to the south. He sent an expedition that built and garrisoned a fort in the borderlands on Elephantine Island, about 80 miles upstream from Hierakonpolis, near the foot of the First Cataract—the rapids and waterfalls at Aswan. His forces then attacked Nubia. A First Dynasty relief carved on

The Narmer palette.

cliffs overlooking the river near the Second Cataract, more than 200 miles upstream from the garrison at Elephantine Island, depicted a Nubian prisoner bound to the prow of an Egyptian boat.

While the institutions and trappings of a class structure and an imperial dynasty were crystallizing in Upper Egypt toward the end of the fourth millennium B.C., the contemporary communities of Nubia, known as the A-Group culture, followed a different historical trajectory. About 3500 B.C., many of the A-Group settlements were riverbank campsites inhabited by small numbers of people with diverse, mixed subsistence economies. They herded livestock, farmed a little, fished, hunted, and harvested wild plant foods. They buried their dead in graves on high ground above the floodplain. The early A-Group tombs contained a range of goods manufactured in Upper Egypt: pottery vessels that probably arrived filled with cheese and oil, copper tools, and linen cloth, to name only a few. Bruce Trigger (1976:38–44) believes that some Nubian merchants profited in late predynastic times by virtue of their position astride a trade route that brought ivory, panther and leopard skins, incense, and oils northward to Egypt from the wealthy, cattle-rich areas to the south.

The prosperity of the communities in Nubia climaxed during the First Dynasty. Some Nubian communities may have been trading partners of the Upper Egyptian elite, whereas others were merchants or mercenaries who gained materially by providing goods and slaves or securing the trade route for the rapidly developing state-based society to the north. However, their prosperity was short-lived, for many of the Nubian communities fled to avoid the raids and exactions of the Egyptian state and/or its local clients. As a result, Nubia was effectively abandoned by the end of the First Dynasty.

Six features of Egyptian state society during the First and Second Dynasties merit special mention. First, the royal courts rejected outside influences and created an indigenous court culture and a set of artistic canons that influenced the development of Egyptian art for the next three millennia. Second, the traditional leaders of local communities incorporated into the state were brought into the state apparatus as its local representatives. Third, succession to the throne, which was not fixed, was usually pressed by an individual's kin relations with the mothers, wives, and daughters of rulers; as a result, women in the royal court wielded considerable power by virtue of their kin connections with the ruler and their roles as priestesses in various state and local cults. Fourth, since royal power was typically weak shortly after new rulers had ascended to the throne, these were usually the times when local leaders revolted and attempted to reassert the autonomy of the communities. Fifth, the contradiction created by the attempts of local communities to reassert their independence and the state's aim to consolidate its hegemony over them was reproduced through time. Sixth, the royal court was relocated to Memphis, located near Cairo, after a number of communities in the delta revolted during the Second Dynasty.

The Old Kingdom

The rulers of the Old Kingdom—the Third to the Sixth Dynasties (c. 3000 to 2470 B.C.)—resided in palaces in Lower Egypt at the head of the delta and attempted to concentrate political power, first in the hands of the royal household, and then in a bureaucracy that developed out of the royal household. The countryside was divided into a series of *nomes*—administrative territories whose boundaries coincided closely with those of established village communities. They were administered by local leaders, whose positions of power were made hereditary by their relationship with the king and whose authority derived from their interactions with their kin and neighbors. At first, the literate palace and state officials were usually members or close kin of the royal family; later, commoners were incorporated into the bureaucracy and supported by fields that were attached to their offices. Although the ruler retained the right to dismiss these officials, their positions were increasingly passed from father to son. Thus, by the beginning of the Third Dynasty, there was an emerging, relatively independent class of functionaries, whose members accumulated wealth, purchased land from the king's men, and had the capacity to threaten the state's attempt to concentrate and centralize political power. At this time, the state was held together symbolically by the ruler's biennial tours of the domain and in reality by the army, whose officers played no administrative role in the state bureaucracy.

The processes of class formation that occurred in the Third Dynasty drew a sharper distinction between the rulers and the ruled. Artisans of various sorts were attached to the households of the royal families, of the most powerful state officials, and of provincial leaders who had prospered by virtue of their ties to the state. The tombs of these individuals became much larger and more lavishly furnished. For instance, the tomb of an early queen was enclosed in a 185-by–83-foot structure consisting of five rooms, each with storage magazines containing gold, pottery, and other objects the queen had used or accumulated during her lifetime. Outside the structure were 62 graves, each containing the remains of a slave who was sacrificed and buried at the time the queen was interred. The mausoleum of another ruler, King Djer, contained the remains of 580 individuals who were entombed when the crypt was sealed. The royal tombs contained goods that would satisfy every need of their occupants in the afterlife—servants, gardens, and even lavatories. The tombs of minor officials located across the river from the Memphis cemetery at Saqqara and in the provincial capitals were small-scale versions of the royal tombs. Artisans were buried next to their masters and mistresses; their graves contained a few pots and the tools they had used during their lifetimes.

The construction of elaborate tombs culminated in the Fourth Dynasty, when the three great pyramids of Giza were built. The largest is more than 750 feet a side at the base and covers 13 acres. There are more than 2 million limestone blocks in the pyramid weighing up to 15 tons each; the nine slabs that form the roof of the king's burial chamber each weigh 50 tons. Workers' barracks located next to the construction site housed 2,500 to 4,000 individuals, who were engaged full time in the construction work at the building site. In addition, gangs of men and women worked in the quarries, transported blocks to the sorting area at the foot of the pyramids, and supplied the artisans with food. Herodotus tells us that it took 100,000 persons, one-tenth of Egypt's entire population, working twenty years to complete just one of the pyramids. This was an incredible burden on the people of the Nile, who provided the labor and goods that sustained the ruling class.

The construction of the great pyramids coincided with a number of other developments during the Fourth Dynasty. First, King Sneferu sent an armed expedition into Nubia to acquire cattle and slaves; he and his successors also sent several expeditions into the Levant to acquire raw materials and, with the aid of Nubian mercenaries, to suppress the activities of the desert nomads and inhabitants of southern Palestine. Second, the royal family began to eliminate the local leaders of the *nomes* and replace them with officials whose position depended on their loyalty to the king; some of the new administrators were responsible for raising taxes and corvée labor from

Reconstruction of how the pyramids at Giza were built.

the peasant populations. Third, the cult dedicated to the sun god, Re, became increasingly important during the Fourth and Fifth Dynasties, as rulers began to refer to themselves as the "son of the sun" rather than with the earlier Horus appellation. In one instance, the ruler's mother was a priestess in the sun cult.

Centrifugal forces countered the kings' attempts to centralize political power in the state. By the Fifth Dynasty, governors and local leaders were having tombs built for themselves in the provinces they controlled, where they had growing economic and political interests and loyalties. This was one sign that the power of the king and the highest level of the state apparatus were beginning to erode. The popular uprisings that occurred with increasing frequency during the Sixth Dynasty were another sign of the processes of political and economic decentralization that were already under way.

By 2470 B.C., the end of the Sixth Dynasty and the Old Kingdom, the central state had disintegrated. The Egyptian landscape was made up of a number of small, independent political units, each centered at an old provincial capital. Goods, such as copper, lapis lazuli, and turquoise, that were formerly acquired by agents of the state were not as common as they had been earlier. Pottery vessels, which used to be standardized in size and shape throughout the state, now varied from place to place. Some of the provincial capitals were fortified, and weapons appeared in tombs with increasing frequency. A papyrus, *The Admonition of the Prophet Ipuwer*, described the conditions that prevailed when centralized political rule collapsed: The poor were jubilant, wrote its author, whereas the wealthy lamented. Public offices had been sacked; some fields were not planted; others were not harvested; and there were shortages of everything from cloth, perfume, and oil to the Lebanese resin that was used for embalming the dead. The poor were better off than they had been earlier, judging by the fact that their graves contained a wider range of objects than those of their ancestors. Thus they may also have had access to more of the goods that were available in the country at the time.

The time following the collapse of the centralized state, which coincided with the reassertion of local autonomy, is known as the First Intermediate period (2470 to 2140 B.C.). It lasted more than three centuries, during which various regional rulers and former provincial governors proclaimed themselves kings and founded dynasties of their own. They struggled with one another to assert hegemony over their contemporaries and over the nomadic peoples that were moving into the Nile Valley from the deserts to the east and west and from Nubia to the south.

The Middle Kingdom

By 2200 B.C., the rulers of two provinces that had been minor political centers in the Old Kingdom became dominant political figures. The rulers of Thebes in the south and Heracleopolis in the north had gradually subdued the lords or neighboring *nomes* and put together uneasy coalitions. The two rulers fought sporadically as each sought to assert his rule over the entire valley. In 2140 B.C., a Theban king broke the power of his northern rival, founded a new dynasty, and unified the state. This marked the beginning of the Middle Kingdom, which eventually disintegrated about 1800 B.C.

The new king wore his crown uneasily, for he was little more than first among equals. His first act was to establish effective control over national affairs. He abolished hereditary governorships; removed dissidents from office; appointed Thebans to every key position in the new government; moved the capital from Memphis to Thebes; and installed Amun, the patron god of Thebes, as the state deity. Even with these measures, it took Theban rulers more than a century and a half to suppress the local lords. At that time, the rulers turned their attention to Nubia and built a series of forts between the First and Second Cataracts to safeguard the frontier and provide trading emporia for goods from the south. Several of the king's successors sent expeditions across the Eastern Desert to reestablish maritime trade with Punt on the Red Sea; these expeditions built boats and a harbor town, where cargoes of myrrh and gum were unloaded and carried by donkeys across the desert to Thebes.

The power of the Theban rulers waned as various local leaders challenged their hegemony and founded rival dynasties. Several successor states were located in or near the delta, including one that was founded by immigrants from Palestine called the Hyksos. Another of the successor states, Kush, which was established between the Third and Fourth Cataracts, produced gold, controlled commerce with the interior of Africa, and adopted pharaonic court culture. This period of decentralized political power, known as the Second Intermediate Period (1800 to 1570 B.C.), lasted more than two centuries.

The New Kingdom and Later Episodes of Class and State Formation

The Theban rulers reasserted their hegemony over Egypt from the Nile River Delta to Nubia, along the Red Sea, and in the Levant as far north as Syria in the early years of the Eighteenth Dynasty and the New Kingdom (1570 to 1069 B.C). The goal may have been political and military rather than economic gain; the impetus for the reunification of the pharaonic state may have been the threat potentially posed by diplomatic contacts that were established between the Hyksos in the north and the Kushite state in the south. After they were subjugated, the two regions were incorporated in different ways into the new imperial state. Kush was treated as a province; the sons of its rulers were brought to Thebes to enhance their understanding and appreciation of pharaonic statecraft and court culture and to become part of the Egyptian ruling class. The Egyptian state divided the lands it controlled in the Levant into three districts, each headed by a governor who had the power to settle disputes among the princes of the subordinated city-states and polities in the region and to counter the Mitanni state, a powerful, commerce-based rival centered in Syria and Anatolia. The New Kingdom reached its greatest extent in the mid-fifteenth century B.C., when the ruler of the conquesting state launched expeditions southward into the area around the Fourth Cataract and northward to the Euphrates River in Syria. After 1400 B.C., Egypt's control over the frontier regions began to wane.

Akhenaten, who reigned from 1353 to 1335 B.C., is perhaps the best known of the New Kingdom rulers. Before ascending to the throne, Akhenaten was a high priest in the state's sun-god cult. He redefined the attributes of the sun god in such a way that no space was left for any of the other traditional, regionally based deities of Egypt. After assuming the crown and the trappings of divine kingship, he established a new capital at El Amarna; built a new temple dedicated to the sun disc, the reconstituted sun god, at Karnak; and closed the cult centers and shrines of other deities, which were located throughout the country. Akhenaten had the support of the military but not of the local populations and village communities whose shrines had been closed by the state. He died unexpectedly, perhaps at the hands of his enemies, and was followed on the throne by his son, Tutankhamun, who abandoned the sun-disc cult and ordered the closed cult centers to be reopened. His successors ultimately dismantled the sun-disc temple at Karnak.

A great deal of land and movable property passed into the hands of various cult centers, especially the Amun Temple at Karnak, during the reign of Rameses III in the early twelfth century B.C. State and temple became inextricably intertwined in the years that followed. By 1100 B.C., the hereditary priests of the Amun cult had established their own dynasty to rival that of the ruling family, and they controlled much of Upper Egypt. The power of the pharaohs during the waning years of the Twentieth Dynasty had dwindled significantly. They exerted direct control only over Middle and Lower Egypt, and even this was soon challenged and usurped as the hereditary kings, princes, and chieftains of various polities in and around the valley asserted or reclaimed their independence. The royal government remained weak throughout the Third Intermediate period (1069 to 664 B.C.), unable to deal with the formation of successor states; the decentralization of political power; external threats; and the appearance of warlords, royal kin, who ensconced themselves in heavily fortified provincial centers and established their own collateral dynasties. By the beginning of the seventh century B.C., Egypt consisted of at least eleven independent political units, which maintained complex relations with one another and with their neighbors.

Both the Kushite state in Lower Nubia and the merchant princes who founded the Saite Dynasty in the agriculturally impoverished western delta attempted to reunify portions of Egypt during the seventh century B.C. The Saite kings reclaimed their independence from the Assyrian state and used Greek and Phoenician-speaking mercenaries to fend off the ambitions of their contemporaries in Thebes. Even though the Saite rulers slavishly copied the court culture and art of earlier periods in pharaonic history, they failed to gain the support of their own subjects because of the favoritism they showed toward various Greek oracles and eastern cults and because of the positions occupied by foreign mercenaries and merchants in the emerging class structure. Thus, the class struggles that shaped the various state-based societies of Egypt made them ripe for conquest and incorporation as provincial areas in new imperial states: the Persian Empire; the Ptolemaic successor state that appeared after the Macedonian king, Alexander the Great, easily defeated the despised Persian administration in Egypt in 331 B.C.; and finally Rome in the first century B.C. Independent states persisted or appeared and flourished along and beyond the southern margins of Egypt during the period of its encapsulation and incorporation into imperial states centered in Asia or the Mediterranean world. These included the kingdom of Kush; Meroe, located downstream from Khartoum above the Fifth Cataract; and Axun, located 500 miles southeast in the Ethiopian highlands overlooking the Red Sea. The deserts and grasslands of North Africa were also the remote areas to which various peoples, including heretical Christian communities, have fled repeatedly during the last 2,500 years to avoid the exactions of states.

AFRICA OUTSIDE THE NILE VALLEY AND ITS ENVIRONS

The Greeks and Phoenicians established colonies on the Mediterranean coast of North Africa after about 800 B.C. and ports of trade on the Atlantic coast west of the Straits of Gibraltar a century or so later. There they encountered coastal fishing communities and peoples from the interior, whom they engaged in silent barter, exchanging beads and perhaps other goods from the Mediterranean for gold, animal skins, and ivory from the Sahara, Sahel, and beyond. This maritime trade gradually withered and disappeared altogether after the second century B.C.

Unlike their contemporaries in the Nile Valley and Ethiopian highlands to the east, the agropastoral communities of the Sahara and the Sahel either had not experienced conditions and circumstances that could potentially precipitate class and state formation or they had successfully resisted the claims of individuals or groups who argued that their kin and neighbors should provide the labor and goods needed to support them in a particular lifestyle.

Differences in burial practices, perhaps marking status or wealth differentials, appeared in parts of the Niger grasslands about 2000 B.C. Although most individuals were interred in pits or small burial mounds, the tombs of a few individuals buried near Agadez were embellished. They contained the remains of a goat or cow, were marked with a standing stone, stood inside a stone enclosure, or were located near geometric alignments.

During the first millennium B.C., the inhabitants of the area around the Dhar Titchitt escarpment in eastern Mauritania, more than 1,000 miles west of Agadez, moved from dispersed settlements around the foot of the cliffs to palisaded hilltop forts that overlooked their millet fields and pastures. Raiding may have played an important role in determining the location of settlements for a century or so; however, by 700 B.C., the inhabitants of the area were once again residing in villages that lacked defensive features.

Between about 800 and 400 B.C., the inhabitants of some communities in northern Nigeria, Niger, Ghana, and Mali began to smelt iron. This event occurred about the same time that smiths began to smelt and work iron ores in Europe, and a controversy has raged over whether they were independent or related developments. The archaeological remains are particularly abundant at Taruga, Nigeria, and at Agadez and Do Dimmi in Niger. Thirteen smelting furnaces; extensive slag deposits; and fragments of wrought iron figurines, some 30 inches tall, have been found at Taruga. At first, the bellow-driven smelters were located in villages; however, by the end of the first century B.C., the furnaces were parts of specialized smelting sites located close to the iron ores and to fuel. Smelting and ironworking were the activities of craft specialists, who burned so much fuel that large parts of the plateau were effectively deforested about 2,000 years ago.

The smelters and specialized ironworking sites or villages near the rich iron ore deposits in the Cameroons and on the west and southwest shores of Lake Victoria in Rwanda and Zaire are probably as old as those in West

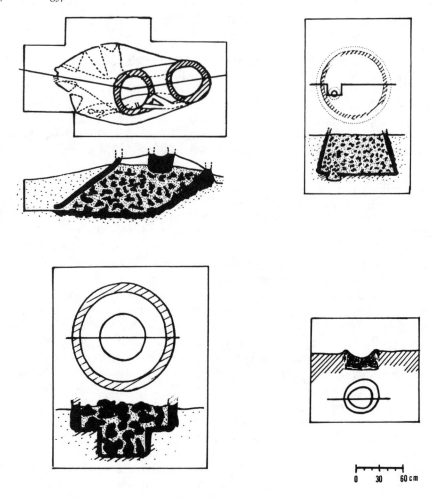

Reconstructions of early iron-working furnaces in Nigeria

Africa. The ironworking settlements on the upper Zambezi and Limpopo rivers in southern Africa and those in East Africa are more recent and date to the early part of the first millennium A.D. Objects made by the smiths were circulated to regions and peoples who lived long distances from their workshops or from the furnaces they built in the forests to smelt ores.

Class and state formation occurred during the middle of the first millennium A.D. in four regions of West Africa: along the lower and middle reaches of the Senegal River, at Jenne-jeno in the inland Niger Delta, around Lake Chad, and in the forested region around Igbo-Ukwu near the mouth of the Niger River in southern Nigeria. This burst of activity predated the expansion of Arab-speaking merchants across North Africa in the eighth century and the subsequent construction of commercial centers on the Mediterranean littoral and trans-Saharan trade routes that linked them with peoples living along the western and southern margins of the desert. The ruling elites of the West African states benefited from these linkages and probably derived revenues by controlling certain kinds of production and the markets where buying and selling took place.

Three distinct kinds of evidence indicate that state formation occurred; however, they do not clarify the conditions or events that precipitated the development of exploitative and oppressive social relations in this part of the world. First, burial practices became differentiated toward the middle of the first millennium A.D., and some individuals were interred in lavishly furnished tombs. For example, the largest burial mounds along the middle Senegal River were 250 feet in diameter and 40 feet high and contained both single and multiple inhumations. Contemporary burial mounds along the middle Niger River contained wooden chambers, human sacrifices, and an array of objects. The individual buried in the royal tomb at Igbo-Ukwe in southeastern Nigeria was interred in a grave lined with wooden planks; he sat on a copper-studded wooden stool, clutching a bronze fanholder and staff. An ivory tusk was placed at his feet along with nearly 700 copper and bronze vessels; more than 100,000 glass and carnelian objects were also recovered from the tomb and three nearby sites.

Second, population concentration occurred in areas around Lake Chad, the inland Niger Delta, and possibly in southern Nigeria during the early and middle parts of the first millennium A.D. Jenne-jeno, a settlement in the inland Niger Delta that was first occupied in the second century B.C., covered more than 100 acres by A.D. 800. It was a center for the small hamlets and villages that dotted the surrounding countryside and whose inhabitants used the same kind of pottery as the townspeople. Gold and copper began to be used about A.D. 300 in the town, which suggests that mining and exchange played increasingly important roles in the creation of wealth.

Third, specialized iron-producing zones appeared during this period along the Senegal River. The 35,000 furnaces and slag heaps identified in this region alone attest to the importance of ironworking around the western and southern edges of the desert in West Africa. There clearly were technical divisions of labor in these societies; in later periods, the knowledge required to smelt iron was a secret possessed by a hereditary group of ironworkers. By the ninth century A.D., the iron they produced may well have been taxed by the local rulers before it was moved along the trade routes that crossed the Sahara. Human beings were another commodity that moved along the trans-Saharan trade routes; slave raiders may well have transformed the frontier regions of these states as the technical and social divisions of labor were elaborated and whole village communities fled to avoid capture.

Like states elsewhere in the world, those in West Africa were inherently unstable, and their fortunes waxed and waned through time. The early ones disappeared or were consolidated in later polities that crystallized to avail themselves of the opportunities provided by new trade routes and new sources of labor drawn from areas inhabited by kin-organized communities. These workers, many of whom presumably toiled in fields and mines controlled by the rulers, enriched the local merchant princes and their trading partners in other areas.

A Chinese source provides insights into the conditions that prevailed in East Africa during the ninth century A.D. This account describes pastoralists in the interior, who subsisted on milk, meat, and the blood drawn from live cattle. It also mentions that the pastoralists were kidnapped by neighboring peoples and sold to foreign merchants who visited the numerous commercial centers on the coast; the foreign merchants occasionally ventured inland, in large caravans comprising several thousand individuals, to barter cloth for ivory and other products of the grasslands and ambergris collected along the coast. Trade with the interior was monopolized, however, by Swahili-speaking merchants who dwelled in the coastal towns; controlled rituals; minted coins; and controlled the production of craft goods, like cloth, in the urban neighborhoods. The social and political organization of the coastal towns was varied, according to William Fawcett (1990), ranging from class-stratified communities along the Mozambican coast to councils of elders whose members had authority and wielded power in the coastal towns of Kenya and Somalia.

Powerful kingdoms developed inland during the later half of the first millennium A.D. These included the Luba state in Katanga; Zimbabwe, located between the Zambezi and Limpopo rivers; Mapungubwe, on the Limpopo River; and another state on a plateau near Harare. Like their counterparts in West Africa, the rulers of these protostates derived their revenues by controlling local production and exchange. Some, like the ruler of Great Zimbabwe, extracted tribute in goods and labor from their own subjects and from communities in the surrounding countryside, a portion of

Zimbabwe.

which was devoted to the construction of monumental structures, like the Great Enclosure at Zimbabwe. Judging by the written account of the ninth century, the merchant princes of some states and their retainers raided for slaves that were sold in the coastal markets.

FURTHER READINGS: A BRIEF GUIDE

For insightful discussions of the interconnections of racism, civilization, and science, see St. Clair Drake, *Black Folk Here and There: An Essay in History and Anthropology*, Center for Afro-American Studies Monograph Series, vol. 7 (Los Angeles: University of California, 1987); and Martin Bernal, *Black Athena: The Afroasiatic Roots of Classical Civilization*, vols. 1 and 2 (New Brunswick, NJ: Rutgers University Press, 1987, 1991).

For the development of food production, see Gordon C. Hillman, "Late Palaeolithic Plant Foods from the Wadi Kubbaniya in Upper Egypt: Dietary Diversity, Infant Weaning, and Seasonality in a Riverine Environment," in *Foraging and Farming: The Evolution of Plant Exploitation*, ed. David R. Harris and Gordon C. Hillman (London: Unwin Hyman, 1989), pp. 207–239; J. Desmond Clark and Steven A. Brandt, eds., *From Hunters to Farmers: The Causes and Consequences of Food Production in Africa* (Berkeley: University of California Press, 1984); John Bower, "The Pastoral Neolithic of East Africa," *Journal of World Prehistory*, vol. 5, no. 1 (1991), 49–82; J. E. G. Sutton, "The Aquatic Civilization of Middle Africa," *The Journal of African History*, vol. XV, no. 4 (1974), 527–546; Thurston Shaw, "Hunters, Gatherers and the First Farmers in West Africa," in *Hunters, Gatherers and the First Farmers Beyond Europe*, ed. J. V. S. Megaw (Leicester, Eng.: Leicester University Press, 1977), pp. 69–126; Fred Wendorf, Angela Close, and Romuald Schild, "Prehistoric Settlements in the Nubian Desert," *American Scientist*, vol. 73, no. 2 (1985), 132–141; Randi Haaland, *Socio-economic Differentiation in the Neolithic Sudan*, British Archaeological Reports, International Series 350 (Oxford, 1987); and Fekri A. Hassan, "Desert Environments and the Origins of Agriculture in Egypt," *Norwegian Archaeological Review*, vol. 19, no. 2 (1986), 63–76.

For overviews of the historical development of Egyptian society, see Cyril Aldred, *The Egyptians* (London: Thames & Hudson, 1984); Alan K. Bowman, *Egypt after the Pharaohs: 332 BC-AD 642* (Berkeley: University of California Press, 1989); and Dorothy J. Thompson, *Memphis under the Ptolemies* (Princeton, NJ: Princeton University Press, 1988).

State formation in the Nile Valley is discussed by Richard Lobban, "Cattle and the Rise of the Egyptian State," paper presented at the ICAES, Zagreb, Yugoslavia, 1988; Fekri A. Hassan, "The Predynastic of Egypt," *Journal of World Prehistory*, vol. 2, no. 2 (1988), 135–186; Bruce G. Trigger, "Egypt: A Fledgling Nation," *Journal of the Society for the Study of Egyptian Antiquities*, vol. XVII, no. 1–2 (Toronto, 1990), pp. 58–66; Erika Endesfelder, "Social and Economic Development Towards the End of the Predynastic Period in Egypt," and Bruce G. Trigger, "The Mainlines of Socio-economic Development in Dynastic Egypt to the End of the Old Kingdom," both in *Origin and Early Development of Food-producing Cultures in North-eastern Africa*, ed. Lech Krzyzaniak and Michal Kobusiewicz (Poznań: Poznań Archaeological Museuem, Poznań Branch, Polish Academy of Sciences, 1984), pp. 95–100 and 101–109; Lech Krzyzaniak, "Trends in the Socio-economic Development of Egyptian Predynastic Societies," *Acts of the First International Congress of Egyptologists* (Cairo, 1979), pp. 407–412; Michael A. Hoffman, *Egypt before the Pharaohs* (London: Ark Paperbacks, 1984); Jac. J. Janssen, "The Early State in Ancient Egypt," in *The Early State*, ed. Henri J. M. Claessen and Peter Skalník (The Hague: Mouton Publishers, 1978), pp. 213–234; Hans Goedicke, "The Origin of Royal Administration," *Colloques Internationaux du Centre National de la Recherche Scientifique*, no. 595, tome II (Paris, 1982), pp. 123–130; and Barry J. Kemp, "Old Kingdom, Middle Kingdom, and Second Intermediate Perio *c.* 2686–1552 B.C.," in *Ancient Egypt: A Social History*, ed. Bruce G. Trigger, Barry J. Kemp, David O'Connor, and A. B. Lloyd, (Cambridge: Cambridge University Press, 1983), pp. 71–182.

Early state formation and/or its effects in Nubia are debated by Bruce Williams, "The Lost Pharaohs of Nubia," *Archaeology*, vol. 33, no. 5 (1980), 14–21, and "Forebears of Menes in Nubia: Myth or Reality?" *Journal of Near Eastern Studies*, vol. 46, no. 1 (1987), 15–26; William Y. Adams, "Doubts about the 'Lost Pharaohs,'" *Journal of Near Eastern Studies*, vol. 44, no. 3 (1985), 185–192; Peter L. Shinnie, "The Mainlines of Socio-economic Development in the Sudan in Post-Neolithic Times," in *Origin and Early Development of Food-producing Cultures in North-eastern Africa*, ed. Lech Krzyzaniak and Michal Kobusiewicz (Poznań: Poznań Archaeological Museuem, Poznań Branck, Polish Academy of Sciences, 1984), pp. 110–115. See also Bruce G. Trigger, *Nubia under the Pharaohs* (London: Thames & Hudson, 1976).

The Middle and New Kingdoms are examined by William C. Hayes, "The Middle Kingdom in Egypt," in *The Cambridge Ancient History*, ed. I. E. S. Edwards, C. J. Gadd, and N. G. L. Hammond, vol. I, pt. 2 (Cambridge: Cambridge University Press, 1971), pp. 464–531; David O'Connor, "New Kingdom and Third Intermediate Period," in *Ancient Egypt: A Social History*, ed. Bruce G. Trigger, Barry J. Kemp, David O'Connor, and A. B. Lloyd, (Cambridge: Cambridge University Press, 1983), pp. 183–278; Paul John Frandsen, "Egyptian Imperialism," in *Power and Propaganda: A Symposium on Ancient Empires*, ed. Mogens T. Larsen (Copenhagen: Akademisk Forlag, 1979), pp. 167–190; Barry J. Kemp, "Imperialism and Empire in New Kingdom Egypt," in *Imperialism in the Ancient World*, ed. Peter D. A. Garnsey and C. R. Whittaker (Cambridge: Cambridge University Press, 1978), pp. 1–58; Donald B. Redford, *Akhenaten: The Heretic King* (Princeton, NJ: Princeton University Press, 1984); Jac. J. Janssen, "The Role of the Temple in the Egyptian Economy during the New Kingdom," in *State and Temple Economy in the Ancient Near East*, ed. Edward Lipinski, vol. II (Louvain, Belg.: Departement Oriëntalistiek, 1979), pp. 507–515; W. F. Edgerton, "The Strikes in Ramesses III's Twenty-ninth year," *Journal of Near Eastern Studies*, vol. X, no. 3 (1951), 137–145; and J. Capart, A. H. Gardiner, and B. van de Walle, "New Light on the Ramesside Tomb Robberies," *Journal of Egyptian Archaeology*, vol. XXII (1936), 169–193.

For surveys of historical developments in Africa outside the Nile Valley, see various articles in J. D. Fage, ed., *The Cambridge History of Africa*, vol. 2 (Cambridge: Cambridge University Press, 1978); Samir Amin, *The Arab Nation* (London: Zed Books, 1978); David W. Phillipson, *African Archaeology* (Cambridge: Cambridge University Press, 1985); and Graham Connah, *African Civilizations: Precolonial Cities and States in Tropical Africa* (Cambridge: Cambridge University Press, 1987).

Historical developments in West Africa are discussed by Patrick Munson, "Archaeological Data on the Origins of Cultivation in the Southwestern Sahara and Their Implications for West Africa," in *Origins of African Plant Domestication*, ed. Jack R. Harlan, J. R. de Wet, and Ann B. Stamler (The Hague: Mouton Publishers, 1976), pp. 187–209; Susan K. McIntosh and Roderick J. McIntosh, "From Stone to Metal: New Perspectives on the Later Prehistory of West Africa," *Journal of World Prehistory*, vol. 2, no. 1 (1988), 89–133; and A. Holl, "Background to the Ghana Empire: Archaeological Investigations on the Transition to Statehood in the Dhar Tichitt Region (Mauritania)," *Journal of Anthropological Archaeology*, vol. 4, no. 1 (1985), 73–115.

East Africa is discussed by Peter Rigby, "Class Formation among East African Pastoralists: Maasai of Tanzania and Kenya," in *Power Relations and State Formation*, ed. Thomas C. Patterson and Christine W. Gailey (Washington, DC: Archeology Division, American Anthropological Association, 1987), pp. 57–80; H. Neville Chittick, "The East Coast, Madagascar, and the Indian Ocean," in *Cambridge History of Africa*, ed. Roland Oliver, vol. 3 (Cambridge: Cambridge University Press, 1977), pp. 183–231; Mark C. Horton, "The Swahili Corridor," *Scientific American*, vol. 257, no. 3 (1987), 86–93; Paul Sinclair, "Chibuene—An Early Trading Site in Southern Mozambique," *Paideuma*, vol. 28 (1982), 150–164; and William Fawcett, "Beyond Row House, Neighborhood, and City," paper presented at Temple University, Philadelphia, 1990.

For insightful discussions of how the slave trade was organized and its consequences, see Joseph Miller, *Way of Death: Merchant Capitalism and the Angolan Slave-Trade 1730–1830* (Madison: University of Wisconsin Press, 1988).

chapter 10

The Levant
and Asia Minor

So Samuel told all the words of the Lord to the people who were asking a king from him. He said, "These will be the ways of the king who will reign over you: he will take your sons and appoint them to his chariots and to be his horsemen and to run before his chariots; and he will appoint for himself commanders of thousands and commanders of fifties, and some to plow his ground and to reap his harvest, and to make his implements of war and the equipment of his chariots. He will take your daughters to be perfumers and cooks and bakers. He will take the best of your fields and vineyards and olive orchards and give them to his servants. He will take the tenth of your grain and of your vineyards and give it to his officers and to his servants. He will take your male and female slaves, your choice young men, and your asses, and put them to work. He will take a tenth of your flocks, and you shall become his slaves." (I Samuel 8:7–18)

Tampering with history in the interests of the present is just as reprehensible as any other kind of misrepresentation. . . . The manipulation of ancient history for present purposes is an unusually bold deception (Glen W. Bowersock, "Palestine: Ancient History and Modern Politics")

The one chosen by God is not the one chosen by people. (Maasai proverb)

The rolling plains and low mountains of the Levant and the rugged mountains and high plateau of Asia Minor lie on the eastern shore of the Mediterranean Sea. The evergreen woodlands of Lebanon and Syria, long famous for their cedar trees, merge to the north with the deciduous and coniferous woodlands of the Taurus and Pontic mountains and the Anatolian Plateau and to the east and south with the semiarid grassland, steppe, and desert habitats that cover the gently rolling landscape.

The region has been shaped over time by complex geological processes. The Tethys Sea, which long separated the African and Eurasian landmasses, was closed when the two plates collided more than 15 million years ago. The waters of the Mediterranean basin and of the great arm of the Tethys that stretched eastward from the Black Sea to the Aral Sea slowly evaporated, leaving a series of lakes and salt flats. Parallel mountain ranges, the Taurus and Pontic, separated by the inland basin of Anatolia were thrust upward in Asia Minor when the plates collided. For several million years, these overlooked the deep lakes lying north of the peninsula and the salt lakes and mountains in the Aegean, until Atlantic Ocean waters spilled through the Straits of Gibraltar and slowly inundated the Mediterranean basin.

Although human populations have resided in or moved through western Asia for the last million years, our understanding of the early stages of human history there is shrouded by the mists of time. The image of everyday life gradually comes into focus during the last 20 millennia. About 12,000

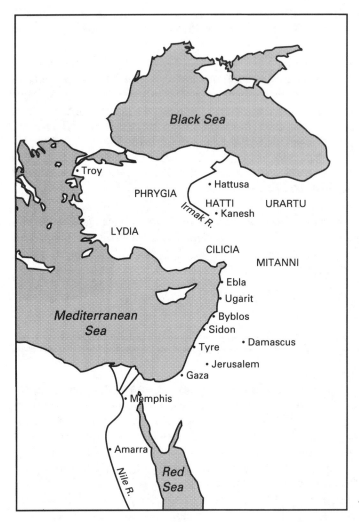

The Levant and Asia Minor.

years ago, sedentary communities in the Levant were harvesting abundant wild cereals and storing the surplus, along with wood and other raw materials, for the season when foodstuffs were scarce. They cultivated and eventually domesticated these cereals as well as lentils and peas around 8500 B.C. A millennium and a half later, they were keeping small herds of goats and sheep, which they fed on crop stubble and the plant communities of nearby nonagricultural habitats.

The burial practices of early settlements in both the Levant and Anatolia indicate that besides place of residence, ancestors, descent, and kinship played important roles in constituting the membership of social groups. Individuals publicly asserted and reaffirmed their membership in the village community by repeatedly participating in those shared activities that reminded them of their responsibilities and privileges. Such acts maintained the cohesion of the group, and recognition of the mutual responsibilities by the members constituted insurance against the uncertainties that each of them confronted in everyday life. Participation in the shared activities of the community also defined who could use its collectively held means of production and raw materials. Many of the village communities in western Asia, even early ones like Jericho or Çatal Hüyük, mentioned in Chapter 6, had several thousand residents and, thus, presented circumstances in which craft specialization and technical divisions of labor might develop and flourish.

CITY-STATES, COMMERCIAL EMPIRES, AND REFUGEES

Up to the early third millennium B.C., the members of various communities of the Levant and Asia Minor resided in villages and hamlets in which the houses were separated from one another by open spaces. These settlements lacked palisades or other kinds of fortifications, and the residents of one village produced and used pottery that was generically similar to that found in other villages throughout the area. However, significant changes occurred in the Levant, but apparently not in Asia Minor, after about 3000 B.C. Distinctive local pottery styles began to mark boundaries between contemporary production-exchange-consumption units. More important, walled towns or cities appeared suddenly, and their residents began to live in houses that were much closer together than those of their ancestors. The palisades of the fortified towns in the Levant were up to 25 feet thick and studded with towers and easily defended gates. The area north of the Judean hills was more densely inhabited than the Sinai, where a few nomadic herders moved their goats and sheep from one pasture to another and Egyptian miners came to acquire turquoise.

Although some walled towns were abandoned during the middle of the third millennium B.C., the inhabitants strengthened the fortifications of other settlements—like Byblos and Ugarit on the coast and Hama, Mari, and Ebla inland—that continued to be occupied. Many settlements near the west coast of Asia Minor—for example, Beycesultan—were also destroyed and/or abandoned at about the same time; the people who remained in the area built fortifications around towns, like Troy, that continued to be occupied. These events were apparently associated with the relatively rapid crystallization of a number of small, semiautonomous polities in what had become the frontier area of states that had developed a few centuries earlier in Mesopotamia and northeastern Africa.

Mari, Ebla, Byblos, and the other city-states that developed in the Levant and Asia Minor during the mid-third millennium B.C. were enmeshed in a complex web of political, tributary, marital, and commercial relations that linked them to one another and to the merchants and ruling classes of states outside the area. Artifacts and textual remains recovered at various sites put flesh on the bare skeleton constructed of political-economic relations. For instance, the domain of Mari, a city-state centered on the west bank of the Euphrates River near Aleppo, included the city itself and an unknown number of towns and hamlets in northern Syria. It was an independent political unit at certain times and under certain circumstances. At other times and under different circumstances, it was incorporated into the Akkadian state by Sargon and his successor; it was linked with the Ur III Dynasty but was not an integral part of the economic structure of that Mesopotamian state; and it paid tribute to the rulers of Ebla, located 250 miles northwest.

By 2400 B.C., Ebla's domain was an oval-shaped territory no more than 70 miles across. It included the townspeople; the inhabitants of villages and hamlets in the surrounding countryside; the residents of colonies that provided raw materials; and the merchants who lived in several of Mesopotamian city-states, most notably Lagash. An alabaster jar made in Egypt during the reign of a Sixth Dynasty pharaoh and recovered from the palace at Ebla suggests that the kingdom also had ties with the royal court in Egypt. Most of the 16,000 cuneiform tablets in the palace archives described the administrations of three successive rulers and various economic transactions that involved flax and wool. Ebla exported textiles, sheep, metals, perfumes, and olive oil to the coastal city of Byblos and received linen, gold, and silver in return. The king of Ebla, who owned 80,000 sheep, played a role of unknown dimensions in the city's commerce at this time. Pasturing herds of this size in the semiarid steppe must also have presented the king with a potential problem: the possibility of conflicts with other rulers or communities that were seeking to pasture their own livestock in an area where the available grazing lands may have been inadequate for the task.

Each year, the Ebla ruler received 11 pounds of gold and 1,100 pounds of silver from his subjects, who presumably included not only the inhabitants of the town and the countryside but also vassals in those polities over which he exercised suzerainty. Political relations between rival kingdoms were cemented not only by military action and commerce but also by marriage. The rulers of Ebla and Byblos cemented their relationship when the daughter of the Ebla ruler married the king of Byblos. She journeyed to the coastal city with an entourage of 1,200 persons, 600 loaves of bread for the wedding, and 3,000 loaves consigned to Byblos. In return, the king of Byblos contributed 940 loaves for the 300 persons at the ceremony and for the 880 emissaries from his city. Thus, the royal couple, as well as the bride's father, contributed food to the wedding.

State formation creates uneven development—a continually shifting mosaic of different kinds of societies, each of which is characterized by distinctive social and political-economic structures and shaped by particular, often diverse, sociohistorical conditions. Neither Mesopotamia nor Africa were wholly responsible for the network of interconnected communities and polities that developed during the third millennium B.C. in the Levant and Asia Minor. The autonomous and semiautonomous peoples on the margins of the civilized world contributed to the construction of their own political-economic, social, and cultural reality. In shaping their own destinies, the communities and polities of the borderlands often pitted rival powers against one another for their own gain.

The end of the third and the early second millennia B.C. produced tumultuous times in the Levant and Asia Minor. The influence of the kingdom of Akkad and the Ur III Dynasty had waned; the Egyptian court and its imitators no longer acquired the wood, perfumes, and oil they had received earlier during the Old Kingdom and the early years of the Middle Kingdom. Towns in southern Palestine and Asia Minor were abandoned and destroyed. Some states withered and eventually collapsed; new ones coalesced on their margins; and others continued to flourish, often after the appearance of new dynasties. Many of the political leaders of the time must have shared the wishes and sentiments of Zimri-Lim, an early eighteenth-century ruler of Mari, who pleaded with the nomads and mountain people to settle down and acknowledge his authority. His plea fell largely on deaf ears. Two decades later, Mari itself was destroyed around 1750 B.C. by Hammurabi of Babylon. The nomads and mountain folk founded a number of petty city-states and kingdoms on its margins.

In 1500 B.C., the politics of western Asia were dominated by several strong, centralized states: the early dynasties of New Kingdom Egypt; the Kassite Dynasty, which was slowly loosing its grasp on Babylonia and western Iran; the Hittite ruler who, a few decades earlier, had enveloped neighboring polities and established hegemony in Anatolia; and Mitanni, a loose confederation of polities that emerged in northern Mesopotamia in the power vacuum created by the collapse of Ashur, the waning of Kassite power, and the destruction of the Aleppo state by the formidable Hittite charioteers. Besides the aforementioned large states, whose rulers acknowledged one another as "great kings," numerous minor states with small spheres of influence were located on the margins of the great states and in their interstices. Although these petty kingdoms retained their traditional political institutions and dynasties in some instances, their rulers were often vassals of the great lords or related to them through the kin and diplomatic ties of royal marriage.

Mitanni reached its zenith around 1440 B.C., when its warrior elite exerted control across northern Mesopotamia from the Mediterranean to the Zagros Mountains. Relations with Egypt were strengthened when a New Kingdom pharaoh, Amenophis III, married a Mitanni princess. The ruling estate consisted of charioteers who received land and political authority in return for service to the king; they gained wealth through trade and agriculture, and they sold or acquired land by adopting the potential buyers or being adopted by owners who were disposing of land.

The political circumstances of Mitanni waned rapidly in the mid-fourteenth century B.C. Diplomatic relations with Egypt were stretched beyond the breaking point when the Egyptian court entertained emissaries from Assur, a city-state on the eastern frontier of Mitanni that had begun to flex its might, claim prominence, and thus threaten Mitanni in the early fourteenth century. The fate of Mitanni was all but sealed when its charioteers lost a series of battles with the Hittites in the ill-defined borderlands between the two states. By the end of the century, the Hittite and Assyrian states had absorbed much of Mitanni's territory and productive capacity. In the process, it became a buffer between the two states, and its ruler became no more than a puppet married to the daughter of the Hittite king.

The states that developed during the fourteenth and thirteenth centuries B.C. had different political-economic structures. In some ways, the Hittite state resembled Mitanni. For example, the Hittite rulers assigned inalienable fiefs of land, labor, and authority to an estate of warrior aristocrats that owed them personal loyalty and military service. The rulers traveled throughout the domain during the winter to pay homage and officiate at the cult ceremonies performed at the shrines of local deities and, more important, to renew political and social relations. In at least one instance, the queen's power rivaled and was apparently independent of that of her husband. In the early fourteenth century B.C., Queen Purduhepa was regularly mentioned along with her husband in treaties and state documents; she maintained an independent correspondence with the male and female rulers of other domains, and she remained in office after her husband died.

The Assyrian state was dominated by a group of old families who controlled the city and provincial governments, administered them as profit-making ventures, and controlled commerce; membership in this ruling council was hereditary in some instances. Unlike the Hittite ruling class, which derived its wealth primarily from land and the labor and production of its subjects, the Assyrian state derived its revenues primarily from commerce. The trade was organized by private individuals, who acted alone; as agents for the king or the public and religious institutions of the city; and occasionally in partnership with them or with other individuals or groups, including at times the slaves who journeyed with the caravans. After the collapse of Mitanni, the position of the old ruling families declined as their power was usurped and centralized in the hands of the king, who appointed retainers to administrative positions, became head of the state cult, nominated temple officials, and tried to break up the landholdings of the old families. The fortunes of the new ruling class were closely linked with their position in the bureaucracy and with the prosperity of the state. The fortunes of the old families depended on their ability to resist the efforts of the new rulers.

Shortly after 1200 B.C., the centralized political structures of both the Hittite and Kassite states fragmented and were replaced by the relatively sudden appearance of a number of autonomous, small kingdoms whose petty rulers resided in castles and controlled what happened in the surrounding countryside. Although the precise circumstances and events that precipitated the decentralization of power remain obscure, the processes are fairly clear. In the Levant, the palaces had typically controlled long-distance commerce during the thirteenth century; this practice benefited the kings and a class of functionaries closely linked to the palace and the state—administrators, governors, scribes, and merchants—whose well-being depended on the extraction of labor and goods from subject populations and on the steady flow of exotic goods that were used or consumed by the court. As their demands and exactions increased, growing numbers of individuals and groups fled to avoid debt bondage and other consequences of the commoditization of their lands and labor—that is, they became items that could be bought and sold. They deserted their homes and fields, and growing numbers of them became the nomadic peoples who inhabited the borderland areas beyond the grasp of states and their agents.

This development meant, as Mario Liverani (1987) observed, that the royal courts found it increasingly difficult to acquire the goods and services required to maintain the standards of living to which they had become accustomed. To do so meant that they had to increase the levels of the labor and goods they siphoned from their subjects—an act that only encouraged people to run away. From the courts' perspective, this was not an especially desirable or viable solution. In many instances, the palace administrators and governors struggled for the adoption of an alternative: the transformation of their offices and salaries into hereditary positions that involved no responsibility other than an annual cash payment to the king in lieu of service. This change, of course, eroded the kings' power. It also transformed the role of the merchants, who remained linked with the court but separated from the direct producers whose goods and labor were controlled increasingly by local, hereditary nobles. The merchants responded to the new circumstances by adding moneylending and other financial services to their institutional activities; they obtained various kinds of exemptions as a result of their dealings with the nobility.

The resistance of village communities and subject populations to greater exactions by the king and increasingly independent local lords was an important factor in the collapse of the palace economies and centralized political power in the twelfth century. It coincided with the emergence of new patterns of maritime trade in the Mediterranean and Red seas, the creation of colonies in Sicily and North Africa, and the search for new sources of gold and other exotic items.

In the Levant and Asia Minor, class and state formation constituted distinctive regional political-economies and linked them into a single, unstable, spatially organized division of labor through tribute extraction and/or commerce. At the regional level, this development created a distinction between the subsistence sector, which produced goods for local consumption, and a tribute or export sector geared to satisfying the demands of the states, their ruling classes, and allied groups—which were not necessarily uniform and which frequently emanated from different areas. That is, goods appearing in the tribute or export sector were used in both the heartland areas and the frontier provinces by classes and/or groups that relied heavily on tribute and taxes for their maintenance.

The commercial transactions that occurred in the borderland areas and linked them with Mesopotamia and northeastern Africa meant that there was some production beyond the immediate requirements for subsistence and for the conditions that sustained the class structures of the states and kin-based village communities in western Asia. However, it is not clear that a commodity sector—that is, production for exchange—existed during the third or second millennia B.C. If one did, it must have resembled a very small island in a vast sea of subsistence production—that is, the production of use-values for consumption. As a result, it is necessary to clarify the circumstances and the conditions that would promote the development of petty commodity production and the formation of internal markets.

STATE FORMATION, ETHNOGENESIS, AND RESISTANCE: THE LEVANT IN THE FIRST MILLENNIUM B.C.

State formation triggers uneven development—that is, it both creates and perpetuates circumstances in which societies can develop at different rates and along different trajectories. Uneven development provides a rich medium for ethnocide and ethnogenesis. The former involves the destruction of a way of life; the latter results when a people, who share the historical experience of occupying the same position in a class- and state-structured system of oppressive social relations, attempt to escape entrapment and forge a collective identity out of those shared experiences and circumstances. Let us examine two instances of ethnogenesis that occurred in the Levant between about 1250 and 750 B.C. and a third that occurred later during the first and second centuries A.D.

The Canaanite and Phoenician Commercial Cities

By the sixteenth century B.C., the coastal cities of the Levant—like Sidon, Tyre, Byblos, and Ugarit—already occupied central places in a regional economy that linked Egypt, Cyprus, Syria, Anatolia, and the Aegean. They existed on the margins of the great states and provided them with raw materials, finished goods, and services that were not easily acquired or readily available. The merchants were navigators, the owners of boats fashioned by shipbuilders from the hardwoods that grew in the tree-covered hills overlooking the coast. In the workshop districts of the cities, artisans crafted luxury commodities, like ivory-inlaid furniture, that were used by various royal courts; more important, the cities produced cloth, dyes, and garments that were exchanged for raw materials and used as tribute. The merchant captains hired crews of sailors, moved bulky commodities and raw materials along the coast, and used gifts and diplomatic skills to forge relations that guaranteed them independent access to raw materials and markets in distant lands. After the fourteenth century B.C., the coastal commerce of the Levantine cities was controlled by merchant firms that provided capital, built ships, and sponsored and protected merchant fleets.

The tin, copper, and other raw materials obtained during the voyages of the Canaanite merchants and the Phoenician sea venturers who followed them were made into finished goods by artisans who resided in the various cities. These items were given as tribute payments, were exchanged for additional raw materials in local or foreign markets, or were sold for profit in one of the region's royal courts. The merchant firms employed certain kinds of artisans—shipbuilders, carpenters, divers, and perhaps weavers—who were probably a mixture of free laborers, debt bondsmen, and slaves and uprooted landless peasants from the surrounding countryside. By the eleventh century B.C., the merchant firms, notably those of Tyre, were investing their profits in new ventures: fishing, the production of dyes made from marine mollusks, weaving, and the construction of temples. While they continued to ship the goods they had been famous for earlier, they began to export new commodities, including artisans and the technical skills they possessed. The merchants severed their ties with the countryside and began to rely increasingly on the foodstuffs and raw materials they produced, imported, or purchased.

The Phoenician merchants, the artisans they employed to produce commodities, and perhaps others who catered to their needs became increasingly differentiated from the remaining residents of the cities and from those of the rural hinterlands. They represented the materialization of a monetary economy in societies whose members were primarily engaged in the production of use-values. They constituted a distinctive, internally differentiated, economically specialized people-class, analogous to the Jews in medieval Europe or the overseas Chinese in Southeast Asia today. The merchants' position became more prominent during the early part of the first millennium B.C. as the use of money spread and the demand for silver specie increased. The merchant firms extended their control over the flow and availability of silver and expanded their moneylending, banking, and other financial services.

What ultimately limited the spread of a monetary economy was the fact that many of the direct producers in the countryside around the Phoenician cities maintained significant levels of control over their own means of production, the use-values they produced, and their labor power. The local nobles who exacted tribute typically demanded payment in kind or labor service rather than cash during the first half of the first millennium B.C. The Phoenician cities began to supply increasing quantities of iron and other raw materials to the Neo-Assyrian state, which established hegemony over much of the Near East late in the eighth century B.C. This exchange involved forging treaties with neighboring peoples to protect overland caravan routes; establishing overseas colonies in those parts of the Mediterranean where the raw materials were abundant; and building a shipyard at Ezion-geber on the Gulf of Aqaba which was the base for maritime expeditions in the Red Sea to acquire gold from the principalities of southern Arabia and ivory from Africa.

The linkages between the independent Phoenician city-states and their colonies were expressed through a complex web of kin relations. For example, the city of Tyre was described as the daughter of Sidon, and Carthage was the daughter of Tyre. Thus, the Phoenician merchants and artisans from Tyre who resided in the colonies it established in Cyprus, Carthage, Cadiz, and other places on the Mediterranean around 700 B.C. also expressed their relationship to the founders in terms of kinship and descent. The colonists also reaffirmed their connections with the Levantine cities by building temples dedicated to the major deities of Tyre and the other Phoenician kingdoms related to it and by participating in the rituals and activities of those shrines. These practices enmeshed the colonists in that complex, ideologically constructed web that simultaneously linked and explained the connections of the cities and colonies to one another.

The Israelites: From Tribal Confederacy to Dynastic State

During the early twelfth century B.C., the Egyptian ruler, Ramesses III, established five fortified garrison-cities in the plains and foothills of southern Palestine: Gaza, Askkalon, Ekron, Ashdod, and Gath. Unlike the commercial cities of the Phoenicians, these were located a few miles from the sea and straddled important inland caravan routes. The garrisons were staffed by chariot-using mercenaries, administrators, and enough retainers to keep the chariots running efficiently. They were an imposed ruling elite. The mercenaries came from Crete, judging by both written accounts and the kinds of pottery they used, and were called Philistines by the authors of the Old Testament. They were employed by the Egyptian rulers to guard the frontiers of the state and to protect merchants and caravans traveling overland on the trade route from the outlaws—fugitives, refugees, bandits, and rebels—who had fled into the remote areas of southern Palestine and threatened both commerce and the dominant social order.

The outlaws, called 'apiru in numerous texts, were not a homogeneous group, ethnically or any other way. They had moved to remote, inaccessible areas in southern Palestine and elsewhere at various times and for different reasons. Their numbers included criminals, escaped slaves, priests, and deposed officials, as well as peasants and town dwellers who had fled to avoid taxes in kind and corvée labor demands. What united them were the simultaneous experiences of being recognizably outside the existing state-based social order and of having to rely on the wider society to the extent that it provided their livelihood. At the same time as the outlaw communities provided individual contract laborers and groups hired as soldiers, agricultural workers, or construction gangs, they also fought to retain their self-sufficiency by growing their own food and making or stealing the goods they required. The 'apiru communities maintained varying relations with the states around them. In Canaan, they were armed and described as either mercenaries or renegades who were familiar with guerrilla tactics. The outlaws, with their often fiercely egalitarian worldviews, were perceived as threats to the existing social order and were frequently hired by the ruler of one city-state to harrass other polities.

Attacks from the outside, the counterattacks that followed, internal power struggles, and defections combined to weaken the city-states in southern Palestine during the twelfth century B.C. Egypt's control over the region completely disintegrated, creating new political arenas and opportunities for the Philistines and the *'apiru* bands. The Philistines became the de facto rulers of the garrison-cities and quickly established hegemony over the Canaanite city-states of the region. The membership of the outlaw bands was fed by steadily growing numbers of fugitives and refugees from areas controlled by the states. In such circumstances, the line between the *'apiru* and the farmers and pastoralists on the margins of the states became increasingly blurred. The latter, in some instances, undoubtedly provided covert aid to the outlaws and may not even have abandoned their homes and fields when they themselves joined the renegade bands—that is, after they stopped paying taxes and providing labor service to the state's representatives.

Not all of the *'apiru* bands were Israelites, according to both Philistine and Israelite contemporaries (Gottwald 1979:419–425). That is, there were non-Israelite *'apiru* communities scattered throughout the area on the margins and in the interstices of the existing territorially organized Philistine and Canaanite kingdoms in southern Palestine and in the small tribal or nation states of Moab, Edom, and Ammon, which appeared in the Jordan River Valley after 1300 B.C. and were organized around core groups, each of whose members shared a conscious, collective national identity.

The Israelite tribal confederation and, later, the kingdom came into existence in circumstances that disrupted the power of the states and their ability to coordinate their actions. It permitted the interests of various anti-statist elements and groups to converge. As Israelite *'apiru* groups broke free from their association with the Egyptian state, centered at Amarna, the similarities between their "outlaw" form of everyday life and that pursued by other bands in the area became apparent and ultimately the basis for a new social order, which the various states in the region deemed illegitimate. What emerged was an eclectic coalition of communities that were constituted in opposition to the states and made up of diverse underclass and outlaw elements. The communities were bound together by their identity as a single people. They increasingly used the name Israel to designate the coalition that had crystallized over a period of years; at the same time, they retained their own distinctive names and identities. What bound the communities together were the shared religious cult and similar, diffusely egalitarian, antistatist ideologies. Conversion to Israel occurred as the Canaanite ruling classes lost control, first over the rural populations in the countryside and then over the city dwellers, and the various outcasts and underclasses collaborated and identified themselves with the tribal communities.

The tribal confederacy collapsed in the eleventh century B.C., as the Philistines defeated its army, sacked its shrine, placed garrisons at strategic points, and deprived the tribal peoples of the metals they needed to make weapons. These were the circumstances that propelled the tribes to elect a king. Saul, the first monarch, was a charismatic war chief—that is, he understood the situation clearly enough to act decisively when opportunities presented themselves. He was elected to serve for the duration of the crisis, which persisted throughout his entire adult life. Saul made little or no effort to create a bureaucracy, except for employing kinsmen to collect taxes; however, he did assemble an entourage of young soldiers, who formed the backbone of the army and warrior aristocracy. One of the soldiers was David, who married Saul's daughter and eventually succeeded him as king.

David fled into the hills of Judah when his father-in-law attempted to murder him. He assembled an 'apiru band that attacked the Philistines, avoided Saul's soldiers, and extorted support from wealthy citizens. This was not a viable position, so David allied himself with the Philistine kingdom of Gath and became a vassal, whose soldiers raided 'apiru groups that bothered the Israelite tribes. David redistributed the spoils of his victories to groups in Judah. At about the same time, the Philistines defeated the Israelite army; Saul's sons died in battle, and Saul killed himself. Within a few years, David, the Philistine vassal, consolidated his position by repairing relations with the loyal supporters of the dead leader, establishing marital and diplomatic relations with neighboring kingdoms, and out-maneuvering his only rival. He united the tribes when he was proclaimed king in Hebron; however, sectional disputes and the animosity of some of Saul's kin continued.

The Philistines, realizing what David had accomplished, attacked the Israelite monarchy and were ultimately defeated, their power broken. David then built a palace in Jerusalem, the new capital, and moved the Ark, the major religious symbol of the Israelite tribal confederacy, and its priests into an official national shrine. Within months, he attacked neighboring polities throughout Palestine and southward toward the Gulf of Aqaba; the term "Israel," originally used to designate the tribal confederation, now became the name of a territorial state, an empire, whose officials included a military commander, a commander of mercenaries, a secretary, a tax collector who supervised foreigners forced to work on royal projects, and two priests.

Solomon ascended to the throne as his father's coregent; however, since there were no rules of succession, the whole affair was surrounded by palace intrigues and civil unrest. When his father finally died, Solomon eliminated everyone who might threaten his authority. His armies adopted chariots and fortified cities—like Megiddo and Hazor—that marked the periphery of the core area of the state. The king also undertook a number of commercial and industrial ventures, which enriched the state's coffers: maritime trade in the Red Sea, undertaken with the aid of the Phoenicians; caravan trade with Arabia; the creation of a copper industry; and the acquisition of horses from the foothills of northern Syria and chariots from Egypt. The state also built a national temple—a shrine for the Ark and royal chapel for the high priest appointed by Solomon.

Solomon's expenditures outstripped the state's revenues, and he eventually reorganized the land into twelve administrative districts headed by governors whom he appointed to increase revenues and collect taxes more efficiently. Since the old tribal territories were largely ignored when the lands were reapportioned, tax levies, which had formerly fallen most heavily on subjugated populations, now fell on the members of the tribal groupings as well. Priests associated with the state cult, merchants, and others who benefited from the new forms of exploitation initiated by the state continued to

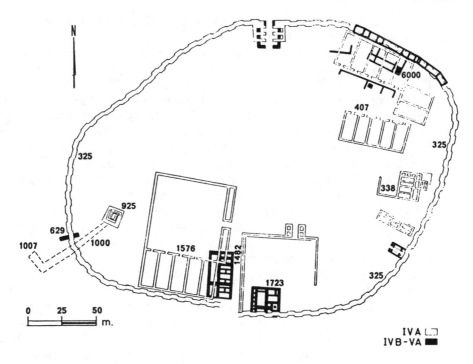

N

6000

407

325

325

338

925

629

1007   1000

1576

1482

1723

325

0   25   50
m.

IVA ⬜
IVB-VA ⬛

Plan of the fortified settlement of Megiddo.

support its goals. However, the reorganization and rationalization of the state apparatus to improve revenues and tax collection alienated the tribal communities, especially the poorer ones in the north. The northern tribes found the new policies increasingly oppressive, and one of their prophets attempted to foment a rebellion against the king and state. He represented sentiments that favored dismantling the state and returning to the old tribal order. The plot was crushed, but the sources of the discontent continued to fester.

Shortly after Solomon's death in the late tenth century B.C., the imperial state fell apart, as the northern tribes created a new identity and dressed it up in the clothes of tradition. They asserted their independence from the southern kingdom. For fifty years, the two kingdoms were rivals that quarreled and fought. Judah, the southern state, maintained the dynastic tradition, whereas the rulers in Israel, the northern kingdom, had to create a state where none existed, where there was no army, no capital, and no state shrine. Jeroboam, the charismatic leader designated by the prophets as its first ruler, established a capital near the center of the domain and set up official shrines at both ends, which could lay claim to traditions that existed before the monarchy of David and Solomon. The shrines ultimately challenged the legitimacy of the official cult in the southern kingdom and put Jeroboam in the role of reformer, who could criticize the failure of Solomon and the state religion in the south to deal forcefully with the pagan cults of the foreigners and merchants.

Omri, who ascended to the throne of the northern kingdom in 876 B.C., established peaceful relations with the southern state and close ties with the Phoenicians, especially those of Tyre. He cemented the alliance by having his son marry Jezebel, the Tyrian king's daughter, who had shrines dedicated to Phoenician deities built on Israelite soil so that she, her retainers, and the Phoenician merchants could attend to their religious obligations. She also had the Phoenician cult made the official cult of the king's court. Thus, many members of the court, the ruling class, and the merchants of the northern kingdom were paganized, and for a time, cults dedicated to different deities crosscut and related to one another in a myriad of ways. Jezebel also persecuted the classes and groups—mostly the urban and rural poor, the priests, and the prophets—that remained loyal to the traditional Israelite shrines. Her persecution and, in some instances, execution of the loyalists hardened their resistance and exacerbated class differences between the poor and the prophets—some of whom gave voice to their sentiments, and those with access to the power of the state.

In 722 B.C., Israel and Judah were subjugated by the neo-Assyrian state and became entangled in complex webs of tributary relations, whose centers of gravity were located to the east, first in Assur, then Babylon (612 to 539 B.C.), and finally Persia (539 to 333 B.C.). The Levant then fell under the sway of the Ptolemies in Egypt (323 to 198 B.C.) and eventually the Romans. This was the period when Hellenistic culture crystallized in the eastern Mediterranean; an overseas Jewish people-class dominated by merchants and finance capitalists became prominent as a result of the eastward shift of economic activity into the Greco-Roman world, where occupations linked with commerce and banking were usually, but not always, loathed by the local ruling classes; and the seeds of Christianity were sown among the diverse Eastern, Egyptian, Greek, Jewish, and Roman cults and sects that thrived between Athens and Alexandria.

Early Christian Communities in the Hellenistic World

The early Christian sects of the second and third centuries A.D. developed under the continually shifting conditions and circumstances of the internationalist, Hellenistic cultural milieu of the Mediterranean world, where a common spoken Greek dialect, not the classical language of Athens, was the lingua franca. This implies that some or all of the inhabitants of many areas were multilingual. They spoke the indigenous language(s) of their households and local communities and *koine,* the spoken Greek dialect, which gave them access to the various intellectual currents and practices of the larger Hellenistic speech community. Thus, a *koine*-speaker in Jerusalem, whose native language was Aramaic, had the ability to gain very detailed knowledge of events and practices in other parts of the Mediterranean world merely by talking with other Greek-speakers.

In these circumstances, orthodoxy was continually being constructed and defended in the face of internal conflicts, mutual accusations of heresy, and the schismatic communities that emerged almost as soon as the Apostles undertook their mission among the Aramaic-speaking peasants of rural Galilee. In the internationalist Hellenistic world, syncreticism, the blending of beliefs and practices from different cults, Judeo-Christian and pagan, was a common, almost everyday event.

By the second century, the Christian communities were located mainly in the cities rather than in the rural areas around the Mediterranean. The latter remained largely pagan well into the fourth century. The early Christians were largely members of the urban middle classes: artisans who moved back and forth between urban areas and villages, merchants, bankers, farmers who lived in the cities, urban wage workers, and freedmen and freedwomen with aspirations of social mobility. Many members of the communities were educated or, at least, exposed to learning since their teachers and clerics often came from the educated classes and groups of Hellenistic society. They maintained both business and personal relations with pagans in their pursuit of self-improvement and wealth. The financial positions of the communities were based on the offerings of their members, banking and moneylending, the rental of urban buildings to artisans and lodgers, and the sale of plots in community-owned cemeteries.

There were fluidity and movement among the various Christian and Jewish sects of the first century; consequently, the boundaries were blurred on some matters. However, the differences were clear in the Levant by A.D. 100, after the revolt by the indigenous ruling class of Judaea, which had occupied a favored position in the province, provoked the Roman state and fueled its antagonism toward Judaism as a cult. Whereas the Jews were persecuted in Judaea, the Christian communities were not. Their practices and beliefs had become distinctive enough from those of the Jews to avoid identification with them and persecution. Earlier laws that expelled the Jews from Rome in 139 B.C., in A.D. 19, and again in A.D. 49 probably had less to do with Roman hostility to Judaism than with the desire of the Roman state to appropriate property or with the wishes of segments of the native upper classes to enter the low-status but very lucrative•commercial and financial professions of the Jewish people-class.

Both the composition of the early Christian communities and their relations to one another, to other sects, and to the state were complex. As Dimitris Kyrtatas (1987:186) has observed, "What requires further investigation, perhaps, is not so much the social character of early Christianity as the social factors which allowed religion to take on such importance in late antiquity."

FURTHER READINGS: A BRIEF GUIDE

For overviews of the area, see A. Bernard Knapp, *The History and Culture of Ancient Western Asia and Egypt* (Belmont, CA: Wadsworth, 1988); N. K. Sandars, *The Sea Peoples: Warriors of the Ancient Mediterranean* (London: Thames & Hudson, 1985); and Martin Bernal, *Black Athena: The Afroasiatic Roots of Classical Civilization, vol. II, The Archaeological and Documentary Evidence* (New Brunswick, NJ: Rutgers University Press, 1991).

For discussions of historical developments during the third millennium B.C., see Michael Roaf, *Cultural Atlas of Mesopotamia and the Ancient Near East* (Oxford: Equinox, 1990); Roland de Vaux, "Palestine in the Early Bronze Age," and James Mellaart, "Anatolia, *c.* 4000–2300 B.C.," both in *The Cambridge Ancient History*, ed. I. E. S. Edwards, C. J. Gadd, and N. G. L. Hammond, vol. I, pt. 2 (Cambridge: Cambridge University Press, 1971), pp. 208–237 and 363–410; Giovanni Pettinato, *Ebla: A New Look at History* (Baltimore: Johns Hopkins University Press, 1991); and Paolo Matthiae, "A New Palatial Building and the Princely Tombs of Middle Bronze I–II at Ebla," in *Gesellschaft und Kultur im alten Vorderasien*, Schriften zur Geschichte und Kultur des alten Orients 15, ed. Horst Klengel (Berlin, 1982), 187–194, and *Ebla in the Period of the Amorite Dynasties and the Dynasty of Akkad*, Monographs on the Ancient Near East, vol. 1, fasc. 6 (Malibu, CA: Undena Publications, 1979).

Mogens T. Larsen, "The Tradition of Empire in Mesopotamia," in *Power and Propaganda: A Symposium on Ancient Empires*, ed. Mogens T. Larsen (Copenhagen: Akademisk Forlag, 1979), pp. 75–106; Pierre Briant, *Etat et Pasteurs au Moyen-Orient Ancien* (Cambridge: Cambridge University Press, 1982); and Mario Liverani, "Communautés de Village et Palais Royal dans la Syrie du IIème Millénaire," *Journal of the Social and Economic History of the Orient*, vol. XVIII, pt. 2 (1975), 146–164, provide an excellent overview to the empires and commercial states of the second millennium B.C. For the role of nomadism in the Levant, see M. B. Rowton, "Autonomy and Nomadism in Western Asia," *Orientalia*, vol. 42, fasc. 1–2 (1973), 247–258, "Enclosed Nomadism," *Journal of the Economic and Social History of the Orient*, vol. XVI, pt. 1 (1974), 1–30, and "Urban Autonomy in a Nomadic Environment," *Journal of Near Eastern Studies*, vol. 32, no. 1–2 (1973), 201–215.

For the Mitanni state, see Ignace J. Gelb, *Hurrians and Subarians* (Chicago: University of Chicago Press, 1944).

The Hittite kingdoms are examined by O. R. Gurney, *The Hittite Empire* (Harmondsworth, Eng.: Penguin Books, 1975); J. G. Macqueen, *The Hittites and Their Contemporaries in Asia Minor* (London: Thames & Hudson, 1986); Alberto R. Green, "Social Stratification and Cultural Continuity at Alalakh," in *The Quest for the Kingdom of God: Studies in Honor of George E. Mendenhall*, ed. H. B. Huffmon, F. A. Spina, and A. R. W. Green (Winona Lake, MN: Eisenbrauns, 1983), pp. 181–203; and Nana V. Khazaradze, "Royal Power in Late Hittite Political Entities," in *Gesellschaft und Kultur im alten Vorderasien*,

Schriften zur Geschichte und Kultur des alten Orients 15, ed. Horst Klengel (Berlin, 1982), pp. 121–126.

For the Assyrian state, see Mogens T. Larsen, *The Old Assyrian City-State and Its Colonies* (Copenhagen: Akademisk Forlag, 1976), and "Your Money or Your Life! A Portrait of an Assyrian Businessman," in *Societies and Languages of the Ancient Near East: Studies in Honour of I. M. Diakonoff* (London: Aris & Phillips, 1982), pp. 214–242; John N. Postgate, "The Economic Structure of the Assyrian Empire," and John A. Brinkman, "Babylonia under the Assyrian Empire, 745–627 B.C.," both in *Power and Propaganda: A Symposium on Ancient Empires*, ed. Mogens T. Larsen (Copenhagen: Akademisk Forlag, 1979), pp. 193–222 and 223–250; Jana Pecírková, "The Development of the Assyrian State," in *Gesellschaft und Kultur im alten Vorderasien*, Schriften zur Geschichte und Kultur des alten Orients 15, ed. Horst Klengel (Berlin, 1982), pp. 201–212.

For the Kassite state, see John A. Brinkman, "Provincial Administration in Babylonia under the Second Dynasty of Isin," *Journal of the Economic and Social History of the Orient*, vol. VI, pt. 3 (1963), 233–242; "Kudurru," *Reallexikon der Assyriologie*, Band 6 (1981), 267–274; "Kassiten," *Reallexikon der Assyriologie*, Band 5 (1980), 464–473; "The Monarchy in the Time of the Kassite Dynasty," in *Le Palais et la Royaute*, ed. P. Garelli (Paris: Geuthner, 1974), pp. 395–408; and *A Political History of Post-Kassite Babylonia, 1158–722 B.C.* (Rome: Pontifical Biblical Institute, 1968).

Commercial and political linkages and transformations are discussed by Mario Liverani, "The Collapse of the Near Eastern Regional System at the End of the Bronze Age: The Case of Syria," and Mogens T. Larsen, "Commercial Networks in the Ancient Near East," both in *Centre and Periphery in the Ancient World*, ed. Michael Rowlands, Mogens Larsen, and Kristian Kristiansen (Cambridge: Cambridge University Press, 1987), pp. 74–86 and 47–56; John M. Halligan, "The Role of the Peasant in the Amarna Period," in *Palestine in Transition; The Emergence of Ancient Israel*, ed. David N. Freedman and David F. Graf (Sheffield, Eng.: Almond Press, 1983), pp. 15–24; Donald B. Redford, "The Relations between Egypt and Israel from El-Amarna to the Babylonian Conquest," *Biblical Archaeology Today: Proceedings of the International Congress on Biblical Archaeology, Jerusalem, April 1984* (Jerusalem: Israel Exploration Society, 1985), pp. 192–205; and Susan Frankenstein, "The Phoenicians in the Far West: A Function of Neo-Assyrian Imperialism," in *Power and Propaganda: A Symposium on Ancient Empires*, ed. Mogens T. Larsen (Copenhagen: Akademisk Forlag, 1979), pp. 263–294.

For discussions of the Levant and Palestine during the late second and first millennia B.C., see Norman K. Gottwald, *The Tribes of Yahweh: A Sociology of the Religion of Liberated Israel, 1250–1050 B.C.E.* (Maryknoll, NY: Orbis Books, 1979); see also Norman Gottwald, "Two Models for the Origins of Ancient Israel: Social Revolution or Frontier Development," and Robert R. Wilson, "Enforcing the Covenant: The Mechanisms of Judicial Authority in Early Israel," both in *The Quest for the Kingdom of God*, ed. H. B. Huffmon, F. A.

Spina, and A. R. W. Green (Winona Lake, MN: Eisenbrauns, 1983), pp. 5–24 and 59–75; George E. Mendenhall, "The Hebrew Conquest of Palestine," *The Biblical Archaeologist*, vol. XXV, no. 3 (1962), 66–87; Norman Gottwald, "Early Israel and the Canaanite Socio-economic System," in *Palestine in Transition*, ed. David N. Freedman and David F. Graf (Sheffield, Eng.: Almond Press, 1983), pp. 25–37; Albrecht Alt, *Essays on Old Testament History and Religion* (Oxford: B. H. Blackwell, 1966); and John Bright, *A History of Israel* (Philadelphia: Westminister Press, 1981).

Events in the waning centuries of the first millennium B.C. and the early part of the first millennium A.D. are discussed by Abram Leon, *The Jewish Question: A Marxist Interpretation* (New York: Pathfinder Press, 1970); Hugo Echegaray, *The Practice of Jesus* (Maryknoll, NY: Orbis Books, 1984); Martin Goodman, *The Ruling Class of Judaea: The Origins of the Jewish Revolt against Rome A.D. 66–70* (Cambridge: Cambridge University Press, 1987); Martin Hengel, *Jews, Greeks and Barbarians: Aspects of the Hellenization of Judaism in the Pre-Christian Period* (Philadelphia: Fortress Press, 1980); Arnaldo Momigliano, *Alien Wisdom: The Limits of Hellenization* (Cambridge: Cambridge University Press, 1975); Dimitris J. Kyrtatas, *The Social Structure of the Early Christian Communities* (London: Verso, 1987); William H. C. Frend, *The Rise of Christianity* (Philadelphia: Fortress Press, 1984), and *Archaeology and History in the Study of Early Christianity* (London: Variorum Reprints, 1988); Karl Kautsky, *Foundations of Christianity* (New York: Monthly Review Press, 1972); Geoffrey E. M. de Ste. Croix, *The Class Struggle in the Ancient Greek World* (Ithaca, NY: Cornell University Press, 1981); Robin Lane Fox, *Pagans and Christians* (New York: Knopf, 1987); A. H. M. Jones, "Were Ancient Heresies National or Social Movements in Disguise?" *The Journal of Theological Studies*, vol. X, pt. 2 (1959), 280–298, and "The Social Background of the Struggle between Paganism and Christianity," in *The Conflict between Paganism and Christianity in the Fourth Century*, ed. Arnoldo Momigliano (Oxford: Clarendon Press, 1964), pp. 17–37; Peter Brown, *Society and the Holy in Late Antiquity* (Berkeley: University of California Press, 1982); and Eric R. Dodds, *Pagan and Christian in an Age of Anxiety* (Cambridge: Cambridge University Press, 1965), and *The Ancient Concept of Progress and Other Essays on Greek Literature and Belief* (Oxford: Oxford University Press, 1973).

chapter 11

The Mediterranean World

For tyranny is monarchy for the benefit of the monarch, oligarchy for the benefit of the men of means, democracy for the benefit of the men without means. (Aristotle, The Politics)

The disappearance of tributary relationships . . . was accompanied by the massive growth of chattel slavery in those parts of Greece where the liberation of the peasant was most complete. (Ellen M. Wood, Peasant-Citizen and Slave: The Foundations of Athenian Democracy)

What distinguished Rome was neither economic inequality nor exploitation but the enormity in scale of both. (P. A. Brunt, Social Conflicts in the Roman Republic)

The really distinctive feature of each society is . . . how the extraction of the surplus from the immediate producer is secured. (Geoffrey E. M. de Ste. Croix, The Class Struggle in the Ancient Greek World)

Mountains dominate the Mediterranean world. They stretch almost uninterrupted along the coast from Asia Minor and Greece to Spain and northward to the Alps and the Carpathians, which seal off the Mediterranean lands from those lying to the north. Some of the mountains are high; others are parts of old ranges with deep, almost inaccessible valleys. The climatic regime of the Mediterranean is produced by the interplay of weather systems centered over the Atlantic and the continents; the homogeneity of the climate is broken up and sculpted by the mountain ranges that enclose the basin. Winters are long and severe in the mountains and 10 or more feet of snow can fall in a single night, whereas 100 miles away flowers bloom in the villages and towns that fringe the Mediterranean coast. Although gentle sea breezes cool the coastal towns during the hot, dry summers, the combination of heat and humidity becomes oppressive a few miles from the shore. The climate, the mountains, and the way in which the people have used various landscapes have also combined to create locally and regionally diverse vegetation.

EARLY FOOD-PRODUCING COMMUNITIES

The earliest farming communities appeared in the low-lying areas of Greece, which have semiarid environments resembling those of the Levant, and the Near East, where food production developed early. Agriculture did not develop independently in southeastern Europe; it was an extension of the food-producing practices that had originated earlier in the east. Many of the species grown by the early European farmers—sheep and goats, wheat and

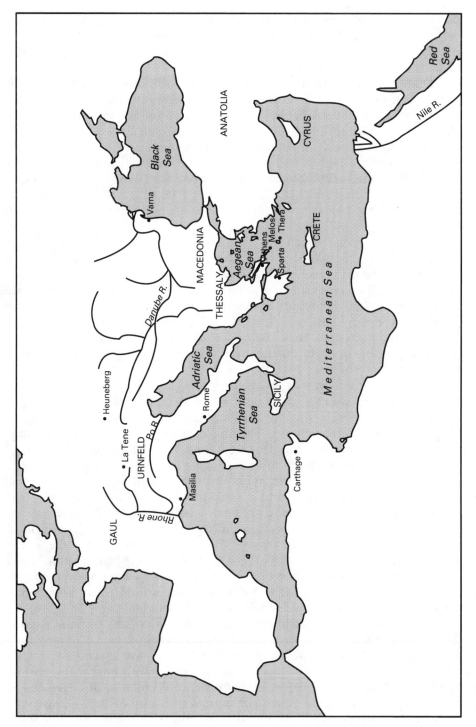

The Mediterranean world.

barley—were first domesticated in the Near East; others, notably cattle, may well have been tamed and domesticated in southeastern Europe during the seventh millennium B.C. while their wild relatives were still being hunted in Anatolia and northern Europe.

During the seventh millennium B.C., the early food-producing community at Argissa in Thessaly kept small herds of sheep and cattle; cultivated wheat, barley, peas, vetch, and lentils; and harvested acorns, pistachios, and wild olives. At Franchthi Cave, overlooking the Gulf of Argolis a few hundred miles to the south, their contemporaries hunted wild cattle, deer, and pigs and collected almonds and pistachios; they also built boats, caught deep-sea fish like tuna, and brought obsidian from the island of Melos, located more than a hundred miles out to sea. After 5900 B.C., when the inhabitants of Franchthi Cave began to keep sheep and goats, they relied less on wild game.

Nea Nikomedeia, which lies on a knoll overlooking a lake in Macedonia, is one of the best-known early farming communities. During the mid-sixth millennium B.C., its inhabitants lived in half a dozen single-roomed, wattle-and-daub houses clustered around a larger building. They grew cereal grains, kept a few domesticated animals, gathered wild fruits and nuts, fished in the nearby lake, and hunted. The pollen rain captured in the lake sediments indicates that they did not clear enough woodland for garden plots and grazing lands to disturb the development of climax forests in the region; this fact suggests that they may have intensively cultivated small garden plots on the edges of wooded areas.

Farming communities appeared in the Balkans—Yugoslavia, Hungary, Rumania, and Bulgaria—during the later half of the fifth millennium B.C. They were quite variable in size, ranging from single homesteads to villages of 400 houses, regularly spaced along both sides of lanes that led into the countryside. Villages with 100 to 150 residents were common. In many of the settlements, ritual or cultic activities, involving small figurines, were practiced at both the household and community levels in most villages. There were general similarities in much of the material culture—the pottery, figurines, and chipped stone tools—used in early village communities of northern Greece and the central Balkans. This does not mean that the pottery manufactured and used in one village was identical with that produced in another, for there were subtle differences; it does mean, however, that the boundaries were often blurred and that the potters of different communities throughout the region shared similar aesthetic standards.

The early food-producing communities are known by various names—Körös, Cris, Starcevo, and Kremikovci—which reflect regional differences in the mixes of subsistence practices, work activities, and associated forms of everyday life. The relative importance of cultivation, husbandry, fishing, hunting, and foraging varied in the subsistence economies of different communities. For instance, the Körös communities of southeastern Hungary and northern Yugoslavia, which pastured their sheep and goats on floodplains during the winter, relied heavily on the local wildlife. The food-producing, village communities of the Bug and Dneister River Valleys of northeastern Rumania relied heavily on hunting, fishing, and gathering wild plants; they resided in year-round settlements but moved every few years. The inhabitants at Anza in southeastern Yugoslavia slaughtered pigs when the animals were young, whereas their sheep, goats, and cattle—which they kept for their wool, milk, and hides—died as adults.

Village communities in the rest of the Mediterranean world, from the Adriatic coast of Italy to France and Spain, adopted various food-producing technologies during the later part of the fifth millennium B.C. and integrated them into existing lifestyles and economic patterns. For example, about 4700 B.C., the communities in central Italy depended on wild pigs, red deer, and cattle. During the summer months, they followed herds of red deer into the mountains, taking a few domesticated sheep and goats with them. They returned to the coastal plains during the fall, rounded up the pigs that rooted in wooded areas, and harvested the wild plant foods of aquatic and woodland habitats. Over time, sheep and goats became more important than deer because they reproduced faster and needed far less pasture to provide the same amount of meat.

Plant cultivation played a different role in the subsistence economy of central Italy. During the spring, the Italian pastoralists may have sown wheat around their coastal lakeside settlements before they went into the mountains with their herds to hunt deer. When they returned to the lowlands in the fall, they harvested what was left of the crops they had planted, rounded up pigs, and harvested water chestnuts and other wild plants. Cereal agriculture became steadily more important as time passed, and patches of forests were cleared and burned so that fields could be planted. As a result, pigs and deer found their natural habitats becoming smaller and smaller, whereas sheep and goats had steadily increasing amounts of open grazing land as more forests were cleared for agriculture.

In the fifth millennium B.C. and later, subsistence economies that incorporated various food-producing practices appeared north of the Alps and the Carpathians. Agriculture and animal husbandry were introduced by immigrants from the Mediterranean area and adopted by the indigenous populations of the temperate regions of central and northern Europe. The practices were integrated into local economies in different ways, yielding diverse forms of everyday life. The complexity of this cultural mosaic was increased by the elaboration of community-level social relations—which involved the exchange of exotic goods by the inhabitants of different settlements—and by the appearance of village communities in which place of residence rather than common descent or membership in the same kin unit began to structure allegiances.

The social relations of the early food-producing village communities were clearly complex. Some communities were internally differentiated, their members occupying different statuses defined by age, kinship, gender, or life experience. In other communities, social relations were more egalitarian or were structured around prestigious men and women who attracted followers by redistributing exotic goods. Within these primitive communities, organized by kinship and sometimes by residence, there were emerging technical divisions of labor organized in part by gender distinctions. At one level, women's activities involved food preparation in the household, spinning and weaving, and presumably milking, while men hunted and farmed. At another level, women were also ritual specialists, while men mined and exchanged metals and exotic materials.

THE AEGEAN AND GREEK WORLDS

A series of far-reaching changes occurred in the Aegean world during and after the fourth millennium B.C. The first set of changes consisted of a shift in the locus of food storage from individual households to the village; the emergence of villages and hamlets along the coast; and the appearance of palisaded or fortified settlements throughout the interior of southeastern Europe, especially after 3000 B.C. The changes involved elaborations of the community-level relations of production in kin-organized communities to deal with new forms of agrarian production, greater control over the movement of the villagers and the goods they produced, and the appearance of new forms of exchange.

The other changes involved the appearance of new kinds of settlements, first at Varna on the Black Sea during the fourth millennium B.C. and, later, at Lerna and other coastal localities on the Aegean between 3000 and 2400 B.C. Varna is best known from the cemetery located south of the Danube Delta, where about sixty graves have yielded enormous numbers of gold objects: stone and copper axe handles covered with gold leaf, scepters, diadems, and earrings. More than twenty of the tombs were cenotaphs—that is, the contents and arrangement of the grave goods were identical to those tombs with bodies—and three of the cenotaphs contained hundreds of small gold objects and clay masks. The gold came from the Carpathian Mountains to the northwest.

Fortified corridor houses were built at Lerna, at Messenia, on the island of Aigina between the Argolid and Attica, and possibly at Thebes. The House of the Tiles, as the structure at Lerna is called, was one of several buildings inside a citadel with double encircling walls and projecting towers that overlooked the Gulf of Argos. The incorporation of certain Egyptian and Levantine design elements into the pottery produced locally at Lerna suggests that its inhabitants were in fairly regular contact with merchants and traders from those regions. The Dodos shipwreck, which dates to the late third millennium B.C., indicates that (1) the coastal sea trade was already thriving and (2) silver and lead ingots were already being shipped from the Laurion silver mines in Greece to Asia Minor, the Levant, and Egypt.

It appears that Varna and then the sites on the Aegean were trading emporia that linked southeastern Europe directly with the Levant, Northeast Africa, and the Near East. The richly furnished burials suggest that the rulers

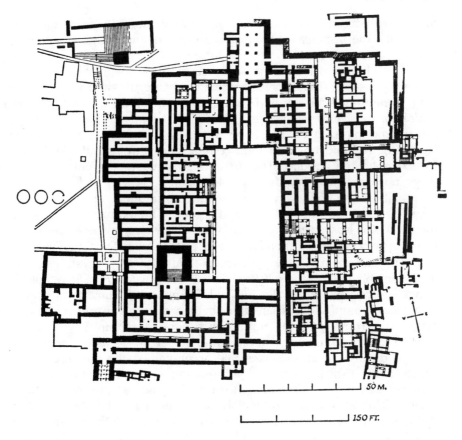

Palace of Knossos, Crete.

of these communities entered into alliances with their kin and neighbors to raid for slaves in the interior in order to acquire workers who toiled in mines for metals that were conspicuously consumed and exported by sea. Lerna was burned to the ground around 2400 B.C., and the exploitative social relations supported by its weakly developed state structures were apparently destroyed with it.

State-based societies, known as Early Minoan civilization, were reestablished, quite suddenly it seems, on Crete shortly after about 2000 B.C. The appearance of these semiautonomous polities was marked by the construction of three palaces on the island during the next two centuries. Each Minoan palace—Knossos, Mallia, and Phaistos—consisted of throne rooms, domestic quarters, workshops, and large storerooms built around a courtyard. Each palace stood at the center of a domain composed of villages, hamlets, and isolated farmhouses, whose inhabitants engaged in food production for themselves and provided labor and/or goods for the rulers, administrators, lapidaries, bronzesmiths, and other artisans who labored full time at the three seats of power. Scribes employed at the palaces used clay tablets with hieroglyphic and Linear A inscriptions to keep track of tribute payments, the dispersal of foodstuffs and goods, and other economic transactions.

The Minoan palaces organized maritime trade with other islands in the Aegean—notably Thera, Melos, Aigina, and Cyprus—and with various mainland communities in southern Europe, Anatolia, the Levant, and northern Africa. Some Minoan merchants resided in island villages—like the one on Thera, and perhaps on the mainland as well—where they acquired gold, silver, copper, and tin from local communities throughout the Aegean area, for example, the Argolid. The artisans attached to the palaces transformed these raw materials into fine jewelry, dishes, bowls, and other items that eventually found their way to mainland communities or royal courts in the Argolid, Anatolia, the Levant, and Egypt. The bronze weapons found in tombs at Knossos resembled those used elsewhere in the eastern Mediterranean, especially by the merchants and pirates from the Syro-Palestine coast.

The Minoan palaces were burned about 1730 B.C., possibly as a result of a local revolt or an attack by outsiders. They were quickly rebuilt and displayed even more Syro-Palestine and Egyptian influence than they had before; for example, Egyptian-style bathrooms and banquet halls became standard features and the murals incorporated certain Egyptian and Near Eastern conventions. Excavations in a house at Knossos, which was destroyed during the earthquakes that accompanied the volcanic explosion on Thera about 1628 B.C., yielded information suggesting that the sacrifice of children was one element of Minoan cultic practices during the New Palace Period. This information ultimately sheds light on the social and political-economic structure of Minoan society in the seventeenth and sixteenth centuries B.C.

Minoan society of this period is usually understood as a highly stratified society in which (1) power resided in the hands of a ruling class and (2) the residents of Knossos had established their hegemony over the inhabitants of the other palaces. Grave associations and representations in various media suggest that the ruling class consisted of gendered, complementary spheres of action. Ruling-class men were merchants, warriors, and pirates; elite women, by virtue of their gender and class position rather than their marital relations, held sway over cultic practices performed at the palaces and various hilltop sanctuaries.

Profound social transformations occurred on the Greek mainland between 1730 and 1670 B.C. These events shaped Aegean history for the next seven centuries. Mycenae, located in the Argolid, became a center of considerable wealth and influence. Two clusters of tombs were enclosed in stone walls; the older grave circle contained twenty-four stone-lined cists and shaft tombs, the newer one, six shaft graves. Both circles were part of a cemetery; however, no traces of the settlements where these people lived have yet been found. The shaft tombs at Mycenae contained several bodies, each of which was surrounded by bronze swords, spears, and daggers; vessels made from gold, silver, and bronze; gold masks; alabaster and rock crystal vases; pottery; and an array of small objects, such as lapis lazuli, faience, or ostrich eggs that came from as far away as Afghanistan, Egypt, and the Sudan. Stone slabs depicting chariots marked the entrances of the later shaft tombs. Several centuries later, the rulers who had the citadel built at Mycenae brought the more recent grave circle into the area enclosed by the massive, 3,000-foot-long fortification wall, which protected the hilltop. Other shaft tombs, similar to those at Mycenae and roughly the same age, were built at Eleusis in Attica, on the islands of Skopelos and Leukas, and on Crete.

The men and women interred in the shaft graves at Mycenae clearly stood at the pinnacle of the regional power structure. However, the shaft graves were not the only kind of ruling or elite tomb found in the cemetery. *Tholoi* (enormous beehive-shaped structures) were also built at Mycenae at about this time, one of which contained an array of goods that resembled those found in the later shaft graves. Other *tholoi* have been found to the south in Sparta and Messenia. Tumuli (burial mounds), the other kind of elite tomb found on the mainland in the seventeenth century B.C., have been found at several localities in Attica on the other side of the Gulf of Argos. Horses were sacrificed in two tumuli excavated at Marathon: on the roof of one tomb and in front of another.

About 1450 B.C., around the time Mycenae was fortified, citadels were also built at several other localities on the Greek mainland: Pylos in Messenia, Tiryns near the head of the Gulf of Argos, probably Thebes in Boiotia, and possibly Athens and Corinth. The citadels were the political centers of small states, which were also enmeshed in extensive trading networks that stretched eastward from the mainland and the islands of the Aegean and eastern Mediterranean to the shores of Asia Minor, the Levant, and North Africa and westward to Sicily and the Italian Peninsula. Scribes employed in the palaces used Linear B script to record tribute payments, the distribution of raw materials and food, anticipated returns from particular communities or artisans, and other transactions. Thus, the palace archives, especially the one at Pylos, provide information about the political-economic structures of the Mycenaean states as well as insights into the nature of uneven social development and history in the Aegean and eastern Mediterranean during the later half of the second millennium B.C. The Mycenaean states—which were linked at points by their class structures, marital ties, and diplomacy—were potentially or actually antagonistic to one another.

The palaces received tribute in kind and small amounts of labor service from free individuals who lived in the towns, villages, and hamlets. The grain sent to the palaces fed the ruling elite and their retainers and provided rations for the palace staff, artisans, corvée laborers, and slaves who toiled in the fields and workshops producing luxury goods for exchange or for consumption by the ruling classes and cults. The Pylian palace also employed and fed about 650 adult women slaves and nearly the same number of their sons and daughters. There was a great deal of occupational specialization in the Pylian state, and both free and servile workers engaged in some of the same occupations. For example, slave women made perfumed oil in the palace, and more than 400 bronzesmiths received ingots of copper and tin from the state and directions regarding the objects they should fashion from the metals.

The Mycenaean states also mobilized armies to acquire slaves from communities and polities located on their periphery, for example, the Balkans or Troy. Women and children captured in the slave raids toiled for the states, their rulers, and their soldiers; the men captured during the raids were either sold or sent to perform dangerous tasks, such as mining the ores at Laurion and other places, which were smelted, cast into ingots, and transformed into commodities or luxury goods that were conspicuously consumed by the elite or state-supported cults. Much of the metal produced in this manner entered into the maritime trade, which made the Mycenaean states wealthy and desirable commercial partners in the eyes of powerful contemporaries in the lands at the eastern end of the Mediterranean.

To summarize, between about 1720 and 1550 B.C., warlords, possibly from outside the Aegean world, founded local dynasties on the mainland at regions where shaft graves and, later, citadels were built. Their position in the political economy of the eastern Mediterranean was based on procuring slaves and mineral ores and trafficking in metals. They established marital alliances and diplomatic relations with communities on the mainland that disposed of their dead elite in *tholoi* and tumuli. The Aegean polities, both on Crete and on the mainland, were less connected with the outside from 1550 to 1470 B.C. During this period, the mainland states established hegemony over those on Crete. Maritime commerce increased significantly after 1470 B.C., but there were new trade routes and ports, judging by the growing quantities of Mycenaean and the dwindling numbers of Minoan goods found outside the Aegean world. The Minoan states on Crete were marginalized as the Mycenaean states and merchants came to dominate overseas commerce in the Aegean.

The royal economies of the Minoan and Mycenaean states were based on production for and control of the market. When the markets declined or were eliminated altogether in some instances, for whatever historically specific reasons, the political superstructures of the states were undermined. The ruling elite's hold on local officials, merchants, and artisans waned in the thirteenth century—that is, at roughly the same time that similar events and processes were unfolding in the Levant. Some Mycenaean towns were sacked and abandoned; others continued to function; and a few new centers, which were formerly provincial towns of secondary importance, rose to prominence. The states at Pylos and Knossos collapsed, whereas other states—Thebes, for instance—continued to function on a diminished scale until about 1200 B.C. The elaborate class structures, especially characteristic of the capitals, either disintegrated altogether or were dramatically simplified in those instances in which the ruling class succeeded in retaining vestiges of its former power.

The expansion of the Assyrian commercial empire and the collapse of the Minoan and Mycenaean states, which dominated Mediterranean trade until the end of the thirteenth century B.C., had two immediate consequences: The Phoenician city-states subsequently claimed control of the maritime trade, and the Greeks were largely excluded from the overland trade routes that began or passed through Anatolia. After the twelfth century, the importance of stock raising and agriculture was renewed among the reconstituted communities and polities of the Aegean; pastoral herding, in particular, was more important than it had been earlier, as many households and communities freed themselves from the tributary relations of the old collapsed states and attempted to avoid the clutches of groups trying to establish and enforce new forms of exploitation. Exchange relations were established with central Europe, colonies were settled from the Black Sea to the Atlantic Ocean, and what little remained of the maritime trade in the eastern Mediterranean was controlled by foreign merchants.

Societies in various parts of the Aegean developed along different trajectories after the institution of kingship collapsed in the eleventh century. As a result, a patchwork—a political-economic mosaic—emerged during the next five hundred years. The Aegean world was a mixture of tributary states with varying capacities to extract surplus from their own subjects and neighbors and kin-organized communities, which struggled to resist the exactions of neighboring states. In some instances, entire regions, like Attica, were organized under the dominion of a single state; in other areas, like Boeotia, Thebes, the largest and most powerful state, was unable to subordinate any of the twelve polities that were its closest neighbors.

The term *basilies* was used to describe a multitude of posts in which political power was vested; these included the aristocratic descendants of regional administrators under the old Mycenaean regimes, chieftains, village elders, and bigmen. The *basilies* were influential men, who had the capacity by virtue of their prominence to make decisions and resolve disputes, and they occasionally succeeded in portraying the authority they possessed as real power. Through the exchange of friendship and gifts, they were able to attract bands of male companions, the *hetairoi*, who would accompany them in traditional activities of primitive accumulation like cattle rustling, piracy, and slave raiding. Under these circumstances, some *basilies* and their retainers were able to concentrate landholdings in the domains where they had power; this act facilitated the appearance of a weakly developed class structure in which there were households with more or less extensive landholdings and domestic groups with little or no land, whose members were sharecroppers, tenants, or debt bondsmen who toiled on the estates of the wealthy to feed themselves and their children.

There were three responses to the crises provoked by class formation. Some households fled or emigrated to establish overseas colonies; however, this response left the emerging class structures intact. A second response involved the intensification of hostilities with neighboring polities and the creation of cross-class alliances, which ensured the participation of small landholders, who had heavily armed themselves; these were the *hoplites*, who manned the infantry phalanxes and who were promised that the labor power and goods required by the city-states and their ruling classes would be

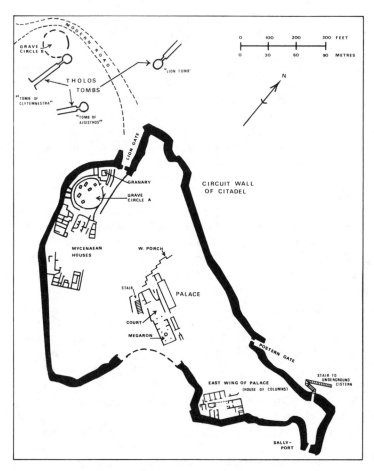

Citadel of Mycenae, Greece.

appropriated from defeated neighbors. The third response involved a cross-class alliance of a different kind. It occurred when the small landholders and artisans supported an outsider, usually a member of the aristocracy, who usurped power from the traditional *basilies* and promised to reform or contain the contradictions of class formation. Such individuals were called tyrants. Their solutions to the problems created when estate and class structure cross-cut one another typically involved the elaboration of various state institutions and practices—for example, the Athenian constitution of Solon.

Each response generated its own problems. Tyrants intervened when the internal disputes of the aristocracy threatened the fabric of everyday life in the city-states; these were usually over inheritance or succession and frequently involved attempts to eliminate collateral kin with claims to land or title. The tyrants who promised reform secured their positions with the support of the small landholders and artisans who were armed; they consolidated their power with armed guards and maintained it by intensifying wars with neighbors; they often legitimated their position by marrying a woman from the deposed ruling elite, as Oedipus did (Stritmatter 1987). The views different classes had about the relative merits and liabilities of tyrannies, monarchies, aristocracies, and democracies as forms of government have survived in various philosophical tracts and plays. For example, the small landholder Hesiod complained about the abuses of the *basilies*, who used their offices for personal gain; Plato, the scion of an aristocratic family fallen on hard times and contemptuous of work, criticized tyranny in *The Republic*; and Aristotle, the Confucius of the Aegean and the tutor of Alexander the Great, claimed that social inequalities were natural and exalted those who were destined to rule by virtue of their position in society and access to state power. In other words, the poems, comedies, and tragedies, as well as the philosophical views of diverse schools, refract in complex ways the class struggles of the Aegean world.

Numerous variations of nondynastic, territorially organized states appeared at several hundred localities in the Aegean during the mid-first millennium B.C. These were *poleis*, or city-states, made up of working peasants and artisans who resided in the town and countryside. The men of this class were citizens and soldiers who worked for a living and took pride in what

The Aegean world.

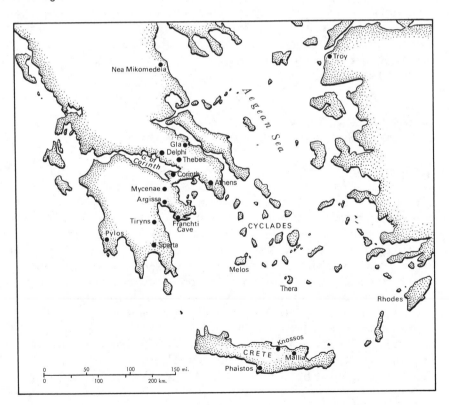

they produced. There were aristocrats, who disdained work. There were slaves taken in wars: the men sent to the mines, fields, and shops; the women to domestic service. Gender relations varied from class to class and from one polis to another. The saber-rattling aristocrats of Athens attempted to enforce the most oppressive gender hierarchy on their wives and daughters by sequestering them in their homes. The upper-class women responded by joining cults and by cutting the penises off the *hermes*, male statues, that decorated the city in 411 B.C.

Although political power was generally decentralized in the Aegean during the first millennium B.C., regional political groupings occurred on several occasions. Coalitions known as the Hellenic and Delian Leagues crystallized during the fifth century B.C. in response to the threat of invasion by the Persian Empire and to disintegrating relations between Athens and Sparta, which fueled the Peloponnesian wars (460 to 404 B.C.). There was a continually shifting balance of forces among various independent and allied poleis during the first half of the fourth century. After 346 B.C., Philip II, the monarch of Macedonia, encapsulated cities on the northern Aegean and threatened those of central Greece. Macedonia, the country on the edge of the Aegean world, soon subordinated Greece and extended its empire as far east as India and Bactria. Because of internal strife over succession, the empire disintegrated rapidly after Alexander's death in 323 B.C., when various provincial governors seized power and attempted to make it hereditary. Ptolemy, who was appointed governor of Egypt and Libya, subordinated the *satrap* (governor) of the Levant and laid the foundations for the Ptolemaic Dynasty, which struggled during the next several centuries to retain its position, power, and control.

ETRURIA AND ROME: CLASS AND STATE FORMATION ON THE ITALIAN PENINSULA IN THE FIRST MILLENNIUM B.C.

The tenth century B.C. was a period when nonstratified, relatively homogeneous, self-sufficient societies occupied a considerable portion of the Italian Peninsula. These circumstances began to change after 900 B.C. on the coastal plains of Tuscany and Liguria in northwestern Italy. Communities abandoned several regions during the ninth century B.C. and settled in a number of relatively large, fortified Villanovan settlements; the shift in population was also accompanied by the development of regionally diverse styles.

Two distinct but interconnected processes of class and state formation occurred soon after in the area. One involved the implantation of a number of settler-colonies and trading emporia by various Greek city-states in Sicily and southern Italy between 750 and 580 B.C. The other involved the rapid consolidation of a dozen semiautonomous city-states in Etruria, several of which were built on the old Villanovan settlements. These developments were accompanied by an increase in the number of fortified villages located in the remote, less accessible mountain valleys of the interior, which were inhabited three centuries later by tribal communities that were struggling to retain their autonomy and independence from their state-based neighbors. The interplay of class and state formative processes and resistance produced a patchwork of different kinds of societies: some class-stratified, others estate-ordered, and many others still kin-based.

The class structures of the semiautonomous Etruscan city-states broadly resembled those of the archaic poleis of Greece. There was a small ruling class, whose members owned agricultural lands and mines; they attempted to control the acquisition, production, and availability of commodities that were exchanged with the Phoenician, Carthaginian, and Greek merchants who ventured onto the Tyrrhenian Sea in search of slaves and precious metals. There was a subordinated underclass, whose members worked their own fields or labored in the fields and workshops of the wealthy. There were also slaves, war captives who were probably taken prisoner north of the Alps and brought southward through slave markets in the Late Hallstatt polities in Switzerland and Austria or through the trading emporia established at Massilia near the mouth of the Rhone River in southern France around 540 B.C.

The ruling classes of the Etruscan city-states maintained their privileged position and ensured the flow of goods and labor with heavily armored foot soldiers, who resembled the hoplites of the Aegean states; with marital and diplomatic alliances among themselves and with foreign states like Carthage; and with short-lived confederations led by one of their number to resolve particular crises. In 540 B.C., they allied themselves with Carthaginian merchants and pirates and seized control of Massilia, driving the Phocaean Greeks out of the Etruscan-controlled Tyrrhenian Sea. Small groups of Etruscan aristocrats and their heavily armored retainers entered the Po Valley to the north and established new cities and local dynasties. Rome also fell under the sway of Etruscans when the son of a Roman aristocrat and an Etruscan woman seized power in the late sixth century B.C. and reorganized the military into hoplite units based on census and tribal groups; they also established a civil bureaucracy, installed caretakers or priests at certain cults, and instituted legal and judicial reforms. Tarquinius Superbus, the last of the Etruscan rulers of Rome, was expelled by the aristocracy in 508 B.C., and the deposed leader was unable to construct a cross-class alliance of slaves and freedmen and freedwomen that would restore his power and position as a tyrant. The Roman aristocrats abolished the monarchy and divided power among the supreme commander, judges, and priests.

From 494 to 287 B.C., Roman society was caught in "the conflict of the orders"—that is, the attempt to resolve the tensions created by crosscutting kin, estate, and class structures that were constituted on different, often contradictory bases. The kin-based structures consisted of corporate land-holding groups whose members defined their relation in terms of descent from a shared ancestor, lived in the same location, worked common lands, and participated in the same local cult. Juridically recognized orders or categories of citizens divided the society into patricians and plebeians: The former held hereditary public offices and/or were the leaders of prominent clans; the latter were largely gainfully employed urban workers, artisans, merchants, and smallholders, who were excluded from government but were obliged to serve as soldiers—and required to provide their own armor and weapons. However, not all of the patricians were wealthy and powerful, nor were all of the plebeians poor. The class structure distinguished the large landholders who monopolized political power and control of the institutions and practices of the state apparatus of this still largely agrarian society, a less homogeneous group that sought to protect itself from economic exploitation and political oppression by the state, and slaves, composed of several categories of unfree, servile workers.

In the struggle of the orders, the plebeians desired to lighten the burdens placed on them by the patricians who constituted the state apparatus. Their principal weapon during the fifth century B.C., the period when Rome began to subordinate neighboring states and communities, was refusing military service and remaining at home to pursue their own activities. Such acts of resistance and even the threat of them weakened the capacity of the state to wage war against its neighbors. The tensions were heightened by the state's practice of distributing land in the newly conquered territories to those who already held landed estates. The position of the patrician state apparatus was weakened in 387 B.C., when a band of Gauls from northern Italy and France sacked Rome and stole movable property from the wealthy. This event created conditions in which the patricians and plebeians forged an alliance out of enlightened self-interest. In 367 B.C., the original patrician oligarchy was replaced by one made up of patricians and the few wealthy plebeians who succeeded in gaining political office and becoming senators. The new oligarchy, in reality a reconstituted ruling class, continued to act in much the same manner as its predecessor.

The less affluent layers of the old plebeian order also benefited economically from the reforms implemented during the early years of the Republic. Debts were canceled and land-reform legislation redistributed land from the large landowners to the free urban poor. However, these gains came with a price: Many of the free men were required to serve in the army for half of each year, and their wives and children were forced to endure the hardships created by the diminished productivity and income of the domestic production-consumption units. Rome launched a series of diplomatic and military campaigns against its neighbors toward the middle of the fourth century B.C., which culminated in 270 B.C. when the mountain tribes and the Etruscans were finally defeated and the entire peninsula was under Roman control. During this period, there was hardly a year in which the army was not mobilized. These wars of conquest were an attempt to displace the internal contradictions—that is, economic exploitation—of a tributary state shaped by a cross-class alliance onto the peoples of the newly incorporated periphery. Although the free artisans, merchants, and smallholders of Rome benefited in some ways by the enslavement or conquest of other peoples, their political influence was challenged in new ways as the foundations of the Roman economy were transformed and class differences were sharpened.

The new nobility was distinguished by its wealth; property; privileges; control of the state's decision-making apparatus; and awareness of its own collective, senatorial identity. Although inherited wealth and position were prominent, the new nobility was not a hereditary order or estate per se but a clearly defined social class that admitted members who by virtue of particular skills they possessed could further its interests. The new ruling class of the third century B.C. used the various state-supported cults to convince the citizens of Rome—that is, its free men—that the Roman state was not only divinely inspired but also the property of Roman society as a whole. The priests of these cults sought to discover what the divine will was and to prescribe the forms of behavior that were appropriate in different situations.

Roman imperial expansion, first in Italy and then through the western Mediterranean during the First Punic War (264 to 241 B.C.) with Carthage, occurred with the support of the landed peasantry and the urban poor, who received land for their service. It also provided new avenues for social mobility for those merchants, moneylenders, and bankers—that is, merchant and

Roman imperial expansion.

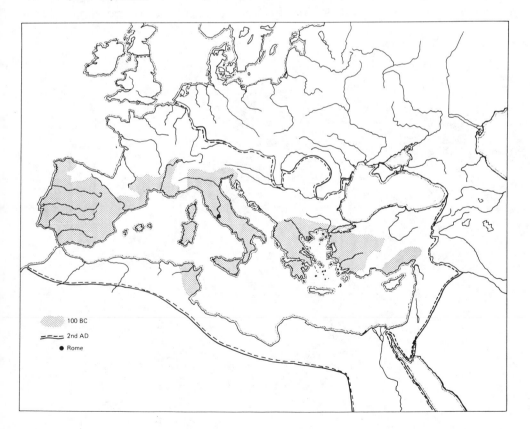

finance capitalists—who either possessed or could mobilize the resources—
the artisans, boats, or capital—that allowed the state to wage war overseas.
This group had enough political power after the Second Punic War (218 to
201 B.C.) to prevent the senatorial aristocracy, the landed ruling class, from
engaging in commerce. The nouveau riche who profited from the wars by
assisting the state and taking over certain of its functions—for example,
feeding the army, collecting taxes, building roads, or leasing mines—were
widely despised, especially in the rural areas and provinces, for their ruth-
less, cutthroat practices in circumstances in which the state made no effort to
control their actions. The peasant-soldiers and their families were the real
losers in the war. Whole armies recruited from the peasantry were destroyed,
as were 400 settlements and hundreds of thousands of people who resided in
the Italian core area of the Roman state.

The disastrous Second Punic War marked the beginning of a major
episode of class formation in the Roman imperial state. It involved (1) the
greatly expanded use of slaves captured in the foreign wars; (2) the reconstitution of an imperial ruling class that included elements of the senatorial
nobility, wealthy merchants and landowners, and loyal elements of the provincial elite in the new areas of the empire; (3) the expulsion of peasants
from the land by wealthy landowners in order to create large estates that
were worked by slaves; (4) the appearance of a landless, rural proletariat

Reconstruction of a Roman villa.

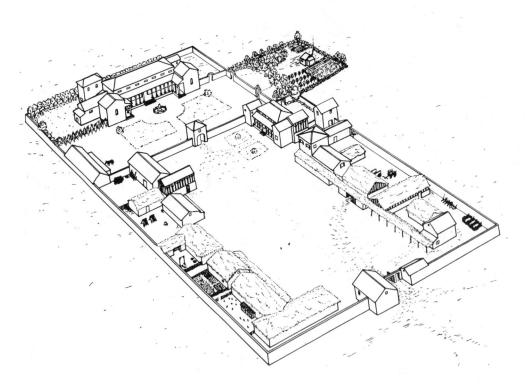

whose members supported themselves and their families with wage labor; (5) the movement of landless or poor peasants to the cities; and (6) an increasing variety of urban occupations and professionals: prostitutes, weavers, cobblers, potters, blacksmiths, and beggars, to name only a few. The sudden appearance of large numbers of people uprooted and dispossessed from their homes; of foreign slaves; and of a small, incredibly cruel ruling class, which regarded the world and its inhabitants as sources of wealth to be exploited for its pleasure, was a volatile mix. During the second and first centuries B.C., there was almost continuous civil unrest: Rebellions erupted in the provincial areas, particularly in Spain and Greece; slave revolts in Rome as well as in the provinces were often built on the collaboration of escaped slaves and poor peasants; and the urban poor resisted ill treatment by the state's representatives and rulers. Political conflict within the ruling class broke out in 133 B.C. when a tribune, who had to provide recruits for the army, attempted to restore the peasantry by passing legislation that limited the size of landed estates and released land for redistribution to the poor; the tribune and his supporters were assassinated a few years later.

Civil conflict within the ruling class was institutionalized in a new form after 100 B.C., when the reformers in the popular assembly created a regular army filled with landless poor from the cities and countryside. The state supplied their equipment and moved them out of the cities; the politicians who commanded the armies ensured that the recruits were paid—a fact that led to strong ties of loyalty between the soldiers and their politician-commanders. From the ruling class's perspective, this was potentially a very dangerous set of conditions. The soldiers were armed and could return to the cities to press their demands, especially for the cancellation of debts, the redistribution of land, or the distribution of food to the urban poor. The politicians who led the armies and paid the wages of their soldiers also had a potent weapon to use against their enemies. The new form of civil conflict erupted in 91 B.C., when a civil war broke out between rival factions of the ruling class, each of which mobilized veterans and recruits to support its cause. The composition of warring camps changed as old issues were either resolved or became unimportant and new ones appeared on the horizon.

Two politicians rose to prominence toward the middle of the first century B.C. One was Pompey, who gained fame and influence following his conquests in the east; the other was Julius Caesar, who conquered Gaul. The civil war that erupted between them in 49 B.C. was a struggle for power within the ruling class. One of the issues was whether the oligarchy should be maintained or a monarchy established. Caesar's victory in the civil war was a triumph for those who supported the idea of a strong monarch; it was not overturned when Caesar was assassinated by Mark Antony and Octavian, who supported the institutional forms of oligarchy. The only unresolved issue at that point was who would become emperor. The struggle lasted fifteen years before Octavian, the future Caesar Augustus, emerged victorious.

At this point, the Roman ruling class wanted peace, opportunities to accumulate new wealth, and their positions made hereditary. They also wanted the system of patronage, and the power it gave them, to continue. However, this was the issue over which the members of the ruling class found themselves potentially at odds with the emperor. Emperors could not afford to grant power indiscriminately; they doled it out instead in small portions to individuals who had proven their loyalty. Most important, they ensured that the army was either under their direct control or under the control of provincial administrators whom they had appointed.

The Roman imperial state reached its greatest extent between 27 B.C. and A.D. 161. However, its economic foundations and social structure remained relatively unchanged during this period. The economy continued to be based on agrarian production, and new organizational forms were occasionally introduced into provincial areas, like Dacia, usually to the detriment of the native communities, which typically resisted the state's attempts to usurp their traditional practices. The commodities produced by the artisans who resided in one of the nine hundred or so cities incorporated into the empire were largely consumed by the ruling class, wealthy individuals, and/or the state. Merchants and moneylenders continued to profit, often exorbitantly, from the transport and circulation of commodities.

By the fourth century A.D., the population of the empire, regardless of class, was indifferent to or alienated from the imperial regime. Many members of the always quite small ruling classes had retired to the self-sufficiency of their country estates. Some peasants and artisans placed themselves under the protection of powerful persons to avoid the exactions of the state apparatus. Large areas on the margins of the state were abandoned as other individuals emigrated and expressed their preference for everyday life in one of the barbarian states that was developing along the empire's Celtic and eastern frontiers.

FURTHER READINGS: A BRIEF GUIDE

For contrasting understandings of the Aegean and Greek worlds and their relations with the Near East and the rest of Europe, see Michael Rowlands, "Conceptualizing the European Bronze and Early Iron Age," in *European Social Evolution: Archaeological Perspectives*, ed. John Bintliff (Bradford, Eng.: University of Bradford, 1984), pp. 147–156; Colin Renfrew, *The Emergence of Civilization: The Cyclades and the Aegean in the Third Millennium B.C.* (London: Methuen, 1972), and *Before Civilization: The Radiocarbon Revolution and Prehistoric Europe* (Cambridge: Cambridge University Press, 1973); and Martin Bernal, *Black Athena: The Afroasiatic Roots of Classical Civilization, vol. II, The Archaeological and Documentary Evidence* (New Brunswick, NJ: Rutgers University Press, 1991).

Early food-producing communities in the Mediterranean and southeastern Europe are discussed by Paul Dolukhanov, *Ecology and Economy in Neo-*

lithic Eastern Europe (London: Gerald Duckworth, 1979); Alasdair Whittle, *Neolithic Europe: A Survey* (Cambridge: Cambridge University Press, 1985); James Lewthwaite, "The Transition to Food Production: A Mediterranean Perspective," in *Hunters in Transition: Mesolithic Societies of Temperate Eurasia and Their Transition to Farming*, ed. Mark Zvelebil (Cambridge: Cambridge University Press, 1986), pp. 53–66; and Andrew G. Sherratt, "Plough and Pastoralism: Aspects of the Secondary Products Revolution," in *Patterns of the Past: Studies in Honour of David Clarke*, ed. Ian Hodder, Glynn Isaac, and Norman Hammond (Cambridge: Cambridge University Press, 1981), pp. 261–305, and "Social Evolution: Europe in the Later Neolithic and Copper Ages," in *European Social Evolution: Archaeological Perspectives*, ed. John Bintliff (Bradford, Eng.: University of Bradford, 1984), pp. 123–134.

For insightful discussions of social organization in the food-producing village communities, see Susan Shennan, "From Minimal to Moderate Ranking," Andrew Sherratt, "Mobile Resources: Settlement and Exchange in Early Agricultural Europe," and Paul Halstead and John O'Shea, "A Friend in Need Is a Friend Indeed: Social Storage and the Origins of Social Ranking," all in *Ranking, Resource and Exchange: Aspects of the Archaeology of Early European Society*, ed. Colin Renfrew and Stephen Shennan (Cambridge: Cambridge University Press, 1982), pp. 27–32, 13–26, and 92–99; and Ian Hodder, *The Domestication of Europe* (Oxford: B. H. Blackwell, 1990).

For discussions of Varna and Lerna, see I. S. Ivanov, "Les Fouilles Archéologiques de la Nécropole à Varna (1972–1975)," *Studia Praehistoria*, Band 1–2 (1978), 13–26; John L. Caskey, "Greece, Crete, and the Aegean Islands in the Early Bronze Age," in *The Cambridge Ancient History*, ed. I. E. S. Edwards, C. J. Gadd, and N. G. L. Hammond, vol. 1, pt. 2 (Cambridge: Cambridge University Press, 1971), pp. 771–807; and J. W. Shaw, "The Early Helladic II Corridor House: Development and Form," *American Journal of Archaeology*, vol. 91, no. 1 (1987), 59–79.

Minoan civilization is examined in Olga Krzyszkowska and L. Nixon, eds., *Minoan Society: Proceedings of the Cambridge Colloquium 1981* (Bristol, Eng.: Bristol Classical Press, 1983); Keith Branigan, *The Foundations of Palatial Crete: A Survey of Crete in the Early Bronze Age* (London: Routlege & Kegan Paul, 1975); John F. Cherry, "Polities and Palaces: Some Problems in Minoan State Formation," in *Peer Polity Interaction and Socio-political Change*, ed. Colin Renfrew and John F. Cherry (Cambridge: Cambridge University Press, 1986), pp. 19–45; Peter Warren, "Knossos: New Excavations and Discoveries," *Archaeology*, vol. 37, no. 4 (1984), 48–57; Monique Saliou, "The Processes of Women's Subordination in Primitive and Archaic Greece," in *Women's Work, Men's Property: The Origins of Gender and Class*, ed. Stephanie Coontz and Peta Henderson (London: Verso, 1986), pp. 169–206; and Robin Hágg and Nanno Marinatos, eds., *The Minoan Thallassocracy: Myth and Reality* (Stockholm: Paul Astróms Förlag, 1984), and *Sanctuaries and Cults in the Aegean Bronze Age* (Stockholm: Paul Astróms Förlag, 1981). For discussions of Minoan and Mycenaean religions, see Lucy Goodison, *Death, Women and the Sun* (London:

Institute of Classical Studies, 1989); and Martin Nilsson, *The Minoan-Mycenaean Religion and Its Survival in Greek Religion* (Lund, Swed.: C. W. K. Gleerup, 1952).

For convenient overviews of Mycenaean social formation and history, see James T. Hooker, *Mycenaean Greece* (London: Routledge & Kegan Paul, 1976); John Chadwick, *The Mycenaean World* (Cambridge: Cambridge University Press, 1976); Emily Vermeule, *Greece in the Bronze Age* (Chicago: University of Chicago Press, 1964); T. G. Palaima and C. W. Shelmerdine, "Mycenaean Archaeology and the Pylos Texts," *Archaeological Review from Cambridge*, vol. 3, no. 2 (1984), 76–89; and Alexander Uchitel, "Women at Work: Pylos and Knossos, Lagash and Ur," *Historia*, Band XXXIII, Heft 3 (1984), 257–282.

Social developments in the Aegean during the early and mid-first millennium B.C. are discussed by J. Sarkady, "Outlines of the Development of Greek Society in the Period between the 12th and 8th Centuries B.C.," *Acta Antiqua Academiae Scientiarum Hungaricae*, vol. 23, no. 1 (Budapest, 1975), pp. 107–125; Robert Drews, *Basileus: The Evidence for Kingship in Ancient Greece* (New Haven, CT: Yale University Press, 1983); Anthony Snodgrass, *Archaeology and the Rise of the Greek State* (Cambridge: Cambridge University Press, 1977); Oswyn Murray, *Early Greece* (London: Fontana Press, 1980); Paul Cartledge, " 'Trade and Politics' Revisited: Archaic Greece," in *Trade in the Ancient Economy*, ed. Peter Garnsey, Keith Hopkins, and C. R. Whittaker (Berkeley: University of California Press, 1983), pp. 1–15; W. G. Forrest, "Colonization and the Rise of Delphi," *Historia*, Band VI, Heft 2 (1957), 160–175; R. C. T. Parker, "Greek States and Greek Oracles," in *Crux; Essays presented to G. E. M. de Ste. Croix*, ed. P. A. Cartledge and F. D. Harvey (London: Gerald Duckworth, 1985), pp. 298–326; Roger Stritmatter, "Oedipus, Akhnaton and the Greek State: An Archaeology of the Oedipus Complex," *Dialectical Anthropology*, vol. 12, no. 1 (1987), 45–63; Richard B. Lee, "Greeks and Victorians: A Reexamination of Engels' Theory of the Athenian Polis," *Culture*, vol. V, no. 1 (1985), 63–73; B. Quiller, "The Dynamics of Homeric Society," *Symbolae Osloenses*, vol. 56 (1981), 109–155; and Moses I. Finley, *Early Greece: The Bronze and Archaic Ages* (New York: W. W. Norton, 1970), and *The World of Odysseus* (Harmondsworth, Eng.: Penguin Books, 1979).

For overviews of the social formations of Greece from the mid-eighth to the late fourth centuries, see Andrew Lintott, *Violence, Civil Strife and Revolution in the Classical City* (London: Croom Helm, 1982); Raphael Sealey, *Women and Law in Classical Greece* (Chapel Hill: University of North Carolina Press, 1990), and *A History of the Greek City States, 700–338 B.C.* (Berkeley: University of California Press, 1976); Eva C. Keus, *The Reign of the Phallus: Sexual Politics in Ancient Athens* (New York: Harper & Row, 1985); Moses Finley, *The Ancient Economy* (Berkeley: University of California Press, 1985); W. K. Lacey, *The Family in Classical Greece* (Ithaca, NY: Cornell University Press, 1968); Martin P. Nilsson, *Greek Folk Religion* (Philadelphia: University of Pennsylvania Press, 1961); Walter Burkert, *Ancient Mystery Cults* (Cambridge, MA: Harvard University Press, 1987); Paul McKechnie, *Outsiders in the Greek Cities in the Fourth Century B.C.* (London: Routledge, 1989); and Thomas Wiederman, *Greek and Roman Slavery* (London: Croom Helm, 1983).

For the background and imperial expansion of Macedonia in the late fourth century, see R. Malcolm Errington, *A History of Macedonia* (Berkeley: University of California Press, 1990); J. R. Ellis, *Philip II and Macedonian Imperialism* (Princeton, NJ: Princeton University Press, 1976); A. R. Bosworth, *Conquest and Empire: The Reign of Alexander the Great* (Cambridge: Cambridge University Press, 1988); F. L. Holt, *Alexander the Great and Bactria* (Leiden, Neth.: E. J. Brill, 1988); and F. W. Walbank, *The Hellenistic World* (London: Fontana Press, 1981).

For overviews of the historical development of state-based societies on the Italian Peninsula, see Simon Stoddart, "Divergent Trajectories in Central Italy, 1200–500 B.C.," in *Centre and Periphery: Comparative Studies in Archaeology*, ed. Timothy C. Champion (London: Unwin Hyman, 1989), pp. 88–101; H. H. Scullard, *The Etruscan Cities and Rome* (Ithaca, NY: Cornell University Press, 1967); Massimo Pallottino, *A History of Earliest Italy* (Ann Arbor: University of Michigan Press, 1991), and *The Etruscans* (Harmonsworth, Eng.: Penguin Books, 1979); D. Ridgeway and F. R. Ridgeway, eds., *Italy before the Romans: The Iron Age, Orientalizing and Etruscan Periods* (New York: Academic Press, 1979); Bettina Arnold, "Slavery in Late Prehistoric Europe: Recovering the Evidence for Social Structure in Iron Age Society," and Stephen L. Dyson, "Rise of Complex Societies in Italy: Historical Versus Archaeological Perspectives," both in *Tribe and Polity in Late Prehistoric Europe: Demography, Production, and Exchange in the Evolution of Complex Social Systems*, ed. D. Blair Gibson and Michael N. Geselowitz (New York: Plenum Press, 1988), pp. 179–192 and 193–203; Daphne Nash, "Celtic Territorial Expansion and the Mediterranean World," in *Settlement and Society: Aspects of Western European Prehistory in the First Millennium B.C.*, ed. Timothy Champion and J. V. S. Megaw (Leicester, Eng.: Leicester University Press, 1985), pp. 45–67; and E. J. Bickerman, "Some Reflections on Early Roman History," *Rivista di Filologia e di Istruzione Classica*, vol. 97, fasc. 4 (1969), 393–408.

The literature on ancient Rome is enormous and well developed. For overviews of the topics discussed, see Géza Alföldy, *The Social History of Rome* (London: Croom Helm, 1985); Richard E. Mitchell, *Patricians and Plebians: The Origin of the Roman State* (Ithaca, NY: Cornell University Press, 1990); Mary Beard and Michael Crawford, *Rome in the Late Republic* (Ithaca, NY: Cornell University Press, 1985); William V. Harris, *War and Imperialism in Republican Rome, 327–70 B.C.* (Oxford: Clarendon Press, 1979); Peter Garnsey and Richard Saller, *The Roman Empire: Economy, Society and Culture* (Berkeley: University of California Press, 1987); Stephen L. Dyson, *The Creation of the Roman Frontier* (Princeton, NJ: Princeton University Press, 1985); David Braund, ed., *The Administration of the Roman Empire, 241 B.C.–A.D. 193* (Exeter, Eng.: Exeter University Press, 1988); Moses Finley, ed., *Studies in Roman Property* (Cambridge: Cambridge University Press, 1976); Keith R. Bradley, *Slavery and Rebellion in the Roman World, 140 B.C.–70 B.C.* (London: B. T. Batsford, 1989), and

Slaves and Masters in the Roman Empire: A Study in Social Control (Oxford: Oxford University Press, 1984); Jane F. Gardner, *Women in Roman Law and Society* (London: Croom Helm, 1986); John K. Evans, *War, Women and Children in Ancient Rome* (London: Routledge, 1991); Peter Brown, *Society and the Holy in Late Antiquity* (Berkeley: University of California Press, 1982); S. R. F. Price, *Rituals and Power: The Roman Imperial Cult in Asia Minor* (Cambridge: Cambridge University Press, 1984); and Ramsey MacMullen, *Roman Social Relations, 50 B.C. to A.D. 284* (New Haven, CT: Yale University Press, 1974), *Paganism in the Roman Empire* (New Haven, CT: Yale University Press, 1981), *Christianizing the Roman Empire, A.D. 100–400* (New Haven, CT: Yale University Press, 1984), and *Changes in the Roman Empire: Essays in the Ordinary* (Princeton, NJ: Princeton University Press, 1990).

chapter 12

Europe

War was indeed a central occupation of the ancient state. . . . Successful ancient wars produced profits . . . booty (of which captives were normally the most valuable), indemnities, and confiscated land. (Moses I. Finley, Ancient History: Evidence and Models*)*

He who commands becomes depraved, he who obeys becomes smaller. Either way, as a tyrant or a slave, as an officer or an underling, man is diminished. The morality which is born out of the present conception of the state and the social hierarchy is necessarily corrupt. (Elisée Reclus, "Bad Blood")

If I were in search of a metaphor to describe the great and growing concentration of wealth in the hands of the upper classes, I would not incline toward anything so innocent as drainage: I should want to think in terms of something much more purposive and deliberate—perhaps the vampire bat. (Geoffrey E. M. de Ste. Croix, The Class Struggle in the Ancient Greek World*)*

Europe is a peninsula that juts into the sea. This ancient landmass narrows as it stretches westward from the vast plains of Russia. The Mediterranean Sea borders it on the south, and the North Atlantic, the Baltic, and the Arctic enclose it on the north. Like Caesar's Gaul, Europe is divided into three parts: the Mediterranean world, Europe north of the mountain ranges—the Carpathians, Alps, and Pyrenees—that bisect the continent, and the rugged Scandinavian Peninsula.

North of the alpine barrier lies the great plain that stretches from France to the Ural Mountains in eastern Russia. For long periods of its history, portions of this vast plain were underwater, and thick limestone deposits accumulated on their surfaces. Now vast forests and farmlands cover the plain. The climate is milder in the coastal regions and the lower latitudes, where mixed evergreen and deciduous forests predominate. The winters become more severe in the interior and the upland areas, where coniferous trees still provide the dominant ground cover. Wide rivers, rising along the northern slopes of the Alps and Carpathians, cross the plain and empty into the North and Baltic seas. The Rhine, Elbe, Oder, and Vistula are only a few of the waterways that have provided communication and transportation links between the peoples of the plain and those living further south.

The Scandinavian Peninsula projects into the North Sea, its gaping mouth seemingly poised before swallowing Jutland. Mixed oak and pine forests cover the lowland areas at the southern end of the peninsula. Further north, these give way to evergreen forests in the low-lying areas around the Baltic Sea and the Gulf of Bothnia, and to fir trees and tundra in the mountains that form the backbone of Scandinavia. Arctic grasslands with occasional stands of fir trees in protected areas cover virtually all of the northern

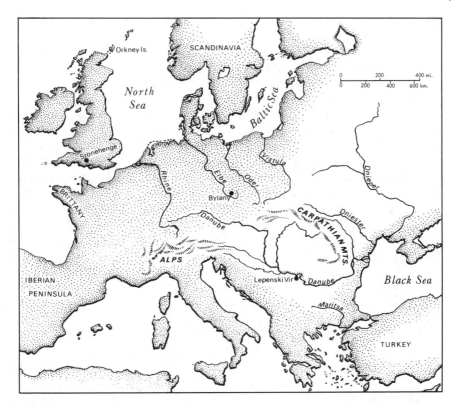

Europe.

half of the peninsula and line the edges of the deep fiords that open into the Arctic and North seas. The winters are long and cold; the summer is mild, and only a few months have average temperatures above 50° F.

EARLY FOOD-PRODUCING COMMUNITIES
IN TEMPERATE EUROPE

The first communities to transform the land from an object into a means of production lived in the Danube Basin, south of the Carpathian Mountains, toward the end of sixth millennium B.C. As we saw in the preceding chapter, they had highly varied subsistence economies that included, besides farming and stockraising, hunting, foraging, and fishing; the diversity also reflected subtle differences in the local availability of raw materials and the organization of work. Not all of the communities residing in the Danube adopted agriculture and herding at this time. Some, like the inhabitants of Lepenski Vir, who resided on the banks of the Danube overlooking the whirlpools at the bottom of the Iron Gates gorges, fished and hunted, while their contemporaries a few hundred miles away tilled the soil and herded small numbers of sheep and goats.

The domesticated plants and animals raised in southeastern Europe were introduced north of the Carpathian Mountains during the early fifth millennium B.C. This practice involved the establishment of new settlements north of the mountains by offshoots of the Danube Basin communities and the adoption of new subsistence activities by some of the indigenous communities of the northern plain. The extension was widespread and rapid, judging by the underlying similarity of pottery made and used by communities in the Paris Basin, Holland, Poland, Czechoslovakia, and Hungary. As a result of the resemblances, these fifth-millennium farming communities are referred to as the Linear Pottery, or Linearbandkeramik (LBK), cultures.

Linear Pottery settlements were usually located in the middle of areas with rich windblown soils. This fact suggests that the people were mainly interested in the easily worked soils rather than the plant and animal resources of the light oak forests that grew on them. The farmers cleared the trees with polished stone axes and planted emmer and einkorn wheat. The rich foliage and underbrush of the nearby forests provided excellent fodder for their cattle and pigs as well as food for wild pigs, oxen, and deer. The inhabitants of the settlements occasionally ventured into the forests to hunt, but their herds ultimately provided most of the meat they consumed.

Bylany, in western Czechoslovakia, was a typical Linear Pottery settlement. It had five to ten houses, some of which were more than 100 feet long and 20 feet wide. They housed a number of people—possibly the members of an extended family—as well as granaries and probably the livestock during the winter. The 100 to 200 individuals who dwelled in Bylany at any given time kept about 100 to 125 animals. The kind of slash-and-burn agriculture they practiced can produce fairly high yields if the fields are rotated every three or four years. Areas of the Russian Plain, where slash-and-burn agriculture was pursued during the nineteenth-century, suggest that the inhabitants of Bylany may have cropped about 70 to 100 acres each year to produce the grain they needed for food and for sowing the next year's crop. However, the windblown soils around the Linear Pottery settlements eroded quickly once they were stripped of natural ground cover.

As a result, some villages may have been occupied for relatively short periods of time, perhaps only ten to fifteen years, before their residents moved to new localities where the soils were still rich or had been fallow long enough to regain their fertility. If this were the case, it is possible that once the soils were restored, households returned to the same longhouse settlements their ancestors had left years earlier, when the productivity of their fields had begun to decline. Other settlements, particularly those located on floodplains, where the soils are replenished each year, may have been occupied continuously for several centuries or more.

Food production was adopted and adapted in the alpine region of central Europe, in northern Europe—Denmark, southern Sweden and Norway, northwestern France, and the British Isles—and in the interior of the Iberian

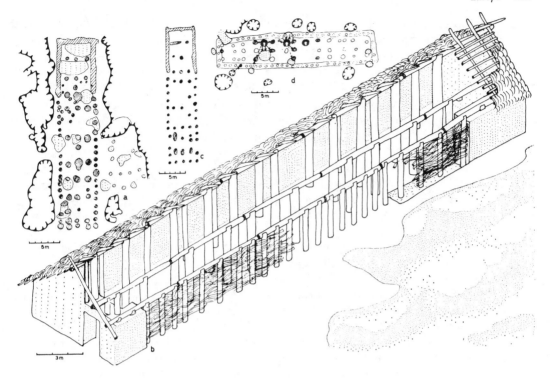

LBK longhouse.

Peninsula during the fourth millennium B.C. For example, the subsistence economies of the Ertebølle communities of southern Scandinavia were dominated by fishing and littoral harvesting, with some hunting and plant foraging in the interiors. After 3500 B.C., a number of them supplemented their subsistence activities with pig and cattle husbandry and with slash-and-burn gardening. At first, the food-producing activities probably added very little to the diet; however, the communities were soon engaged in widespread clearing of the forests to open fields for gardens and pastures. These were labor-intensive activities, and given the scale on which they occurred, they undoubtedly required the cooperation of a number of household production-consumption units and the stabilization of residence. These practices involved (1) an elaboration of the community-level relations of production in ways that facilitated the mobilization of labor for activities that ensured the social reproduction of the community as a whole and (2) a reorganized technical division of labor that enmeshed new work activities into the fabric of everyday life. The result was that the varied, mobile lifeways of the Ertebølle communities were replaced by the more sedentary forms of everyday life associated with the Funnel Beaker cultures of the Middle Neolithic farming communities found throughout temperate Europe and the British Isles.

There were two broad patterns of social organization among the food-producing Neolithic communities of temperate Europe. In the earlier pattern, represented at the Linear Pottery settlements of the fifth and fourth millennia B.C., the villages were probably made up of a core group of brothers and sisters, their spouses, and their children. This pattern reflected a kind of matrimonial mobility, in which, depending on the circumstances, either a man or a woman might move to the residence of a new spouse; thus, the residents of these egalitarian villages were linked by kin and matrimonial ties to the inhabitants of nearby settlements. Grave goods indicate that certain aspects of work were organized into complementary gender spheres. Polished stone axes and adzes and projectile points suggest that men chopped trees, tilled fields, and hunted; stone blades and ornaments—bracelets, beads, and pendants—suggest that women processed raw materials and foodstuffs and may have initiated ritual practices that ensured bountiful harvests.

The residents of a Linear Pottery village, and perhaps those from neighboring settlements as well, cooperated on projects, like building houses, that were beyond the labor capacities of single domestic groups. Toward the end of the fourth millennium B.C., these collectively organized labor activities included the construction of palisades, earthworks, and ditches around some villages and open spaces in the Rhineland, Bavaria, and Bohemia. Such enclosures were most likely corrals; however, later they would come to delineate ritual precincts and provide protection from marauders.

The later pattern of social organization was confined largely to the third millennium B.C. and later, though there were elements of it a few centuries earlier in some localities. This pattern consisted of (1) the "secondary-products revolution," in which animals were bred mainly for milk, wool, or labor rather than meat; (2) the intensification of agricultural production; (3) new technical divisions of labor in which work activities were organized into complementary spheres structured increasingly by gender; (4) the construction of palisaded settlements, causeways, communal and/or family tombs, and public monuments that required investments of labor power surpassing the capacities of single households; and (5) the crystallization of diverse forms of the kin-based communal mode of production in response to class and state formation.

The secondary-products revolution reflected the increased importance of livestock and the fact that European communities began to use animals, their energy, and their products in new ways. Oxen were harnessed to plows and carts; cows were milked; sheep were shorn, and their wool was spun, woven into cloth, and exchanged with peoples living in areas where agriculture rather than livestock constituted the major means of production. Secondary products—like milk or wool—made larger herds economical in some areas where farming was a marginal activity at best, and they may actually have fostered the development of pastoral economies involving transhumance or nomadism.

The means of production, the acquisition of raw materials, and the technical division of labor were structured by gender relations in many societies during the third millennium B.C. Burial data from various regions suggest that women owned or controlled the products of livestock. For example, in the Elbe-Saale region, pairs of oxen, already being used to plow fields, were interred with women; furthermore, spinning and weaving implements, amber jewelry, and ritual paraphernalia were placed in women's graves in Denmark during the third millennium B.C. At the same time, the tombs of Danish men contained agricultural implements, battleaxes, projectile points, beakers, and pieces of unworked amber. The contents of the men's burials reflected the increased importance of raiding and hunting in many parts of temperate Europe—the former activity marked by the increased number of fortified settlements and the latter by a significant increase in the quantities of wild animal bones found in garbage dumps. Men and women were clearly involved in agricultural production but in different ways; the sharing or exchanges that occurred between them ensured the reproduction of household production-consumption units and provided each with goods that they could exchange with individuals or groups living beyond the bounds of the local village or community.

The intensification of exchange relations was an important feature of temperate European societies in the third millennium B.C. Around 3000 B.C., some men in Brittany used their authority or influence to gain control over the production and circulation of hard-stone axes and finely decorated pottery beakers or, more important, what was in the pots. They established relations with men in distant communities, who provided them with goods that were not available locally. They then distributed these items to kin or neighbors or to clients or followers in their own villages. Several of these prestigious persons were ultimately buried in tombs that required 3,000 or more person-days of labor, an amount that would have stretched the human resources of single domestic groups. However, in this instance, both fame and the ability to organize communal labor for elaborate mortuary practices were temporary; several centuries later, the burials in Brittany were more homogeneous and egalitarian than they had been earlier.

Some of the tombs built during the third millennium B.C. were quite large and required significant labor investments by domestic groups and/or the community as a whole. For example, one was entered through a 100-foot-long passage. The capstone of another weighed more than 50 tons and probably required the labor of 200 individuals working together to raise it into place. Some of the tombs may have been family crypts, judging from the fact that they contained the remains of a number of individuals interred at different times; others, like several in southern Sweden, contained piles of bones—skulls in one place, long bones in another—and seem to have been places where the identity, sex, or age of a particular body was less important than membership in the community that built them.

Megalithic passage tombs, wood or stone-lined barrows, cists, and various other kinds of graves, containing single individuals and multiple inhumations, were erected during the third millennium B.C. In some instances, they were easily accessible; in others, placed in remote areas, entry was more difficult. However, mortuary monuments were not the only kinds of communally organized construction activities that occurred during this period. Villages in several parts of Europe—notably in the Danube and the mountains and foothill regions ringing the Aegean and northern Italy—were located in easily defended places and/or fortified with earthworks, palisades, and encircling ditches. A community in the Rhine Valley fortified a 250 acre enclosure at Urmitz.

In southern England, a number of regionally organized communities, each with several thousand members, built large henge and stone circle monuments at a number of places. The henges were large single or concentric earthen rings, surrounded by ditches, that enclosed wooden or stone structures. The Avebury henge involved several million person-hours of labor; it could have been built by about 400 individuals working 3 months each year for 5 years. The most famous of the stone circle monuments is Stonehenge, the construction of which required at least 30 million person-hours of labor and may ultimately have involved a number of the communities residing in southern England. Pig feasting was one activity that occurred at some, but not all, of the henge monuments in England.

Between 5000 and 2000 B.C., the natural and human landscapes of temperate Europe were transformed. Forests were cleared and replaced with agricultural fields and pastures; plants and animals domesticated in other parts of the world were incorporated into varied, regionally diverse subsistence economies. Toward the end of the third millennium, the social relations of relatively nonhierarchical, kin-organized communities were distorted and deformed in many regions; they were ensnared in the webs of tributary relations emanating from state-organized societies along the margins of the

Stonehenge.

Mediterranean and Black seas, or they were enmeshed in exchange relations with the ranked societies and chiefdoms of northwestern Europe.

POLITICAL INSTABILITY AND RESISTANCE
DURING THE SECOND MILLENNIUM B.C.

Temperate Europe at 2000 B.C., roughly the end of the Early Bronze Age, was a political-economic and social mosaic. Timothy Champion, Clive Gamble, Stephen Shennan, and Alisdair Whittle (1984:209–221) have characterized this social and cultural diversity in the following manner. Large-scale, communally organized construction projects had stopped in southern England, except for some renovations and additions at Stonehenge; this was accompanied by the rapid appearance of a small number of richly furnished graves in the Wessex region during the early half of the second millennium B.C. A similar pattern of change occurred in Brittany, where the rich barrow graves dating to the end of the third millennium were replaced by less lavishly furnished barrows erected between about 2000 and 1500 B.C. In contrast, differences in status and wealth were not discernible until about 2100 B.C. in Bohemia and the Elbe-Saale region. During the next three centuries, a few individuals were interred in richly furnished tombs that contained a few exotic items obtained from distant lands, whereas the vast majority of the people were buried in graves, the contents of which were largely undifferentiated. Further east, the relatively egalitarian communities that inhabited the Danube Basin during the third millennium B.C. moved to easily defended, fortified villages around 2000 B.C., many of which had been abandoned a thousand years earlier by their predecessors in the region; these communities acquired amber from groups around the Baltic Sea. Thus, by 1800 B.C., fortified settlements existed from Rumania to western Germany, and the burials from the region provide evidence of social differences. North of the palisaded villages, some individuals in Danish communities were beginning to acquire small quantities of metal daggers from Germany at about this time.

What were the political-economic and social structures of the societies that produced this configuration of archaeological evidence during the early second millennium B.C.? What were the historical conditions and processes that produced the diversity, the uneven development, exhibited by these societies? How were the societies north of the Alps connected to one another and to those of the Mediterranean world? By posing these and similar questions, archaeologists working in Europe have begun to explore the conditions and dynamics produced in communities and polities on the margins of areas where class-stratified, state-based societies precipitated, crystallized, and collapsed.

The trading emporia established on the Black and Aegean seas in the third millennium B.C. and the tributary states that formed in the Aegean during the second millennium B.C. helped to create a patchwork of different kinds of societies, each of which was characterized by distinctive political-economic and social structures and shaped by particular, often diverse historical conditions. However, the civilizations, the state-based societies on the margins of Europe, were not wholly responsible for the network of interconnected communities and polities that developed in Europe between 2000 and 1400 B.C. The autonomous and semiautonomous peoples living in temperate Europe contributed to the formation of that reality. The forms of tribute extraction and resistance that developed shaped the relations within the encapsulated communities and among them, their neighbors, and the various state-based societies that emerged. As these structures crossed, merged, interlocked, and separated in various combinations, the social relations within and among the societies were also transformed and enmeshed in new forms

Changes in burial practices in northern Europe.

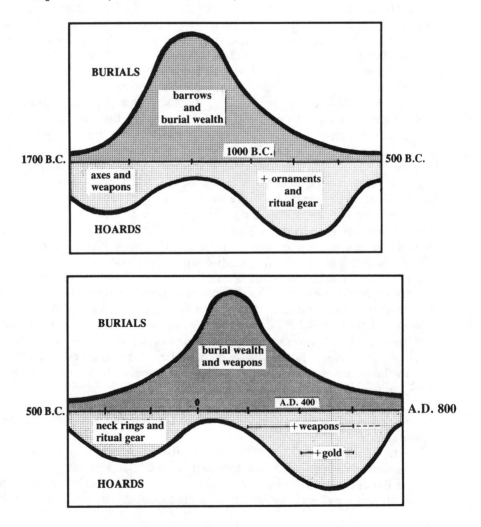

of social reproduction and resistance. They provided people with certain opportunities for making their own history and, at the same time, placed constraints on their actions.

In southern England, there was a marked contrast between the communities of the late third millennium B.C., which invested enormous amounts of communally organized labor power in the construction of henges and stone circles like Stonehenge, and their successors, which did not build large structures. A few members of the later communities placed quantities of goods, often requiring substantial amounts of time and skill to fashion, in tombs containing men, women, and children that were integrated into barrow cemeteries. The fact that rich grave goods were often buried with children suggests that wealth or status was, in significant ways, inherited. There was a breakdown in the community-level relations of production. Surplus labor power, formerly used by the community to build monuments and to ensure its own reproduction, was being employed by domestic groups to guarantee their own reputation and/or reproduction by transferring portions of their wealth from one generation to the next or by removing it from circulation. Differences in herd size and the number of workers a domestic group could count on were the real sources of wealth differences in Wessex society. However, wealth differences were apparently not translated into either hereditary status differences—such as chiefly and nonchiefly estates—or class relations. This fact has led some archaeologists to conclude that the social relations of this kin-based community were stretched to their limits by the bigmen and bigwomen who used wealth and generosity to gain clients and build personal followings.

Different processes and social relations developed in Denmark during the early second millennium B.C. Grave goods suggest that there were hereditary chieftains in Zealand and Jutland, who were buried with wooden stools; drinking cups; and large, elaborately decorated swords that were rarely, if ever, sharpened or used. These swords can be contrasted with the well-used and frequently sharpened weapons found in the graves of some adult males. Women were interred with ritual paraphernalia; some had a complete set of gold discs, bronze collars, and belt plates, whereas others had only partial sets consisting of one or two pieces. In this instance, the differences in the grave goods represent the status differences of a ranked society and a technical division of labor between political, military, and ritual activities that was structured by gender. One issue currently being investigated by Viana Muller (1989) is whether the status of women depended on or was independent of the rank held by their husbands. Did their labor count as part of the family effort and contribute to their husbands' ranks? Or did they, by virtue of their position as ritual specialists, receive gifts for ritual services or offerings that were unrelated to their roles in domestic groups? Furthermore, she is also concerned with how women acquired the ritual paraphernalia they used, since neither gold, copper, nor tin were available locally.

Hierarchically organized estate structures—the division of the community into chiefly and nonchiefly groups—appeared in some of the ranked societies in Denmark and southern Sweden around 1500 B.C. The increased number of raids, the intensification and elaboration of the roles played by armed men, and the creation of patron-client relations with the political leaders led to the formation of military retinues and to distinctions that could be drawn between their members and the rest of the community. The warrior aristocracy ensured the social reproduction of its place in the emerging estate structure by plundering and pillaging nearby communities, enslaving their members, employing artisans to fashion and repair their weapons and armor, and receiving gifts from their unarmed kin in return for protection—that is, what anthropologists call unbalanced kin reciprocity. This shift was marked in the archaeological record by the appearance of (1) new forms of weapons and military technology; (2) new kinds of houses and settlements; (3) craft specialization, most notably metallurgy and woodworking; (4) new agriculture lands and pastures; (5) restricted use or consumption of certain items; and (6) variations in the kinds and quantities of objects placed in different tombs.

There is nothing inherent in the chiefdoms that emerged in Europe during the second millennium B.C. that necessarily and unerringly propelled them along a trajectory culminating in class stratification and statehood. To the contrary, societies characterized by status hierarchies and hereditary access to those positions continuously appeared and dissolved in many regions of Europe—for instance, southern England and the middle Danube Basin. The institutions and practices associated with the ranked or estate-ordered societies were replaced with ones that reestablished the ambiguity and fluidity of earlier, kin-organized communities with more egalitarian social and interpersonal relations. Hierarchies were toppled when new conditions developed; resistance was accompanied by the reappearance in the archaeological record of traditional forms of burial, weaponry, and consumption patterns that must have recalled earlier times, before chiefs had proclaimed themselves kings and gods. However, the dissolution of social hierarchies in Europe around 1000 B.C. occurred at about the same time that there were new demands for land, metals, raw materials, and slaves. As a result, a new cycle of class and state formation, resistance, and uneven development was set in motion.

UNEVEN DEVELOPMENT: STATES, CHIEFDOMS, AND NOMADS ON THE CELTIC PERIPHERY AND BEYOND

This new cycle of uneven development, which became apparent during the eighth century B.C., was shaped by political-economic and social processes operating at the local level and by new trade routes—new patterns of interregional exchange. The alpine area of southern Germany, Austria, and Slovenia was central to these developments. During the opening centuries of the first millennium B.C., the inhabitants of this region were organized into a number of local communities, ranked societies, and small chiefdoms. They lived in rectangular wooden houses in villages defended by palisades or earthworks. They cremated the dead, placed their remains in urns, and buried the urns in large cemeteries. The creators of these "Urnfield Cultures" farmed, raised livestock, fished, and hunted. They also exported salt and copper extracted from mines in the mountains of Land Salzburg and Tirol. The mines were extensive. A pair of miners chiseling at rock faces removed material at a rate of about 3 feet a month. The steep shafts and narrow galleries they cut into the mountains had a combined length of more than 12,000 feet and yielded 1.3 million tons of salt and copper-bearing ores. The 400 to 600 workers at each of the mines engaged in a variety of tasks: mining ore; cutting wood for supports; separating ore from rock; smelting; making the bronze-pointed picks, the wooden mallets, the shovels, the leather and woolen clothes worn by the miners, and the animal-skin knapsacks they used to carry rocks; and providing the meat, grains, apples, and other foods they consumed.

The chiefdoms and communities of southern Bavaria, which were peripheral to the major Urnfield centers to the east during the early centuries of the first millennium B.C., rose to prominence in the seventh and sixth centuries. This was a result of the direct access their caravans of packhorses had through mountain passes and down the Rhone River Valley to the new trading emporia and commercial empires of the western Mediterranean. The formerly autonomous chiefdoms and communities of the Hallstatt region of southern Bavaria were incorporated into a paramount chiefdom or protostate, centered at the fortified stronghold of Heuneberg, which overlooked the Danube River in upper Austria about 200 miles east of the headwaters of the Rhone River.

By virtue of access to the trade routes, the chiefly estate of the Hallstatt protostate at Heuneberg succeeded in reorganizing commerce and production for commerce in the alpine region. Its members controlled the flow of commodities—like ivory, fine pots, and wine—that came from the south. They distributed these and other goods to chiefly families and communities that had less direct access to the trade routes. The local leaders provided iron, lignite, hides, fleeces, and slaves in return. The artisans of Heuneberg made painted pottery; spun wool and wove cloth; and produced bronze and iron tools, weapons, and ornaments from the raw materials they received. The chiefly people, their armed warrior-merchant retainers, and the artisans and slaves who lived at Heuneberg were fed from the large granaries that were filled by the labor power of the nonchiefly settlements and communities in the region.

The emergence and consolidation of the chiefly estate in the Hallstatt region of upper Austria and southern Bavaria were marked by the appearance of a new form of elite burial practices. The highest-ranking members of the chiefly estate were cremated and their remains were placed in metal urns that were interred in wood-lined tombs along with four-wheeled carts, weapons, insignias of office, and other objects. The fact that the same insignias were found in the cemeteries of different settlements suggests that the high-ranking families and individuals constituted a single chiefly estate, whose members were related by marriage and descent. Men and women of the chiefly estate married and resided in the stronghold of the one whose parents had the higher social rank. In estate-ordered societies, there are usually several ways of determining social rank; as a result, the social rank of a particular individual is usually somewhat ambiguous until claims are established for the priority of one principal over the others in a particular circumstance. In class-stratified societies, the ambiguities are eliminated.

The timber-lined graves of the Hallstatt elite, which contained bridles, mouth bits, and harness apparatus as well as the remains of horses, bear striking similarities in concept and content to the timbered graves, dating to the middle of the first millennium B.C., that were built from the Danube Basin through the Ukrainian and Moldavian plains north of the Black Sea to Bactria and Mongolia. The resemblances suggest that there were linkages between the chieftains and emerging ruling classes of polities bordering on the state-based societies that had crystallized in different forms from the Mediterranean world to the inner Asian frontiers of China.

The crystallization of the Hallstatt protostate in the seventh or sixth centuries B.C. was accompanied not only by the increased use of iron but also by social changes affecting the settlements' size and location in northwestern Europe. In southern and eastern England, for instance, there was a great deal of local diversity. Many of the self-sufficient local communities built hilltop forts or refuges in addition to the walled villages in which their members lived, and there were sharply defined stylistic differences in the pottery used by the members of various local or regional groupings. Other kinds of evidence provide additional information about the nature of English society during the Early Iron Age: (1) Immigrant communities from northern France resettled in southern England; (2) many of the forts were burned; and (3) burials associated with additional human heads were interred at a number of settlements. The picture that emerges is one of a series of relatively autonomous, kin-organized communities residing in a tribalized area, where their knife-wielding warriors episodically pillaged, plundered, and raided neighboring communities for booty and slaves and defended themselves from such incursions by building labor-intensive forts or defenses around their settlements. Individuals or groups from northern France had fled to England, where slaving may have been slightly less intense than on the mainland. Slaves captured in the British Isles or northern France may well have been the miners who toiled in the cold, damp salt, copper, and iron mines of Land Salzberg and Tirol under the supervision of armed overseers.

The dominant position, or suzerainty, of the Heuneberg elite was challenged and ultimately replaced during the fifth century by new regional groupings of estate-ordered communities on the periphery of its dominion. One group occupied the region from Champagne to the middle Rhine; the other was centered in Switzerland near the headwaters of the Rhine and Danube rivers. These were Early La Tène polities or protostates. Many of the same kinds of goods were placed in their elite burials, which suggests that the two regional groupings shared a single elite or courtly culture. The goods

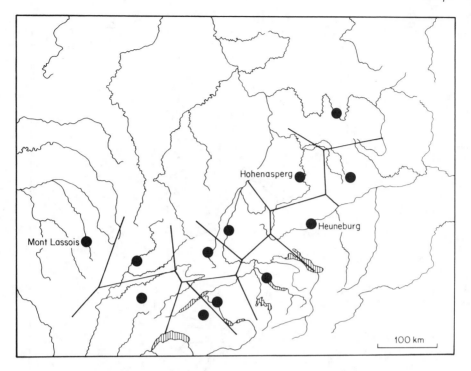

The location of fortified Iron Age villages in the Alps.

placed in the graves of nonchiefly individuals were different. For example, about 30 percent of the graves with weapons in the Champagne-Rhine region typically contain either thrusting or throwing spears. When more than one spear was placed in the tomb, they were usually a combination of the two types. A few individuals, presumably from the chiefly estate, were interred with swords, helmets, and body armor. In contrast, in the Rhine-Danube region, warriors were often buried with a sword and throwing spear; body armor was rare and presumably the property of chiefly individuals. Only adult males were buried with weapons; and only a portion of the adult male burials in each region contained spears or swords. Many of the men who were interred with weapons also wore amulets, or good-luck charms, for protection.

The Early La Tène states emerged out of the ashes and on the margins of the old Heuneberg protostate. Heuneberg itself was destroyed, and many of the lavishly furnished tombs of the Hallstatt chieftains were looted. New settlements, cemeteries, and burial practices severed connections and any continuity with the settlements and customary funerary practices of Hallstatt times. New kinds of settlements—barely fortified farmsteads and rural hamlets—appeared during the fifth century B.C. in southeastern France, southern Germany, and Switzerland. The florescence of the Early La Tène states in the Champagne region and Switzerland was undoubtedly linked

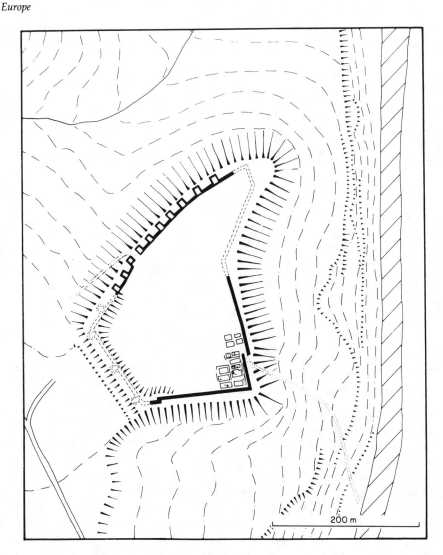

The fortified settlement at Heuneberg, Austria.

with the fact that the Greek colonies and trading emporia on the French Riviera turned their attention to the interior after Carthaginian and Etruscan merchant-pirates established control over the flow of goods through the Tyrrhenian and western Mediterranean seas. Peoples on the margins of regions that provided slaves and goods for the merchants at Massilia were suddenly able to acquire limited ranges of goods from the Mediterranean, and the Greek colonists on the coast began to produce items that their predecessors had imported from the Aegean area a generation or two earlier; they exchanged these goods with their new trading partners in Champagne. Further east, Celtic-speaking merchants from the Early La Tène polities in Switzerland drove slaves and trains of pack horses ladened with metal ingots and other raw materials across the Alps toward settlements in northern Italy. Changes in the location of the trade routes and settlements were undoubtedly accompanied by the movement of peoples—individuals, families, and households—to regions and new population centers that provided political and economic opportunities and security after their old communities were destroyed.

The Early La Tène polities that emerged in the Champagne and Danube-Rhine regions seem to have derived their wealth from taxing commerce and from the export of raw materials, finished goods, and slaves; from stockbreeding; and probably from slave raiding among the less hierarchically organized peoples to the north. By the mid-first century B.C., before Caesar had conquered Gaul and enmeshed its inhabitants in tributary relations with the Roman state, the citizens of the Celtic polities in France controlled their lands and the products of their labor to the extent that the state was not able to lay claim to a portion of its grain production. Patrons linked to the chiefly estate—that is, the incipient ruling class in this instance—provided protection from invaders and juridical relief in legal disputes among citizens or with neighbors. The ruler and the state both cooperated with and taxed merchants; they also organized soldiers to protect trade routes and caravans and to acquire labor power by slave raiding among the communities along their northern peripheries.

The expansion of the Roman state after the Second Punic War (218 to 202 B.C.) had important effects on the political-economic and social landscape of temperate Europe. It created demands for food, raw materials, and finished goods from distant lands and for skilled and unskilled slaves. Polities and communities in frontier areas, like Gaul, were enveloped and their populations enmeshed in various kinds of tributary relations with the central state. The provincial centers established at various places to collect taxes were also market towns, where merchants acting on their own or on behalf of companies acquired foodstuffs, raw materials, finished goods, metals, and slaves from the communities in the borderlands and beyond. One merchant purchased Gallic slaves at the price of one amphora of wine per slave and complained about having to pay transport taxes to the provincial centers and import taxes upon arriving in Rome. The activities of provincial merchants stimulated commerce with independent Celtic communities in Gaul, promoted the development of market towns on the margins of the imperial state, and facilitated the intensification of relations with Rome. As a result, a number of dependent kingdoms and communities flourished along the margins of the empire; however, the identity of these groups changed as the Roman state expanded.

The autonomous polities on the borders of the Roman state typically organized the flow of certain commodities—notably metals and slaves—that were obtained by raids in areas well beyond the frontier. Rome maintained cordial relations with frontier polities; however, it also tended to encapsulate and weaken them as its frontiers expanded outward. Consequently, the im-

Hilltop fort in Gloucestershire, England.

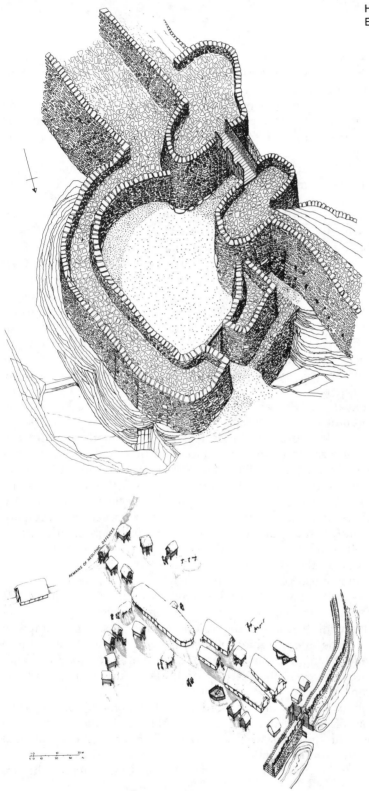

REMAINS OF NEOLITHIC DEFENCES

perial state was continually establishing "new official friends" and crushing old ones. This practice, of course, offered communities suddenly finding themselves on the expanding periphery of the imperial state with commercial opportunities that had not been available earlier. It also created new difficulties and posed very real threats to their continued well-being and existence. As a consequence, many of the frontier states and communities resisted Roman imperial expansion, and revolts erupted after they had been incorporated into the state.

Thus numerous communities beyond the imperial frontiers had no direct linkage with the Roman state but nevertheless provided its ruling class and citizens with various materials and goods. The demand for slaves created the conditions for almost continuous warfare in areas beyond the frontier—circumstances that were described by classical writers, like Strabo, Tacitus, or Julius Caesar. Slave raiding could set off the processes of class and state formation beyond the borders of Rome and its pacified provinces. The class-stratified states that crystallized in southern France used the same coins that circulated in Rome. Their contemporaries beyond the frontiers in north-central France or the Rhine Valley reoccupied the abandoned but heavily fortified settlements of earlier times and rarely used coins, even as a universal exchange value.

Roman goods made their way to Denmark, which was never incorporated into the state. During the first century A.D. the greatest concentrations of Roman goods and the richest graves were located in Lolland, southwest of Zealand. Chieftains residing in Lolland redistributed the imperial goods to vassals residing among the farming communities of the islands located further east. However, the center of authority shifted eastward, and by the fourth century, the richest graves and greatest numbers of Roman imports were found on the east coast of Zealand. What had been a marginal region controlled by vassals during the first century A.D. was the seat of the wealthiest and most powerful chiefdom in Denmark three centuries later, the point of entry for Roman imports, and the port of exit for the amber and war captives that were taken southward.

FURTHER READINGS: A BRIEF GUIDE

Timothy Champion, Clive Gamble, Stephen Shennan, and Alisdair Whittle, *Prehistoric Europe* (Orlando, FL: Academic Press, 1984); John M. Coles and Anthony F. Harding, *The Bronze Age in Europe: An Introduction to the Prehistory of Europe, c. 2000–700 BC* (New York: St. Martin's Press, 1979); Richard Bradley, *The Social Foundations of Prehistoric Britain: Themes and Variations in the Archeology of Power* (London: Longman, 1984); and the articles in John Bintliff, ed., *European Social Evolution: Archaeological Perspectives* (Bradford, Eng.: University of Bradford, 1984)—especially Michael Rowlands, "Conceptualizing the European Bronze and Early Iron Age," pp. 147–156—provide useful overviews of the issues and materials discussed in this chapter.

Ian Hodder, *The Domestication of Europe* (Oxford: Basil Blackwell, 1990) provides an overview of the early food-producing communities of the Balkans. Lepenski Vir is discussed by D. Srejović, *Lepenski Vir* (London: Thames & Hudson, 1972). The literature on the slash-and-burn farmers and herders of the Linear Pottery culture communities is extensive; see Peter I. Bogucki, *Forest Farmers and Stockherders: Early Agriculture and Its Consequences in North-Central Europe* (Cambridge: Cambridge University Press, 1988); and Sarunas Milisauskas, *Early Neolithic Settlements and Society at Olszanica* (Ann Arbor: University of Michigan Press, 1986). The indigenous foraging populations of northern Europe during the fifth millennium B.C. and earlier are considered by Mark Zvelebil, ed., *Hunters in Transition: Mesolithic Societies of Temperate Eurasia and Their Transition to Farming* (Cambridge: Cambridge University Press, 1986).

For the organization of Linear Pottery communities, see W. Startin, "Linear Pottery Culture Houses: Reconstruction and Manpower," *Proceedings of the Prehistoric Society*, vol. 44 (Cambridge, 1987), pp. 144–160; Julian Thomas, "Relations of Production and Social Change in the Neolithic of North-West Europe," *Man*, vol. 22, no. 3 (1985), 405–430; and P. van de Velde, "On Bandkeramik Social Structure," *Analecta Praehistoria Leiden*, vol. 12 (1979), 1–227. The increased importance of livestock and animal husbandry is explored by J. C. Chapman, " 'The Secondary Products Revolution' and the Limitations of the Neolithic," *Bulletin of the Institute of Archaeology, University of London*, vol. 19 (1982), 107–122.

Barbara Bender explores the consequences of intensification in "Gatherer-hunter to Farmer: A Social Perspective," *World Archaeology*, vol. 10, no. 2 (1978), 204–222, "Gatherer-hunter Intensification," in *Economic Archaeology: Towards an Integration of Ecological and Social Approaches*, British Archaeological Reports, International Series 96, ed. Alison Sheridan and Geoff Bailey (Oxford, 1981), pp. 149–157, "Prehistoric Developments in the American Midcontinent and in Brittany, Northwest France," in *Prehistoric Hunter-gatherers: The Emergence of Cultural Complexity*, ed. T. Douglas Price and James A. Brown (Orlando, FL: Academic Press, 1985), pp. 21–57, and "The Dynamics of Nonhierarchical Societies," in *The Evolution of Political Systems: Sociopolitics in Small-scale Societies*, ed. Stedman Upham (Cambridge: Cambridge University Press, 1990), pp. 247–263. The dynamics underlying the crystallization of gender relations during the third and second millennia B.C. are examined by Viana Muller, "Gender and Kinship in Ranked Societies and Chiefdoms of Northwest Europe: 1800 B.C.–A.D. 100," Ph.D. dissertation, New School for Social Research (New York, 1989), "The Formation of the State and the Oppression of Women: A Case Study in England and Wales," *Review of Radical Political Economy*, vol. 9, no. 3 (1977), 7–21. "Origins of Class and Gender Hierarchy in Northwest Europe," *Dialectical Anthropology*, vol. 10, nos. 1–2 (1985), 93–106, and "Kin Reproduction and Elite Accumulation in the Archaic States of Northwest Europe," in *Power Relations and State Formation*, ed. Thomas C. Patterson and Christine W. Gailey (Washington, DC: Archeology Section, American Anthropological Association, 1987), pp. 81–97.

Other features of European social development during the third millennium B.C. are discussed by Michael Shanks and Christopher Tilley, "Ideology, Symbolic Power and Ritual Communication: A Reinterpretation of Neolithic Burial Practices," in *Symbolic and Structural Archaeology*, ed. Ian Hodder (Cambridge: Cambridge University Press, 1982), pp. 129–154; Christopher Tilley, "Ideology and the Legitimation of Power in the Neolithic of Southern Sweden," in *Ideology, Power and Prehistory*, ed. Daniel Miller and Christopher Tilley (Cambridge: Cambridge University Press, 1984), pp. 111–146; Kristian Kristiansen, "The Formation of Tribal Systems in Later European Prehistory: Northern Europe, 4000–500 B.C.," in *Theory and Explanation in Archaeology*, ed. Colin Renfrew, Michael J. Rowlands, and Barbara A. Segraves (New York: Academic Press, 1982), pp. 241–280; Antonio Gilman, "The Development of Social Stratification in Bronze Age Europe," *Current Anthropology*, vol. 22, no. 1 (1981), 1–23; and Colin Renfrew, "Monuments, Mobilization and Social Organization in Neolithic Wessex," in *The Explanation of Culture Change: Models in Prehistory*, ed. Colin Renfrew (London: Gerald Duckworth, 1973), pp. 539–558.

Central to discussions of social organization in Europe during the second millennium B.C. are examinations of the Danish Bronze Age materials by Janet Levy, *Social and Religious Organization in Bronze Age Denmark: An Analysis of Ritual Hoard Finds*, British Archaeological Reports, International Series 124 (Oxford, 1982); Kristian Kristiansen, "From Stone to Bronze—The Evolution of Social Complexity in Northern Europe, 2300–1200 B.C.," in *Specialization, Exchange, and Complex Societies*, ed. Elizabeth M. Brumfiel and Timothy K. Earle (Cambridge: Cambridge University Press, 1987), pp. 30–51, and "The Consumption of Wealth in Bronze Age Denmark. A Study in the Dynamics of Economic Processes in Tribal Societies," in *New Directions in Scandinavian Archaeology*, ed. Kristian Kristiansen and Carsten Paludan-Müller (Copenhagen: National Museum of Denmark, 1978), pp. 158–190; and Klaus Randsborg, "Social Stratification in Early Bronze Age Denmark: A Study in the Regulation of Cultural Systems," *Praehistorische Zeitschrift*, Band 49 (1974), 38–61. Norbert Elias, *The History of Manners* (Oxford: Basil Blackwell, 1982), *Power and Civility* (Oxford: Basil Blackwell, 1982), and *The Court Society* (Oxford: Basil Blackwell, 1983) examines the cultural practices of chiefly estates and ruling courts.

For resistance to and the dissolution of social hierarchies, see Richard Bradley, "Economic Growth and Social Change: Two Examples from Prehistoric Europe," in *Economic Archaeology: Towards an Integration of Ecological and Social Approaches*, British Archaeological Reports, International Series 96, ed. Alison Sheridan and Geoff Bailey (Oxford, 1981), pp. 231–237, and "The Destruction of Wealth in Later European Prehistory," *Man*, vol. 17, no. 1 (1982), 108–122; and Michael Rowlands, "Kinship, Alliance and Exchange in the European Bronze Age," in *The British Later Bronze Age*, British Archaeo-logical Reports, International Series 86, ed. J. Barrett and Richard Bradley (Oxford, 1980), pp. 15–55.

For the structure of first-millennium-B.C. societies, see Susan Franken-stein and Michael J. Rowlands, "The Internal Structure and Regional Context of Early Iron Age Society in South-western Germany," *Bulletin of the Institute of Archaeology, University of London*, no. 15 (1978), 73–112; Peter Wells, *Farms, Villages, and Cities: Commerce and Urban Origins in Late Prehistoric Europe* (Ithaca, NY: Cornell University Press, 1984); Carole L. Crumley and William H. Marquardt, eds., *Regional Dynamics: Burgundian Landscapes in Historical Perspective* (San Diego: Academic Press, 1987); John Collis, *The European Iron Age* (London: B. T. Batsford, 1984); T. G. E. Powell, *The Celts* (London: Thames & Hudson, 1983); and D. Blair Gibson and Michael N. Geselowitz, eds., *Tribe and Polity in Late Prehistoric Europe: Demography, Production, and Exchange in the Evolution of Complex Social Systems* (New York: Plenum, 1988).

An overview of the formation of the Early La Tène and Celtic Iron Age societies is discussed by Daphne Nash, "Celtic Territorial Expansion and the Mediterranean World," Ludwig Pauli, "Early Celtic Society: Two Centuries of Wealth and Turmoil in Central Europe," and H. Lorenz, "Regional Organiza-tion in the Western Early La Tène Province: The Marne-Mosel and Rhine-Danube Groups," all in *Settlement and Society: Aspects of West European Prehistory in the First Millennium B.C.*, ed. T. C. Champion and J. V. S. Megaw (Leicester, Eng.: Leicester University Press, 1985), pp. 45–68, 23–44, and 109–122; and Daphne Nash, "Territory and State Formation in Central Gaul," in *Social Organisation and Settlement*, British Archaeological Reports, International Series 47(ii), ed. David Green, Colin Haselgrove, and Matthew Spriggs (Ox-ford, 1978), pp. 455–476.

Timbered graves with horse sacrifices are discussed by Maurizio Tosi, "The Egalitarian Foundations of Steppe Empires: Facing the Bush of Evolu-tionary Pathways," paper presented at the Wenner-Gren Symposium no. 108, Cascais, 1989; Esther Jacobson, "Burial Ritual, Gender and Status in South Siberian in the Late Bronze-Early Iron Age," *Paper on Inner Asia*, no. 7 (1987); I. Ecsedy, "Ancient Turk (T'u-chueh) Burial Customs," *Acta Orientalia Acade-miae Scientarum Hungaricae*, Tomus XXXVIII, fasc. 3 (Budapest, 1984), pp. 263–287; Maria Gimbutas, *The Bronze Age Cultures in Central and Eastern Europe* (The Hague: Mouton Publishers, 1965); T. Talbot Rice, *The Scythians* (London: Thames & Hudson, 1957); E. D. Phillips, "The Sythian Domination of West-ern Asia," *World Archaeology*, vol. 4, no. 1 (1972), 129–138; and *The Cambridge History of Early Inner Asia*, ed. Denis Sinor (Cambridge, UK: Cambridge Uni-versity Press, 1990).

For social formation on the margins of the Roman state, see Lotte Hedeager, "Processes toward State Formation in Early Iron Age Denmark," in *New Directions in Scandinavian Archaeology*, ed. Kristian Kristiansen and Car-sten Paludan-Müller (Copenhagen: National Museum of Denmark, 1978), pp. 217–223; Lotte Hedeager, "Empire, Frontier, and the Barbarian Hinterland: Rome and Northern Europe from A.D. 1–400," Daphne Nash, "Imperial Expansion under the Roman Republic," and Colin Haselgrove, "Cultural Process on the Periphery: Belgic Gaul and Rome during the Late Republic and Early Empire," all in *Centre and Periphery in the Ancient World*, ed. Michael Rowlands, Mogens Larsen, and Kristian Kristiansen (Cambridge: Cambridge University Press, 1987), pp. 125–140, 87–103, and 104–124; Stephen L. Dyson, "Native Revolts in the Roman Empire," *Historia*, Band XX, Heft 2–3 (1971), 239–274; and Chris Wickham, "The Other Transition: From the Ancient World to Feudalism," *Past and Present*, no. 103 (1984), 3–34.

chapter 13

North America

The colonial world is a world cut in two. The dividing line, the frontiers are shown by barracks and police stations. . . . It is the policeman and the soldier who are the official instituted go-between, the spokesmen of the settler and his rule of oppression. (Frantz Fanon, The Wretched of the Earth*)*

Acculturation has always been a matter of conquest. . . . Refugees from the foundering groups may adopt the standards of the more potent society in order to survive as individuals. But these are the conscripts of civilization, not volunteers. (Stanley Diamond, "Introduction: The Uses of the Primitive")

As soon as the Japanese administration had succeeded in putting down the Formosan rebels in 1902, they turned their attention toward controlling the Aborigines and helping them progress toward civilization. The Aborigines were particularly bothersome because they frequently attacked and took the heads of outsiders who approached their frontiers too closely. (John H. Bodley, Victims of Progress*)*

North America is a wedge-shaped continent. It is widest in the north and tapers toward the south. Most of it lies north of the 30th parallel in temperate and subpolar latitudes. North of the Rio Grande there are mountain ranges along both edges of the continent. The Appalachian chain in the east consists of worn-down mountains that were formed more than 400 million years ago. The Rockies and the coastal ranges of the west consist of high, young mountains that were formed during the past 10 to 15 million years. The lowlands separating the two mountain chains include the Canadian Shield, which is composed of rocks that are more than 2 billion years old; the Great Plains of the western United States, which formed a shallow sea basin about 70 million years ago; and the Mississippi River Basin, which developed after the Great Plains were thrust above the level of the Cretaceous sea that inundated low-lying areas like Texas, Louisiana, and Oklahoma. Rivers rose in the mountains and along the edge of the Canadian Shield and flowed across a mosaic of old and new land surfaces before emptying into the oceans that surround the continent.

Today polar tundra covers the northern part of the continent from Alaska to the coast of Greenland. South of this treeless, frozen area lies the taiga, with evergreen forests that stretch southward to New England. This area gives way to deciduous forests, which covered much of the eastern United States until the beginning of this century; these forests thin out toward the west, where they gradually merge with the grasslands of the Great Plains. West of the grasslands lie the steppe, desert, and alpine environments of the Rockies, the Great Basin, and the American Southwest. Evergreen forests appear again along the Pacific coast of the continent and stretch northward from the middle of California to Alaska.

North America.

For most of their history, human beings lived exclusively in the Old World. No early forms of human beings—such as *Homo erectus* or *Homo sapiens neanderthalensis*—have ever been found in the New World, nor were there fossil or living apes, our closest relatives, in the Americas. Some time after human beings acquired their modern form, between 50,000 and 100,000 years ago, they immigrated across the Bering Strait and settled for the first time in the Western Hemisphere. These immigrants must have closely resembled the ancient inhabitants of northeastern Asia.

The first immigrants to the Americas probably arrived between 30,000 and 40,000 years ago, shortly before the Bering land bridge began to emerge between North America and Siberia as the world's sea levels fell and ice sheets formed in the upper latitudes. This view suggests that the early immigrants crossed the 40-mile stretch of water, called the Bering Strait, that separates Alaska and Siberia. On clear days, Alaska can be seen from Siberia, and both are visible from the Diomedes Islands in the middle of the strait. Today the ice is firm enough about once every decade for people to cross between Alaska and Siberia with dogsleds. The cultural similarities between the American Arctic and Siberia during the past 10,000 years indicate that the peoples of the two areas continued to exchange ideas and techniques long after the land bridge had ceased to exist.

The immigrants moved southward along the coast or the eastern front of the Rockies. People certainly lived south of the continental ice sheets that covered much of Canada during the last glacial maximum. Evidence from Valsequillo, Mexico, indicates that people hunted horses and mastodons as gravels washed into the basin between 18,000 and 15,000 years ago. Chipped stone tools were recovered in a stratum deposited at the Meadowcroft Rockshelter in western Pennsylvania between 19,000 and 14,000 years ago. Several archaeological sites in Mesoamerica, Brazil, and Chile have yielded radiocarbon dates ranging from 32,000 to 20,000 B.P. These antedate by ten millennia or more the well-documented kill and butchering sites in the western United States, where extinct animals have been found in association with fluted spear points in contexts that have been radiocarbon dated from 10,000 to 12,000 years ago.

Archaeologists currently debate three separate issues concerning the early inhabitants of the New World. The first issue involves the approximate time of entry. One group argues that the earliest immigrants crossed the Bering Straits from northeast Asia and arrived in the Americas more than 20,000 years ago. Another group challenges this claim and argues that evidence for people in the New World before about 15,000 years ago is not especially compelling. The second issue concerns the kinds of stone tools the earliest inhabitants made and used. The group advocating the greater antiquity of people in the New World also claims that the first immigrants arrived with a relatively unspecialized stoneworking technology and that there was subsequent independent and very rapid development of an advanced lithic technology, which included the heat treatment of raw materials, pressure flaking, and bifacial thinning. The proponents of the late entry perspective argue that either the first immigrants brought from Asia an advanced stoneworking technology, which included fluted projectile points, or they invented this technology shortly after they arrived in the Arctic. The third issue involves the subsistence economy of the early inhabitants. A group made up mostly of those archaeologists who claim early arrival also argues that the early Americans had mixed subsistence economies that included seasonally based hunting and trapping of a variety of animals. Their opponents claim that the early inhabitants were primarily big-game hunters, who used marshes, arroyos, and other features of the landscape to entrap and kill large game—primarily mammoths and bison—at a rate that eventually led to the extinction of several species toward the end of the Pleistocene.

The last issue, which involves a distinction between broad-spectrum foragers and specialized big-game hunters, is undoubtedly overdrawn. Many of the kill sites, where large animals were butchered, represent single moments—events that yielded food and other materials that must have been consumed relatively quickly. Furthermore, many of the kill and campsite faunas are more diverse than initially supposed: They indicate that the early inhabitants hunted or trapped a variety of amphibians, birds, and small mammals as well as deer, antelopes, horses, camelids, mammoths, and bison. Given the ecological diversity and the amount of environmental change in the Americas, there is also considerable variation in the faunal assemblages found at different times and places in Mesoamerica and elsewhere. The diversity of the faunal resources available to the early inhabitants of the New World and the diversity of the plant and animal resources they actually used raise questions about whether the early Americans were solely or largely responsible for the extinction of certain elements of the Pleistocene megafauna. This is still an open, unresolved question.

The earliest New World communities for which there are significant amounts of evidence were based on variants of the communal mode of production. In these communities, there were collective control and appropriation of raw materials and the means of production. Individuals belonged to the community by virtue of their regular participation in activities and practices that gave meaning to their interdependence. However, archaeologists can say relatively little about the specific social and cultural forms of these early communities because, at this point in their investigations, they know more about the tools they produced and the raw materials they used and consumed.

The subsistence economies of the North American peoples were already diverse by the seventh millennium B.C. For example, by 6500 B.C., the inhabitants of the Great Plains of southeastern Colorado participated in communal buffalo drives during late May or early June. At the Olsen-Chubbuck site, two lines of hunters approached a herd of 200 or so buffalo from downwind, so the animals could not smell them. On a signal, they startled the herd and drove the animals between them toward the edge of a nearby arroyo; by surrounding the herd, the hunters prevented the animals from veering away from the brim of the canyon. The lead animals plunged into the gulch as they were pushed by those behind them. The dead or disabled animals were quickly covered by other animals, who also died in contorted positions. After the stampede was over, more than 200 buffalo lay at the foot of the cliff.

The hunters moved in quickly and began to butcher the animals on top. They removed the forelegs and turned the animals onto their stomachs to skin them; they cut the meat from the hump and then the rib meat and

Bison kill in the Olsen-Chubbuck site in southern Colorado. Ancient hunters drove a bison herd into an arroyo.

internal organs. As each cut was removed, they placed it in a pile with similar pieces from other animals. The hunters then removed the top round steak, the hind legs, the neck meat, and the tongue; finally, they cracked open the skull to get the brains. It took an hour or so to butcher a single animal, so the 75 to 100 individuals who had come together for the bison drive and other collective activities could have carried out the work in a single morning.

Their contemporaries on the California coast near Santa Barbara, who lived in semisubterranean pithouses and covered their dead with red ocher, collected marine shellfish in the intertidal zone and dove for abalone; they caught deep-water fish with baited hooks and shallow-water species with nets that were cast from rocky points and beaches. They hunted deer throughout the year and seals and sea lions in their rookeries during the winter and early spring mating and birthing seasons. In the late summer or early fall, they moved to temporary campsites located a few miles inland to gather acorns and seeds, which were ground in stone mortars and stored for the winter.

From the seventh millennium B.C. onward, communities developed diverse subsistence economies to utilize the varied habitats and resources of the Great Basin. Those that lived near the lakes in northwestern Nevada derived much of their livelihood from fish and migratory waterfowl, which they attracted with decoys that bobbed in the water near the tule, bulrushes, and marsh grasses that fringed the lake. During the fall, they collected pine nuts and acorns, which were ground on flat stone metates or stored for use later in the year. They dispersed during the spring to forage, trap small animals, and hunt deer and other game with spear-throwers and stone-tipped darts. They occasionally stopped and stayed a few days in the lakeside caves to escape the oppressive heat of the hot summer.

THE AMERICAN ARCTIC

Alaska and northern Canada were not abandoned when people moved southward into more temperate areas before, during, and after the last glacial maximum. There is ample evidence that the unglaciated portions of the American Arctic, which were an extension of Eurasia during the waning years of the Pleistocene and for some time afterward, were inhabited more or less continuously. Christy Turner (1987) has argued that there were three waves of immigrants to the New World. The initial settlers came before 15,000 B.P. The second wave occurred about 14,000 years ago and consisted of tundra and forest hunters who moved inland and along the coast of British Columbia, southern Alaska, and the Aleutian Islands. The third wave occurred several millennia later and consisted of maritime hunters who moved along the exposed continental shelf that connected North America, Asia, and the large islands in the Arctic Ocean.

The second group of immigrants, those who moved into the interior and onto the coastal plain of western Canada, made tools on small blades struck from microcores; they camped at such places as Onion Portage in northern Alaska between 14,000 and 12,000 years ago before moving into the interior to pursue the vast caribou herds that roamed central Alaska, the Yukon, and the Northwest Territory. They hunted these animals—as well as elk, bison, and smaller terrestrial mammals—with spears tipped with microblade barbs. The geographical spread of the microblade tool assemblages increased significantly as evergreen forests spread into portions of Canada that had been glaciated during the Pleistocene and became ice free in postglacial time.

By 8500 B.P. numerous small communities had already moved into the Pacific littoral, stretching from the Aleutian Islands to British Columbia. Their members made a variety of stone tools on large flakes, collected marine foods from the intertidal zone, and hunted sea mammals—sea lions, seals, and walrus—while the animals were on land; a few walrus have been found with projectile points still embedded in them. Around 3,000 years ago, the people were beginning to venture out to sea in tiny, skin-covered boats from which they fished and used multibarbed harpoons to kill whales and dolphins during the summer months.

The Arctic Small-Tool tradition, which had appeared on the Bering coast of Alaska by 6000 B.P., was a product of the last wave of immigrants. During the next three millennia people using these tools spread across the Arctic coast from Alaska to Victoria and the Baffin Islands to Greenland and south-eastward along the Canadian coast from the Ungava Peninsula to Labrador and Newfoundland. These people were the ancestors of the modern-day Eskimos, who still inhabit the same coastal areas. They were sea-mammal hunters par excellence. They used thrusting harpoons tipped with slate blades to kill whales, seals, and walrus; they fished with bone and shell fishhooks; and they hunted caribou during the summer with bows and arrows. They burned whale oil in stone lamps to light their houses and carved a variety of tools and decorative objects from walrus ivory and antler. As time passed, these early Eskimo communities became increasingly adept at exploiting the resources of the cold north seas and at living in areas where snow, ice, and subzero temperatures are common for much of the year. Whale hunting, which is perhaps one of the more distinctive subsistence practices of Eskimo communities, was already being pursued 4,000 years ago by a group that camped at Cape Krusenstern in northern Alaska.

By 1000 B.C., whaling peoples lived at a number of places along the Bering Sea and the Arctic Ocean. One settlement overlooking the estuary of a river that emptied into Norton Sound on the northwest coast of Alaska had more than 200 houses; another located on Safety Sound near Cape Nome had nearly 400 houses. During the long winter, the community members lived in sturdy rectangular houses made of driftwood logs covered with earth; they entered their houses through long passageways that kept out the wind and cold. The men hunted seals and walrus from kayaks, fished through holes in the ice, and trapped small land mammals. At night or when the weather was too severe for them to leave their homes, they repaired old tools and made new ones in preparation for the whale hunt that would begin in April. When the ice opened, the men set out in umiaks (large kayaks) in search of the baleen whales. If they harpooned one, the meat ensured that several households would eat for an entire winter. If they were fortunate enough to take three or four whales, the winter would be a very good one indeed.

The villagers dispersed in June as the various households moved inland along the rivers. The women and children set up fishing stations, and the men trekked into the barrens in search of caribou herds. After a month or so they returned to the coast to hunt walrus with the other men of the community. By September the walrus hunt was over, and the men went inland once again to pick up the other members of their households and the fish they had caught. As the first snows began to fall, the households began to congregate again in their winter quarters overlooking the ocean.

By A.D. 1000, communities of efficient whale hunters, referred to as the Thule culture, were living in the coastal regions of the Arctic from the Mackenzie River Delta to eastern Greenland and along the shores of Hudson Bay. Many of the winter settlements were quite small, with perhaps twenty-five households; others, however, were much larger, with a hundred or so domestic groups. The Thule peoples located their winter villages near coastal ponds, where peat, a major building material, was abundant. They were efficient whale hunters, who beached the animals they killed; butchered them; and then moved meat, blubber, and bone by boat or sled to their winter quarters. Toward the end of the first millennium A.D., before the arrival of the first Europeans, some of the Thule communities were already making a few metal implements. They obtained copper in southern Victoria Island and meteoritic and terrestrial iron in the Melville Bay region.

A different lifestyle, known as the Maritime Archaic tradition, devel-

A burial mound erected more than 7000 years ago at l'Anse Amour in southern Labrador. The excavator estimated that it took fifteen to twenty families more than a week to dig and refill the burial pit. *(From James A. Tuck and Robert J. McGhee, "An Archaic Indian Burial Mound in Labrador. Copyright © 1976 by Scientific American, Inc. All rights reserved.)*

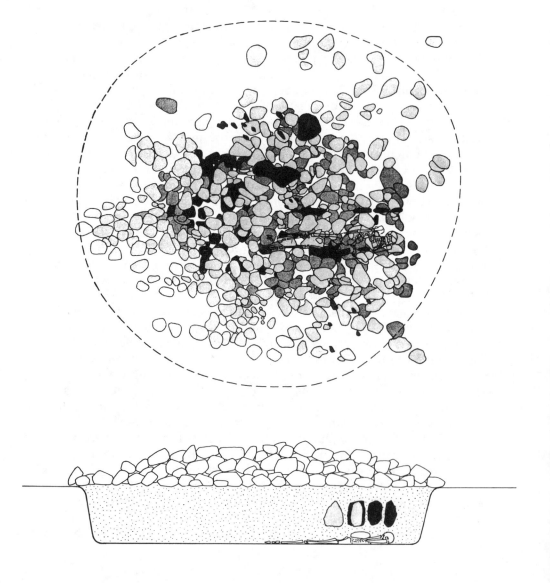

oped in the coastal areas of Labrador, Newfoundland, the Maritime Provinces, eastern Quebec, and northern New England before 5000 B.C. The Maritime Archaic communities produced a relatively homogeneous and widespread material culture—chipped and ground stone implements, bone artifacts, decorated concretions and quartz pebbles, red ocher, and burial mounds. For example, a community of fifteen to twenty households at l'Anse Armour in southern Labrador labored more than a week to dig and refill a large burial pit, which was then marked with a large pile of rocks.

The subsistence economies of the communities were based on birds, fish, and mammals and incorporated differences in the local availability or abundance of particular species; for example, the communities in the southern Maritime Provinces and coastal Maine harpooned swordfish during the summer, whereas their contemporaries in Labrador relied more extensively on Atlantic salmon and cod. The tool inventories of the Maritime Archaic communities resembled those of hunters and foragers who lived in the interior to the east; however, these coastal communities began to exploit seals, walrus, and other marine resources during the summers with increasing efficiency. Households and small bands congregated in settlements like Port aux Choix on the west coast of Newfoundland in the late spring to hunt seals and other marine mammals that were available on the land and pack ice. They also spent the summers on or near the coast to fish, trap birds, and collect berries and other edible plants. When the first snows fell, the coastal settlements broke up as the households and bands retreated inland to favored hunting sites, which overlooked the places where caribou herds crossed rivers or lakes. During the remainder of the winter, they hunted single animals and trapped small animals like beavers. The men and women of the communities made a variety of implements and weapons—toggled and barbed harpoons; slate and bone spears; barbed bone leisters; chipped-stone knives; and fleshers for procuring and processing food and axes, adzes, and gouges that were used to fashion wood into houses, boats, bowls, and tool handles.

Though both the Eskimos of the north and the peoples of the Maritime Archaic tradition exploited marine resources, there were striking differences between them. The Eskimos made extensive use of whales, whereas their contemporaries in eastern Canada and along the Maine coast largely ignored them, in spite of the fact that they occur with some frequency in the waters off Labrador, Newfoundland, and the mouth of the St. Lawrence River. The Eskimos moved inland to fish along the rivers and to hunt caribou during the summer months. This was exactly the same time that the Maritime Archaic communities congregated on the coast to hunt seals, walrus, and migratory birds. The maritime orientation of the two kinds of communities permitted both to congregate in significant numbers on the coast but at different times of the year. The abundance of the marine resources is only part of the reason for the specificity of the two subsistence systems. However, the Marine Archaic subsistence economies were replaced during the second millennium B.C. when these communities or groups, whose tools resembled those found on the Canadian Shield, became littoral harvesters who left deep shell mounds at various places along the Maine coast.

KIN-ORGANIZED COMMUNITIES, CENTRALIZATION, AND RESISTANCE IN THE EASTERN WOODLANDS

Although communities have occupied the eastern woodlands for more than 15,000 years, our knowledge of their lifeways only becomes appreciable for those of the Archaic Period (8000 to 500 B.C.). These groups used the foodstuffs and raw materials afforded by the diverse habitats of eastern North America. During the eighth millennium B.C., small bands camped in the bottomlands and on sandbars along the rivers of Tennessee; their members lived in skin or bark shelters; hunted deer and elk; trapped small animals; captured turtles during the spring; occasionally ate freshwater mollusks; and harvested hickory nuts, acorns, and berries in the late summer and early autumn. The late summer camp at the Koster site in the lower Illinois River Valley north of St. Louis had about twenty-five residents, who dispersed to collect shellfish and harvest and store hickory nuts in the fall; the households hunted deer and relied on their foodstores until they returned to Koster in the following spring.

Between 4500 and 4000 B.C., many communities began to return regularly each year to campsites on rivers and lakes that overlooked rich shellfish beds or spawning grounds. They built relatively permanent houses at Koster and sites on the Tennessee River Valley and along the upper Tombigee River in Mississippi. In some areas, like Rose Island in Tennessee, they abandoned these dwellings when rising waters inundated them and returned after the floods had receded; some of these riverine or lakeside settlements may have had as many as one hundred residents. As a consequence of the settlement and subsistence practices, deep refuse mounds of discarded mollusk shells and debris accumulated around the campsites.

Cemeteries and less formal burial grounds were another aspect of this increased sedentism. Most of the fourth-millennium-B.C. graves contained individuals, only about a quarter of which had grave goods of any kind. Grave goods became somewhat more common during the third millennium B.C. A few graves in Wisconsin and Michigan contained implements that were cold-hammered from the pure native copper that outcrops around Lake Superior. A small number of individuals from the Lamoka Lake and Indian Knoll cemeteries in western New York and southwestern Kentucky, respectively, had projectile points embedded in their bodies, and a few of the Lamoka burials were mutilated—their heads, hands, or feet had been severed from their bodies. The presence of weapons, like spear-throwers, in the graves of women and children suggest that they not only hunted but may also have been involved in the violence and low-level feuds that characterized these kin-organized, relatively egalitarian communities, in which leadership and authority were based largely on age, experience, or skill rather than ascribed status.

The women of the Archaic Period communities played major roles in their subsistence economies, which seem to have consisted of overlapping but complementary spheres of activities that were organized to some extent by gender. Women played a major role in plant cultivation. They adopted gourds and cucurbits around 5000 B.C. and used them as containers in ritual contexts, which suggests that some of these fell within the women's domain. Later, in the second millennium B.C., they cultivated a number of local species—sunflowers, sumpweed, and chenopodium—and used the harvests to supplement the hickory nuts and other wild plant foods they gathered and stored during the fall. Women also harvested freshwater mollusks from the streams and oxbow lakes of the Savannah River watershed in South Carolina and Georgia.

Between 1000 and 700 B.C., peoples in the lower Mississippi River Valley began to erect monumental earthworks at Poverty Point, which overlooked the Mississippi River floodplain, 200 miles upstream from the Gulf of Mexico near the confluences of half a dozen rivers. The earthworks consisted of six

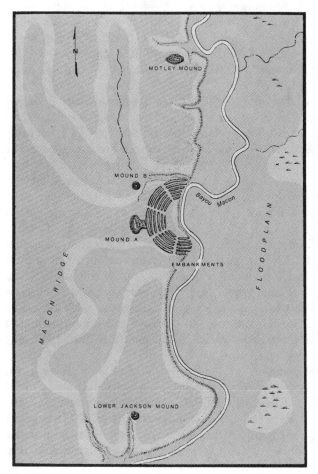

Large earthworks at Poverty Point, Louisiana.

semicircular embankments, 80 feet wide and 10 feet high, and several plat-form mounds, the largest of which rises nearly 70 feet above the surface of the bluff. The construction of the mounds required the labor of an estimated 1,350 persons working for a period of 210 days; this figure does not include the labor of those who provided the food and other necessities to sustain the construction workers during this period. It seems likely that the labor involved was recruited from the 4,000 to 5,000 residents of Poverty Point as well as the inhabitants of nearby hamlets and villages, who gathered a variety of wild foodstuffs and fished in the streams, swamps, and ox-bow lakes.

Poverty Point was probably the center of a widespread exchange system that brought raw materials and finished items from various upstream locali-ties, some of which were more than 600 miles away, and from settlements along the Gulf coast; these materials included argillite, copper, slate, steatite, and mollusk shells. This seemingly sudden elaboration of exchange relations in the lower Mississippi Valley was accompanied by the intensification of social relations; what is not clear is whether the circulation of goods was orchestrated through the traditional social relations of the community—that is, by leaders whose positions were defined in customary terms—or whether it was contrived by big persons who stood outside the traditional framework and whose positions were facilitated by the rapid appearance of new condi-tions and the equally rapid consolidation of new kinds of social relations involving patron-client obligations.

Poverty Point was not the only settlement in eastern North America that witnessed an intensification of construction and exchange activities dur-ing the first millennium B.C. The Adena communities of the Ohio Valley contin-ued the tradition of northern groups—like the Maritime Archaic peoples of Labrador—of erecting burial mounds; by 500 B.C., they had erected another 300 to 500 mounds in the central Ohio River Valley. Although not on the scale of the Poverty Point earthworks, they involved the labor power of a number of local communities, whose members cooperated in digging, mov-ing, and piling the earth that went into the mounds. Some of the mounds were used over considerable periods of time, and their construction was part of elaborate funerary rituals. For instance, when an individual died or was about to be interred, kin and neighbors covered the body with red ocher, placed personal possessions in the grave, and then heaped earth on top of the burial pit. The mound grew in size as more burials were added. Few if any of the Adena burials during the later part of the first millennium exhibited any indication of social differences; the social relations within the communi-ties were still egalitarian rather than ranked.

There were important changes in Adena burial customs about 2,000 years ago: Individuals or small numbers of bodies were placed in burial chambers located in wooden structures that were subsequently covered with earthen mounds and often enclosed with circular earthworks. The grave goods were often lavish and frequently included objects made from raw mate-rials that were obtainable only in distant localities; in some instances, they also included severed human heads—that is, trophy skulls. The later Adena burial mounds suggest the continuing importance of social relations based on kinship and residence and the elaboration of status differences or ranking within some communities.

Between 200 B.C. and A.D. 400, the inhabitants of the small hamlets that lived in the Miami and Scioto valleys of southern Ohio began to erect enormous earthworks. At Hopewell near Chillicothe, thirty-eight mounds spread over 110 acres were enclosed by a rectangular earthwork; a gigantic complex of circles, squares, and octagons connected by causeways, covering about 4 square miles, encloses burial mounds at Newark, Ohio. Several hundred thousand person-hours of labor were involved in digging, moving, and piling the earth that formed a typical Hopewell mound. The mounds contained several thousand burials of diverse types, from cremations to crypts. There were also charnel houses, in which corpses and cremated individuals were interred before the structures were burned to the ground and covered over with earth. The grave goods of the Hopewellian elite were richer than those found in the earlier Adena tombs: copper earspools and breastplates; pearl beads; and ornaments made from mica, tortoiseshell, and silver. Many of the Hopewell tombs contained objects made from raw materials that came from distant localities. The carefully executed objects also suggest that some individuals were part-time artisans who worked with galena, mica, and even obsidian.

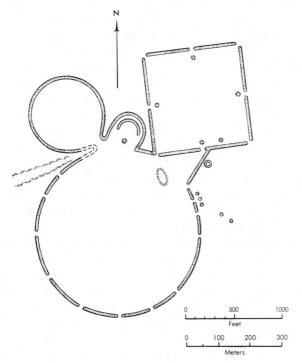

The Hopewell earthworks and mounds of the Edwin Harness group in Ohio.

Pottery vessels and ornaments resembling those from the Hopewell burial mounds in southern Ohio were also placed in elite tombs in villages in the Illinois River Valley. One of these was Scovill, a settlement located in the rich bottomlands of the valley, whose inhabitants hunted mallard ducks and planted squash and gourds in the late spring before they dispersed to hunt deer and other animals in the uplands in the summer. They returned to the bottomlands in the late summer to harvest their crops and to gather other economically important plants—nuts, knotweed, wild rice, marsh elder, grapes, and plums—that grew in the area.

Beginning around A.D. 150, communities in a broad band stretching from northern Louisiana to Georgia performed elaborate burial rituals on the tops of platform mounds, where the residences of important personages and charnel houses for the dead were erected. These rank-ordered kin communities, known as the Weeden Island culture, were contemporary with the Hopewellian groups to the north. Each local Weeden Island community may have had its own ritual specialist, who performed during the burial rituals and whose knowledge was the ideological cement that bound together the members of the community and provided linkages among them, their ancestors, and nature.

Eastern North America was a social and cultural mosaic during this period, the pieces of which were linked together by the exchange of raw materials and/or finished goods, by funerary practices involving burial mounds and charnel houses, and possibly by intertribal or interregional alliances. Communities in the Ohio Valley may well have been perched on the brink of class and state formation, which were ultimately prevented by the opposition of the nonelite members of those groups and their capacity to move away from any potentially exploitative and oppressive relations their kin and neighbors might have sought to impose.

Around A.D. 900, a series of regional groupings, known as Mississippian culture, appeared in various parts of the eastern United States—the lower Mississippi River Valley, the Caddoan area centered in the Arkansas and Red River valleys, the southern Appalachian of Alabama and Georgia, the middle Mississippi and the river basins emptying into that portion of the valley, the Oneota of the upper Mississippi Valley, and the Fort Ancient communities of the middle Ohio River Valley. Of these, the middle Mississippi was the most elaborate and overdeveloped. Cahokia—located in the bottomlands at the confluence of the Mississippi, Missouri, and Illinois rivers near St. Louis—was the center of an autochthonous class-stratified, state-based society that crystallized about A.D. 1050 and collapsed about two centuries later. There were more than 100 mounds at this 3,300-acre settlement; 250 acres near the center, where several of the largest mounds were located, were enclosed by a wooden palisade. More than 30,000 people lived at Cahokia between the eleventh and thirteenth centuries.

During the eleventh century, a small platform was built and aligned along a north-south axis with the largest structure in the settlement. Two individuals were buried in this mound within a century of each other. Little

Reconstruction of Monks Mound and its environs at Cahokia.

is known about the first burial. The second individual, however, was accompanied to his grave by a number of other people. He was buried on a platform made of more than 20,000 shell beads. Near him were bundles of bones from earlier burials. A little further away six men were buried in separate tombs with lavish grave goods—rolls of sheet copper, stacks of mica sheets, semiprecious stones, and finely chipped arrowheads that were never used. More than fifty women—similar in height, weight, and age (eighteen to twenty-three years old)—were possibly strangled and buried at the same time in a nearby pit. Four men, whose heads and hands had been cut off, were buried between the central figure and the young women. As one archaeologist remarked, "The central figure was clearly a guy with class!" The raw materials used to make the goods placed in the tomb came from the Gulf Coast, Yellowstone, the Great Lakes, and the Carolina piedmont.

Cahokia's ruling elite appropriated significant amounts of labor power from its residents and from those of smaller neighboring settlements. It also acquired raw materials that moved up and down the river systems that merged near the city. However, by 1400, the population of Cahokia had dwindled to 4,000 or 5,000 individuals. Three hundred years later, the first French explorers of the region found its mounds overgrown with vegetation. The decline of Cahokia was the outcome of processes in which successor states and warlords proliferated on its periphery, while the inhabitants of outlying settlements and regions reasserted their autonomy and control over the raw materials, goods, and labor power of their own members. There was class struggle, and in this instance, the subordinated communities won and they reclaimed control over their lives. However, there was a cost: The margins were tribalized and exchange and warfare intensified, notably among the proto-Iroquois societies of the eastern Great Lakes region and in the lower Mississippi Valley.

KIN-ORGANIZED COMMUNITIES
IN THE AMERICAN SOUTHWEST

The American Southwest is a small area with diverse habitats. The low-lying deserts, which stretch westward from Tucson and Phoenix to the Colorado River and southward into Chihuahua, Mexico, exhibit little temperature variation from one season to the next. North and east of the desert lie the steep, forest-covered mountains and deep, narrow valleys of the Mogollon Rim, which stretches in a broad band across central Arizona and New Mexico. North of the mountains lie the high mesas and deep canyons of the Four Corners area, where the boundaries of Colorado, Utah, Arizona, and New Mexico converge; much of the land is flat or gently sloping, and the wooded mesas are separated by grass-covered bottomlands.

More than 11,000 years ago, the inhabitants of the Southwest were hunters and gatherers, who camped near springs and killed various animals, including mammoths, that came to drink at the waterholes. Five thousand years later, their descendants were also hunters and foragers, who relied more intensively on plant foods and on fish and birds from the lakes and rivers. They dug up tubers, roots, and whole plants with wooden digging sticks. They carried the plant foods they harvested in tightly woven baskets. They ground the seeds and nuts they collected on flat milling stones; and they boiled their food by dropping hot rocks in baskets that had been waterproofed with a lining of pitch. They wore robes made from animal skins that had been sewn together and sandals woven from plant fibers; a few individuals wore necklaces made from Pacific Ocean seashells.

During the first millennium B.C., communities in various parts of the Southwest—for example, the desert of southern Arizona and Chaco Canyon in northern New Mexico—incorporated plants originally domesticated far to the south into their subsistence economies. The hunter-gatherer bands of Chaco Canyon, which foraged in the open grasslands during the summer months, returned to the canyon in the fall to collect pinyon nuts and to harvest the squash, beans, and maize from the gardens they had planted earlier in the year. For centuries, agriculture remained a relatively minor subsistence activity in the everyday lives of the foraging communities in the Southwest; their agricultural labor merely supplemented their wild food resources. After about A.D. 200, small sedentary hamlets and villages appeared in various parts of the region—the Hohokam area of southern Arizona, the Sonoran Desert, and the Colorado Plateau. The earliest of the permanent settlements varied in size from a few pithouses to 25 or 35 households. Some of the farming towns that were built and occupied after A.D. 700 may have had 500 to 1,000 residents.

Before A.D. 500, a typical pithouse in the Mogollon Rim had a floor area of 330 square feet, which suggests that as many as ten individuals participated in the activities of the household production-consumption units. By A.D. 1000, the settlements contained three times as many rooms as their predecessors but each dwelling was about a third the size, suggesting that the organization of the residential groups was transformed through time. In the earlier settlements, the domestic groups were made up of extended families that lived in a few large dwellings; in the later villages, the households consisted of two to four individuals. The shift in the size and composition of the domestic groups was accompanied by a reduction in the size of the cooking vessels.

Between 1000 B.C. and A.D. 1000, the social organization of the hunter-forager and farming communities of the Southwest was structured by variants of the communal mode of production. The earlier communities consisted of relatively autonomous, largely self-sufficient households—extended families—that were the real units of appropriation; these were linked to one another by a continually shifting web of kinship and marital relations. Many of the later communities were also structured by the communal mode of production, even though members of the constituent households contributed significant amounts of labor to the construction and maintenance of structures, called kivas, that were presumably used by the village as a whole as places where rituals were performed, and where discussions shaped how labor and other resources would be allocated and how they could obtain raw materials and finished goods—like turquoise, copper bells, or seashells—from distant places in Mexico or on the Gulf and Pacific coasts. Such items were usually obtained when individuals in one community exchanged gifts with friends, kin, or partners who lived elsewhere or with visitors from distant settlements.

Around A.D. 700, peoples in various parts of the Southwest began to abandon their pithouses and to build rectangular, above-ground structures. The later villages—that is, those dating to the tenth century and after—consisted of one or more apartment houses, often with two or three stories and several hundred rooms, which were variously used for the activities of everyday life and for storage.

During the tenth century, the inhabitants of Chaco Canyon in northwestern New Mexico built 12 towns, the largest of which was Pueblo Bonito. The 800 rooms that made up this crescent-shaped apartment block rose 4 stories above the ground and overlooked an enclosed plaza and more than 30 semisubterranean kivas that were roofed with pine logs carried down from the mesa tops. The residents entered the rooms by ladders that were placed against the outside walls of the building. The large towns—Pueblo Bonito,

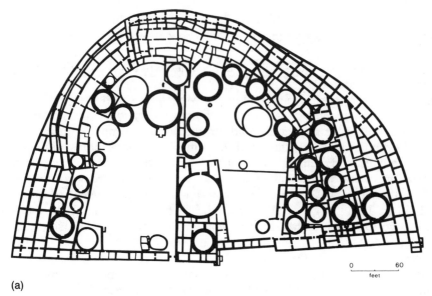

(a)

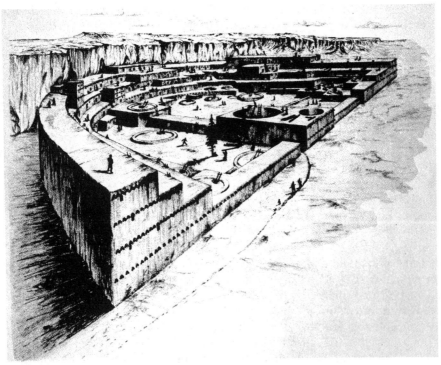

(b)

Pueblo Bonito, Chaco Canyon, New Mexico. (a) Plan. (b) Reconstruction of its appearance about A.D. 1050.

292

Penasco Blanco, and Una Vida—may well have served mainly as food storage areas and ritual centers for the inhabitants of the isolated households and the 70 or so small hamlets located throughout the 20-mile-long canyon, on the mesas overlooking its bottomlands, and in areas linked by an extensive road system. Besides the towns and roads, the inhabitants of the canyon, between the tenth and thirteenth centuries, also built an elaborate water-control system.

The inhabitants of Chaco Canyon and its environs were farmers. The women planted and tended crops and foraged for wild plant foods, and the men hunted and acquired raw materials and finished goods from distant areas. Between A.D. 920 and 1120, the Chaco community made turquoise ornaments from raw materials they brought from sources near Santa Fe, which was about 100 miles to the east. These objects were manufactured not only in the towns but also in the smaller outlying settlements and isolated homesteads. The other exotic materials they acquired during the tenth and eleventh centuries were seashells from the Gulf of California and copper bells, cotton fabrics, macaws, and parrots from Mexico. Some of the objects produced in the canyon found their way to Hohokam communities in the deserts of southern Arizona and to Mexico, probably through Casas Grandes, an important town in Chihuahua that rose to prominence at this time. It has been suggested that slaves were also exported to the south from Chaco Canyon. Their source may have been the cliff-dwelling communities of southern Colorado—for example, Mesa Verde—and beyond.

The social conditions and exchange networks that sustained the settlements in Chaco Canyon collapsed after A.D. 1130. Some inhabitants of the canyon abandoned their homes and moved to new localities; others remained and relied increasingly on hunting and foraging to supplement the crops tended by the women. Those who remained, either in the small hamlets or in the outlying settlements north of the canyon, began to develop new linkages or new kinds of social relations with the communities from the Mesa Verde region of southern Colorado.

The Hohokam communities, centered in the Gila and Snake River valleys of the southern Arizona desert, also rose to prominence during the later part of the first millennium A.D. The population of several of the pithouse villages located along the rivers increased, presumably after their inhabitants dug irrigation canals to extend the amount of land under cultivation. These kin-organized, possibly rank-ordered communities began to rely increasingly on the water-management systems they built during the eighth and ninth centuries. The construction and maintenance of these systems required significant inputs of labor each year. During the eleventh century, the communities may have attempted to recruit this labor from groups that occupied fortified or easily defended hilltop settlements in the Phoenix area.

There was some degree of village specialization: Settlements in the Tucson Basin made large numbers of shell objects; those in localities where good clays were available fired pottery; and those in southern Arizona, where cotton grows, spun thread and made weft-wrapped textiles. However, few of the Hohokam settlements were large enough to be self-sufficient, and their inhabitants depended on other communities for mates, raw materials, and finished goods.

Around 1250, a new type of architecture and social grouping appeared in the Hohokam settlement at Casa Grande in the Phoenix Basin: Residential structures with extensive storage facilities were built on old palisaded platform mounds. The residents of these large households had greater access to labor power and to wealth than their contemporaries in the same community. This fact suggests that large households may have been wealthier than smaller ones, by virtue of having more individuals who could contribute labor power, and that social ranking may have intensified during the thirteenth century, after the communities in the Tucson Basin and the Mimbres area had rejected the kinds of objects and styles associated with the Hohokam communities around Phoenix.

Often the intensification of social relations means that the members of certain households or domestic groups expect to receive gifts from their kin and neighbors. Under some conditions, the latter may make these prestations or gifts to higher-ranking individuals or families; however, in other circumstances, when they distinguish between a gift and a demand, and refuse to make prestations, they cease to participate in exchange relations that have the capacity to become oppressive and exploitative. Communities throughout North America repeatedly made the choice not to enmesh themselves for long periods of time in tributary relations. They typically resisted attempts to turn gifts into tribute.

FURTHER READINGS: A BRIEF GUIDE

Brian Fagan, *Ancient North America: The Archaeology of a Continent* (London: Thames & Hudson, 1991) provides an excellent overview of North American archaeology and a guide to the rapidly growing literature.

For discussions of the earliest inhabitants of the Americas, see John Benditt, "Earliest Americans," *Scientific American*, vol. 258, no. 6 (1988), 28–30; Tom Dillehay, "The Peopling of the Americas: New Sites and Old Problems," *Past: Newsletter of the Prehistoric Society*, no. 4 (Cambridge, 1988), pp. 7–9; James Adovasio, J. Donahue, and Robert Stuckenrath, "The Meadowcroft Rockshelter Radiocarbon Chronology, 1975–1990," *American Antiquity*, vol. 44, no. 2 (1990), 348–354; Alan L. Bryan, ed., *New Evidence for the Pleistocene Peopling of the Americas* (Orono, ME: Center for the Study of Early Man, 1986); Dena Dinacauze, "An Archaeo-Logical Evaluation of the Case for Pre-Clovis Occupations," *Advances in World Archaeology*, vol. 3 (1984), 275–324; George Frison, *Prehistoric Hunters of the High Plains* (New York: Academic Press, 1978); and David J. Meltzer, "Late Pleistocene Human Adaptations in Eastern North America," *Journal of World Prehistory*, vol. 2, no. 1 (1988), 1–52.

For more detailed discussions of the various kinds of subsistence economies that appeared during and after the seventh millennium B.C., see Joe Ben

Wheat, *The Olsen-Chubbuck Site: A Paleo-Indian Bison Kill*, Memoirs of the Society for American Archaeology, no. 26 (Washington, DC, 1972); Michael A. Glassow, Larry R. Wilcoxon, and Jon Erlandson, "Cultural and Environmental Change during the Early Period of Santa Barbara Channel Prehistory," in *The Archaeology of Prehistoric Coastlines*, ed. Geoff Bailey and John Parkington (Cambridge: Cambridge University Press, 1988), pp. 64–77; and C. Melvin Aikens, "The Far West," in *Ancient Native Americans*, ed. Jesse D. Jennings (San Francisco: W. H. Freeman, 1978), pp. 131–182.

For the far north, see Christy Turner II, "Telltale Teeth," *Natural History*, vol. 96, no. 1 (1987), 6–10; Don Dumond, *The Eskimos and Aleuts* (London: Thames & Hudson, 1987); Robert J. McGhee, *Canadian Arctic Prehistory* (Ottawa: National Museums of Canada, 1978); James A. Tuck and Robert J. McGhee, "An Archaic Indian Burial Mound in Labrador," *Scientific American*, vol. 235, no. 5 (1977), 122–129; Moreau Maxwell, *The Prehistory of the Eastern Arctic* (New York: Academic Press, 1985); James Tuck, *Newfoundland and Labrador Prehistory* (Ottawa: National Museums of Canada, 1976), "Regional Cultural Development, 3000 to 300 B.C.," in *Handbook of North American Indians, vol. 15, Northeast*, ed. Bruce G. Trigger (Washington, DC: Smithsonian Institution, 1978), pp. 28–43, and "An Archaic Indian Cemetery in Newfoundland," *Scientific American*, vol. 222, no. 6 (1970), 112–221; and Elmer J. Harp, Jr., "Pioneer Cultures of the Subarctic and the Arctic," in *Ancient Native Americans*, ed. Jesse D. Jennings (San Francisco: W. H. Freeman, 1978), pp. 95–129.

For discussions of the Archaic communities of eastern North America, see Bruce D. Smith, "The Archaeology of the Southeastern United States: From Dalton to de Soto, 10,500 to 500 B.P.," *Advances in Archaeology*, vol. 5 (1986), 1–92; Jefferson Chapman, *Tellico Archaeology* (Knoxville: Department of Anthropology, University of Tennessee, 1980); David G. Anderson and Glen T. Hanson, "Early Archaic Settlement in the Southeastern United States: A Case Study from the Savannah River," *American Antiquity*, vol. 53, no. 3 (1988), 262–286; James L. Phillips and James A. Brown, eds., *Archaic Hunters and Gatherers in the Midwest* (New York: Academic Press, 1983); Ronald Mason, *Great Lakes Archeology* (New York: Academic Press, 1981); Nan A. Rothschild, "Mortuary Behavior and Social Organization at Indian Knoll and Dickson Mounds," *American Antiquity*, vol. 44, no. 4 (1979), 658–675; William F. Keegan, ed., *Emergent Horticultural Economies of the Eastern Woodlands* (Carbondale: Center for Archaeological Investigations, Southern Illinois University, 1987); Richard Jefferies, *Carrier Mills* (Carbondale: Southern Illinois University Press, 1987); Patty Jo Watson and Mary C. Kennedy, "The Development of Horticulture in the Eastern Woodlands," and Cheryl P. Claessen, "Gender, Shellfishing, and the Shell Mound Archaic," both in *Engendering Archaeology: Women and Prehistory*, ed. Joan M. Gero and Margaret W. Conkey (Oxford: Basil Blackwell, 1990), pp. 255–275 and 276–300; and Howard Winters, "Value Systems and Trade Cycles of the Late Archaic in the Midwest," in *New Perspectives in Archeology*, ed. Sally R. Binford and Lewis R. Binford (Chicago: Aldine, 1968), pp. 175–227.

For Hopewell and its contemporaries in eastern North America, see

David S. Brose and N'omi Greber, eds., *Hopewell Archaeology* (Kent, OH: Kent State University, 1979); David P. Braun, "Midwestern Hopewellian Exchange and Supralocal Interaction," in *Peer Polity Interaction and Socio-political Change,* ed. Colin Renfrew and John F. Cherry (Cambridge: Cambridge University Press, 1986), pp. 117–126, and "Ceramic Decorative Diversity and Illinois Woodland Regional Integration," in *Prehistoric Ceramics,* ed. Ben A. Nelson (Carbondale: Center for Archaeological Investigations, Southern Illinois University, 1985), pp. 128–153; Jon Muller, *Archaeology of the Lower Ohio River Valley* (New York: Academic Press, 1986); M. F. Seeman, *The Hopewell Interaction Sphere: The Evidence for Interregional Trade and Structural Complexity* (Indianapolis: Indiana Historical Society, 1979), and "Ohio Hopewell Trophy-Skull in Middle Woodland Societies circa 50 B.C.–A.D. 350," *American Antiquity,* vol. 53, no. 4 (1988), 565–577; Patrick J. Munson, Paul W. Parmalee, and Richard A. Yarnell, "Subsistence Ecology at Scovill, a Terminal Woodland Village," *American Antiquity,* vol. 36, no. 4 (1971), 410–431; Jerald T. Milanich, Ann S. Cordell, Vernon J. Knight, Timothy A. Kohler, and Brenda J. Sigler-Lavelle, *McKeithen Island: The Culture of Northern Florida, A.D. 200–900* (New York: Academic Press, 1984); Frank T. Schnell, Vernon J. Knight, Jr., and Gail S. Schnell, *Chemochobee: Archaeology of a Mississippian Ceremonial Center on the Chattahoochee River* (Gainesville: University Presses of Florida, 1981); and Barbara Bender, "Emergent Tribal Formations in the American Midcontinent," *American Antiquity,* vol. 50, no. 1 (1985), 52–62.

Cahokia and Mississippian culture are described by George R. Milner, "The Lake Prehistoric Cahokia Cultural System of the Mississippi River Valley: Foundations, Florescence, and Fragmentation," *Journal of World Prehistory,* vol. 4, no. 1 (1990), 1–44; Melvin L. Fowler, *Cahokia: Ancient Capital of the Midwest* (Boston: Addison-Wesley, 1974); Patricia J. O'Brien, "Urbanism, Cahokia, and Middle Mississippian," *Archaeology,* vol. 25, no. 3 (1972), 189–197; Bruce D. Smith, ed., *Mississippian Settlement Patterns* (New York: Academic Press, 1978); Vincas Steponaitis, *Ceramics, Chronology, and Community Patterns: An Archaeological Study at Moundville* (New York: Academic Press, 1983); Jon Muller "Salt, Chert, and Shell: Mississippian Exchange," in *Specialization and Exchange in Complex Societies,* ed. Elizabeth M. Brumfiel and Timothy K. Earle, (Cambridge: Cambridge University Press, 1987), pp. 10–21; Bruce G. Trigger, *Natives and Newcomers: Canada's 'Heroic Age' Reconsidered* (Montreal: McGill-Queen's University Press, 1985), and *The Children of Aataentsic: A History of the Huron People to 1660* (Montreal: McGill-Queen's University Press, 1972); and Dena Dincauze and Robert J. Hasenstab, "Explaining the Iroquois: Tribalization on a Prehistoric Periphery," in *Centre and Periphery: Comparative Studies in Archaeology,* ed. Timothy C. Champion (London: Unwin Hyman, 1989), pp. 67–87.

Linda S. Cordell, *Prehistory of the American Southwest* (New York: Academic Press, 1984); and William D. Lipe, "The Southwest," in *Ancient North Americans,* ed. Jesse D. Jennings (San Francisco: W. H. Freeman, 1983), pp. 421–494, provide overviews of Southwest archaeology. Alternative understandings of the Archaic period are presented by Cynthia Irwin-Williams, *Archaic Culture History in the Southwestern United States* (Portales: Eastern New Mexico University, 1968); and Claudia F. Berry and Michael S. Berry, "Chronological and Conceptual Models of the Southwest Archaic," in *Anthropology of the Desert West: Essays in Honor of Jesse D. Jennings*, ed. Carole J. Condie and Don D. Fowler (Salt Lake City: Department of Anthropology, University of Utah, 1986), pp. 253–327. For the development of food-producing economies, see W. H. Wills, "Early Agriculture and Sedentism in the American Southwest: Evidence and Interpretations," *Journal of World Prehistory*, vol. 2, no. 4 (1988), 445–488; and A. H. Simmons, "New Evidence for the Early Use of Cultigens in the American Southwest," *American Antiquity*, vol. 51, no. 1 (1986), 73–88.

For analyses of the political-economic and social organization of early communities in the Southwest, see Christy G. Turner II and Laurel Lofgren, "Household Size and Prehistoric Western Pueblo Indians," *Southwestern Journal of Anthropology*, vol. 22, no. 2 (1966), 117–132; Dean J. Saitta, "Economic Integration and Social Development in Zuni Prehistory," Ph.D. dissertation, University of Massachusetts, Amherst, 1987; Dean J. Saitta and Arthur S. Keene, "Politics and Surplus Flow in Prehistoric Communal Societies," in *The Evolution of Political Systems: Sociopolitics in Small-scale Sedentary Societies*, ed. Stedman Upham (Cambridge: Cambridge University Press, 1990), pp. 203–224; Kent G. Lightfoot, *Prehistoric Political Dynamics: A Case Study from the American Southwest* (DeKalb: Northern Illinois University Press, 1984); and Kent G. Lightfoot and Gary M. Feinman, "Social Differentiation and Leadership Development in Early Pithouse Villages in the Mogollon Region of the American Southwest," *American Antiquity*, vol. 47, no. 1 (1982), 64–86.

For discussions of intensification and alternative modes of production, see John Gledhill, "Formative Development in the North American Southwest," in *Social Organisation and Settlement*, British Archaeological Reports, International Series 47(ii), ed. David Green, Colin Haselgrove, and Matthew Spriggs (Oxford, 1978), pp. 241–284; Randall H. McGuire, "The Greater Southwest as a Periphery of Mesoamerica," in *Centre and Periphery: Comparative Studies in Archaeology*, ed. Timothy C. Champion (London: Unwin Hyman, 1989), pp. 40–66; Patricia L. Crown and W. James Judge, eds., *Chaco and Hohokam: Prehistoric Regional Systems in the American Southwest* (Santa Fe, NM: School of American Research Press, 1991); and Fred Plog, "Political and Economic Alliances on the Colorado Plateaus, A.D. 400 to 1450," *Advances in World Archaeology*, vol. 2 (1983), 289–330. Chaco Canyon social organization is examined by R. Gwinn Vivian, "Kluckhohn Reappraised: The Chacoan System as an Egalitarian Enterprise," *Journal of Anthropological Research*, vol. 45, no. 1 (1988), 101–113; Stephen H. Lekson, Thomas C. Windes, John R. Stein, and W. James Judge, "The Chaco Community," *Scientific American*, vol. 256, no. 7 (1988), 100–109; J. Charles Kelley and Ellen A. Kelley, "An Alternative Hypothesis for the Explanation of Anasazi Culture History," in *Collected Papers in Honor of Florence Hawley Ellis*, Papers of the Archaeological Society of

New Mexico, ed. Theodore R. Frisbie, no. 2 (Albuquerque, 1975), pp. 178–223; Frances J. Mathien and Randall H. McGuire, eds., *Ripples in the Chichimec Sea: New Considerations of Southwestern-Mesoamerican Interactions* (Carbondale: Southern Illinois University Press, 1986); and Carroll L. Riley and Basil C. Hedrick, eds., *Across the Chichimec Sea: Papers in Honor of J. Charles Kelley* (Carbondale: Southern Illinois University Press, 1978).

chapter 14

Mesoamerica

[The producers of the 1492—Clash of Visions series] were informed by NEH that the project would not be funded because of its "lack of evenhandedness." The endowment's letter of rejection said the series downplayed "distressing aspects" of Aztec culture, such as human sacrifice, while highlighting Spanish brutality. (Stephen Salisbury, Philadelphia Inquirer)

When you draw near to a city to fight against it, offer terms of peace to it. . . . But if it makes no peace with you, but makes war against you, then when the Lord your God gives it into your hand you shall put all of its males to the sword, but the women and little ones, the cattle, and everything else in the city, all of its spoils, you shall take as booty for yourselves. . . . But in the cities of these peoples that the Lord your God gives you for an inheritance, you shall save nothing alive that breathes, but you shall utterly destroy them. . . . (Deuteronomy XX:10–17)

There is a close connection between genocide and the rise of civilization. States kill! (placard, Washington, DC, January 19, 1991)

Mesoamerica stretches southward from the Tropic of Cancer in northern Mexico to central Honduras, western Nicaragua, and the Nicoya Peninsula. Mountain ranges form the backbone of Mesoamerica. Snow-clad peaks and volcanoes, many of which are still active, tower above the high plateaus and mountain valleys. The land trembles almost continuously from earthquakes, and volcanoes awakened and driven by forces deep beneath the earth's surface erupt and spew their molten contents over the landscape. These are the shocks and spasms of a world still being born. As the westward-moving continental North American plate overrides the eastward-moving Pacific and Cocos oceanic plates, the landmass buckles and mountains are thrust upward, a few inches each year.

The geological history of Mesoamerica has produced a mosaic of distinct landmasses. The largest, the high, funnel-shaped Mexican Plateau, opens northward from the belt of volcanoes that crosses central Mexico; the Sierra Madre Occidental and Sierra Madre Oriental mark the edges of the eroded land surface. The heavily dissected mountain ranges of the Sierra Madre del Sur, which lie south of the volcanic belt, end abruptly in a pine-covered escarpment that overlooks the Isthmus of Tehuantepec and, 25 miles away, the edge of the Chiapas highlands—the northern end of a chain of volcanoes that have burst an older mountain range. To the northeast, the Chiapas Highlands give way to the limestone platform of the Yucatán Peninsula. Coastal plains fringe the mountainous core of Mesoamerica. The Pacific plain is narrow, and only two of the rivers that cross it—the Lerma and the Balsas—drain the interior; the wider Gulf and Caribbean lowlands are crossed by more than eighty slow-moving rivers, fed by heavy rains that fall along the coast and the slopes behind it. Only the northern Yucatán Penin-

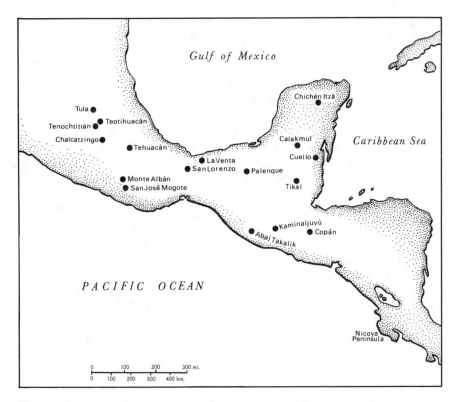

Mesoamerica.

sula lacks rivers because the rains that fall there are immediately absorbed into the porous bedrock.

The structural complexity of Mesoamerica is matched by the diversity of its ecological habitats. The configuration and composition of these zones have been shaped over the years by the subtle interplay of various geological, topographical, climatic, natural, and human agencies. Diverse oak and pine forests cover the high mountain landscapes that stretch from Mexico to Panama. These forests overlook the progressively increasing aridity of the Mexican Plateau with the concomitant shift from thorn thickets to steppe and high desert ground cover. They also overlook the seasonal savannas and rain forests of the Pacific coast of Mexico and Central America as well as the jungles, swamps, and tropical grasslands of the Gulf and Caribbean lowlands. At high elevations, the oak-pine forests give way to alpine grasslands and even tundra above the tree line.

EARLY FARMERS, UNEVEN DEVELOPMENT, AND THE OLMEC

People have lived in Mesoamerica for more than 20,000 years. By 7000 B.C., bands of hunter-foragers relied on hundreds of plant and animal species for subsistence. Their activities were geared to the seasonal availability of various foodstuffs in particular regions. Some food resources—like white-tailed deer—occurred in many habitats; others—acorns, for instance—had more limited distributions. Consequently, groups that occupied different habitats exploited different arrays of locally available foods.

During the seventh millennium B.C., some bands began to plant seeds during wet years, when large quantities and varieties of plant foods were available, to increase their abundance near campsites; once cultivation proved productive, they carried this practice over into drier years, when plant foods were both less plentiful and diverse. By 3000 B.C. the inhabitants of many areas had adopted plant cultivation; however, the rate at which the shift occurred varied from one region to another. It generally took several millennia in highlands areas but was more rapid in coastal regions, like Chiapas, where relatively sedentary groups adopted the domesticated plants and cultivation practices that were developed and honed elsewhere.

The move toward agricultural production occurred in the context of a network of social relations that linked domestic groups and bands into larger communities. These relations involved alliances, exchange, distribution, and reciprocal ties that ensured the demographic and social reproduction of everyday life at the different levels of the community. Groups changed their daily and seasonal routines to produce more foodstuffs in the same amount of time—that is, they intensified their subsistence activities—in order to resolve conflicts between escalating social demands on production and an inadequate production base.

By 2000 B.C., people in many regions had abandoned the highly mobile lifeways of their predecessors and were already residing in permanent villages. This change was marked not only by the appearance of more durable dwellings but also by the fact that the villagers did not fragment into smaller social units and disperse each year during the season of scarcity. They were able to store enough food to satisfy their subsistence during those seasons when food was scarce. Their subsistence economies had shifted from those involved with the immediate consumption of various foodstuffs to ones that involved the storage and consumption of particular foods. Certain conditions are necessary for the development of food-storing subsistence economies: abundant quantities of suitable, seasonally available foodstuffs; efficient harvesting techniques; and the ability to preserve and store large quantities of food resources.

Sedentarism is related to the development of food storage. What distinguished the village farmers from their predecessors, who occasionally planted seeds and harvested those that ripened, was the role of intensive food storage in their calculations. The shift involved new attitudes toward nature, time, and work. Land was transformed into a major means of production that yielded delayed returns only after considerable inputs of labor. The food-storing farmers became more dependent on the results of work performed in the past—cultivating, harvesting, preserving, and storing plant foods—than they were on the bounty nature made available at a particular time. The foods they had acquired or produced in the past became more consequential for survival than those that could be acquired in the present. Food storage probably had less to do with creating a surplus than with intensifying production or increasing productivity to meet some immediate, short-term, socially constructed need. That is, the development of food storage and food production were embedded in the social relations that shaped everyday life in these diverse, kin-based communities.

Toward the end of the fourth millennium B.C., sedentary village societies existed in various parts of Mesoamerica. The residents of the permanent streamside hamlets in the Tehuacán Valley devoted considerable amounts of labor power to planting and harvesting a wide variety of cultivated and/or domesticated plants—fruit trees, like avocados; annuals, like maize; beans; squash; and chili peppers. By 1200 B.C., virtually all of the inhabitants of Tehuacán lived in permanent villages; food remains and desiccated feces indicate that agricultural produce provided 40 percent of their diet. The intensification of plant cultivation occurred at the expense of hunting and gathering. Between 3000 and 1000 B.C., agricultural production facilitated the accumulation of foodstuffs and small durable goods in Tehuacán; however, it did not facilitate the development of craft part-time craft specialization or a social division of labor, in which one group within the community appropriated labor or goods from the other members.

A different process occurred in coastal Chiapas and Guatemala. During the third millennium B.C., the inhabitants of this region typically lived in isolated households near estuaries and lagoons, where they fished, harvested crustaceans and mollusks, hunted in the forests, and cultivated small quantities of maize and other plants. By 1700 B.C., some of the region's inhabitants began to reside in economically specialized fishing villages on the coast and farming hamlets inland. The production relations that developed did not mirror the earlier ones. Although the households continued to be the real units of appropriation and consumption both in the dispersed households and in those of the villages, new, spatially organized social relations emerged at the community-level, which allowed domestic groups to acquire regularly raw materials and foodstuffs from distant localities. This development also facilitated the construction of storage facilities and public buildings that were beyond the capacity of a single household. These social relations constituted the conditions for the reproduction of both the community and the domestic groups it comprised.

Sedentary village life—based, to varying degrees, on the consumption of domesticated plants and dogs—was an established fact in many parts of Mesoamerica by 1200 B.C. Moreover, the circulation of certain raw materials and finished goods—for example, obsidian, jade, marine shell, sharks' teeth, and iron-ore mirrors—had intensified. The Gulf Coast of Veracruz and Tabasco witnessed the crystallization of collective labor processes that operated at the community level and the mobilization of work forces that built large platforms and pyramid complexes and moved several dozen stone sculptures, some weighing more than 35 tons, over distances of 50 miles or more.

Colossal stone Olmec head from Tres Zapotes, Mexico.

However, the intensification of labor processes did not occur uniformly, for in many regions the community-level relations of production and social reproduction continued to operate at the same intensities as they had several centuries earlier. This was the time of the Olmec, a complex phenomenon that spanned 400 to 700 years.

About 1500 B.C., people living along the lower Coatzacoalcos River built a few houses on San Lorenzo, a natural plateau that rose about 150 feet above the surrounding countryside and overlooked agricultural fields planted on the seasonally flooded levees of the river. Between 1350 and 1150 B.C., they brought large quantities of fill to level the top of the plateau and to construct a series of ridges along its western edge. In the process, they created a platform that was more than 3,600 feet long and 1,800 feet wide.

During the next two centuries, they capped these fills with a series of floors made from colored sands and clays and built several stone-lined drains and lagoons on the platform's surface.

An estimated 800 to 1,000 individuals resided at San Lorenzo during the twelfth century in houses that overlooked the river, which flooded their fields, provided the fish they ate, and served as a major avenue for communication and transport. At about this time, they began to acquire obsidian from a dozen or more localities in the mountains and to move the enormous stone monuments from the Tuxtla Mountains, 45 miles to the north. Around 900 B.C., the colossal heads, which may have been portraits of particular individuals, were defaced, and altars and smaller sculptures were broken; however, the settlement itself was neither damaged nor abandoned, and people continued to live on the platform for the next two centuries.

Two coastal settlements were contemporary with San Lorenzo: Laguna de los Cerros near the Tuxtla Mountains and La Venta in the Tabasco lowlands, 70 miles northeast. Between about 1000 and 500 B.C., people living around La Venta cleared the jungle and erected a number of large public buildings, which included a 100-feet high pyramid, shaped like a volcano, and its associated platforms, mounds, and courtyards. They rebuilt the pyramid complex on several occasions. During the second construction, they dug two enormous pits and filled them with layer upon layer of serpentine slabs, the combined weight of which was more than 11,000 tons; the nearest source of serpentine is located about 200 miles away in the Isthmus of Tehuantepec. The people covered the slabs with serpentine masks, which were then covered with layers of adobe brick. During the last building phase in the sixth century, five tombs were placed in the courtyard between the pyramid and the two offering pits.

Some archaeologists view Olmec society as class-stratified because of the scope of the construction; others view it—even in its latest phase, when a few individuals were interred in elaborate tombs that were carefully placed in the architectural monument at La Venta—as an internally ranked but kin-organized community because it lacked most of the trappings and the sud-

Perspective of the main pyramid and accompanying buildings as they appeared at La Venta, Mexico, toward the mid-first millennium B.C.

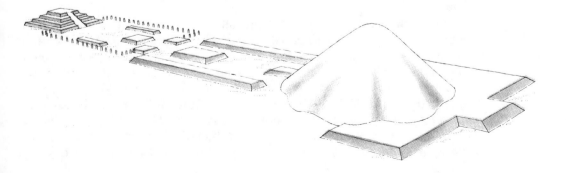

den, dramatic social changes associated with the formation of state-based societies—for example, firm evidence of warfare and/or repression, weapons, fortified settlements, extraction of labor and goods by a ruling elite, or town-country distinctions. In such estate-ordered societies, chieftains and chiefly peoples whose requests for gifts and service exceeded the customary expectations of their kin and neighbors were often killed or left to fend for themselves when the nonchiefly groups moved and established new places of residence, where the threat of extortion was absent.

Between 700 and 500 B.C., artisans carved Olmec-style bas reliefs on rock faces, stelae, and altars at Chalcatzingo in Morelos, just south of the Valley of Mexico. During this period, Chalcatzingo was a gateway through which various raw materials—obsidian and greenstone—from the central Mexican hinterlands were assembled and then carried to the Gulf Coast. This settlement was abandoned at about the same time that the stone monuments at La Venta were mutilated.

From 1000 to 500 B.C., there were more than 20 farming settlements in the Oaxaca Valley. Some were situated to facilitate the extraction of raw materials, like salt or iron ore, and part-time craft specialization; these had 80 to 120 households. There were wealth differentials among the households, judging by differences in domestic architecture, in the contents of associated refuse deposits, and in the kinds and quantities of grave goods. Inhabitants of the better-made households had more shell ornaments and greater access to exotic raw materials than their less affluent neighbors. This difference may mean merely that those households had more members in productive age and gender categories than other domestic groups, that some of their labor was devoted to craft production, and that some of their goods were exchanged for nonlocal items. The wealth of the households was ultimately based on the labor power of their members and on their capacity to divert some of it away from subsistence production into other activities. There is no evidence that these households failed to contribute to demands for the collective labor required to construct public buildings or for other community-wide practices, or that they were dependent on the labor of others for their livelihood.

THE FIRST MESOAMERICAN STATES

By 500 B.C., the social relations that prevailed in a number of Mesoamerican societies had long been structured by kinship, residence, and crosscutting technical divisions of labor based on age and gender that created complementary spheres of men's and women's activities. The small size of many of the settlements meant that there was matrimonial mobility and that some individuals did not reside in their natal villages. However, larger villages were often composed of kin groups whose members resided in spatially distinct wards; their size diminished the need for intervillage marriages. Customary authority in these communities was minimally constituted by intersecting and interdependent principles reflecting kinship and residence. The tensions created by these cleavages were the motors of history and change.

The Oaxaca Valley

The earliest episode of class and state formation now recognized in Mesoamerica occurred in the Oaxaca highlands during the fifth century B.C. The circumstances surrounding it were undoubtedly linked with (1) rebellions on the Gulf Coast and in Morelos, which led to the destruction of Olmec monuments in those regions; (2) the abandonment of settlements where these colossal sculptures were found; and (3) the settlement of the Maya lowlands by refugees from highland Guatemala. In the Oaxaca Valley, the processes involved (4) the construction of lavish homesteads on the tops of public, community-built platforms in two of the established villages; (5) the founding of a new administrative town at Monte Albán about 475 B.C.; and (6) the abandonment or decline of a number of villages as their residents resettled in the new capital.

The rulers of Monte Albán situated their capital on a hilltop overlooking the valley floor; it meant that its residents devoted considerable amounts of time and energy to carrying food and water up the slopes. An enormous plaza, with three buildings on its northern and western sides, dominated the site. One was an elaborate tomb. Another was a rubble-filled platform mound, the Building of the Danzantes, sheathed with stone slabs, each of which contained the carved representation of a single, naked, sprawled fig-

The central plaza at Monte Alban in Oaxaca.

ure; these formed a gallery associated with two stelae that contained the oldest written glyphs in Mesoamerica. The iconography indicates that the figures were representations of captives slain by the Monte Albán rulers.

At this time, the new overlords sought to diminish the mobility of the valley's residents in order to facilitate census taking and tax collection. They encouraged the households to live in more permanent dwellings, to increase the number of individuals in productive age and gender categories to meet the demands placed on them by the state, and to reorganize certain aspects of everyday life. For example, women began to make corn tortillas, which although they were easily carried to other places, was a more time-consuming activity than preparing stews or roasting meat and vegetables.

To reproduce the conditions required for the continued appropriation of labor and goods, the Monte Albán rulers appeased the local population through raids and wars of conquest, in which foreign communities on the periphery were encapsulated by the state and labor and goods were extorted from their members. Expansion outside the Oaxaca Valley began in the fourth century B.C. and continued for several hundred years; objects manufactured in Oaxaca appeared in settlements on the periphery, and new buildings were added to the main plaza at Monte Albán, one of which was adorned with more than fifty conquest slabs with place-name glyphs. One of these was Cuicatlán, located on the northeast margins of the state.

While the Monte Albán state may not have been able to intervene continuously in the subsistence and reproduction of the local communities in Oaxaca during the second century B.C., the conquest of frontier populations provided its rulers and citizen-soldiers with war captives and with the labor and goods they were able to extract from the subordinated communities. These conflicts underwrote and witnessed the transformation of the kin-based communities on the margins of the weak, tribute-based state centered in Oaxaca. In Cuicatlán, the basic production-consumption units prior to its encapsulation were patio groups consisting of three or four contiguous households. The Monte Albán invasion transformed the local society. Villages were abandoned, and the patio production units were fragmented with a concomitant reorganization of work activities, so that individual households, not the patio group, became the main units of production and consumption.

A garrison established on the northern edge of the Cuicatlán domain, housed 400 to 2,000 individuals, many of whom were soldiers fed by food that was grown elsewhere in the region. Although the state was able to intervene directly in the organization of the subsistence sector and perhaps even the demographic reproduction of the Cuicatlán community, it did not control social reproduction since the households maintained and re-created a sense of community in spite of the state's intervention. They accomplished this feat through their continued participation in traditional practices that operated outside those prescribed by the state and above the domestic level.

Teotihuacán

Mesoamerica resembled a continually shifting constellation of city-states and kin-based communities during the first millennium A.D. The term *city-state* projects an image of a landscape dotted with urban centers that were seats of power whose rulers drove politics. However, most residents of these city-states derived their livelihood from farming, regardless of whether they lived in the city or in the dispersed villages near agricultural fields. The whole populations of these polities—those in the city and in the countryside—were involved in the life and production of the rural areas, so that the city dwellers were never independent of the lands around them. At the same time, there were also community life and facilities in the city that no individual village could provide.

Teotihuacán was Mesoamerica's largest urban center and predominant city-state during most of the first millennium A.D. The city appeared about 150 B.C. and quickly became a center of extraordinary size and influence. Its population may already have stood at 80,000 persons between A.D. 1 and 150. The growth of the city involved major demographic shifts in the Valley of Mexico, as the inhabitants of the southern and eastern portions of the basin resettled in the city. By A.D. 150, massive public construction had already occurred: the major north-south axis, the Street of the Dead, was laid out; the Pyramids of the Sun and Moon were built; other structures were also built along the Street of the Dead at this time; and more than 20 three-temple pyramid complexes were erected throughout the city. Construction continued in the city between A.D. 150 and 650. The official residence of the ruling elite was built about A.D. 200, and, during the next 450 years, two thousand apartment compounds were completed and occupied by core groups of brothers and sisters, their spouses, and their children. By A.D. 500, the city housed 125,000 to 200,000 persons—that is, roughly 60 percent of the valley of Mexico's total population.

Although the city seemed to prosper between A.D. 650 and 750, there was a crisis. Like other preindustrial cities, Teotihuacán was not a healthy place to live in, especially for the direct producers who occupied the lowest levels of its class structure. Their members experienced poor nutrition; low birth weights; and high levels of neonatal, juvenile, and adolescent mortality. Thus, from the second to the eighth centuries, the countryside underwrote the demographic replacement of the urban population through the labor power of the rural population, the goods it produced, and the children born by its women. A population decline beginning about A.D. 550 suggests that the city was no longer able to attract immigrants as it had done earlier.

Arable land was the major means of production in Teotihuacán society. At any time, two-thirds of the urban population and virtually all of the rural population farmed and/or collected wild foodstuffs. Their activities were essential; the craft production and the social division of labor were grafted onto this economic base and the labor power of the direct producers. Thus, the

TEOTIHUACAN

CENTRAL PLATEAU
OF MEXICO
ARCHAEOLOGICAL AND
TOPOGRAPHIC MAP

CONTOUR INTERVAL FIVE METERS

SEPTEMBER 1970
COPYRIGHT 1970 BY RENE MILLON

LEGEND

EXCAVATED ROOM COMPLEX
OR OTHER STRUCTURE
UNEXCAVATED ROOM COMPLEX
POSSIBLE ROOM COMPLEX
FLOOR OF ZONE LIMITS UNCLEAR
TEMPLE PLATFORM
SINGLE STAGE PLATFORM
INSUBSTANTIAL STRUCTURES
MAJOR WALL
WATER COURSE
PROBABLE OLD WATER COURSE
METERS ABOVE MEAN SEA LEVEL
MAPPING PROJECT EXCAVATION

KEY

1 PYRAMID OF THE MOON
2 PYRAMID OF THE SUN
3 CIUDADELA
4 TEMPLE OF QUETZALCOATL
5 "STREET OF THE DEAD"
6 GREAT COMPOUND
7 WEST AVENUE
8 EAST AVENUE
9 "MERCHANTS' BARRIO"
10 TLAMIMILOLPA
11 XOLALPAN
12 TEPANTITLA
13 MAGUEY PRIEST MURALS
14 PLAZA ONE
15 HOUSE OF THE EAGLES
16 "OLD CITY"
17 OAXACA BARRIO
18 ATETELCO
19 LA VENTILLA A
20 LA VENTILLA B
21 LA VENTILLA C
22 TETITLA
23 RIO SAN LORENZO
24 RIO SAN JUAN
25,26,27,51 RESERVOIRS
52 ACOMALCO

KEY TO INSET MAP

1 PYRAMID OF THE MOON
2 PYRAMID OF THE SUN
3 CIUDADELA
4 TEMPLE OF QUETZALCOATL
5 "STREET OF THE DEAD"
6 GREAT COMPOUND
24 RIO SAN JUAN
28 PLAZA OF THE MOON
29 QUETZALPAPALOTL PALACE
30 GROUP 5
31 VIKING COMPOUND
32 ZACUALA PATIOS
33 BUILDING OF THE ALTARS
34 TEMPLE OF AGRICULTURE
35 MYTHOLOGICAL ANIMALS MURALS
36 PUMA MURAL
38 PLAZA OF THE COLUMNS
39 EXPLORATIONS OF 1895
40 PALACE OF THE SUN
41 PATIO OF THE FOUR SMALL TEMPLES
42 HOUSE OF THE PRIESTS
43 VIKING GROUP
44 "STREET OF THE DEAD" COMPLEX
45 SUPERPOSED BUILDINGS
46 EXPLORATIONS OF 1917
47 EXPLORATIONS OF 1908
48 TETITLA
49 ZACUALA PALACE
50 YAYAHUALA

GRID IS ORIENTED
CA. 15°25' EAST OF
ASTRONOMIC NORTH.

SUN PYRAMID
19°41'30" N. LAT.
98°50'30" W. LONG.

LOCATION OF INSET MAP

SCALE OF INSET MAP

TEOTIHUACAN MAPPING PROJECT
RENE MILLON, DIRECTOR
DEPARTMENT OF ANTHROPOLOGY
UNIVERSITY OF ROCHESTER
ROCHESTER, NEW YORK

AIDED BY GRANTS FROM THE
NATIONAL SCIENCE FOUNDATION

CHIEF DRAFTSMAN J. ARMANDO GERDA
PRINCIPAL ASSOCIATES, BRUCE DREWITT AND GEORGE COWGILL

TEOTIHUACAN IS 40 KILOMETERS (25 MILES)
NORTHEAST OF MEXICO CITY.

MEXICO

Plan of Teotihuacán, Mexico.

Perspective looking down the Street of the Dead from behind the Pyramid of the Sun. The Pyramid of the Moon and the Ciudadela are the large structures on the left side of the street.

control of labor power, rather than commerce, constituted the state's major source of wealth. Enormous amounts of labor power were appropriated on a regular basis for public construction along the Street of the Dead. After the third century, the apartment complexes may have been the units of taxation from which labor, foodstuffs, and finished goods were extracted.

The social division of labor that had crystallized in Teotihuacán by the third century had several features: (1) It distinguished between old and new residents; (2) it was interwoven with distinct occupations—for example, farmers, warriors, merchants, and ritual practitioners—that occupied different places in the class structure; and (3) the state apparatus, which sustained the class structure, had multiple centers or layers of power. In addition, enclaves of foreigners resided in at least two of the city's districts, and the upper level of Teotihuacán warriors apparently married into the ruling families of Tikal and other communities in borderland areas.

Both the composition of the ruling class and the relative power relations of different fractions of that class were transformed after A.D. 650. This was undoubtedly not the first time in Teotihuacán's history that the fortunes of various cults and social groups changed or that there were political upheavals; however, now the struggles within the urban ruling class were intensified at a time when the state's influence abroad had declined and its capacity to extract surplus labor or products from formerly encapsulated or subordinated populations had declined or ceased altogether. To maintain the existing levels of extraction of labor and goods meant that greater and greater amounts of both were demanded by the state from the direct producers in Teotihuacán society. Thus, there were increased levels of direct and indirect exploitation of the city's residents and those in the hinterland.

The individuals who destroyed Teotihuacán—the groups that burned its temples, palaces, and civic center and that slaughtered the inhabitants of the palace—may have juxtaposed two traditions: one that involved the ritual destruction of monuments and another that burned buildings to achieve a political goal. To accomplish the political goal, the groups involved not only destroyed the palaces, the material manifestation of the ruling class and the state apparatus, but also the vast number of temples and images that provided the ideological cement of this state-based society and made the city a major pilgrimage center for more than 500 years. The city's rulers, as well as its political and religious centers, were the target of their assault. The groups that burned the Street of the Dead and murdered the rulers were *teotihuacanos* (no foreign persons or artifacts have been found). Although they may have had a few allies from the outside, it was the residents who responded violently to the increased burdens the ruling class and the state were attempting to impose on the lower classes; who destroyed the state and the city; who brought about new settlement patterns and a redistribution of wealth; and who eliminated the exploitative relationship that had existed for centuries between the inhabitants of the city and the surrounding countryside.

During the height of its power, the Teotihuacán ruling class and its state apparatus established and maintained far-flung ties with peoples living elsewhere in Mesoamerica and beyond. However, the core area over which the Teotihuacán state exerted direct political control was not large. The inner part consisted of the Valley of Mexico; the outer hinterland included the Tula and southern Hidalgo regions north of Teotihuacán, southeastern Hidalgo and Tlaxcala to the east, the Río Amatzinac region of eastern Morelos to the south, and the Valley of Toluca to the west. The core area covered no more than 10,000 square miles and probably had a population of about 300,000. The state also had direct or indirect connections with a number of regions outside the core area; these included Monte Albán in Oaxaca, various centers in the Maya region, parts of coastal Veracruz, Guerrero to the west, and a number of localities in northwestern Mexico.

The Maya Region

The settlements of the sparsely inhabited Maya lowlands of southern Mesoamerica were transformed from isolated farmsteads and hamlets into a series of competing city-states during the later part of the first millennium B.C. This change was accompanied by intensified subsistence production and by increased community-level appropriations of labor power for the construction of public works—for example, a dry moat surrounding Becan or platform mounds at Kaminaljuyú. By 250 B.C., Komchen on the Yucatán Peninsula already had several thousand inhabitants. The residents of El Mirador, Lamanai, and Tikal were beginning to erect tall pyramids, and those around Cerros and Lamanai in Belize were constructing elaborate networks of canals and raised fields to improve agricultural production.

State-based societies and the institution of kingship appeared during the first century B.C. in the Maya lowlands. Stelae were erected at various localities to commemorate events at this time, and local rulers razed public buildings at Cerros and replaced them with a new structure—a stepped pyramid adorned with stucco masks. The first states that developed in the lowlands were small and apparently centered on settlements—like El Mirador, Cerros, or Tikal—and their hinterlands. Some of the city-states were 15 to 20 miles apart. However, the relationships among the states and between them and their neighbors were not necessarily cordial, judging by the ditch and rampart at Becan and fortifications at other contemporary settlements in the southern Yucatán, which may well have protected their residents from marauders who came from homelands in the Peten, Belize, or the highlands to kidnap and plunder.

The rulers of Tikal established the preeminence of this polity in the Peten lowlands during the first and second centuries A.D. The class structure of Tikal society was marked; the intensity of the exploitation and the nutritional and health problems this created were such that the direct producers were, on the average, 2 inches shorter than the ruling class at this time. It is also likely that the early rulers of Tikal belonged to a different faction of the ruling class than their successors and that they were subordinated by them during the third century.

The stelae erected between A.D. 238 and 435 by various communities in the northern lowlands tell us a number of things about the political history of the area: (1) Tikal and Uaxactun were independent during the third century; however, during the fourth century, a member of the Tikal royal family married into the Uaxactun royal dynasty or was imposed as ruler. (2) Communities like Yaxha were independent of Tikal or parts of other polities at this time. (3) Other communities paid tribute to the Tikal ruling elite. (4) The social reproduction of the ruling classes, which involved wars and interdynastic marriages, operated at an interpolity level. Between the end of the fifth century and the end of the eighth century, the number of autonomous polities in the Maya lowlands increased from nine to twenty-two, as more kin-based communities became enmeshed in tributary relations dominated by already existing polities and as some of the formerly subordinated communities reasserted their autonomy. It appears, however, that several of these formerly subordinated communities failed to shed the exploitative social relations imposed on them by state-based societies; as a result, one set of oppressive rulers was exchanged for another, and the social relations that structured everyday life remained exploitative throughout most of the low-lands.

If class and state formation during the first century B.C. marked the first social crisis in lowland Maya society, then Tikal's rise to preeminence during the third century A.D. was the second, after which the Tikal rulers maintained ties with Teotihuacán that lasted until the middle of the sixth century. The third crisis in lowland Maya society occurred in the ninth century. It began in the west when city-states stopped erecting stelae and large buildings, urban populations dispersed, and kin-based communities reasserted their autonomy. The collapse of state power was accompanied by widespread looting of tombs at Tikal and other settlements. Some of the objects removed from tombs in the Peten region were subsequently thrown into the cenote at Chichén Itzá. Towns in the southern Yucatán were also abandoned or occupied by small bands of squatters, and Belize was marginalized. However, there was a great deal of construction in the northern portions of the Yucatán Peninsula, where city-states centered at Chichén Itzá and Cobá flourished.

The course of history during the later part of the first millennium A.D. in the northern lowlands was influenced by the activities of merchant groups, called the Putun or Itzá, that flourished in settlements on the coastal lowlands from Tabasco to the Yucatán Peninsula and beyond to the Chetamul Bay. They thrived on the frontiers of powerful city-states, like Teotihuacán, and in the borderlands that remained beyond their control. The appearance of the Putun in the northern lowlands during the early sixth century coincided with a shift in the location and importance of particular transport routes. At the time, Teotihuacán's influence was diminishing in the Peten lowlands and becoming more evident in the north. The shift was manifested in various ways; for example, stelae, bearing representations of the local ruler

Chichen Itza, Yucatan.

as warrior wearing a Teotihuacán-style costume, were erected at Piedras Negras on the middle Usumacintla in 729 and 736, roughly fifteen to twenty years before the central Mexican city was destroyed.

By 1000, Chichén Itzá and Cobá were civic and political centers of two city-states on the Yucatán Peninsula. Chichén Itzá grew rapidly between the eighth and tenth centuries; extensive public construction—a number of temples and the largest ballcourt in Mesoamerica—was an expression of the ability of its rulers to appropriate the labor power of others. Toward the end of the tenth century, its rulers attacked communities along the northern frontier of the Cobá domain and were repelled. After encountering resistance in the north, they drove to the south and established settlements on the Peten lakes and enclaves on Chetumal Bay in order to envelop Cobá and to choke off its connections with Belize and the Maya lowlands. Public construction ceased at Cobá in the eleventh century, at about the same time that a number of its satellite communities were abandoned.

MESOAMERICA AFTER THE COLLAPSE OF TEOTIHUACÁN

Teotihuacán remained the largest and most important city in the Valley of Mexico for more than a century after the revolt that destroyed the state apparatus and the power of its old ruling class. After looting and burning the public structures on the Street of the Dead and the temples located elsewhere in the city, its 30,000 inhabitants continued to pursue various craft specializations and to live in the apartment compounds that had been built several centuries earlier. Between about A.D. 750 and 900, they erected more than a dozen pyramids on the edge of the old city. The old political-economic and social relations, as well as the cultural traditions that gave them meaning, were replaced by smaller, more decentralized arrangements. The disintegration and collapse of the Teotihuacán state had various consequences for communities elsewhere in Mesoamerica.

Between about A.D. 650 and 750, the Main Plaza of Monte Albán fell into disuse, and public construction ceased. Many of its 16,000 inhabitants resettled in small villages, hamlets, and isolated farmsteads in the valley floor and piedmont areas where agricultural production occurred. The dispersal of the population and the simultaneous appearance of regional civic and residential centers in various parts of the valley suggest that the political power of the ruling class and its capacity to extract labor or goods from the direct producers were diminishing and that political power was becoming decentralized. By A.D. 900, the inhabitants of the Oaxaca Valley and its environs, including the Mixteca Alta to the west and Mitla and Tehuantepec to the east, were already balkanized; that is, they were divided into a number of small, mutually antagonistic polities and kin-based communities. These were ultimately joined together by raids, wars, kidnappings, usurped thrones, and dynastic marriages. Many of them retained access to fortified mountaintop retreats, where their members fled during moments of crisis.

Two city-states that developed in central Mexico after the disintegration of the Teotihuacán state had ties with the Maya region. They were Xochicalco, which became a regional power in Morelos during the late seventh century, and Cacaxtla, which emerged around 750 in Puebla and southern Tlaxcala. Stone sculptures on the central pyramid at Xochicalco portrayed warriors and the conquest glyphs of tributary communities. The rulers of Xochicalco used central Mexican glyphs and iconographic cannons to communicate with the local population and Maya symbols of authority to proclaim their connections with the Maya ruling class; they used these linkages to support their own claims to power. One of the Cacaxtla murals, apparently painted by Maya muralists from the Usumacintla lowlands, commemorated the destruction of Teotihuacán; this artwork indicates that the ruling elite of this polity either maintained close ties with Gulf Coast merchants or that they emerged from that group.

Another successor state emerged 45 miles northwest of the Valley of Mexico after Teotihuacán collapsed. Some inhabitants of the Teotlalpan region were enmeshed in tributary relations with Teotihuacán, whereas others fled to remote, easily defended localities or to areas beyond the frontier to escape the labor and tribute exactions of the state. After the settlements established by Teotihuacán were abandoned and its control over the region had collapsed, the inhabitants of the hilltop villages moved from their retreats to new settlements located at lower elevations. The largest was the Toltec city of Tula, which was established about A.D. 800.

Historical annals of the Toltecs indicate that power in Tula was divided between sacred and secular rulers. When one of the sacred rulers who reigned during the later half of the tenth century tried illegally to pass his office to a member of his own family, a civil war erupted, and his son-in-law, who belonged to another faction of the ruling class, overthrew his wife's father and drove him and his followers from the city. According to the annals, the vanquished exiles moved southward and attempted to seize control of various polities. Some remained at Cholula, whereas others launched a series of attacks on Maya-speaking polities and communities after 994. These attacks culminated between 1070 and 1090, when the Itzá ruler of Chichén Itzá was defeated and the Puuc polity was incorporated into the loosely structured Toltec state. In the Guatemala highlands, Toltec warlords and their retinues had either seized power from the local ruling families or married into them, and their descendants began to acknowledge and stress the importance of their Toltec ancestors and heritage. The period of Toltec hegemony extended from about 950 to 1200.

After the collapse of Tula, various refugee populations moved into the Valley of Mexico, where they were absorbed into existing polities. In some instances, they swept aside the ruling elites; in other cases, they occupied less powerful positions in the existing class structures. This development paved the way for a new episode of class and state formation in the Valley of Mexico. By the end of the thirteenth century, more than forty small polities— semiautonomous, self-governing city-states—vied for power. Their small size and proximity affected both their internal development and their external relations since none was economically self-sufficient and since each participated from early times onward in periodic markets to obtain staples—like obsidian, firewood, building stone, or certain crops—that were either not available or produced within its borders. The relations among them helped to shape both the processes and the conditions in which they unfolded during the next two centuries.

Historical annals indicate that various Aztec factions arrived in the Valley of Mexico around 1300. Some settled in already existing polities, whereas others eked out their livelihoods by hunting, fishing, and foraging in the reeds and marshes of the lake. In these accounts, one group portrayed itself as a kin-based community, led by a collective of calpulli headmen, that became enmeshed in tributary relations with Colhua overlords and served mercenaries until the Colhua expelled them for brutality. They then made their way to the west side of the lake, where they settled on a small island, which they called Tenochtitlan. Aztec women traded the island's produce in the markets of nearby cities to obtain raw materials and goods that were not available locally. Thirteen years later, they founded a second city, Tlateloco, on a number of small, nearby islands. In 1372, the Aztecs enhanced their position in the basin by selecting as their leader the son of a Aztec man and a ruling-class woman from the Colhua, a group that claimed cultural hegemony in the basin by virtue of its Toltec heritage. The new leader took a number of secondary wives, who were the daughters of the leaders of various corporate landholding groups in the area. By 1400, the Aztecs had become a force to be reckoned with in the valley; they were simultaneously tributaries of the local rulers and in the process of constructing a tributary state of their own, which extracted labor and goods from the communities they subjugated independently from their lords.

During the 1430s, the Aztecs and their allies from Tacuba and Texcoco, the Triple Alliance, conquered the remaining city-states in the Valley of Mexico and began to extract both tribute and land from the subordinated polities. Some of the subject populations paid tribute exclusively to one of the allies, some to all three. Once the Aztecs stripped the commoners of large amounts of their lands, the latter were bound to the soil and required to pay tribute in kind, to perform labor services, and to provide young women for the ruler and the state. The Aztecs permitted vanquished nobles to retain a portion of their landholdings; this practice forced them to rely on the patronage of the Aztec rulers, who believed their dependence would ensure their future loyalty.

Two events etched in the historical accounts of the life of Moctezuma I were the great famine that struck the valley between 1450 and 1454 and the expansion of Aztec power, a result of military campaigns and conquests that consolidated the power of the Aztec state and transformed it into an empire. To obtain food, some Aztecs, presumably the direct producers, sold themselves and their children into slavery; they were purchased by affluent Totonac merchants and lords in coastal Veracruz, an area that had not been touched by the food shortages and whose inhabitants were not tributaries of the Aztecs and their allies. This practice did not noticeably weaken the state. Moctezuma I waged war against recalcitrant neighbors, already subjugated city-states whose rulers were slow to acknowledge his dominance, and the ruling faction of Tlatelolco, whose members attempted to assert their independence from their Tenochtitlan kin. He also initiated the first of the "flowery wars"—a series of battles—against the independent communities and polities of Tlaxcala and Puebla in order to train warriors and acquire war captives for sacrifice.

The great expansion of Aztec power began in 1458, when Moctezuma I and the Triple Alliance sent military expeditions to acquire loot, to establish tributary relations with the subordinated populations, and to ensure the safety of Aztec merchants. The first expedition was launched against a Mixtec city-state in Oaxaca. After defeating it, the Aztecs burned its temple, executed its ruler, and negotiated a treaty with the Mixtec nobles who survived the battle. The treaty permitted the local ruling class to retain control over its subjects; however, its members were obliged to turn over specified quantities and kinds of goods to an Aztec tax collector, who resided in Oaxaca and forwarded the tribute to a counterpart who tallied the items when they arrived in Tenochtitlan. This became a model for subsequent conquests in the Soconusco of coastal Chiapas and the Tehuantepec region in the 1490s, where the Aztec armies forced local lords to provide lavish gifts and tribute. This practice meant that the traditional rulers retained considera-

Reconstruction of the great temple of Tenochtitlan, Mexico.

ble control over the labor power and goods produced by their subjects; it also meant that subject populations often rebelled when Aztec power waned.

In 1502, Moctezuma II, supported by the rulers of Tacuba and Texcoco, succeeded his uncle on the Tenochtitlan throne. He suppressed rebellions, consolidated populations that had already been incorporated into the imperial state by his predecessors, and absorbed various principalities in the Oaxaca region into the empire. He also removed all of the officials who had served with his popular uncle and had received their positions by virtue of their achievements in war, claiming that it was inappropriate for the state to employ nobles by achievement, who were allegedly coarse, crude, and brutal and lacked the social graces and refinement necessary to hold office. He replaced them with the descendants of former rulers, who reputedly possessed these qualities and were more supportive of his policies than the high-ranking warriors he purged from office. Thus, the class position of a group was transformed by royal edict, as the members of his uncle's staff were declassed and possibly subjected to tribute exactions.

During the fifteenth and sixteenth centuries, the westward expansion of the Triple Alliance was halted by the Tarascan state centered in the Pátzcuaro Basin, west of the Valley of Mexico. The state crystallized toward the middle of the fifteenth century in response to Aztec military campaigns launched against its inhabitants. These peoples, who spoke different languages and had different origin myths, allied themselves with a Tarascan war chief. They contributed warriors to the Tarascan chief and his successors. On several occasions, the Tarascans defeated the Aztec armies and inflicted heavy casualties on them.

The first two Tarascan kings were war leaders, elected or at least treated deferentially because of their military prowess and skills. The third Tarascan king, who ascended to the throne around 1500, was also a war leader, elected and aided by a group of appointed officials. However, he or one of his predecessors had also assumed responsibility for several ritual activities, so the office he held became infused with ritual obligations and power as well. By his reign, the Tarascan king was apparently viewed mainly as the representative of the sun god. His duties in the ritual hierarchy were to supply firewood so that the temple fires always burned, to conquer, and to extract the hearts of sacrificial victims.

Two customary practices of Tarascan society that troubled the Spanish friars were (1) the polygynous marriages of noble men with close consanguineal and affinal kin and (2) male homosexuality and prostitution. Both were connected with the emergence of particular kinds of power relations during the period of intensified warfare with the Triple Alliance and the rapid formation of a class structure. Tyrants, like the Tarascan kings, typically consolidated state power against the countervailing claims of traditional leaders; killed their opponents; alleged that they stood above the corrupting influences of kin relations; and then married elite women, who were often close kin, to overcome the contradictions created by undermining the kin groups that made up the state and simultaneously to legitimize their own

positions and reforms. Eva Keuls's (1985) study of sexual politics and homosexuality in ancient Athens points to the importance of understanding the
power dynamics of sexuality in a society that bore some striking resemblances to the Tarascan state—for example, the sequestering of wives and
daughters, homosexuality, prostitution, and rampant saber rattling.

The rulers and subjects of the semiautonomous city-states that made up
Tlaxcala, centered about 65 miles east of the valley of Mexico, retained their
independence from the Aztecs, despite the fact that their territory was eventually surrounded on all sides as the Triple Alliance extended its control
eastward to the Gulf of Mexico. The Aztecs and their allies waged war
against the inhabitants of this frontier area to train warriors. Tlaxcala was
also a refuge area, whose inhabitants allied themselves, at least on one
occasion in 1515, with a dissident faction from Texcoco that challenged Moctezuma II's authority in a successional dispute.

After the 1490s, armed Aztec merchants appeared regularly in the marketplaces of Tzinacantán in highland Chiapas and the Xicalanco, which was
the western end of a vast commercial network that extended eastward to the
Yucatán Peninsula and southward to the Guatemala highlands and Honduras. Merchants on the periphery of this network, in cities like Xicalanco,
exchanged goods with their counterparts from Oaxaca and central Mexico
and with tribal peoples in Nicaragua. The Aztec kings sent merchants, ladened with various kinds of garments obtained as tribute from subject provinces, to Xicalanco to traffic with its rulers, whom the Mexicans considered
enemies. In return for the cotton capes and other goods they brought, the
Aztec merchants acquired a variety of goods: the jade and jadeite quarried in
remote areas of the Guatemala highlands and, more important, slaves from
Yucatán and Honduras. Many of the commodities found in the market at
Xicalanco arrived by water, carried in canoes that were paddled along the
coast as far east as Cozumel and up and down the rivers that both flood and
empty the interior. When the rivers moved too fast or were too small to
navigate, goods were unloaded and carried overland by porters.

Except for the exchange relations they were in the process of establishing, the Aztecs had relatively little direct influence over what happened in
the area beyond the Isthmus of Tehuantepec, and the influence they did
have was recent. However, earlier peoples from the Mexican highlands had
had a significant effect on the course of history in the Maya area since the
ruling elites of many Maya city-states and principalities claimed descent from
Toltec ancestors.

The development of long-distance trade between the Aztecs and the
aristocrats of the Maya frontier changed the historically constituted conditions
that underwrote the reproduction of existing class structures, state institutions and practices, and coercive arrangements that ensured extraction of
goods and labor from subject populations. The political organization of the
Maya area consisted of a continually changing array of city-states, principalities, and kin communities; alliances that were perpetually being made and
broken; and processes that led to the centralization of political power in some

regions and to its disintegration in others. For instance, the ruling Itzá dynasty of Chichén Itzá was destroyed in the 1380s by their close kin, the Cocom family, who were the local lords of Mayapan. The Cocom allied themselves with two patrilineages: the Canul from Tabasco and the Xiu from Uxmal. By the end of the century, the joint government formed by the three lineages at Mayapan was the center of a tributary state that included all of the provinces in the central and western portions of the peninsula. However, this political unity was short-lived. Mayapan was sacked after a coup, and the state soon disintegrated as local leaders asserted control. Two kinds of polities emerged. There was a core area of class-stratified provinces in the interior of northwestern Yucatán, where political power was centralized in the hands of warlords who extracted labor service and goods from their tributaries. The core area was surrounded by a mixture of class-stratified, ranked, and kin-ordered communities, where political power was decentralized.

Portions of the prestations to traditional leaders and the tribute goods extracted by provincial or town rulers were consumed or used locally. Another portion entered the sphere of circulation, which was grafted onto the production sphere and was dominated, at least in its long-distance manifestations, by the rulers themselves or by their close noble kin, who had their own factors, trading canoes, and slave porters and who extended credit and made loans. Some of these merchant princes and their kin undoubtedly became quite wealthy; however, long-distance trade was a risky venture because of unsettled political conditions; hostile neighbors; and the ever-present threat posed by pirates, robbers, and slavers. It was dangerous for itinerant peddlers to travel alone in distant provinces.

Events in the Maya borderlands focus attention on the relationship between long-distance trade and state formation and on the parasitical role of aristocratic merchants who dealt in goods extracted as tribute from the indigenous producing communities or in the enslaved members of those communities. In this region, the various state apparatuses attempted to provide security for the merchants and to maintain or secure the conditions necessary to acquire goods and slaves from kin-organized communities, which retained significant amounts of control over their means of production and reproduction. However, the official histories of the Maya ruling families reveal that from the rulers' view, the kin communities rarely functioned as desired. Some communities, like the Cehache, moved to avoid the demands of the states that were emerging in their midst. Other communities adapted to the changes the ruling classes sought to impose. Sometimes they improvised a facade of support for the demands of the state when its inspectors were present but otherwise continued to do things in their own way, treating the state apparatus as another element in a dangerous world. This practice created a split between public and private life. The kin communities professed conformity in public and pursued their own interests in private. Collective discipline and conformity were the price their members paid for security and survival under adverse conditions.

FURTHER READINGS: A BRIEF GUIDE

For overviews of Mesoamerican archaeology, see Eric Wolf, *Sons of the Shaking Earth* (Chicago: University of Chicago Press, 1959); Linda Schele and David Freidel, *A Forest of Kings: The Untold Story of the Ancient Maya* (New York: William Morrow, 1990); Brigitte Boehm de Lameiras, *Formación del estado en el México prehispánico* (Zamora: El Colegio de Michoacán, 1986); and Richard E. Blanton, Stephen A. Kowalewski, Gary Feinman, and Jill Appel, *Ancient Mesoamerica: A Comparison of Changes in Three Regions* (Cambridge: Cambridge University Press, 1981).

Early hunter-forager and food-producing communities are discussed by Richard S. MacNeish, "Ancient Mesoamerican Civilization," *Science*, vol. 143, no. 3606 (1964), 531–537, and "The Evolution of Community Patterns in the Tehuacán Valley of Mexico and Speculations about the Cultural Processes," in *Man, Settlement and Urbanism*, ed. Peter J. Ucko, Ruth Tringham, and G. W. Dimbleby (London: Gerald Duckworth, 1972), pp. 67–93; Kent V. Flannery, *The Early Mesoamerican Village* (New York: Academic Press, 1976), and *Guilá Naquitz: Archaic Foraging and Early Agriculture in Oaxaca, Mexico* (New York: Academic Press, 1986); and Christine Niederberger, "Early Sedentary Economy in the Basin of Mexico," *Science*, vol. 203, no. 4376 (1979), 131–142.

The intensification of social relations during the second millennium B.C. is discussed by John E. Clark and Michael Blake, "The Pacific Coast Early Formative Project, Chiapas, Mexico: The Implications of Recent Archaeological Research," Arthur A. Demarest, "The Origins of Cultural Complexity in Southeastern Mesoamerica: The Early Formative Societies of Guatemala and El Salvador," and Michael W. Love, "Early Complex Societies of Pacific Guatemala," papers presented at the Circum-Pacific Prehistory Conference, Seattle, 1989; and Gareth Lowe, "The Mixe-Zoque as Competing Neighbors of the Early Lowland Maya," in *The Origins of Maya Civilization*, ed. Richard E. W. Adams (Albuquerque: University of New Mexico Press, 1977), pp. 197–248.

The Olmec phenomena are examined in Michael D. Coe and Richard A. Diehl, *In the Land of the Olmec*, 2 vols. (Austin: University of Texas Press, 1980); Elizabeth Benson, *Dumbarton Oaks Conference on the Olmec* (Washington, DC: Dumbarton Oaks Research Library and Collection, 1968); Richard A. Diehl, "Olmec Architecture: A Comparison of San Lorenzo and La Venta," and Philip Drucker, "On the Nature of the Olmec Polity," both in *The Olmec and Their Neighbors; Essays in Memory of Matthew W. Stirling*, ed. Elizabeth Benson (Washington, DC: Dumbarton Oaks Research Library and Collections, 1981), 49–69 and 29–48; Frederick J. Bove, "Laguna de los Cerros: An Olmec Central Place," *Journal of New World Archaeology*, vol. 2, no. 3 (1978), 1–56; Philip Drucker, Robert F. Heizer, and Robert J. Squier, *Excavations at La Venta, Tabasco, 1955*, Bureau of American Ethnology Bulletin 155 (Washington, DC, 1959); Robert J. Sharer and David C. Grove, (eds.) *Regional Perspectives on the Olmec* (Cambridge: Cambridge University Press, 1989); David C. Grove, *Chalcatzingo: Excavations on the Olmec Frontier* (London: Thames & Hudson,

1984); Ann Cyphers Guillen, "The Possible Role of a Woman in Formative Exchange," in *Trade and Exchange in Early Mesoamerica*, ed. Kenneth G. Hirst (Albuquerque: University of New Mexico Press, 1984), pp. 115–124; and Carl W. Clewlow, Jr., "A Stylistic and Chronological Study of Olmec Monumental Sculpture," *Contributions of the University of California Archaeological Research Facility*, no. 19 (Berkeley, 1974).

Early episodes of class and state formation in Mesoamerica are discussed by Richard E. Blanton, *Monte Albán: Settlement Patterns at the Ancient Zapotec Capital* (New York: Academic Press, 1978); Kent V. Flannery and Joyce Marcus, eds., *The Cloud People: Divergent Evolution of the Zapotec and Mixtec Civilizations* (New York: Academic Press, 1983); Elsa M. Redmond, A fuego y sangre: *Early Zapotec Imperialism in the Cuicatlán Cañada, Oaxaca*, Memoirs of the Museum of Anthropology, University of Michigan, no. 16 (Ann Arbor, 1983); Charles S. Spencer, *The Cuicatlán Cañada and Monte Albán: A Study of Primary State Formation* (New York: Academic Press, 1982); and Joyce Marcus, "The Iconography of Militarism at Monte Albán and Neighboring Sites in the Valley of Oaxaca," in *The Origins of Religious Art and Iconography in Preclassic Mesoamerica*, University of California Latin American Studies Series, ed. Henry B. Nicholson, vol. 31 (Los Angeles, 1976), 123–139.

For Teotihuacán, see René Millon, "Teotihuacan: City, State, and Civilization," in *Supplement to the Handbook of Middle American Indians*, ed. Jeremy A. Sabloff, vol. 1 (Austin: University of Texas Press, 1981), pp. 198–243, "Social Relations in Ancient Teotihuacán," in *The Valley of Mexico: Studies in Pre-Hispanic Ecology and Society*, ed. Eric Wolf (Albuquerque: University of New Mexico Press, 1976), pp. 205–248, and "The Last Years of Teotihuacan Dominance," in *The Collapse of Ancient States and Civilizations*, ed. Norman Yoffee and George L. Cowgill (Tucson: University of Arizona Press, 1988), pp. 102–164; George L. Cowgill, "Teotihuacan, Internal Militaristic Competition, and the Fall of the Classic Maya," in *Maya Archaeology and Ethnohistory*, ed. Norman Hammond and Gordon R. Willey (Austin: University of Texas Press, 1979), pp. 51–62, and "Rulership and the Ciudadela: Political Inferences from Teotihuacan Architecture," in *Civilization in the Ancient Americas: Essays in Honor of Gordon R. Willey*, ed. Richard M. Leventhal and Alan L. Kolata (Albuquerque: University of New Mexico Press, 1983), pp. 313–343; Deborah L. Nichols, "A Middle Formative Irrigation System Near Santa Clara Coatitlán in the Basin of Mexico," *American Antiquity*, vol. 47, no. 1 (1982), pp. 133–144; Esther Pasztory, "A Reinterpretation of Teotihuacan and Its Mural Painting Tradition," in *Feathered Serpents and Flowering Trees: Reconstructing the Murals of Teotihuacan*, ed. Kathleen Berrin (San Francisco: Fine Arts Museum of San Francisco, 1988), pp. 45–77; Michael W. Spence, "Craft Production and Polity in Early Teotihuacan," in *Trade and Exchange in Early Mesoamerica*, ed. Kenneth G. Hirth (Albuquerque: University of New Mexico Press, 1984), pp. 87–114, and "Locational Analysis of Craft Specialization Areas in Teotihuacan," in *Economic Aspects of Prehispanic Highland Mexico*, ed. Barry L. Isaac, (Greenwich, CT: JAI Press, 1986), pp. 75–100; Vincas P. Steponaitis, "Settlement Hierarchies and Political Complexity in Nonmarket Societies: The Formative Period in the Valley of Mexico," *American Anthropologist*, vol. 83, no. 2 (1981), 320–363; William T. Sanders, *The Cultural Ecology of the Teotihuacán Valley* (University Park: Department of Sociology and Anthropology, Pennsylvania State University, 1965); William T. Sanders, Jeffrey R. Parsons, and Robert S. Santley, *The Basin of Mexico: Ecological Processes in the Evolution of Civilization* (New York: Academic Press, 1979); and Kenneth G. Hirth and Jorge Angulo Villaseñor, "Early State Expansion in Central Mexico: Teotihuacan in Morelos," *Journal of Field Archaeology*, vol. 8, no. 2 (1981), 133–150.

For discussions of class and state formation in the Maya region, see Richard E. W. Adams, *The Origins of Maya Civilization* (Albuquerque: University of New Mexico Press, 1977); William T. Sanders, "Chiefdom to State: Political Evolution at Kaminaljuyu, Guatemala," in *Reconstructing Complex Societies: An Archaeological Colloquium*, Supplement to the Bulletin of the American Schools of Oriental Research, ed. Charlotte B. Moore, no. 20 (Philadelphia, 1972), pp. 97–121; Richard E. W. Adams, W. E. Brown, and T. Patrick Culbert, "Radar Mapping, Archeology, and Ancient Maya Land Use," *Science*, vol. 213, no. 4515 (1981), 1457–1463; William L. Rathje, "Sociopolitical Implications of Lowland Maya Burials: Methodology and Tentative Hypotheses," *World Archaeology*, vol. 1, no. 3 (1970), pp. 359–374, and "The Origin and Development of Lowland Classic Maya Civilization," *American Antiquity*, vol. 36, no. 3 (1971), 275–285; Gordon R. Willey, "Ancient Maya Politics," *Proceedings of the American Philosophical Society*, vol. 134, no. 1 (Philadelphia, 1990), pp. 1–9; and Arthur A. Demarest, "Political Evolution in the Maya Borderlands: The Salvadoran Frontier," in *The Southeast Classic Maya Zone*, ed. Elizabeth H. Boone and Gordon R. Willey (Washington, DC: Dumbarton Oaks Research Library and Collection, 1988), pp. 335–394.

For Mesoamerican history after the collapse of Teotihuacán, see Kenneth G. Hirth, "Xochicalco: Urban Growth and State Formation in Central Mexico," *Science*, vol. 225, no. 4662 (1984), 579–586; Richard A. Diehl and Janet C. Berlo, eds., *Mesoamerica after the Decline of Teotihuacan, A.D. 700–900* (Washington, DC: Dumbarton Oaks Research Library and Collection, 1989); Arlen F. Chase and Prudence M. Rice, eds., *The Lowland Maya Postclassic* (Austin: University of Texas Press, 1985); Jeremy A. Sabloff and E. Wyllys Andrews V, eds., *Late Lowland Maya Civilization: Classic to Postclassic* (Albuquerque: University of New Mexico Press, 1986); Edward Calnek, "Patterns of Empire Formation in the Valley of Mexico, Late Postclassic Period, 1200–1521," in *The Inca and Aztec States, 1400–1800; Anthropology and History*, ed. George A. Collier, Renato I. Rosaldo, and John D. Wirth (Stanford: Stanford University Press, 1982), pp. 43–62; Pedro Carrasco, "The Peoples of Central Mexico and Their Historical Traditions," and "Social Organization of Ancient Mexico," in *Handbook of Middle American Indians*, ed. Gordon F. Ekholm and Ignacio Bernal (Austin: University of Texas Press, 1971), vol. 11, pp. 459–473, and vol. 10, pp. 349–375; T. Patrick Culbert, "Political History and the Decipherment of

Maya Glyphs," *Antiquity*, vol. 62, no. 234 (1988), 235–252; Nigel Davies, *The Toltecs until the Fall of Tula* (Norman: University of Oklahoma Press, 1977); Richard A. Diehl, *Tula: The Toltec Capital of Ancient Mexico* (London: Thames & Hudson, 1983); John W. Fox, *Maya Postclassic State Formation: Segmentary Lineage Migration in Advancing Frontiers* (Cambridge: Cambridge University Press, 1987); David A. Freidel and Linda Schele, "Kingship in the Late Preclassic Maya Lowlands: The Instruments and Places of Ritual Power," *American Anthropologist*, vol. 90, no. 3 (1988), 547–567; Eric C. Gibson, "Inferred Sociopolitical Structure," in *A Consideration of the Early Classic Period in the Maya Lowlands*, Institute for Mesoamerican Studies, State University of New York at Albany, ed. Gordon R. Willey and Peter Mathews, Publication no. 10 (Albany, 1985), pp. 161–171; and J. Eric S. Thompson, *Maya History and Religion* (Norman: University of Oklahoma Press, 1970).

For the Aztecs and their contemporaries, see Elizabeth M. Brumfiel, "Aztec State Making: Ecology, Structure, and the Origin of the State," *American Anthropologist*, vol. 85, no. 2 (1983), 261–284, "Factional Competition in Complex Society," in *Domination and Resistance*, ed. Daniel Miller, Michael Rowlands, and Christopher Tilley (London: Unwin Hyman, 1989), pp. 127–139, "Elite and Utilitarian Crafts in the Aztec State," in *Specialization, Exchange, and Complex Societies*, ed. Elizabeth M. Brumfiel and Timothy K. Earle (Cambridge: Cambridge University Press, 1987), pp. 102–118, and "Weaving and Cooking: Women's Production in Aztec Mexico," in *Engendering Archaeology: Women and Prehistory*, ed. Joan M. Gero and Margaret W. Conkey (Oxford: Basil Blackwell, 1990), pp. 224–253; Edward Calnek, "El sistema de mercado en Tenochtitlan," in *Economía política e ideología en el México prehispánico*, ed. Pedro Carrasco and Johanna Broda (Mexico: Editorial Nuevo Imagen, 1978), pp. 97–113; Robert M. Carmack, *The Quiché Mayas of Utatlan* (Norman: University of Oklahoma Press, 1981); Pedro Carrasco, "Royal Marriages in Ancient Mexico," and Frederic Hicks, "Rotational Labor and Urban Development in Prehispanic Tetzcoco," both in *Explorations in Ethnohistory: Indians of Central Mexico in the Sixteenth Century*, ed. H. R. Harvey and Hanns J. Prem (Albuquerque: University of New Mexico Press, 1984), pp. 41–82 and 147–174; John K. Chance, "Colonial Ethnohistory in Oaxaca," and Frederic Hicks, "Prehistoric Background of Colonial Political and Economic Organization in Central Mexico," both in *Supplement to the Handbook of Middle American Indians*, ed. Ronald Spores, vol. 4, (Austin: University of Texas Press, 1986), pp. 165–189 and 35–54; Nigel Davies, *The Aztecs: A History* (Norman: University of Oklahoma Press, 1973), and *The Aztec Empire: The Toltec Resurgence* (Norman: University of Oklahoma Press, 1987); Frederic Hicks, "'Flower War' in Aztec History," *American Ethnologist*, vol. 6, no. 1 (1979), 87–92, and "Tetzcoco in the Early 16th Century: The State, the City, and the *calpolli*," *American Ethnologist*, vol. 9, no. 2 (1982), 230–249; Ralph L. Roys, *The Indian Background of Colonial Yucatan*, Carnegie Institution of Washington Publication 548 (Washington, DC, 1943), and *The Political Geography of the Yucatan Maya*, Carnegie Institution of Washington Publication 613 (Washington, DC, 1957); Frances V.

Scholes and Ralph L. Roys, *The Maya Chontal Indians of Acalan-Tixchel: A Contribution to the History and Ethnography of the Yucatan Peninsula*, Carnegie Institution of Washington Publication 560 (Washington, DC, 1948); J. Benedict Warren, *The Conquest of Michoacán: The Spanish Domination of the Tarascan Kingdom in Western Mexico, 1521–1530* (Norman: University of Oklahoma Press, 1985); Robert Wasserstrom, *Class and Society in Central Chiapas* (Berkeley: University of California Press, 1983); and Eva C. Keuls, *The Reign of the Phallus: Sexual Politics in Ancient Athens* (New York: Harper & Row, 1985).

chapter 15

South America

The moral discipline effected by state formation is therefore not, neutrally, about "integrating society." It is about enforcing rule. (Philip Corrigan and Derek Sayers, The Great Arch: English State Formation as Cultural Revolution)

Just as we often underestimate the ability of many stateless societies to engage in large-scale communal production, so we often underestimate the high degree to which they are able to specialize their labor on a part-time basis. (David Kaplan, "Men, Monuments and Political Systems")

South America is an ancient, triangle-shaped landmass, most of which currently lies in the tropics. The Andes Mountains, which rise abruptly out of the Pacific Ocean, form the continent's backbone. Jagged peaks, many continually capped with snow and ice, tower above high plateaus and deep mountains. The land trembles from earthquakes and tectonic shocks and is thrust upward as the South American continental plate overrides the Nazca oceanic plate. This process has been going on for 10 to 15 million years and has produced a vertical landscape, with one of the steepest gradients in the world, in western South America. The sixteenth-century inhabitants of the Pacific coastal region recognized the connection between these processes and everyday life and attributed them to Pachacamac, the powerful deity who was both the creator of the world and the earthshaker.

East of the Andes lie the Brazilian and Guiana uplands, which are among the most ancient landmasses in the world. More than 100 million years ago, this enormous shield was connected with southern and western Africa; however, they separated and slowly drifted apart after a deep rift developed between them. South of the Brazilian highlands and east of the Andes lies the Patagonian Plateau. The enormous river systems rising in the Andes and the Brazilian and Guiana highlands have sculpted the topography of eastern South America. The Amazon River and its tributaries drain much of the continent east of the mountains. Only a narrow ridge separates the tropical forests of the Amazon Basin from the forests and savannas of the Orinoco to the north; in fact, streams feeding both river systems rise in the Casiquare swamp. A similar situation prevails in the south, where low hills separate the tributaries of the Amazon from the upper reaches of the Paraguay-Paraná drainage system. Consequently, the river systems of eastern South America provided a transportation and communication network that connected the inhabitants of the Amazon Basin with those living elsewhere on the continent.

Tropical rain forests, tree-studded savannas, and grasslands cover much of the eastern lowlands north of the Tropic of Capricorn. These are replaced by the seasonally flooded habitats of the Gran Chaco in Paraguay and northeastern Argentina, which eventually merge with the desert scrub vegetation

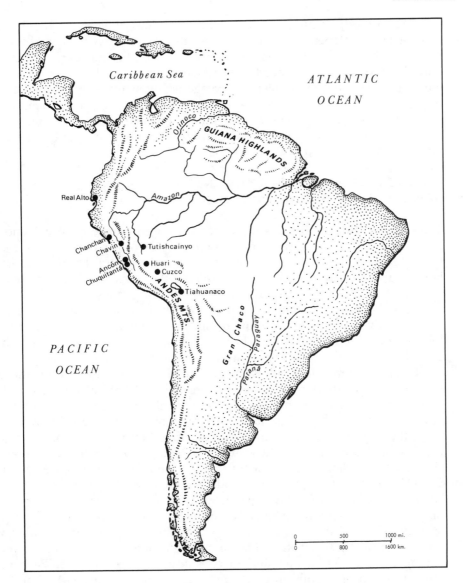

South America.

of Patagonia. West of the mountains, the temperate rain forests of the south coast of Chile give way to a coastal desert that stretches northward to Ecuador, where it merges with the tropical rain forests of Colombia. The Andes Mountains, with vast plateaus 12,000 feet or more above sea level and mountain peaks that rise to heights exceeding 20,000 feet, have an incredible range and variety of alpine environments. Mountain glaciers overlook bleak windswept tundras and the diverse habitats of the river valleys formed by summer precipitation and runoff.

When the first Europeans arrived in the 1520s, they found highly stratified, state-based societies in the Andes, the largest of which was the Inca
Empire, which stretched from northern Ecuador through Peru and Bolivia
into northern Chile and northwestern Argentina. At the same time, they
found bands of hunter-foragers in Patagonia, who lived in much the same
way as their predecessors had 10 millennia earlier. They encountered a variety of food-producing communities in the forested areas of eastern South
America: some with village populations of 5,000 or more and others with
rank- or estate-ordered social relations.

THE DEVELOPMENT OF FOOD PRODUCTION AND THE
CONSTITUTION OF A SPATIAL DIVISION OF LABOR

The earliest Andean societies for which significant amounts of evidence are
available seem to have used the communal mode of production. Information
from Paloma and other contemporary sites on the central Peruvian coast can
be used to establish a baseline for examining the transition from an appropri-
ative to a food-producing economy in the central Andes.

The Paloma communities, which date from before 6000 B.C. to about
3250 B.C., lived in seasonal camps or small permanent villages with twenty-
five to seventy-five residents. Their subsistence economies were dominated
by fishing, littoral harvesting, hunting, and foraging; toward the end of the
fourth millennium, plant cultivation was added. Households were the basic
production-consumption units, and there was a technical division of labor
based on both gender and age. In settlements near the shore, adolescent
boys and young men fished and dove for mollusks in the cold waters that
wash the coast judging by exostoses that formed on their ear bones—a result
of prolonged exposure to cold water; older women and men made mats and
sewed. The division of labor meant that no one in a Paloma phase settlement
procured or produced all of the goods essential for life; they cooperated and
shared the products of their own labor with one or more members of the
opposite sex and with members of different generations. Judging by their
size, the settlements were not autonomous demographic entities; they were
linked instead by the matrimonial mobility of men and women who moved
among them to find mates and to constitute new households. Each settlement was probably built around a nucleus of brothers and sisters and their
spouses and children, as well as more distant kin and even outsiders.

The relations of production and reproduction that shaped everyday life
in this kind of society operated at two levels. Although the real appropriation
of nature occurred at the level of the household and the village, neither was
able to ensure demographic replacement. Each was part of a larger community that underwrote the social and demographic reproduction of the domestic groups, camps, and villages found in the archaeological record.

The subsistence economies of the coastal Peruvian communities of the
third millennium B.C. were still dominated by fishing and littoral harvesting;
however, they were based on new forms of production: (1) Labor processes

associated with the extraction of littoral and marine resources—that is, men's work, given the gender division of labor in Paloma society—and with the cultivation of two inedible plants, cotton and gourds, were intensified; (2) the manufacture of cotton nets, fish line, and textiles—activities associated with women and elderly men in Paloma society—was expanded; (3) labor power was appropriated at the community level to erect platform mounds that were beyond the capacities of single households or villages; and (4) economically important subsistence and industrial goods began to circulate between economically specialized fishing and farming settlements.

In some communities, farming and fishing increasingly were carried out in different localities. In these instances, the relations of production gradually acquired a spatial organization that was not merely superimposed on the existing age- and gender-based division of labor characteristic of Paloma society. The gender-based division of labor was transformed as the activities of men and women residing in economically specialized settlements converged. In fishing villages, both men and women engaged in activities centered on the sea, and both acquired the exostoses; in contrast, those individuals who lived and died in the farming settlements typically lacked exostoses.

The relations of production that developed in these communities did not merely replicate the earlier division of labor. Rather, they involved the elaboration of community-level relations and of their articulation with the domestic level, where the real appropriation of raw materials still occurred. The community-level relations, previously seen in the practices of matrimonial mobility, began to link economically specialized settlements consisting of households whose members were no longer able to produce all of the materials they consumed, given the spatially organized, technical division of labor that had developed in the new kinds of villages. Community-level social relations permitted the inhabitants of the specialized settlements to acquire, on a regular basis, foodstuffs, raw materials, and goods from distant localities. Such relations were also involved in activities or projects that were beyond the capabilities of a single household or a small number of cooperating domestic groups—for example, the construction of platform mounds and fish-drying terraces and the early stages of the large architectural complex at El Paraíso. The labor required for building each of the handful of platform mounds at Aspero or Río Seco exceeded 60,000 person-days, which was conceivably within the range of a few households with large numbers of productive members; however, the 1.9 million person-days of labor minimally expended to build El Paraíso clearly surpassed that capacity and must have been raised at the level of the wider community. At the same time, community-level social relations continued to function as the relations of reproduction.

The shift to a truly agrarian economy in coastal Peru, in which the cultivation of food plants rather than fishing played the determinant role in shaping the economic structure, occurred during the time U-shaped pyramids were built on the central and north-central coasts of Peru, roughly 2350 to 400 B.C. In these communities, agricultural production, previously con-

One of the smaller structures at the early site of El Paraiso (Chuquitanta) on the central coast of Peru.

cerned mainly with cotton and gourds, was expanded to include greater varieties and quantities of cultivated plant foods. This laid the foundations for new forms of production and appropriation that built on the existing community-level relations and spatially organized, technical division of labor. The reproduction of these societies depended on the continued participation of households in community-level institutions and practices—such as the circulation of raw materials and foodstuffs, construction of platform mounds, and participation in the festivities that occurred at these structures.

In terms of the productive forces, the crystallization of these communities involved the formation of additional economically specialized farming hamlets in localities with ecological conditions suited to the production of particular food crops, like avocados, as well as the construction of water-management systems in the mid-valleys and U-shaped platform mounds in inland localities. The mounds, some of which took more than 6 or 7 million person-days of labor to erect, served as the loci for social practices—rituals, predictions, and offerings—that presumably established and maintained the culturally constituted conditions necessary for successful farming. The labor for these building projects was probably recruited at the level of a regional community since none of the known settlements had populations large enough to complete them. The rate at which labor was appropriated for such projects, defined in terms of person-days of labor per year, was two to four times greater than it had been in the third millennium B.C.

Production and the real appropriation of nature continued to occur at the household level. Storage pits and refuse deposits associated with residential structures, as well as tool kits placed in the graves of different individuals, attest to the continued importance of the households in everyday life. However, their composition, at least in some fishing villages, had apparently

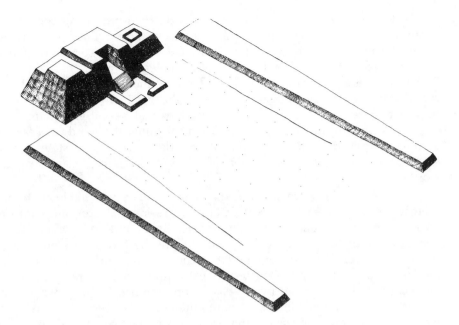

Schematic perspective of the U-shaped pyramid complex at La Florida near Lima, Peru.

changed. At Ancón changes in the size of the cooking vessels indicate a threefold increase in the number of servings prepared, which suggests that the domestic groups increased from about five to fifteen members during the early part of the second millennium B.C. It also suggests that the Ancón consumption units were no longer composed simply of nuclear or stem families, even if they had been earlier. Residential structures at Cardal—a slightly later inland farming settlement—may have been occupied by nuclear or stem families. Thus, domestic groups may have been organized differently in the fishing and farming settlements.

These communities were not class-stratified. There is no evidence of inequalities exhibited by artifacts with restricted distributions in the societies; there is no evidence of a class-based distinction between center and countryside, even though economically specialized farming and fishing settlements existed in some localities; and there is no evidence of centralization or of the kinds of settlement hierarchies, with multiple levels of decision making, posited for class-stratified, state-based societies. There is also no evidence of a social division of labor in which the members of one social class exploited those of another by permanently appropriating either their labor power or their products; however, there is evidence from Cardal of differences in status or rank among its inhabitants—that is, some were interred on the pyramid, whereas others were buried in the residential area. There is also no evidence from any of the settlements dating to the second or the early part of the first millennium B.C. of class struggle—which is a defining feature of state-based societies.

Although the social relations of the early food-producing societies were continually reconstituted and significant social and economic changes occurred through time, the societies themselves exhibited a stability that must be measured in terms of centuries or even millennia rather than generations. Societies manifesting variants of the communal mode of production have the capacity to incorporate transformations of the productive forces at the same time as they resist the formation of hierarchies that permit exploitation. Thus, there was nothing inherent in their social relations that would necessarily or automatically lead to the development of a class structure; a state apparatus; exploitation; and the crystallization of oppositional forces, class struggle, or resistance.

At issue is how small numbers of individuals were able to transform themselves from being members of kin and residential groupings into being masters, able to dominate their kin and neighbors and appropriate labor and goods. In Peru during the waning centuries of the first millennium B.C., this involved uneven development and the consolidation of a number of small, regional entities, integrated by tribute extraction, whose attempted exactions were contested or opposed by kin-based communities on their peripheries. In the initial stages, the kin-based communities of the central Peruvian coast were on the margins of early states. What distinguished early Peruvian states from one another were differences in the capacities of their various ruling classes to extract labor and tribute from their own kin and neighbors and to impose their will over the kin-organized communities on their peripheries.

CLASS AND STATE FORMATION IN THE CENTRAL ANDES

Class and state formation, the expression of exploitation, occurred when the community-level relations of production—which had previously ensured the maintenance and reproduction of a spatially organized economy and mobilized labor for communal construction projects—broke down between 400 and 200 B.C. Labor and goods were no longer appropriated at the community level for the construction of platform mounds and the performance of rituals that guaranteed the agricultural success of the community as a whole; they were directed instead into new channels. Fortified hilltop villages and retreats were built along a 700-mile stretch of the Peruvian coast. Burials contained headless individuals and persons entombed with additional human skulls or trophy heads, stone-headed maces, and spear-throwers. Some interred individuals had depressed skull fractures or dart points embedded in vital areas of their bodies. When taken together, these remains suggest that raiding was rampant and permit us to infer that war leaders had acquired prominence. This configuration coalesced at about the same time that skillfully made pottery styles with marked, largely nonoverlapping regional distributions appeared. These developments suggest (1) the elaboration of craft specialization; (2) the restricted circulation of certain kinds of goods; and (3) the use of cultural elements, like art styles, to mark boundaries between communities that participated in different production-consumption systems. A century or so later, there were tombs with markedly different arrays and quantities of grave goods and individuals interred with retainers. Such a configuration under the circumstances that prevailed in the central Andes indicates the development of class-based social differences that began with "conquest abroad and repression at home" (Diamond 1974:1). The archaeological evidence indicates that class-stratified, state-based societies and class struggle crystallized rapidly during this period, in a matter of years or decades rather than centuries or millennia.

Class structures crystallized during the fourth century B.C. at Chavin de Huantar, Kunturwasi, and possibly a few other localities in the north highlands of Peru and at Pucara in the northern end of the Lake Titicaca Basin. At Chavin de Huantar, the ruling class resided near public buildings, consumed more marine fish and younger llamas than their lower-class neighbors or the residents of farming hamlets, used exotic pottery vessels, and had exclusive rights to gold or spondylus jewelry. At Kunturwasi, they buried their dead, often adorned with gold jewelry, in stone-lined cists. They established a garrison at Atalla, near Huancavelica in the central highlands, and resettled the rural, kin-based communities of the area, transforming their members, for a century or so, into townspeople.

The early Andean states seem to have lacked massive infrastructures and large, luxuriously leisured privileged classes; there were apparently no great disparities of wealth between the direct producers and their rulers— especially in societies in which the burden of tribute was light or in which the direct producers either had successfully resisted the attempted extortions of their leaders or had joined with them in military adventures against neighboring peoples. Such attacks provided an alternative to subsistence production, a way of making up deficits in the combatants' own supplies. The participation of direct producers in these raids limited the extent to which they could be exploited, protecting them from certain forms of surplus extraction by the dominant class or state institutions of their own society. It also mitigated against the formation of a warrior elite supported either by plunder or by the tribute payments of a subordinated class of direct producers.

This perspective emphasizes the relations between tributary states, whose dominant classes were frequently unable to appropriate goods and labor in sufficient amounts from their own direct producers, and neighboring communities. Some of these neighboring groups were probably class-stratified, but others remained kin-organized groups that were relatively autonomous or were allied, to varying degrees, with communities that were quite similar to themselves. The states focused on these villages and local communities when they attempted to exact goods and labor from their members. Tribute extraction deformed the kin organization of the communities as their members and the state struggled to control the conditions of production and distribution. Social relations within the communities were transformed and enmeshed in new forms of social reproduction and resistance.

The south coast of Peru provides information about the interrelations of

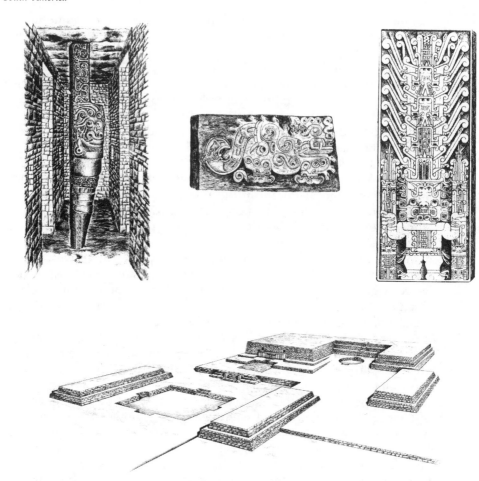

Perspective representation of the mid first-millennium B.C. structures and sculptures at Chavin de Huantar in the north highlands of Peru.

state formation and ethnogenesis. During the second century B.C., the inhabitants of the Ica and Nazca valleys were subject to influences from two state-based societies: the Pucará in the northern Lake Titicaca Basin and Topará on the south-central coast of Peru. Judging by shared iconographic themes and artistic preferences, they were more closely involved at this time with the distant Pucará state than with the neighboring Topará polity. The oculate being—a mythical figure—was depicted in the art styles of the south coast communities as well as in the contemporary materials from the Titicaca Basin and Marajo Island at the mouth of the Amazon River; however, it was not found in the Topará styles. The polychrome pottery used in the Pucará polity and by the inhabitants of Nazca and Ica is easily distinguished from each other and contrasts markedly with the monochrome Topará ceramics.

Groups on the margins of the Topará state had continually shifting affiliations during the period of its dominance. For example, the inhabitants of the upper Ica and Pisco valleys, who were independent when the state crystallized during the second century B.C., were enmeshed in its tributary relations a century later. This condition persisted until the beginning of the second century A.D., when their inhabitants were incorporated into a state-based society, centered 60 miles south in the Nazca Valley, that emerged following the collapse of the Pucará polity. When the Nazca state disintegrated about A.D. 250, these communities were once again allied with or incorporated into the Topará state.

Class and state formation followed a different trajectory on the north coast. An urban culture crystallized in the lower Virú Valley during the first century B.C. when 30,000 residential structures were erected within a few decades in the Gallinazo Group. The valley's irrigation system was also enlarged, and fortresses were built on hills overlooking portions of the river where water was diverted into large canals.

A major episode of class and state formation began about A.D. 350. It coincided with the collapse of Topará and witnessed the consolidation of agrarian, tributary states centered in Nazca, around Lima on the central coast, and in the Nepeña-Moche-Lambayeque region of the north coast. Evidence for both raiding and for class stratification is more pronounced than it had been earlier. Elaborately furnished tombs dating to this period were recently excavated at Sipan in the Lambayeque Valley. At Pachacamac, near Lima, an individual was interred with oversized grave goods and more than one hundred retainers.

These states derived their revenues from labor. Since the wealth of their ruling classes depended on the control of labor and, ultimately, on extending the agricultural base, the administrative and economic restructuring that occurred during their formation and subsequent development was organized primarily to assess and collect tribute from subject communities. Some of the labor appropriated was used to weave textiles, which were put in storehouses; to build pyramids; or to expand existing water-management systems.

The class-stratified Moche, Lima, and Nazca societies that flourished in coastal Peru are usually portrayed as being relatively homogeneous entities. Such representations implicitly accept the dominant ideology thesis: the idea that social order is promoted and maintained when all layers of a class-stratified society have the same beliefs, values, and culture. There are two versions of this thesis. One is that the beliefs of the dominant class have swamped and infected the consciousness of the subordinate groups so that the culture of the society constitutes a seamless whole. The other is that the ruling class, although its members are unable to promote a homogeneous culture shared by all classes, can prevent the subordinate groups from developing countercultures and counterideologies. A frequent corollary of the dominant ideology thesis is that since religion was intimately linked with the state and served to safeguard the interests of the ruling class and the state, its institutions and practices were uniform throughout the society and reflected in some mediated way the interests of both the dominant class and the state.

Characterizations that create illusions about the uniformity of the archaeological records left by these tributary states are misleading. For example, different arrays of pottery were produced and used in the northern and southern regions of Moche society during the fourth and fifth centuries; this diversity has led some archaeologists to question whether the two regions had common political institutions and practices or whether they constituted separate states, a northern one centered in Lambayeque and a southern one centered in Moche. On the central coast, there were at least four, and possibly as many as eight, pottery-making centers that produced vessels for different regional communities.

In class-stratified societies, like Moche, where there may have been kin-based groups within the ruling class that competed for political power and control of the state apparatus, we should expect to find evidence of their attempts to legitimate their claims by evoking historical depth and continuity, that is, by constructing a heritage and representing it on various objects. In fact, Moche Valley potters imitated earlier representations of particular cult-associated, supernatural beings to create or promote an illusion about the continuity of old institutions and practices. They did so not once but twice: first in the late fourth or early fifth century and again during the sixth century. The imitation of something old and its incorporation into new contexts is called archaism. It seems to be especially common during major episodes of class and state formation, when people are making their own histories and the existing social order is actively being decomposed and reconstituted. Archaeologists have documented a number of instances of archaism in ancient Peru. The earliest archaisms known so far occurred during the second century B.C., when the inhabitants of the fortified villages in the middle Ica Valley revived stylistic features from pottery vessels used two centuries earlier; this revival occurred at the time when their neighbors in the upper valley were being encapsulated by the Topará state.

The states that developed during the fifth and sixth centuries—both on the Peruvian coast and in highland areas like Huamachuco, Huari, or Tiahuanaco at the southern end of the Lake Titicaca Basin—were based on production for local use or consumption. Their subsistence economies were dominated by the agriculture sector, while pastoralism and fishing varied in importance from one state to another. These states were mainly organized to collect tribute either in labor or in kind from direct producers. When tribute was extracted in kind, a relatively narrow range of goods from direct producers was demanded. For example, when the pastoral communities of the upper Mantaro Valley were incorporated into the Huari state during the early seventh century, pastoral production was disrupted and its importance diminished significantly as the herders were transformed into farmers. The taxes levied on the local communities were apparently based on agricultural rather than pastoral production and labor.

The transformation of the Mantaro pastoralists into farmers, who produced the same range of goods as subject populations in the core area of the Huari state, focuses attention on the form of state revenues. It suggests that

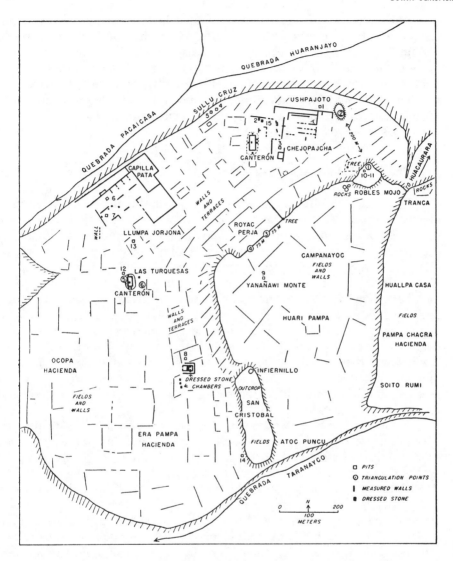

Plan showing the unexcavated compounds at Huari, Peru—an important middle and late first-millennium A.D. settlement and capital in the south-central highlands of Peru.

the Huari state was less concerned with gaining access to something that was not readily available in its core area than with reorganizing the subsistence economy of encapsulated or subjugated communities so that they would provide greater quantities of those goods already produced for and desired by the state. The Huari state was not intent on creating a highly differentiated subsistence economy in which surplus revenues moved toward the metropolitan area. The goods produced by encapsulated communities and subject populations were apparently used or consumed locally. This practice meant that the various regions incorporated into the state were economically self-sufficient. It suggests also that they had the capacity to be politically autonomous as well, especially when disgruntled peasants and their local leaders threatened or disassembled the veneer of state power. Thus, the political economies of states, like Huari or Tiahuanaco, were easily fragmented and could be reconstituted around autonomous productive regions. This is part of the reason why Andean states, including the Inca Empire, were so short-lived.

The Inca Empire and Resistance

The Inca state that crystallized in the Central Andes during the fifteenth century displays the never-ending dance between centralizing tendencies and centrifugal forces that minimize the possibility of dominating structures and practices becoming permanent fixtures. Around 1400, the Incas were merely one of a number of small, class-stratified polities in the Peruvian highlands. They raided neighboring communities, stealing food and kidnapping their members; however, they were not able to extract either goods or labor from their neighbors in a regular or systematic fashion. New forms of exploitation appeared in the 1430s, when the Incas established permanent garrisons and overseers in neighboring areas to ensure that the inhabitants contributed the labor power demanded by the Inca state. Extending the conditions of exploitation to neighboring communities was the ruling class's attempt to resolve internal contradictions within the ruling class and between its members and the direct producers in Inca society.

Each successive generation of the Inca ruling class had to devise new ways of extracting labor and products from the communities incorporated into an imperial state that grew explosively between 1438 and the 1470s and was still expanding, though much more slowly, in the early 1500s. Pachakuti 'Inka Yupanki, the first ruler of the imperial state, secured the loyalty of his collateral relatives by allowing them to extort labor from the inhabitants of the core areas of the empire. As a result, subsequent rulers were forced to seek wealth—that is, land and labor—in areas and among peoples they incorporated into the state. Thus, Topa 'Inka, the second emperor, who came to prominence in the 1460s and died in the early 1490s, extended his own power and that of the Inca state northward into Ecuador and southward to central Chile and northwestern Argentina. He acquired estates and forged alliances with the traditional leaders of polities and spokespersons of powerful shrines located outside the old core area of the empire. He appropriated land and servants for his own use as well as for the state, for his collateral relatives, and most especially for his allies. His son, Wayna Qhapaq, who succeeded him on the throne and ruled until his death in the late 1520s, established estates in the frontier areas incorporated into the state during his reign and around the imperial capital because of the alliances he was able to forge, through his mother's kin, with subordinate factions of the Inca ruling class. He also consolidated his power and that of the state through the state management of lands seized from subject populations, the creation of a professionalized army whose members were full-time soldiers, personal servitude to the state, and grants of private estates to kin and allies.

The composition of the ruling class was in flux as successive rulers devised new ways of extracting labor from subject communities. In the process of creating alliances with the traditional leaders of recently subjugated peoples, the rulers transformed them into local representatives of the state and often cemented the alliances by marrying their sisters or daughters. The

Plan of the Inca capital, Cuzco, Peru.

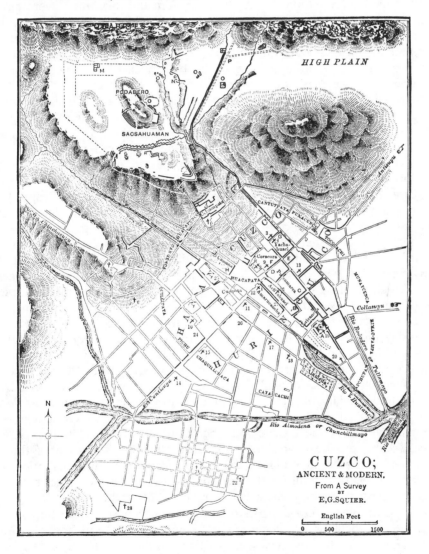

offspring of these unions belonged to the royal corporation of their fathers and, hence, had a legitimate claim on its wealth. The offspring of unions with women from other factions of the Inca ruling class also belonged to their corporations and had legitimate claims to the throne itself. The second emperor also established close ties with the spokespersons of powerful shrines in central Peru, which benefited materially from their alliance with the Inca ruler and state. As a result, the dominant class of the empire increasingly came to consist of individuals and institutions from various communities who were not Incas by birth and whose interests and activities were linked but not necessarily identical with those of the state.

At the same time that the composition of the dominant class was being transformed, new middle layers, distinct from the peasantry, were also emerging. They comprised various categories of retainers, specialists, and resident colonists who were detached from their kin in subjugated polities and separated from their traditional means of production. Some were attached to the corporate landholding groups established by each Inca ruler; others were assigned to state institutions, shrines, and ethnic chieftains. They became increasingly dependent on the state, and those groups and institutions incorporated into the emerging dominant class, for the production and reproduction of their lives; their traditional relations of production and reproduction were transformed as new patterns of dependency developed.

The state pursued a number of policies to establish conditions that permitted it to appropriate land and labor from subject populations and to obscure the fact that their customary modes of production and reproduction were being dramatically transformed in the process. These included resident tax collectors and inspectors in the provinces, military garrisons, resettled colonists, strategic hamlets, cooption of traditional leaders, educational instruction for future leaders, holding traditional leaders for ransom, a particularly repressive legal code, and the ever-present threat of armed reprisals and the implementation of scorched-earth policies. The state even attempted to recast the myths and practices of encapsulated communities, which prescribed proper behavior and perpetuated socially acceptable explanations of everyday life; however, these efforts were never completely successful.

Although the Inca state attempted to intervene in the everyday lives of subject populations to ensure compliance with its demands, its capacity to do so effectively and successfully was hampered in significant ways by the virtual impossibility of rapid communication over the long distances separating the imperial capital from the provincial centers. This capacity was also limited by the political structures the state put together in the provincial areas. Although the governors were close allies and kinsmen of the ruler, members of the dominant class, the layers of provincial administration immediately below them built on the existing local social and political hierarchies, incorporating them into the decimal organization of the state.

Border wars were a persistent feature of imperial expansion into new territories; rebellions erupted unexpectedly; and civil wars were an integral part of everyday life, especially after the death of an emperor. Clearly, not all of the communities on the margins of the state or even those already incorporated into it recognized the value of *pax incaica*, acknowledged the superiority of Inca beliefs and norms, viewed imperial demands in the same way as coopted traditional leaders, or were at times even particularly intimidated by the force the state could muster or the severity of its legal code. The consequence was that the Inca state was engaged almost continuously in armed struggle from before its inception in 1438 through the Spanish invasion in 1532 to its final collapse in the 1570s; relatively tranquil conditions prevailed for about a decade during this period. Revolts in the frontier regions and rebellions in the core areas were often sparked by rumors of the emperor's death and by the civil disruption caused by the successional disputes that inevitably followed. As a result, the state frequently had to reconquer peoples that had already been incorporated into the empire.

Civil unrest or rebellions in the borderlands usually broke out when the state suffered setbacks in its domestic or foreign policies or when it attempted to impose new forms of surplus extraction. For instance, when Huarco successfully resisted Inca efforts to incorporate it into the imperial state in the late 1470s, other groups rebelled when its forces were not immediately defeated. The state was forced not only to continue its struggle with Huarco, which ultimately lasted three years, but also to suppress the unrest it fomented among other peoples. The state reproached these groups for the resistance they displayed and urged them to remain loyal friends or else they would be visited by a cruel war. At the same time, it enlarged the garrison located in the foothills on the edge of Huarco.

Class and state formation in frontier areas created contradictions and opportunities not only for the empire but also for the indigenous people. It led to the constitution of new alliances, the merging of formerly independent communities into new groups, and even the appearance of border states where none had existed before, as people recognized their shared position in the emerging system of production and examined the implications of such infringements on their traditional use-rights and practices. This does not mean that all frontier communities automatically opposed the state either passively or actively; in a number of them, both the peasants and their leaders benefited materially, though differentially, from their new dependent relationship with the empire. Even though the frontier policies of the Incas were narrow, they succeeded in many instances in transforming customary use-rights, in separating traditional leaders from their kin or subjects, in linking the fortunes of subject groups with those of the state, and in recasting old enmities so that communities remained pitted against one another and their neighbors.

In his memoirs, written in 1571, Pedro Pizarro (1963:181) assessed the importance of the civil war for the Spaniards' cause.

> Had Wayna Qhapaq [the Inca ruler who died in the 1520s] been alive when we Spaniards entered this land it would have been impossible to win it. . . . Also, if the land had not been divided by the war between Washkar and 'Ataw

Wallpa [two of his sons with equal claims to the throne] we could not have entered or conquered it. . . .

The hegemony of the imperial state that existed when Wayna Qhapaq died collapsed in less than a decade. It was rapidly replaced by a devastating civil war between factions of the imperial ruling class; a series of insurrections along the frontiers, as recently encapsulated peoples fought to reassert their autonomy; and an invasion by foreigners, whose numbers and influence grew steadily after 1532. By 1536, segments of the old ruling class had transformed the civil war into a protracted, armed struggle whose goal was to dislodge the invading forces and to eliminate their hold on the native peoples. At the same time, the apparent unity of the outsiders crumbled as internal disputes erupted and plunged them headlong into their own civil war.

BEYOND THE FRONTIERS OF CIVILIZATION

Civilization—that is, state-based societies—is often portrayed as the end product of a line of historical development that culminates in the emergence of a form of social organization characterized by acquisition of social order and a certain level of refinement. It is typically contrasted with societies that lack its distinctive features—rule by law, writing, government, and the exploitation and oppression of their direct producers. Most South American societies outside the Andes were not afflicted with civilization before the sixteenth century; those that were infected generally succeeded in fighting off or reversing the appearance and crystallization of exploitative social relations. In some instances, communities accomplished this goal with their feet. They simply moved to new localities to avoid having their gifts transformed into tribute that was expected and demanded at periodic intervals. This response was pervasive in the sixteenth century, when communities in southern Colombia retreated to remote areas to avoid taxation; when Guarani-speaking peoples left their homes in search of a world where exploitation and domination were not aspects of everyday life; and when escaped slaves joined indigenous peoples in the Caribbean, Mexico, and the Andes to resist the exactions of the emerging colonial regimes.

This means that many of the communities outside the Andean area were typically structured by variants of the communal mode of production. It does not mean that all of them exhibited egalitarian social relations. Many, in fact, were rank- or estate-ordered, and bigmen and -women certainly appeared in border areas of the Inca state to profit from the new conditions created by the sudden juxtaposition of state-based and kin-organized societies. These were the frontier merchants, the cultural brokers, who enhanced their own position among the border peoples by trafficking with the state. They were the intermediaries in the process of surplus extraction, who transferred labor and goods received as gifts by local chieftains to the ruling class and institutions of the Inca state, usually in designated marketplaces. They profited by returning goods to the local chieftains or by redistributing them directly to their clients in the borderland communities. Their position ultimately depended on their ability to ensure that the flow of goods from the state continued. When they failed to do so, their followers aligned themselves with others who could provide the exotic items.

Mercantile states, whose revenues derived from controlling trade or taxing merchants, flourished episodically on the margins of agrarian states. In the Andes, they may be discerned in areas like northern Ecuador, when it was on the periphery of the Inca Empire, or perhaps in the Atacama Desert of northern Chile and in the Hualfín Valley of northwestern Argentina, when the inhabitants of these areas lived on the margins of the Tiwanaku state during the sixth and seventh centuries. If the agrarian states were expanding, as was the Inca state during the fifteenth century, and enveloping frontier communities, enmeshing them into their web of tribute relations, then the actual geographical locations of the mercantile states on their peripheries may be displaced steadily outward from the core areas. Similar situations, of course, occurred in Europe during the fifteenth century; for example, Christopher Columbus, a merchant from Genoâ, moved to Lisbon and then Seville to ply his wares and seek his fortune in the slave trade.

To argue that the central Andean states were based on the control of labor rather than on commerce does not mean that trade was nonexistent. The members of various communities clearly trafficked in goods, sometimes far beyond their boundaries. What has not been satisfactorily demonstrated in these instances is that they trafficked in commodities—that is, goods that were deliberately produced for exchange. What appear to be more certain about the circulation of goods and ideas within and among pre-Incaic states were some of the conditions in which it occurred. Cults, shrines, and in some instances perhaps even pilgrimages provided one framework that permitted this kind of horizontal integration. The observation of classicists that "gods travel on the backs of people who are also engaged in other activities" is appropriate for Andean societies as well.

FURTHER READINGS: A BRIEF GUIDE

The articles in Jesse D. Jenning, ed., *Ancient South Americans* (San Francisco: W. H. Freeman, 1983), provide an overview to the archaeology of South America.

The advent of food production is discussed by Michael E. Moseley, *The Maritime Foundations of Andean Civilization* (Menlo Park, CA: Cummings Publishing Company, 1975) and *Pre-Agricultural Coastal Civilizations of Peru* (Burlington, VT: Carolina Biological Supply Company, 1978); Jeffrey Quilter and Terry Stocker, "Subsistence Economies and the Origins of Andean Complex Societies," *American Anthropologist*, vol. 85, no. 3 (1983), 545–562; David J. Wilson, "Of Maize and Men: A Critique of the Maritime Hypothesis of

State Origins on the Coast of Peru," *American Anthropologist*, vol. 83, no. 1 (1981), 83–120; Jeffrey Quilter, *Life and Death at Paloma: Society and Mortuary Practices in a Preceramic Peruvian Village* (Iowa City: University of Iowa Press, 1988); Thomas C. Patterson, "The Historical Development of a Coastal Andean Social Formation in Central Peru, 6000 to 500 B.C.," in *Investigations of the Andean Past*, ed. Daniel Sandweiss (Ithaca, NY: Latin American Studies Program, Cornell University, 1983), pp. 21–37; Robert Benfer, "The Challenges and Rewards of Sedentism: The Preceramic Village of Paloma, Peru," in *Paleopathology at the Origins of Agriculture*, ed. Mark N. Cohen and George J. Armelagos (New York: Academic Press, 1984), pp. 531–558; Richard L. Burger, "The U-Shaped Pyramid Complex, Cardal, Peru," *National Geographic Research*, vol. 3, no. 3 (1987), 363–375; and Robert A. Feldman, "Preceramic Corporate Architectural Evidence for the Development of Non-Egalitarian Social Systems in Coastal Peru," in *Early Ceremonial Architecture in the Andes*, ed. Christopher B. Donnan (Washington, DC: Dumbarton Oaks Research Library and Collection, 1985), pp. 71–92.

Class and state formation in the central Andes are examined by Jonathan Haas, Sheila Pozorski, and Thomas Pozorski, eds., *The Origins and Development of the Andean State* (Cambridge: Cambridge University Press, 1987); Thomas C. Patterson, "Class and State Formation: The Case of Pre-Incaic Peru," *Dialectical Anthropology*, vol. 10, no. 3–4 (1966), 275–282; Richard L. Burger, "Unity and Heterogeneity within the Chavín Horizon," in *Peruvian Prehistory*, ed. Richard W. Keatinge (Cambridge: Cambridge University Press, 1988), pp. 99–144; Elías Mujica, "*Altiplano*-coast Relationships in the South-central Andes: From Indirect to Direct Complementarity," in *Andean Ecology and Civilization: An Interdisciplinary Perspective on Andean Ecological Complementarity*, ed. Shozo Masuda, Izumi Shimada, and Craig Morris (Tokyo: University of Tokyo, 1985), pp. 103–140; Dwight T. Wallace, "The Topará Tradition: An Overview," in *Perspectives on Andean Prehistory and Protohistory*, ed. Daniel Sandweiss and D. Peter Kvietok (Ithaca, NY: Latin American Studies Program, Cornell University, 1986), pp. 35–48; Thomas C. Patterson, John P. McCarthy, and Robert A. Dunn, "Polities in the Lurín Valley, Peru during the Early Intermediate Period," *Ñawpa Pacha*, vol. 20 (1982), 61–82; Donald Proulx, "Cultural Relationships between the Ica and Nazca Valleys, Peru during the Early Intermediate Period," paper presented at the annual meeting of the Society for American Archaeology, Reno, NV 1966; Walter Alva, "Discovering the New World's Richest Unlooted Tomb," *National Geographic*, vol. 174, no. 4 (1988), 510–550; Richard P. Schaedel, "The Transition from Chiefdom to State in Northern Peru," in *Development and Decline: The Evolution of Sociopolitical Organization*, ed. Henri J. M. Claessen, Pieter van de Velde, and M. Estellie Smith (South Hadley, MA: Bergen & Garvey, 1985), pp. 156–169; David L. Browman, "Demographic Correlations of the Wari Conquest of Junin," *American Antiquity*, vol. 41, no. 4 (1976), 465–477, and "New Light on Andean Tiwanaku," *American Scientist*, vol. 69, no. 4 (1981), 408–419; William H. Isbell, "El origen del estado en el valle de Ayacucho," *Revista Andina*, no. 3 (1985), 57–106; Dorothy Menzel, "Style and Time in the Middle Horizon,"

Ñawpa Pacha, vol. 2 (1964), 1–105, and "New Data on the Huari Empire in Middle Horizon Epoch 2A," *Ñawpa Pacha*, vol. 6 (1966), 57–114; and Alan L. Kolata, "The Agricultural Foundations of Tiwanaku: A View from the Heartland," *American Antiquity*, vol. 51, no. 4 (1986), 748–762, and "Tiwanaku and Its Hinterland," *Archaeology*, vol. 40, no. 1 (1987), 36–41.

For the Inca state, see John Hemming, *The Conquest of the Incas* (New York: Harcourt Brace Jovanovich, 1970); John Hyslop, *Inkawasi, the New Cuzco, Cañete, Lunahuaná, Peru*, British Archaeological Reports, International Series no. S234 (Oxford, 1985); Friedrich Katz, *The Ancient American Civilizations* (London: Weidenfeld & Nicolson, 1966); Dorothy Menzel, "The Inca Occupation of the South Coast of Peru," *Southwestern Journal of Anthropology*, vol. 15, no. 2 (1959), 125–142; Dorothy Menzel and John H. Rowe, "The Role of Chincha in Late Pre-Spanish Peru," *Ñawpa Pacha*, vol. 4 (1966), 63–76; Sally F. Moore, *Power and Property in Inca Peru* (New York: Columbia University Press, 1958); Craig Morris, "State Settlements in Tawantinsuyu: A Strategy of Compulsory Urbanism," in *Contemporary Archaeology: A Guide to Theory and Contributions*, ed. Mark Leone (Carbondale: Southern Illinois University Press, 1972), pp. 49–60, and "The Infrastructure of Inka Control in the Peruvian Central Highlands," in *The Inca and Aztec States, 1400–1800: Anthropology and History*, ed. George A. Collier, Renato I. Rosaldo, and John D. Wirth (New York: Academic Press, 1982), pp. 153–171; John V. Murra, "Social Structural and Economic Themes in Andean Ethnohistory," *Anthropological Quarterly*, vol. 34, no. 2 (1961), 47–59, "New Data on Retainer and Servile Populations in Tawantinsuyu," *Actas y memorias del XXXVI Congreso Internacional de Americanistas, Sevilla, 1964*, tomo II, (Madrid: Instituto "Gonzalo Fernandez de Oviedo," 1966), pp. 35–45, and *The Economic Organization of the Inka State*, Research in Economic Anthropology, Supplement 1 (Greenwich, CT: JAI Press, 1980); Thomas C. Patterson, *The Inca Empire: The Formation and Disintegration of a Pre-capitalist State* (Oxford: Berg Publishers, 1991), "Pachacamac— An Andean Oracle under Inca Rule," in *Recent Studies in Andean Prehistory and Protohistory*, ed. Daniel Sandweiss and D. Peter Kvietok (Ithaca, NY: Latin American Studies Program, Cornell University, 1985), pp. 159–176, and "Merchant Capital and the Formation of the Inca State," *Dialectical Anthropology*, vol. 12, no. 2 (1987), 217–227; Pedro Pizarro, "Relación del descubrimiento y conquista de los reinos del Perú," *Biblioteca de Autores Españoles*, tomo 168 (Madrid: Ediciones Atlas, 1963), pp. 161–244; María Rostworowski de Diez Canseco, "Succession, Coöption to Kingship, and Royal Incest among the Incas," *Southwestern Journal of Anthropology*, vol. 16, no. 4 (1960), 417–427, and *Historia del Tawantinsuyu* (Lima: Instituto de Estudios Peruanos, 1988); John H. Rowe, "Inca Culture at the Time of the Spanish Conquest," in *Handbook of South American Indians*, Bureau of American Ethnology Bulletin 145, ed. Julian H. Steward, vol. 2 (Washington, DC, 1946), pp. 183–330, "The Kingdom of Chimor," *Acta Americana*, tomo VI, no. 1–2 (1948), 26–59, and "The Origins of Inca Creator Worship," in *Culture in History: Essays in Honor of Paul Radin*, ed. Stanley Diamond (New York: Columbia University Press, 1960); Frank Salomon, "Pochteca and Mindalá: A Comparison of Long-distance Traders in

Ecuador and Mesoamerica," *Journal of the Steward Anthropological Society*, vol. 9, no. 2 (Urbana, 1978), pp. 231–246, and *Native Lords of Quito in the Age of the Incas: Political Economy of a North Andean Chiefdom* (Cambridge: Cambridge University Press, 1986); Janet Sherbondy, "Les réseaux d'irrigation dans la géographie politique de Cuzco," *Journal de la Société des Américanistes*, tome LXVI (Paris, 1977), pp. 45–66; Irene Silverblatt, "Andean Women in Inca Society," *Feminist Studies*, vol. 4, no. 3 (1978), 37–61, *Moon, Sun, and Witches: Gender Ideologies and Class in Inca and Colonial Peru* (Princeton, NJ: Princeton University Press, 1987), and "Imperial Dilemmas, the Politics of Kinship, and Inca Reconstructions of History," *Comparative Studies in Society and History*, vol. 30, no. 1 (1988), 83–102; Karen Spalding, "Social Climbers: Changing Patterns of Nobility among the Indians of Colonial Peru," *Hispanic American Historical Review*, vol. L, no. 4 (1970), 645–664, "Kurakas and Commerce: A Chapter in the Evolution of Andean Society," *Hispanic American Historical Review*, vol. LIII, no. 4 (1973), 581–599, and *Huarochirí: An Andean Society under Inca and Spanish Rule* (Stanford, CA: Stanford University Press, 1984); and Tom R. Zuidema, *The Ceque System of Cuzco: The Social Organization of the Capital of the Inca* (Leiden, Neth.: E. J. Brill, 1964), and "Hierarchy and Space in Incaic Social Organization," *Ethnohistory*, vol. 30, no. 2 (1983), 49–75.

For a discussion of exchange relations between the Andes and the eastern lowlands, see Donald W. Lathrap, Angelika Gebart-Sayer, and Ann M. Mester, "The Roots of the Shipibo Art Style: Three Waves on Imiríracocha, or There Were 'Incas' before the Incas," *Journal of Latin American Lore*, vol. 11, no. 1 (1985), 31–119.

chapter 16

Civilization and Its Discontents: The Archaeology of Capitalism

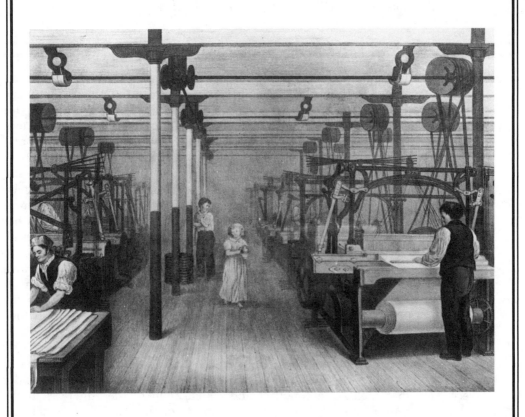

The price we pay for our advance in civilization is a loss of happiness. . . . (Sigmund Freud, Civilization and Its Discontents*)*

It is hard to call capitalism successful, when two-thirds of the world's people live in poverty. (placard, Guadalajara, Mexico, July 18, 1991)

The drive to political accumulation, *to* state building, *is the* pre-capitalist *analogue to the capitalist drive to* accumulate capital. *(Robert Brenner, "The Social Basis of Economic Development")*

The state is the distinctive collective misrepresentation of capitalist societies. . . . [It] is a bid to elicit support for or tolerance of the insupportable and intolerable by presenting them as something other than themselves, namely, legitimate, disinterested domination. The study of the state, seen thus, would begin with the cardinal activity involved in the presentation of the state: the legitimating of the illegitimate. (Philip Abrams, "Notes on the Difficulty of Studying the State")

Capitalism as an economic system is concerned with the production and sale of commodities in markets. Commodities are goods that are produced for sale rather than use by the people who made them. The roots of modern capitalism lie in the sixteenth century with the expansion of commerce and markets that eventually enveloped the entire world. Commercial or merchant capital is different from the barter, or traffic in goods, that occurred, and still takes place, among precapitalist communities. In these societies, the circulation of goods is aimed at the satisfaction of wants or needs. In capitalist societies, the goal is making profit, the expansion of money value, rather than the pleasure of using or consuming the commodities acquired through exchange. In noncapitalist societies, if money is used at all, it is used to facilitate exchange. In capitalist societies, value is continually being transformed from money into commodities and then back into a larger sum of money; value becomes capital by virtue of the fact that it is involved in the process of expanding, of creating extra value. However, there is only one commodity that can actually create extra value: human labor power.

Thus, the origins of capitalism must also be sought in those activities that provided the money that permitted the early commercial capitalists to purchase human labor power. Two come immediately to mind: the plunder economy that fueled the conquest and colonization of the Americas in the sixteenth century and the rapid redevelopment of the African slave trade.

The antecedents for Spanish commercial expansion, colonization, and conquest in the Americas and North Africa are to be found in the political-economic events and developments that occurred on the Iberian Peninsula during the fifteenth century. These included (1) the decline of the

Mbanza, capital of the Kongo Kingdom and a source of war slaves, captives who were subsequently sold into slavery and shipped to islands in the Caribbean.

Mediterranean-oriented economies of Catalonia and Aragon and the emergence of Genoa as an important commercial center; (2) the growth of large ranch-based wool production in Castile and export to textile factories in Flanders; (3) the expansion of shipbuilding on Spain's north coast in conjunction with the wool trade; (4) the marriage of Isabella and Ferdinand, which linked the interests of two dynastic states; (5) the 1488–1492 civil war in Granada, the last Moorish state on the peninsula, which facilitated the final phase of the reconquest; and (6) Castile's demand for new sources of raw materials, slave labor, and finished goods.

The first expeditions to the Americas were commercial ventures. Although the Spanish crown provided no financial support for Columbus's first two voyages, it did grant him the post of governor-general and one-tenth of the merchandise it produced. However, his investors quickly lost confidence when he failed to produce the quantities of gold and silver he promised; the 2,000 native Americans he sold in the slave markets of Europe and the Canary Islands, which made him one of the world's largest slave dealers in the late 1490s, did not satisfy their desire for profits.

By the end of the century, other expeditions were organized, fi-

Olandus carauellam, & cafas ædificare curat.　XIX.

VERAGVA PARS.

Shipbuilding in Panama during the early 16th century.

nanced, and sent out to search for gold. The locus of their activities gradually expanded from the islands to the "pearl coast" of Venezuela and then to Mexico and Peru. In 1519, Hernán Cortés, who led the expedition against the Aztec state, sent gifts from the Mexican ruler and plunder to the Spanish court. In 1532, Francisco Pizarro, who led the Spanish expedition against the Inca state, kidnapped the Inca ruler and held him for ransom. The amount of gold, silver, and precious jewels collected to pay the ransom exceeded anything previously encountered in the Americas: more than 13,400 pounds of pure gold and 26,000 pounds of pure silver. At today's prices, the ransom amounted to $86 million. If this were viewed as a loan with a 10 percent interest rate, which is lower than the rates charged by the International Monetary Fund and the World Bank, Spain and the other states that profited from the ransom now owe the Andean people about $860,000,000,000,000,000,000,000,000,000, or 86×10^{25}. It is important to note that the ransom constituted only a small fraction of 1

An early 17th-century representation of the execution and mutilation of the Inca ruler, Ataw Wallpa, by Pizarro and his soldiers of fortune.

percent of the gold and silver that were extorted from the Andean peoples before 1600.

The gold and silver mined in the Americas with forced Indian labor provided the bulk of the money that fueled the European economies during the sixteenth and seventeenth centuries. The 50 million to 100 million people who were forcibly removed against their will from Africa between about 1450 and 1800 and sold into slavery provided enormous amounts of labor power, which created surplus value for their owners and for capitalist merchants and bankers.

The unevenness of the political economies and cultural practices of Europe were also being reconstituted and reorganized by 1600. Merchant and finance capital flourished in Holland and the city-states of the Hanseatic League. The producers of woolen goods in Flanders and England began to

An early 17th-century representation of a mining center in
the highlands of south-central Peru.

challenge those in northern Italy for control of the European market. Peasant
farmers in England were being stripped of their means of production as
common lands were expropriated and enclosed by local members of the
ruling class; those in eastern Europe were once again being enmeshed in
tributary relations that bound them to the estates of large landowners, who
acquired grain and other agricultural produce for markets throughout Europe. As the European economies were becoming increasingly differentiated
and interconnected, power relations and cultural practices were also transformed. In various parts of central Europe north of the Alps, as well as in
Scandinavia and England, members of newly emerging power blocs used
Protestantism to challenge the power of the established ruling class and its
linkages with the Catholic church.

   This struggle for power took different forms and had various outcomes
at different times and places. In eastern Europe—Poland, the Ukraine, and

Prussia—the large, noble landowners succeeded in passing laws that severely restricted the mobility of independent peasant households and subjected them to heavier levies. In the sixteenth century, they also promulgated laws that "rationalized" the spatial organization of peasant villages to make them more productive; these laws effectively disrupted community-level social relations and production, alienated households from their neighbors, and separated the village communities from their lands and means of production. Serfdom was reestablished in eastern Europe when the large landowners created new forms of tributary states and employed extra-economic means to extract agricultural labor and money from peasant households, which were increasingly bound to the land. Power—ownership of land and instruments of production and control of various legal institutions and practices—became concentrated in the hands of a progressively smaller number of feudal lords, who exchanged the agricultural produce extracted from servile populations for items manufactured in northwestern Europe and the Mediterranean. Thus, the refeudalization of eastern Europe created conditions for the growth of manufactures in western Europe at the same time as it diminished the demand for those goods in the market towns on the Baltic where east European grain was sold.

The struggle for power erupted into a civil war in southern England in the 1640s, which pitted the king and his supporters, mostly landowners from the north and west, against an unstable alliance of townsfolk, Presbyterian merchants, artisans, and independent yeoman farmers. Once the monarchists were defeated and the state bureaucracy weakened, the allies quickly found themselves at odds with one another. The merchants, many of whom purchased landed estates, claimed a position of privilege, which would allow them to extract labor and goods from the yeoman farmers and their neighbors in the towns as the king had done; the peasants and artisans, who made up the Levellers and Diggers, demanded the distribution of land; political equality; and the reestablishment of the village communities, whose very existence was already being threatened. Their demands were crushed in the 1650s by the powerful townspeople and the old large landowners, who then proceeded to conquer Ireland and Scotland in order to open them to English traders.

The Navigation Act, which was promulgated in 1651, underwrote English commercial expansion during the next century, the construction of a large merchant fleet and strong navy, and wars with Holland and Spain. Other legislation abolished feudal land tenures, taxed some of the royalists almost out of existence, and confiscated the lands of a steadily growing number of yeomen farmers, thereby creating a class of landless individuals who were separated from the means of production and driven increasingly into wage labor to support themselves and their families. The monarchy was restored in 1660, but the new king ruled in name only, for real power was held by the large merchants and squires and administered through their representatives.

The dynamic created by the linkage of economically specialized regions—

the accumulation of gold and silver by Spain; the export agriculture of eastern Europe; and the merchants, bankers, and commodity producers of northwestern Europe—promoted uneven development even further during the seventeenth and eighteenth centuries. In England, some of the large landowners hired laborers to mine peat, coal, and minerals to meet a growing demand for fuel and metal; some of the large merchants purchased looms and rented them to peasant households to produce cloth, which they subsequently purchased and sold in the market; and some of the commodity producers, who already owned looms and other means of production, hired wage workers to manufacture cloth and other goods, which they took to markets and sold directly for money without the intervention of merchants.

The activities of the merchants and the petty producers both promoted the production of commodities for the market and provided underpinnings for the development of industrial capitalism. However, a closer examination of their circumstances reveals a difference of fundamental importance between the merchants and those owners who sold goods produced by their employees. The former derived their income by purchasing finished goods cheap and selling them at a profit in the market. The latter appropriated part of the value created by their workers during the production process; they realized these profits once the commodities were sold. The activities of the merchants added no value to goods already produced; those of the commodity producer, the incipient industrial capitalist, did.

This practice laid the foundations for the Industrial Revolution in northwestern Europe, especially in England, where there was already a large number of yeoman farmers, artisans, and wage workers who purchased and sold food and other commodities in their local markets. The landscapes of England and other regions in the northwest were irrevocably transformed during the eighteenth and early nineteenth centuries as forests were cleared; roads and canals were built; and factory towns, like Manchester, appeared almost overnight and grew explosively into large, unhealthy industrial cities with smoke-belching chimneys, dangerous workplaces, and slums that contained and constrained unbelievably impoverished men, women, and children.

The producers of woolen textiles and the cloth made from cotton grown in India and Egypt and on slave plantations in the Caribbean and American South competed with one another to increase their share of the local and national markets and to expand their profits. In capitalist production, merely maintaining the same share of a market of fixed size is not sufficient since the motor driving this mode of production necessitates continual economic growth—that is, larger shares of the market or larger markets created by the incorporation of new consumers into their relations. The competition also led the early industrial capitalists to seek new ways of reducing their costs to maximize their profits. They accomplished this by replacing their male employees with increasing numbers of women and children, who were paid significantly lower wages for longer workdays. They also began to purchase new kinds of machines and to organize their factories in ways that increased

The mass production of pens.

productivity and allowed them to produce more goods in the same amount time for the same or lower labor costs. The demand for greater productivity is the basis for the steadily increasing rate of technological innovation during the last two centuries. This is one of the truly distinctive features of industrial capitalism; it is not characteristic of any precapitalist mode of production.

The English state supported the early industrialists' desire for ever-expanding markets through overseas expansion and colonization. It suppressed other industrial revolutions—that is, the industrialization and development of local industries—in colonies that were already enmeshed in its webs of tributary relations; for instance, local textile production was virtually destroyed in India and Egypt and prevented from crystallizing in the North American colonies before they broke away and proclaimed their political independence in 1776. England also supported various revolutionary movements in Latin America during the early nineteenth century in order to pry the Spanish colonies away from European masters. Although this practice culminated in the political independence and formation of a number of autonomous states in the New World, it also led to their incorporation into a free trade market that was dominated and virtually monopolized in many areas until the 1890s by English merchants, whose activities were sustained by the power of the imperial state and its navy.

A second phase of industrialization began to develop around 1850, first in England and then in the United States, Germany, and France. It involved the manufacture of large amounts of iron and steel, chemicals, and machines that were used to produce other commodities. Its success depended on the development of new mining technologies, the construction of railroads, and the demand for machines and capital goods in states whose industrial development lagged behind that of England. This phase of the Industrial Revolution was propelled by the need to invest the enormous amounts of capital accumulated during the preceding century in new, profitable ventures. For instance, railroad construction between 1850 and 1880 stimulated the development of iron and steel industries in the industrializing countries and opened areas like the prairies of the American Midwest or the pampas of Argentina to export agriculture. The railway systems built in countries on the margins of the capitalist world opened them to foreign markets and laid the foundations for the development of extractive industries, mining and monocrop export agriculture; these often followed in the wake of military threats or armed incursions that broke the invaded countries' resistance, as was the case in China, Japan, and Cuba.

The heavy industries that appeared after 1850 required enormous capital investments in comparison to those of the early phase of the Industrial Revolution. This change meant that the firms producing these capital goods were better financed and larger than their predecessors; it also meant that there were generally fewer of them. Whereas a hundred firms might have competed for a share of textile trade fifty years earlier, only two or three firms might have possessed the financial resources to produce steel and compete for a share of that market. In other words, capital was becoming increasingly concentrated in the hands of a continually shrinking number of firms that were getting larger and larger with the passage of time. These firms made use of new products and stimulated technological innovation; they also promoted the expansion of science and engineering and fostered the reorganization of work, transforming the spatial arrangement of the workplace and the pace at which labor was performed in order to gain and exercise more control over the labor processes.

Increasing numbers of unskilled workers were drawn to the developing industries from the rural and nonindustrialized areas of the capitalist countries as well as from foreign lands; growing numbers of skilled workers were employed to work the expensive equipment and machines housed in the new factories. The reconstitution of the industrial work force also involved the appearance of leadmen and supervisors, who organized and oversaw work practices and performances on the shop floor, and the extension and increased technical divisions of labor, which sharpened distinctions between manual and mental labor and between workers and managers. Thus in the industrialized states, there was some transfer of workers from lower- to higher-paying jobs; however, it did not ameliorate the squalid conditions and low standard of living experienced by most of the newly arrived immigrants, who toiled as unskilled factory workers, or those marginally employed or unemployed men, women, and children who eked out livelihoods in the informal or underground economies of industrial cities like Essen, Birmingham, or Pittsburgh.

The development of industrial capitalist economies in Europe and the United States during the nineteenth century involved the crystallization of three structural contradictions: (1) between owners and workers, (2) among

(a)

(b)

Immigration is an essential feature of capitalism. (a) European immigrants to the United States circa 1900; (b) Latin American and Southeast Asian immigrants in 1970s.

capitalists competing for control of the same market, and (3) between capitalists and the inhabitants of those precapitalist societies that were resisting absorption into capitalist markets or the incursion of extractive industries into their homelands. The first contradiction—that between capitalists who owned the means of production and workers who, by virtue of being separated from any means of production, were forced to sell their labor power to gain a livelihood—was intimately linked with class struggle. This was the motor that drove the development of trade unions, which sought to ameliorate the

dangerous and deplorable conditions in which many factory and farm workers toiled. The capitalist owners of industry have historically used their influence with state officials to suppress trade unions and the demands of their
workers; unions have historically sought to insert themselves in arenas of
debate and decision making controlled by the state to improve the working
conditions and quality of life of their members.

The second structural contradiction of the modern era is the one that
exists between the capitalist firms themselves. Although firms actually make
their profits in the production process, since only workers create value, they
realize, or acquire, these profits only after the commodities are sold in the
market. Historically, these markets have operated at different levels: regional,
national, and international. Some industrial firms produced largely for regional or national markets; others sold their commodities nationally and in
foreign markets. They entered into competition with one another during
these circuits of exchange. Competing firms used the judicial and legislative
apparatuses of states to gain control of markets located within particular
boundaries. This practice quickly strengthened the linkages between capitalist
firms and the states in which their factories were located. By the end of the
nineteenth century, economists and historians were already clear about the
existence of various national capitals—for example, those centered in England, Germany, France, or the United States. Typically, each capitalist state
passed legislation that protected local firms by prohibiting or taxing the sale
of goods produced in another country. This fueled the rise of nationalist
sentiments throughout the nineteenth and twentieth centuries. The combination of intercapitalist rivalries and nationalism underwrote two devastating
world wars during the twentieth century; this potent combination has the
capacity to underwrite a third war in the 1990s as the political-economic
circumstances of the United States, Europe, and Japan are transformed, as
they continue to struggle for markets, and as the hegemonic position that the
United States held after World War II continues to decline.

The creation of overseas empires by England, the United States, France,
Germany, Belgium, Italy, and Russia in the nineteenth century was one facet
of the third contradiction, the one between states with capitalist economies
and noncapitalist societies on the margins of those polities. The imperial
states secured political and economic control through military intervention,
conquest, and the support they gave their local representatives. The encapsulated peoples of the nineteenth-century colonies provided markets for goods
manufactured in the metropolitan centers and furnished them with a steady
supply of inexpensive raw materials, foodstuffs, and labor. Areas inhabited
by these peoples were frequently the loci of struggle between competing
capitalist powers—for example, the United States and England nearly went
to war over control of the Mosquito Coast of Central America during the
mid-nineteenth century.

The other facet of the contradiction between the imperialist powers and
the noncapitalist societies on their margins has been the two century-long
attempts of the latter to retain or to reclaim their autonomy and indepen-

Zulu attack on a British regiment in South Africa in the late 19th century. (*The Granger Collection, New York.*)

dence. These include the Great Mutiny of 1859 in India, the Wounded Knee massacre of 1890 and the Sioux occupation of that site in 1972, the Russian Revolution of 1917, the Chinese Revolution from 1935 to 1949, the various anticolonial and decolonization struggles in Africa during the 1960s, and the wars of national liberation that were waged against England and France in

Southeast Asia after 1946. These are only a few of the encounters; for instance, there were more than two hundred armed, antiimperialist conflicts between 1945 and 1975 alone. These struggles have typically been complex, drawn-out processes that pass through various stages: Unwilling compliance, passive resistance, political dissent, and armed resistance are only a few of the more obvious. They led the capitalist powers to send expeditionary forces to the Soviet Union after World War I; to spend billions of dollars propping up puppet governments; and in recent decades, to wage costly, highly destructive wars in places like Algeria, the Congo, Vietnam, and Malaysia.

Although many former colonies gained political independence after World War II, most of them have continued to participate in capitalist market relations. They were unable to assert and maintain their economic autonomy in the face of capitalist competition and the changing economic conditions of the modern world. Consequently, many of the new states have remained dependent on the productive capacities and policies of the capitalist states; since the economic crisis of the mid-1970s, they have become increasingly enmeshed in financial webs woven by the capitalist powers. For example, the Latin American countries had a total combined debt of about $220 billion in 1979 and paid $365 billion in principal and interest during the 1980s. However, in 1990, they were even deeper in debt; they now owed more than $420 billion, even though they had just paid an amount equal to 164 percent of their debt ten years earlier. The economic policies driving debt repayment have had devastating effects on the health and well-being of the region's population. More than 60 percent of its people now live in poverty, and probably no more than 10,000 individuals out of the 450 million people who live there have benefited materially from the policies imposed by the International Monetary Fund, the World Bank, and the local governments forced to do their bidding. Similar, if not worse, circumstances prevail on much of the African continent.

Currently, some states on the margins of the capitalist world—most notably certain regions of the former USSR and the Peoples Republic of China, which were once excluded to some extent from capitalist markets— seem propelled, largely by the present configurations and balance of internal forces, toward some form of economic integration and expanded market relations with the capitalist states. These tendencies are fragile, they are not supported by all sectors of the populations, and they are easily reversible in contexts created by class formation and class struggle and by continual changes in the balance of forces. At the same time, social movements in other countries, often with quite different perspectives and understandings of the world, advocate neutralizing external economic interactions in favor of various domestic priorities. These movements also function in contexts that are still marginal being reshaped by new forms of struggle in contested political and ideological arenas.

In the early 1990s, capitalist economies—built on commodity production, the extraction of surplus value, market exchange, and crises—persist in many parts of the world, as do political regimes that promote both their spread into still marginal societies and their more profound penetration of those societies in which capitalist social relations already exist. This does not mean that the spread of capitalism is inevitable but rather that it is on the offensive at the same time that peoples in different parts of the capitalist world—for example, the United States, Germany, and Mexico—are experiencing severe economic crises and contractions in the quality of their everyday lives and increasing numbers of them are disenfranchised or excluded from the political process. If archaeology has conclusively shown only one thing, it is that social relations change, often more rapidly and drastically than we typically assume. As a result, the archaeology of capitalism, modern civilization, and the political regimes that support their structures and practices is necessarily an ongoing story of social relations that are still very much alive.

As you will recall from the first chapter, modern archaeology was itself nurtured by circumstances that were shaped by the development of capitalism, imperialism, and nationalism. It was part of the increasingly complex technical division of labor that was created by the development of industrial capitalism. The professionalization of archaeology in the 1870s and 1880s occurred at the same time that other intellectual disciplines were also professionalized and that university education was transformed in ways that facilitated the certification of technical proficiency in one of the newly constituted fields of learning. In other words, archaeologists are both participants and creators of modern society and civilization. They are not passive observers who peer in from the outside and make value-neutral pronouncements about past societies.

This book has made certain theoretical, methodological, and epistemological points about the rise of civilization. Theoretically, it implies that tributary states are unstable; they consolidate very rapidly, in a matter of months or years rather than decades or centuries. However, the pieces incorporated into them keep falling apart, and the states must struggle continuously to keep subject communities under their control. They attempt to put the pieces back together, often in new combinations and configurations, until they are overwhelmed by the very contradictions they generate. The disintegration of states is often triggered by peoples who have become conscious of the violence and exploitation states attempt to disguise as civilization and enlightenment.

Methodologically, this book suggests that carefully constructed comparisons of different episodes of state formation open new, potentially productive lines of questioning about what happened in particular historical instances; they have the capacity to shed new light on those instances and to extend our understanding of the underlying processes. Such an approach allows us to address systematically and historically the issues of uneven development, the formation of class and state structures, resistance, ethnogenesis, and fragmentation.

Epistemologically, one of the implications of this book is that a limited relativism must also be embraced. That is, archaeologists must investigate the archaeological record itself, not only in order to explain past societies and their historical development, but also to account for the concrete cultural, social, and historical conditions in which their descriptions and explanations are conceived and deployed. Since our own civilization is a totality character-ized by uneven development, class and state structures, fragmentation, re-sistance, ethnogenesis, and multiple understandings of that reality, we must examine how our own masters and managers have shaped current debates about civilization. We must consider how our scientifically informed views support or challenge their perspectives and how they resonate with the standpoints of the various subordinated communities. In this endeavor, it is essential to retain the positive findings of interpretive systems, which claim that science is a continually changing body of knowledge that tells us about reality. It is also essential to situate the proponents of these views in the complex webs of social and power relations that characterize society today, as members of socially constituted historic blocs, social classes, and class frag-ments in states where capitalist development has often taken different trajec-tories. Finally, it is necessary to historicize the operation of their views, to recognize the historical specificity of their claims, and to examine closely whose interests are ultimately served by the claim that exploitative and op-pressive social relations and violence are the natural and inevitable outcomes of human history.

FURTHER READINGS: A BRIEF GUIDE

For discussions of the development of capitalism in Europe, see T. H. Aston and C. H. E. Philpin, *The Brenner Debate: Agrarian Class Structure and Economic Development in Pre-Industrial Europe* (Cambridge: Cambridge University Press, 1984); Eric J. Hobsbawm, "The Crisis of the Seventeenth Century," in *Crisis in Europe, 1560–1660*, ed. Trevor Aston (New York: Anchor Books, 1967), pp. 5–62, and *Industry and Empire* (Middlesex, Eng.: Penguin Books, 1969); Chris-topher Hill, *Reformation to Industrial Revolution* (Middlesex, Eng.: Penguin Books, 1969); Victor G. Kiernan, *State and Society in Europe, 1550–1650* (Ox-ford: Basil Blackwell, 1980), and *The Lords of Human Kind: Black Men, Yellow Men, and White Men in an Age of Empire* (New York: Columbia University Press, 1986); and Walter Rodney, *How Europe Underdeveloped Africa* (London: Bogle-L'Ouverture, 1972). Karl Marx's *Capital: A Critique of Political Economy*, 3 vols. (New York: International Publishers, [1867–1894], 1967) is still the most insightful analysis of the capitalist economic system. It is usefully supple-mented with Ernest Mandel, *Late Capitalism* (London: Verso Books, [1972] 1978).

The archaeology of conquest and colonization is pursued by Kathleen Deagan, *Spanish St. Augustine: The Archaeology of a Colonial Creole Community* (New York: Academic Press, 1983); Carmel Shrire, "The Historical Archaeol-ogy of the Impact of Colonialism in Seventeenth-Century South Africa," and Carmel Shrire and Donna Merwick, "Dutch-Indigenous Relations in New

Netherlands and the Cape in the Seventeenth Century," both in *Historical Archaeology in Global Perspective*, ed. Lisa Falk (Washington, DC: Smithsonian Institution Press, 1991), pp. 69–96 and 11–20; Juan J. Arrom and Manuel García-Arevalo, *Cimarrón* (Santo Domingo: Ediciones Fundación García-Arevalo, 1986); Alaric Faulkner and Gretchen Faulkner, *The French at Pentagoet: 1635–1674: An Archaeological Portrait of the Acadian Frontier* (Augusta: Maine Historic Preservation Commission, 1987); Jerald T. Milanich and Susan Milbrath, eds., *First Encounters: Spanish Explorations in the Caribbean and the United States, 1492–1570* (Gainesville: University of Florida Press, 1989); Elise M. Brenner, "Sociopolitical Implications of Mortuary Remains in 17th-Century Native Southern New England," in *The Recovery of Meaning: Historical Archaeology in the Eastern United States*, ed. Mark P. Leone and Parker B. Potter, Jr. (Washington, DC: Smithsonian Institution Press, 1988), pp. 147–182; A. Adu Boahen, *African Perspectives on Colonialism* (Baltimore: Johns Hopkins University Press, 1987); and Thomas C. Patterson, "Early Colonial Encounters and Identities in the Caribbean: A Review of Some Recent Works and Their Implications," *Dialectical Anthropology*, vol. 16, no. 1 (1991), 1–14.

Discussions of the Atlantic slave trade should begin with Joseph C. Miller, *Way of Death: Merchant Capitalism and the Angolan Slave Trade, 1730–1830* (Madison: University of Wisconsin Press, 1988). Terrence W. Epperson, *"To Fix a Perpetual Brand": The Social Construction of Race in Virginia, 1675–1750* (Philadelphia: Temple University Press, 1992), and "Race and the Disciplines of the Plantation," *Historic Archaeology*, vol. 24, no. 4 (1990), 29–38, discusses the social construction of race, the organization of plantation work, and resistance in the Chesapeake region. For further discussions of slavery and plantation archaeology, see Charles E. Orser, Jr., ed., "Historical Archaeology on Southern Plantations and Farms," *Historical Archaeology*, vol. 24, no. 4 (1990); and Theresa Singleton, ed., *The Archaeology of Slavery and Plantation Life* (Orlando, FL: Academic Press, 1985), and *Studies in African American Archaeology* (Charlottesville: University of Virginia Press, 1992).

The destruction of local industry and efforts to thwart industrial capitalist development in colonial areas are examined by Frank Parkin, "Proto-Industrialization and Pre-Colonial South Asia," *Past and Present*, no. 98 (1983), 30–95; and Peter Gran, *Islamic Roots of Capitalism: Egypt, 1760–1840* (Austin: University of Texas Press, 1979).

The consolidation of class structures in capitalist states and their colonies is investigated by Robert Paynter, "Steps to an Archaeology of Capitalism: Material Change and Class Analysis," and Mark P. Leone, "The Georgian Order as the Order of Merchant Capitalism in Annapolis, Maryland," both in *The Recovery of Meaning*, ed. Mark P. Leone and Parker B. Potter, Jr. (Washington, DC: Smithsonian Institution Press, 1988), pp. 407–434 and 235–261; Mark P. Leone, "Interpreting Ideology in Historical Archaeology: The William Paca Garden in Annapolis, Maryland," in *Ideology, Power and Prehistory*, ed. Daniel Miller and Christopher Tilley (Cambridge: Cambridge University Press, 1984), pp. 25–36; Randall McGuire, "Building Power in the Cultural Landscape of Broome County, New York," and "'Employees

Must Be of Moral and Temperate Habits': Rural and Urban Elite Ideologies," both in *The Archaeology of Inequality*, ed. Randall McGuire and Robert Paynter (Oxford: Basil Blackwell, 1991), pp. 102–124; Suzanne Spencer-Wood, ed., *Consumer Choice in Historical Archeology* (New York: Plenum Press, 1987); and Mary C. Beaudry and Stephen A. Mrozowski, "The Archaeology of Work and Home Life in Lowell, Massachusetts: An Interdisciplinary Study of the Boott Cotton Mills Corporation," *IA, The Journal of the Society for Industrial Archaeology*, vol. 14, no. 2 (Washington, 1988) pp. 1–22.

The construction of gender relations and their intersection with class are addressed by Leith Mullings, "Uneven Development: Class, Race, and Gender in the United States before 1900," in *Women's Work: Development and the Division of Labor by Gender*, ed. Eleanor B. Leacock and Helen I. Safa (South Hadley, MA: Bergin & Garvey, 1987), pp. 41–57; and Ann Yentsch, "The Symbolic Divisions of Pottery: Sex-related Attributes of English and Anglo-American Household Pots," in *The Archaeology of Inequality*, ed. Randall McGuire and Robert Paynter (Oxford: Basil Blackwell, 1991), pp. 150–191.

Discussions of the spatial arrangement of class structures and their concomitants, exploitation and resistance, are initiated by Robert Paynter, *Models of Spatial Inequality: Settlement Patterns in Historical Archeology* (New York: Academic Press, 1982); Stephen A. Mrozowski, "Landscapes of Inequality," in *The Archaeology of Inequality*, ed. Randall McGuire and Robert Paynter (Oxford: Basil Blackwell, 1991), pp. 79–101; and Laurence F. Gross, "Building on Success: Lowell Mill Construction and Its Results," *IA, The Journal of the Society for Industrial Archaeology*, vol. 14, no. 2 (Washington, DC, 1988), pp. 23–34.

U. R. Q. Henriques, "The Rise and Decline of the Separate System of Prison Discipline," *Past and Present*, no. 54 (1972), pp. 61–93, and Dario Melossi and Massimo Pavarini, *The Prison and the Factory: Origins of the Penitentiary System* (London: Macmillan, 1981), deal with the development of prisons, an important aspect of the suppression of resistance and class struggle.

The attempts of factory owners to organize and control labor processes in the workplace and resistance to their efforts are discussed by Edward P. Thompson, "Time, Work-Discipline, and Industrial Capitalism," *Past and Present*, no. 38 (1967), pp. 56–97; Janet Siskind, "Class Discourse in an Early 19th-Century New England Factory," *Dialectical Anthropology*, vol. 16, no. 1, pp. 35–50; Russell G. Handsman and Mark P. Leone, "Living History and Critical Archaeology in the Reconstruction of the Past," in *Critical Traditions in Contemporary Archaeology*, ed. Valerie Pinsky and Alison Wylie (Cambridge: Cambridge University Press, 1989), pp. 117–135; Mary C. Beaudry, ed., *Documentary Archaeology in the New World* (Cambridge: Cambridge University Press, 1988); and Richard M. Candee, "The 1822 Allendale Mill and Slow-Burning Construction: A Case Study in the Transmission of an Architectural Technology," *IA, The Journal of the Society for Industrial Archaeology*, vol. 14, no. 3 (Washington, DC, 1988), pp. 21–34.

The structural contradictions of capitalism and their implications can be developed from LouAnn Wurst, "'Employees Must Be of Moral and Temperate Habits': Rural and Urban Elite Ideologies," in *The Archaeology of Inequality*, ed. Randall McGuire and Robert Paynter (Oxford: Basil Blackwell, 1991), pp. 125–149; Gary Kulik, "Dams, Fish, and Farmers: Defense of Public Rights in Eighteenth-Century Rhode Island," in *The Countryside in the Age of Capitalist Transformation: Essays in the Social History of Rural America*, ed. Steven Hahn and Jonathan Prude (Chapel Hill: University of North Carolina Press, 1985), pp. 25–50; Peter R. Schmidt and Stephen A. Mrozowski, "History, Smugglers, Change, and Shipwrecks," in *Shipwreck Archaeology*, ed. Richard A. Gould (Albuquerque: University of New Mexico Press, 1983), pp. 143–171; Jim Allen, "The Archaeology of Nineteenth-Century British Imperialism: An Australian Case Study," *World Archaeology*, vol. 5, no. 1 (1973), 44–59; J. Douglas McDonald, Larry J. Zimmerman, A. L. McDonald, William Tall Bull, and Ted Rising Sun, "The Northern Cheyenne Outbreak of 1879: Using Oral History and Archaeology as Tools of Resistance," in *The Archaeology of Inequality*, ed. Randall McGuire and Robert Paynter (Oxford: Basil Blackwell, 1991), pp. 64–79; and Michael Rowlands, "The Archaeology of Colonialism and Constituting the African Peasantry," in *Domination and Resistance*, ed. Daniel Miller, Michael Rowlands, and Christopher Tilley (London: Unwin Hyman, 1989), pp. 261–283.

appendix A

Chronometric Dating Methods

Chronometric, or absolute, dates are those expressed in terms of years, centuries, or millennia, those that are related to a calendrical system, usually the Christian calendar. These dates are obtained by measuring the rates at which natural phenomena occur—the annual growth of tree rings, the disintegration of radioactive carbon in a timber beam, or the formation of argon gas from potassium. Over the years, archaeologists have experimented with a number of chronometric dating techniques, but they rely on a few that provide relatively consistent results.

Dendrochronology, or tree-ring dating as it is more commonly known, is based on the fact that trees add concentric growth rings each year, especially where there are marked seasonal changes in the weather, and therefore, the tree grows only during a few months of the year. When a tree is cut down or a core is taken from it, the age of the tree can be determined by counting the number of rings. The width of the rings can vary from year to year and reflect variations in the weather. The rings tend to be wider in years in which the climatic conditions favor growth and narrower in those in which conditions were less favorable. By comparing the ring sequences from different trees with overlapping ages and matching the pattern of wide and narrow rings, scientists can build a master chronology. This technique was first used by A. E. Douglass in the American Southwest with sequoia, ponderosa pine, and other slow-growing trees to construct a calendar that could be used to determine the ages of beams found in pueblos. That calendar now stretches back to 322 B.C.

Scientists have constructed a tree-ring sequence by using California bristlecone pine that now extends 8,200 years into the past. They have also established a calendar in northern Ireland that begins more than 7,200 years ago and another in Germany that extends back 6,000 years. Tree-ring calendars established in Europe and the American Southwest have also been used to calibrate radiocarbon dates.

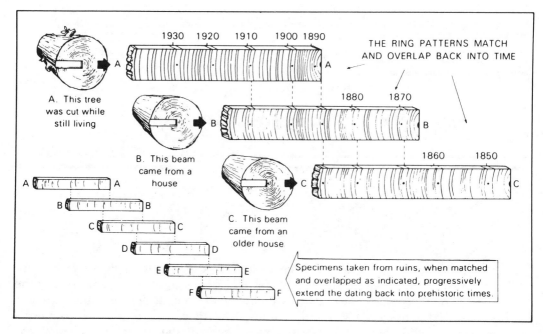

A. This tree was cut while still living

B. This beam came from a house

C. This beam came from an older house

1930 1920 1910 1900 1890

THE RING PATTERNS MATCH AND OVERLAP BACK INTO TIME

1880 1870

1860 1850

Specimens taken from ruins, when matched and overlapped as indicated, progressively extend the dating back into prehistoric times.

Archaeologists use absolute chronologies established by matching ring patterns on trees cut at different times in the past.

Archaeologists have used dendrochronology effectively in the American Southwest and, to a lesser extent, in Alaska; the American Southeast; Greece; Ireland; and Germany, where a combination of Celtic and Roman beams provide a calendar that extends from about 700 B.C. to A.D. 339. For a ring-dated piece of wood to be useful to archaeologists, they must know its archaeological significance. Did the members of an ancient community chop down a tree and use it immediately as a house beam, or did they pick up and use a piece of wood that had fallen many years earlier?

Radiocarbon dating can be used to date assemblages that have ages of about 60 to 70,000 years. Radiocarbon dating, developed in 1949 by Willard Libby and J. R. Arnold, is the chronometric method most widely used by archaeologists. The method is based on the fact that a radioactive isotope of carbon—carbon 14—is produced by the cosmic ray bombardment of nitrogen atoms in the upper atmosphere and is eventually absorbed by every living thing on earth. Since living organisms are continually absorbing and eliminating carbon 14, they all contain roughly the same percentage that is found in the atmosphere and in other living organisms. When the organisms die, they no longer absorb carbon compounds from the environment, and their proportion of carbon 14 begins to diminish as the radioactive atoms disintegrate. After 5,730 years they have lost half of their carbon 14 atoms. Since the disintegration of radioactive atoms occurs at a known rate, called the half-life, scientists can obtain the age of an organic material by measuring its radioactivity—that is, by counting the number of particles emitted by a known amount of material over a given period. By doing so, they can calculate how much radiocarbon is still present in the material and, as a result, determine how old the material is.

Archaeologists can collect radiocarbon samples from a wide range of organic materials that occur in archaeological assemblages. These include charcoal from a fireplace, burned bone or shell, wood, or any other organic material that is clearly associated with the assemblage. Scientists in a laboratory convert the sample into an organic compound and place it in a chamber surrounded by devices that count radioactive decay. Dates obtained by this technique are expressed as probability statements. For example, a sample of organic material might yield an age of 1,000 ± 200 radiocarbon years B.P. This statement means a number of things: B.P. means "before the present," which is arbitrarily defined as A.D. 1950. The phrase *radiocarbon years* indicates that scientists are aware that a radiocarbon year does not necessarily have the same duration or even a consistent duration as a year defined by the Christian calendar. The statement 1,000 ± 200 indicates that there is a 67 percent chance that the actual age of the sample falls between 800 and 1,200 radiocarbon years and that there is a 95 percent probability that it falls between 600 and 1,400 radiocarbon years.

The radiocarbon dating method involves a number of assumptions, the most important of which is that the amount of carbon 14 produced in the upper atmosphere is relatively constant from one year to the next. At least three factors affect this assumption. First, the use of coal, oil, and other fossil fuels has tremendously increased the amount of ancient carbon in the atmosphere since the beginning of the Industrial Revolution in the later half of the eighteenth century. Second, the hydrogen bomb explosions that occurred in the 1950s and 1960s greatly increased the amount of carbon 14 and other radioactive debris in the atmosphere and elsewhere. Unfortunately, the "industrial effect" and the "atom bomb effect" do not cancel each other out. Third, there have been long-term variations in the intensity of the earth's magnetic field and, hence, fluctuations in the amounts of solar energy reaching the upper atmosphere. Thus there were times in the past when more carbon 14 was being produced in the atmosphere as well as times when less was being produced. Scientists discovered these variations by dating samples of known age from slow-growing bristlecone pines or European oak trees and comparing the radiocarbon and tree-ring ages. Using these dates, they have also worked out correction curves and tables in which carbon 14 ages are calibrated with those obtained by dendrochronologists. These are presented in a very abbreviated form in Table A–1.

Potassium-argon dating has been used to date rocks that range in age from about half a million to more than 4 billion years. It is based on the fact that a radioactive isotope of potassium disintegrates into the inert gas argon 40. By measuring the amount of argon that has been trapped in the crystal structures of potassium-bearing minerals—such as many volcanic rocks and ashes—in a mass spectrometer, scientists can determine the age of the sam-

Table A-1   Radiocarbon Measurements and Calibrated Ages

Radiocarbon Date	Range of Calibrated Ages
A.D. 1500	A.D. 1300 to 1515
A.D. 1000	A.D. 870 to 1230
A.D. 500	A.D. 265 to 640
A.D. 1	5 B.C. to A.D. 420
500 B.C.	820 to 400 B.C.
1000 B.C.	1530 to 905 B.C.
1500 B.C.	2345 to 1660 B.C.
2000 B.C.	2830 to 2305 B.C.
2500 B.C.	3505 to 2925 B.C.
3000 B.C.	3950 to 3640 B.C.
3500 B.C.	4545 to 3960 B.C.
4000 B.C.	5235 to 4575 B.C.
4500 B.C.	5705 to 5205 B.C.
5000 B.C.	6285 to 5445 B.C.

ple. The value of this technique is that it can be used to date materials that are well beyond the range of the radiocarbon method. In fact, the older the sample, the more accurate the technique becomes. Its limitations are that it can be used only in areas where there was once volcanic activity and that the crystal structures of the rock samples cannot be porous (otherwise argon gas could have been added or lost through holes in the crystals). Archaeologists and geologists have used the potassium-argon method to data samples from Olduvai Gorge in Tanzania and other sites associated with our early ancestors.

Thermoluminescence dating is based on the fact that many minerals contain naturally occurring, radioactive impurities and that radiation distorts the distribution of electrons in their crystal lattices. When pottery or burned flint, for example, are heated or stimulated with light, the electrons that have accumulated over time because of naturally occurring radiation are released from traps in the crystal structure—a process accompanied by the emission of light, which can be detected and measured by a sensitive photomultiplier device. Electrons begin to accumulate once again as the sample cools; thus, there is a relationship between the luminescence and the electron buildup in the traps. Determining the age of the sample involves counting the number of trapped electrons. This figure is established by heating the object, measuring the amount of light emitted, and comparing this amount with the luminescence of the same object after it has been heated and exposed to a known level of radiation for a given period of time.

Scientists are refining these techniques to improve their accuracy. In addition, they are experimenting with others—like obsidian hydration, fission-track dating, or electron spin resonance—that will increase the range and variety of materials that can be used for absolute dating.

Obsidian hydration dating is based on the fact that fresh surfaces of volcanic glass absorb water from their surroundings, forming a hydrate layer that accumulates through time at a measurable rate. The thickness of the hydrate layer, measured in microns, represents the amount of time that has passed since the fresh surface was originally exposed. The thicker the layer, the older the surface. Temperature and other factors affect the rates at which hydrate layers accumulate; as a result, the rates of accumulation vary from one region to another. The technique may be useful for dating surfaces with ages up to about 800,000 years.

Fission-track dating is based on the fact that obsidian and many minerals contain small amounts of radioactive uranium, which decays, emitting alpha particles at a constant rate. These scratch the material, leaving narrow tracks, which can be counted. The older the material, the more tracks it has. The technique is applicable to objects with ages between 100,000 and 1 million years.

Electron spin resonance (ESR) is also based on the fact that many minerals contain small amounts of radioactive impurities. It resembles thermoluminescence dating in that both techniques attempt to measure radiation damage caused by ionizing radiation, which is also a function of the age of the sample. This technique involves dividing a sample into several parts and comparing their ESR spectra after each has been heated to a particular temperature and irradiated in order to determine the duration or mean life of the electron traps under different conditions. If the signals have a linear relationship, it is possible to compare them with the signal emitted by an unmodified portion of the sample to estimate its age.

In spite of the problems with the methods of absolute dating currently being used and others that are now being developed, archaeologists have to rely on them to determine the age and duration of most assemblages. Consequently, it is important to be aware of their limitations and not to accept their results uncritically or use them carelessly.

FURTHER READINGS: A BRIEF GUIDE

Absolute dating techniques used by archaeologists are discussed by Brian M. Fagan, *In the Beginning: An Introduction to Archaeology* (Boston: Scott, Foresman, 1988); Joseph W. Michels, *Dating Methods in Archaeology* (New York: Seminar Press, 1973); Bryant Bannister and William J. Robinson, "Tree Ring Dating in Archaeology," *World Archaeology*, vol. 7 (1975), 210–225; David L. Browman, "Isotopic Discrimination and Correction Factors in Radiocarbon Dating," in *Advances in Archaeological Method and Theory*, ed. Michael B. Schiffer, vol. 4 (New York, Academic Press, 1981), pp. 241–295; Jeffrey Klein, J. C. Lerman, P. E. Damon, and E. K. Ralph, "Calibration of Radiocarbon Dating: Tables Based on the Consensus Data of the Workshop on Calibrating the Radiocarbon Time Scale," *Radiocarbon*, vol. 24 (1982), 103–153; G. W. Pearson and M. Stuiver, "High-precision Calibration of the Radiocarbon Time Scale 500–2500 BC," and M. Stuiver and G. W. Pearson, "High-precision Calibration of the Radiocarbon Time Scale, AD 1950–500 BC," both in *Radiocarbon*, vol. 28B

(1986), 839–862 and 805–838; G. Brett Dalrymple and Mason A. Lamphere, *Potassium Argon Dating* (San Francisco: W. A. Freeman, 1970); M. J. Aitken, "Luminescence Dating: A Guide for Non-specialists," *Archaeometry*, vol. 31, no. 2 (1989), 147–159; and M. Ikeya, "Electron Spin Resonance as a Method of Dating," *Archaeometry*, vol. 20, no. 2 (1978), 147–158.

appendix B

Human Origins: An Evolutionary Biology Perspective

People are animals. They share a remarkable number of anatomical and behavioral features with other kinds of animals. They have bilateral symmetry; an internal skeleton, including vertebrae that protect the spinal nerve and a skull that encloses the brain and protects the sense organs of the head; a complex circulation system in which oxygenated blood is pumped throughout the body by a chambered heart; powerful muscles along the sides of the body that are used for locomotion; well-developed sense organs; and bisexual reproduction. All of these features are also characteristic of fish, amphibians, reptiles, and birds.

More specifically, people are mammals because they share features characteristic of this particular group of animals. They have body hair, their body temperature is constant, they give birth to live infants, and the females suckle their young. There are many different kinds, or orders, of mammals, each of which has its own characteristics. For example, dogs, cats, and members of the carnivores are flesh eaters and have teeth that are specialized for biting, tearing, and shredding flesh; rats, beavers, and other rodents have teeth that are well suited for gnawing hard materials, like wood or nuts.

People belong to an order called the *primates*, which also includes apes, monkeys, and prosimians. The primates have very large brains and skulls, small snouts and relatively flat faces, eyes that have rotated toward the front of the skull, small bony structures around the eyes, nails instead of claws, and paired breasts located high on the chest. Classifying human beings as primates is a way of saying that their closest relatives in the animal kingdom are the other animals of this order. That is, the different kinds of primates living today evolved from a common ancestor that lived in the distant past—65 to 70 million years ago, according to the fossil record—and that the order diversified through time. Some lineages became extinct, while others survived, diversified, and changed through time. How did these processes of change, diversification, and extinction take place? How did human beings evolve from their primate ancestors? And what changes have taken place in human beings?

THE ECOLOGICAL THEATER AND THE EVOLUTIONARY PLAY

The title of this section comes from a book by G. Evelyn Hutchinson (1965). It is an elegant statement of some fundamental aspects of the history of life. The evolution of life has taken place in a wide variety of environmental situations that are themselves continually changing. The evolutionary process, then, is like a long play being performed on a stage of global proportions. The theater is essential for the performance; without it, the play could not take place. In other words, evolution can be understood only in terms of what is happening in the environment. Ecology and evolution are interdependent; they are two ways of looking at the same story. Ecology focuses on the relationships and interactions among the performers on stage at a particular moment in time; evolution is concerned with how the plot developed to allow those particular characters to be there at that particular moment.

When biologists use the term *ecology* they are referring to the relationships between organisms and their environments. Any environment is a complex situation produced by the interaction of a number of factors. For example, one part of the environment, the biogeographic region, is defined by the intersection of such physical factors as temperature, topography, soil conditions, and the availability of water. These and other circumstances interact to produce situations in which some kinds of plants and animals can live and others cannot. The other part of the environment is a social one; it is produced by the interrelationships and interactions among the organisms that reside there and what happens between them and their physically defined surroundings.

For biologists, the word *evolution* means change through time or descent with modification. That is, the different kinds of plants and animals that exist today are the modified descendants of different kinds of organisms that lived in the past. These changes may be morphological ones, which affect the appearance of the organisms, or behavioral ones, which influence how they interact with their contemporaries. Evolution can also be defined as changes in the genetic composition of a population. This definition is different from that of Charles Darwin. Such a description is useful, however, because it focuses on the ideas of population, heredity, and variation. It also forces us to pose questions: Where does variation come from? How is it transmitted from one generation to the next? What causes it to change through time?

Although the individual is a basic unit of life—it is the individual who is born, nurtured, and grows to maturity—the actions of individuals can begin to be understood only in terms of connections with other members of their group. Biologists deal with two levels of groups: populations and species. Briefly, a *population* consists of individuals that live in the same region at a particular time and mate successfully with one another. For example, the people of Pitcairn Island form one population and those of Philadelphia constitute another. A *species* is a more inclusive group; it consists of a number of similar but spatially isolated populations whose members are capable of mating and producing viable offspring. Thus, individuals from Pitcairn Island and Philadelphia could mate and have a child, even though they come from different populations.

We are all aware that like produces like. Dogs mate and have puppies; cats mate and produce kittens. That is, individuals resemble their parents physically—or phenotypically, as biologists say—but they are not identical with them. The important question is, how does this inheritance take place? Gregor Mendel, who raised garden peas and bred them over a number of successive generations, provided the answer. He noted the relationships among seven visible characteristics, such as seed form and color, of each plant and the patterns of inheritance between them and each of their offspring. He concluded that hereditary features are transmitted by a number of independent particles that we now call genes. These are contributed in roughly equal numbers by each of the individual's parents. Furthermore, the genes that affect the appearance of one trait are inherited independently from those that determine the appearance of other features.

All of the genes of the individuals of a particular local population constitute what is called a *gene pool*. The genes of individuals whose parents belong to this population are derived from its gene pool. Thus, the gene pool is a reservoir of hereditary material that is passed from one generation to the next. Many individuals or only a few may contribute to and share in the gene pool. It may be distributed over a wide area or a small one. It may be stable through time or change from one generation to the next.

No two individuals in a population have exactly the same combination of genes, including identical siblings—who are born with identical genetic systems but are subjected to different environmental and historical circumstances so that different genes have mutated. This genetic variation contributes to the fact that the people of a population are physically different from one another.

There are three reasons for the amount of genetic variation in a population: recombination, gene flow, and mutation. *Recombination* is what occurs when two individuals mate and their offspring receive half of their genes from each parent. The mathematics of this process are impressive when we consider that any two individuals probably differ by 30,000 genes. The continual reshuffling of genes through recombination is a major source of the genetic variation that exists in a population. *Gene flow* is the second source of genetic variation; it occurs when there is some exchange of genetic material between populations—that is, when a person from one population mates with one from another population, thereby potentially introducing new genes into one of the gene pools. *Mutation*, the third source of variation, is the ultimate source of every new gene.

If recombination, gene flow, and mutation operated without checks, the genetic diversity of populations would far exceed anything that exists naturally. The continued increase in the genetic diversity of a population is limited by natural selection and sampling accidents. These forces restrict the potential for unlimited variation and channel it into certain pathways or directions.

Natural selection is by far the more important and effective of the two forces that limit variation. It is based on four fundamental facts of life: (1) survival is limited—the number of eggs and sperm produced greatly exceeds the number of individuals born, which in turn exceeds the number who survive to the reproductive stage and can contribute genetic material to the next generation by producing viable offspring; (2) there is hereditary variation among the individuals of a population because of genetic differences; (3) there is differential survival—some individuals have a greater chance of becoming adults and reproducing than others because they possess genes that are advantageous in the environments in which they live; and (4) these advantageous genes have a greater chance of being inherited because more individuals with them are likely to reach adulthood and contribute genetic material to the next generation.

Natural selection permits any advantageous gene or combination of genes to accumulate in a population at the expense of those that are less favorable or are deleterious. This may be a long process requiring many generations. Differential survival and reproduction are the testing ground for natural selection, in which genes with survival value are either fixed in or eliminated from the gene pool. Natural selection modifies the gene pool to increase the congruity, or harmony, between the population and its environment.

Any hereditary characteristic that increases this congruity—that is, that promotes survival at the level of the individual or the population—is called an *adaptation*. Adaptations enable individuals to obtain food, avoid predators, survive to the reproductive stage, and produce offspring. They take many different forms and may involve morphological, physiological, or behavioral features. They make it possible for the members of a population to function more efficiently in an environment. Natural selection is the driving force that produces adaptations, which it does by using the opportunities provided by the population's gene pool.

There is an important relationship among the genetic variability of a population, its adaptation at a given time, and its potential for change in an environment in flux. Populations with low variability—in which most of the members are similar to one another, and atypical individuals are few—are usually well adapted to their environments; however, they are usually not very successful in adapting to slight changes in these conditions because of the homogeneity of their members. Populations with a great deal of variability and wide ranges of variation—in which there are relatively few typical individuals and a lot of unusual ones—may be less well adapted to a particular set of environmental conditions, but they have a greater chance of adapting to new conditions and occupying previously unoccupied environments. Thus populations with low variability and limited ranges of variation are potentially disadvantaged in a continually changing world since they have fewer available options for coping with change. The most successful groups with regards to survival are those with wide ranges of variation and the ability to adapt productively to many different environmental settings.

Most populations live in environments that offer them a greater range of habitats than they are willing to occupy and many more resources than they are willing or able to exploit effectively. Another way of viewing evolution, therefore, is to see it as a series of changes in the kinds of interactions that occur between a population and its environment. From this perspective, a major feature of evolution is the entrance of a population into a new environmental niche; this move may be real or figurative. Often the population does not really go anywhere; the new environment comes to it as a result of climatic change or the appearance of new plants or animals. If the population can utilize these new resources, its members have "moved" in an evolutionary sense. The fossil record shows numerous instances in which, once a group of animals has entered a new environmental zone, its descendants often become highly diversified. This process is called *adaptive radiation*. The new populations become increasingly specialized by focusing their activities on certain parts of the new environment and using them more efficiently than their predecessors did or their contemporaries are able to do.

Richard Levins and Richard Lewontin (1985) have conceptualized nature as a multileveled totality or whole, "a [historically] contingent structure in reciprocal interaction with its own parts and with the greater whole of which it is a part." In their view, the heterogeneous parts of the totality acquire their characteristic properties in the interactions that constitute the whole. The various elements of the totality—its parts and levels—as well as the whole itself are continually changing, though at different rates; consequently, at a given moment, one element might appear to be fixed in relation to another. The fact that this totality is constantly in flux means not only that it may destroy the very conditions that put it into existence in the first place but also that the transformations create possibilities for new historically contingent structures that did not exist previously. The changes that occur in a totality and its components arise from both the internal heterogeneity of the parts and the diversity of their interconnections as well as from their development in relation to larger totalities, which influence and are influenced by those changes. The whole is where the internal and external intersect.

Nature, as Levins and Lewontin (1985) point out, is a unity of contradictions characterized by the interplay of elements and dynamics that operate at different levels of the totality—local species populations, communities composed of a number of local species populations, and biogeographic regions. Consequently, natural totalities exhibit spontaneous activity and change, which can be conceptualized in terms of (1) positive and negative feedback, (2) the interpenetration and interaction of categories from different levels of the whole, and (3) the coexistence of opposing principles that shape interaction.

A community, in this perspective, is a totality—an intermediate, historically contingent entity constituted by the reciprocal interactions of populations of different species residing in the same biogeographical region. It is also the locus of the interactions between higher- and lower-level wholes. Although the local demographic interactions take place against a backdrop of the biogeographic and population genetic parameters, the community level is not epiphenomenal because it has its own distinctive properties and dynamics, which are incompletely determined by its connections with other levels of reality.

The composition of a community depends to some extent on the origin of the plants and animal populations that reside there. It is linked to the biogeographic region by the dynamics of colonization and local extinction and to the biological characteristics of the constituent populations by the rate at which they enter the region and by their interactions with one another and with various ecological parameters. The interconnections of communities and their constituent populations are composed by various forms of linkages, which ensure that different examples of the same kind of community are not identical.

THE ORIGIN AND EVOLUTION OF THE PRIMATES

Traditional investigations of primate evolution and the relationships between living and fossil primates were based largely on comparisons of anatomical features. Since the late 1960s, however, molecular genetic studies based on the degree of similarity of immune systems, molecular sequences on chromosomes, and DNA hybridization have been used successfully to assess the degree or proximity of relationship of living humans, apes, and monkeys. The two methods, which examine different kinds of evidence, yield generally similar conclusions.

The first primates appeared more than 65 million years ago in the tropical forests that covered North America and Europe, which were beginning to separate from each other because of ocean-floor spreading and the formation of the Atlantic Ocean. The earliest primates evolved from ground-dwelling, shrewlike insectivores that had well-developed senses of touch and smell. They moved into the lower canopy and shrub layer of the tropical forests—an environmental niche that was unoccupied earlier—and diversified rapidly.

During the Eocene (58 to 34 million years ago), at least one group began to rely on eyesight rather than touch or smell. A number of adaptations allowed these animals to achieve better control over their movements among the branches and vines, to grasp narrow supports, and to use their hands to catch and hold prey. These adaptations included the following: (1) Their eyes rotated forward, producing stereoscopic vision and depth perception; (2) bony sockets surrounding their eyes protected the eyes from injury; (3) larger and reorganized middle ears improved balance; (4) their hands and feet had opposable thumbs and big toes; and (5) their digits had nails instead of claws.

This group, which shared anatomical and behavioral features with modern prosimians, diversified rapidly during the Middle Eocene. Perhaps the most important dichotomy that appeared was the time of day when different kinds of primates were active. Although some continued to be nocturnal, others moved into the daytime niche. This change selected for improved vision among the diurnal primates, which had relatively larger visual centers than their nocturnal relatives. The ancestors of the anthropoids—a taxonomic unit comprising fossil and living monkeys, apes, and humans—are to be found among the diurnal prosimians of the Eocene. Two poorly known jaw fragments with a few teeth from Late Eocene deposits in central Burma may represent transitional forms.

Although the Burmese fossils suggest that anthropoids may have evolved in the Late Eocene, fossils from the 37- to 31-million-year-old Oligocene deposits in the Fayum Depression of northern Egypt provide more information. At the time, several different kinds of anthropoids lived in the Fayum, which had a warm, wet, and seasonal climate and was crossed by slow, vegetation-clogged streams that emptied into brackish estuaries and lagoons. Since most of the Fayum anthropoids were immature, the young animals fell out of trees lining the river banks and drowned and then were incorporated—along with leaves, branches, and other animals—into the mucky stream bottoms.

The anthropoids had diverged into two lineage groups by the Early Miocene (23 to 18 million years ago). One branch gave rise to modern Old World monkeys. The fossil and living species of this branch are remarkably uniform: They are sexually dimorphic (males are larger than females); quadrupedal walkers; fruit- and leaf-eaters; and adapted to conditions found in diverse forest, woodland, and grassland environments. The other branch gave rise to the hominoids—a taxonomic group composed of the modern apes (gibbons, orangutans, chimpanzees, and gorillas), humans, and their fossil ancestors. Molecular genetic and anatomical studies indicate that the ancestors of gibbons were the first to diverge from the common hominoid stock; this may have occurred 17 to 20 million years ago. Fossil data from Asia suggest that orangutan ancestors diverged about 10 to 15 million years ago, which suggests that hominids (human beings and their ancestors) diverged from the African apes, chimpanzees, and gorillas between 6 and 10 million years ago in Africa.

The first hominoids appeared at about the time that the Indian subcontinent collided with Asia, forming the Himalaya Mountains; the Tehtys Sea was cut off from the Indian Ocean by the emergence of the Arabian Peninsula; and volcanic eruptions began along the great East African rift valley. The Early Miocene apes, the proconsulids, of East Africa appeared after the ape and monkey lineages had separated but before the hominoids themselves diversified. They were fruit- and leaf-eating, arboreal quadrupeds capable of a wide range of movements: arm swinging, vertical climbing, and quadrupedal running. They occupied a variety of forest and woodland habitats. Most of the Early Miocene apes weighed 20 pounds or less; the smallest species was cat-sized, and adults of the largest species weighed about 120 pounds.

Apes spread out of Africa into the forests and woodlands of Eurasia during the Middle and Late Miocene (18.0 to 5.2 million years ago), a period marked by significant climatic, geographic, and environmental changes as well as one that is almost unrepresented in the fossil record of Africa. The Eurasian apes belonged to several distinct lineages, each of which consisted of a cluster of species in space and time. They were sexually dimorphic; had varied locomotor habits; and developed a variety of feeding strategies, judging from differences in the shapes of their teeth. They also varied considerably in size; adults of the smallest species weighed about 15 pounds, and those of largest were heavier than modern male gorillas. Modern orangutans most likely derive from one of Late Miocene *Sivapithecus* species found in Asia. Many of the Eurasian apes became locally extinct around 7 million years ago, probably as a result of further changes in their habitats.

Molecular studies indicate that gorillas, chimpanzees, and human beings are closely related and suggest that they diverged between 6 and 10 million years ago. African fossil apes from this period are exceedingly rare, and none can be linked securely with any of the modern species. David Pilbeam (1986) has assembled the various lines of evidence to construct a scenario that accounts for the array of African apes and hominids that appear in the Pliocene (5.2 to 1.8 million years ago) and later fossil deposits. A first radiation, which occurred in the Late Miocene, led to gorilla and a protohuman/ protochimpanzee species. Both were sexually dimorphic, arboreal quadrupeds; the former consumed leafy plants, whereas the latter depended on arboreal resources.

The protohuman/protochimpanzee species divided into eastern and western parts around 5 million years ago, at a time when major shifts were occurring in the configuration and composition of plant communities as a consequence of mountain building, changes in the patterns of atmospheric and oceanic circulation, and the formation of permanent polar ice. The western population—the protochimpanzees—continued to reside in forests and woodlands where the trees were separated by open spaces. They remained dependent on fruits and other arboreal resources; consequently, both arboreal and terrestrial locomotor habits were essential since they climbed trees and moved on the ground between them. The eastern populations—the protohumans—resided in the wooded savannas and more open habitats that were appearing in eastern and southern Africa. They became increasingly more bipedal as they spent more and more time on the ground.

HOMINID ORIGINS AND EVOLUTION

Hominids appeared during the Pliocene and evolved a number of morphological and behavioral characteristics that distinguish them from their hominoid relatives: they have upright posture and walk bipedally; they have smaller front teeth; they have enlarged and reorganized brains; they have opposable thumbs and the motor skills to make tools; they have less body hair than their nonhuman contemporaries and, presumably, than their ancestors; they use spoken language as an effective mode of communication; and they have culture. This complex of traits, which appeared at different times in the fossil record and evolved at different rates, reflects a progressive adjustment to conditions that were emerging in a continually changing and increasingly terrestrial environment. To maintain themselves in this environment, the hominids not only had to adapt to the conditions that existed at any given moment but also had to be flexible enough—both genetically and behaviorally—to respond to the changes that were taking place.

Although paleoanthropologists generally agree on the overall features of human evolution, they hold divergent views about the specific features during the Pliocene and Pleistocene (1.8 million to about 10,000 years ago) periods. The reason for the discrepancies is that different paleoanthropologists interpret the fossil evidence differently. That is, they hold different views about the meaning of variations in the size and shape of particular anatomical structures in different specimens; they emphasize the importance of some specimens and deemphasize that of others for interpreting the human fossil record; and they have different ideas about the relationships among the various fossil remains, their significance, and how they should be classified.

Essentially, there are three positions. The first is that there were two parallel lineages of hominids—*Australopithecus* and *Homo*—that diverged from each other about 2.5 to 3.0 million years ago and coexisted until 1.2 million years ago, when the former became extinct. The second is that there were three parallel hominid lineages that diverged from their common ancestor about 5 million years; these were *Homo*, a small australopithecine, and a large australopithecine—all of which coexisted until about a million years ago, when the latter two became extinct. The third view is that there was never more than one hominid lineage at any time in the past. In the remainder of this section, I will follow those paleoanthropologists who expound the first position because it seems to offer the best explanation of the evidence that is now available.

The earliest undoubted hominid fossils belong to *Australopithecus afarensis*, a sexually dimorphic, small-brained, big-toothed, frugivorous or omnivorous hominid that lived 4.5 to 2.8 million years ago in East Africa. Remains have been found at Laetoli in northern Tanzania, along with two sets of footprints, and at several locations around Hadar in Ethiopia.

Anatomically, *A. afarensis* was midway between apes and humans. They possessed diverse locomotor habits. Their long, curved digits indicate that they were skilled climbers that foraged, escaped predators, and perhaps even slept in trees; the structure of lower limbs, ankles, and feet indicates that they walked upright with a knock-kneed gait, their toes pointed in, and their torsos probably swayed from side to side when they moved rapidly. They exhibited marked sexual dimorphism. The females were 3 to 4 feet tall and weighed about 60 pounds. The taller males weighed about twice as much. Their jaws were set under their faces, which improved the efficiency with which they chewed, ground, and sliced food by facilitating the rotary and lateral movement of the lower jaw. Their teeth had flat crowns and thick enamel, which suggests that they were basically vegetarians who ate the fruits, tough seeds, shoots, and stems provided by their open woodland and savanna environment. Their molars show differential wear, which indicates a delayed sequence of tooth eruption that must have been associated with a prolonged period of maturation. Finally, they probably sweated a lot to dissipate heat and drank small amounts of liquid frequently during the daytime to prevent dehydration under the tropical sun.

This species split into two distinct lineages about 2.5 to 3.0 million years ago. One was *Homo*, the direct ancestor of modern human beings; the other was *Australopithecus*, a lineage that retained many of the primitive anatomical characteristics of *A. afarensis* and became extinct about a million years ago. What this split means, in biological terms, is that the members of one lineage could mate successfully with their contemporaries in that lineage but not with individuals from the other. In other words, the members of the two lineages were reproductively isolated.

A question of considerable interest is this: How did this reproductive isolation develop? The process is called *speciation*. What probably happened is that different populations of *A. afarensis* began to make use of the food resources found in slightly different environments in the same area. At first there may have been some gene exchange between them. However, as each population became better adapted to the conditions that prevailed in its environment, the amount of gene exchange decreased because of less frequent interactions between the two populations. Eventually the reproductive isolation was complete in the sense that the members of the two species could not mate successfully.

The australopithecine lineage consists of three species: an earlier gracile form known as *A. africanus* and two later, more robust forms, *A. robustus* and *A. boisei*. They are essentially smaller and larger versions of the same creature. The differences in the size of their brains, cheek teeth, and musculature associated with chewing and grinding food were directly related to differences in their body size and dietary adaptations. The sexually dimorphic individuals of this lineage shared a number of features that were not found in *A. afarensis*; these included relatively larger cheek teeth and increased robustness and buttressing of the lower jaw and musculature associated with chewing. The members of the lineage seem to have developed an increasingly specialized feeding strategy that involved a diet—presumably fruit, nuts, seeds, stems, and shoots—that required heavy mastication.

A. africanus, the earlier member of the lineage, is best known from a series of South African sites that date between 3.0 and 2.5 million years ago. With the exception of the changes in their facial structure because of their increasingly specialized chewing apparatus, the members of this species were

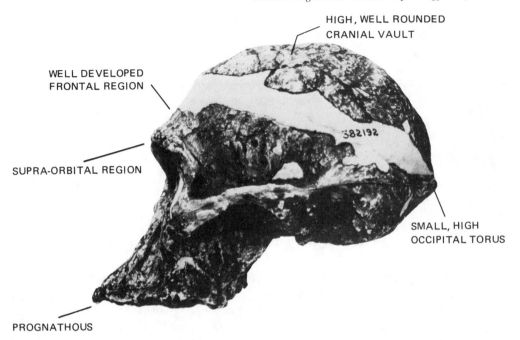

HIGH, WELL ROUNDED
CRANIAL VAULT

WELL DEVELOPED
FRONTAL REGION

SUPRA-ORBITAL REGION

SMALL, HIGH
OCCIPITAL TORUS

PROGNATHOUS

The cranium of *Australopithecus africanus*, the small gracile australopithecine that appeared in the fossil record about 2.5 million years ago.

probably not too different in appearance from their immediate ancestors. *A. robustus* and *A. boisei*, the later members of the lineage, are known, respectively, from South and East African fossil deposits, which date between about 2.4 and 1.0 million years ago. These species were also sexually dimorphic, and some individuals weighed between 70 and 100 pounds. They had enormous cheek teeth and jaws, compared with those of modern human beings. The muscles that supported these structures and provided the power for chewing were attached well up on the top of the skull; the result was that a number of the robust australopithecines had a sagittal crest on the top of the skull.

The australopithecines became extinct about a million years ago. It is clear that these tropical hominids were preyed on by large cats and packs of wild dogs. However, predation was probably not why they ultimately became extinct. It is one way in which population size is regulated, but predator and prey do not compete with each other for food. It is more likely that competition was the major factor in the extinction of the australopithecines. Their competitors may well have been terrestrial cercopithecine monkeys—like baboons—that radiated at this time and were able to use the plant food resources of the park savannas of eastern and southern Africa more efficiently than the australopithecines.

The other hominid lineage, which appeared about 2.5 million years ago, evolved into modern human beings. The three species, *Homo habilis, H. erec-*

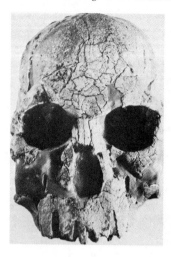

Front view of the skull of *Homo habilis*.

tus, and *H. sapiens*, form a single continuum characterized by considerable geographic variation through time. The members of this lineage gradually created a new, distinctly human ecological niche. *H. habilis*, the earliest representative of the lineage, is known from a series of East African localities that date between 1.5 and 2.5 million years ago. Their teeth—relatively small molars and broader incisors—suggest that their food required less mastication than that of their robust australopithecine contemporaries and imply that the feeding strategies of the two lineages were becoming increasingly differentiated. Their brains had volumes of 635 to 780 cubic centimeters—roughly 25 to 50 percent larger than those of the australopithecines. The presence of an indentation on the interior surface of a *H. habilis* skull corresponds to Broca's area of the brain—a center that controls the production of words and word sequences—and suggests that *H. habilis* were already using spoken language to communicate information. The presence of chipped-stone tools at 2-million-year-old archaeological sites indicates that they had the intellectual capacity and motor skills to make and use these tools on a regular basis.

   H. erectus, the next structural stage in human evolution, ranges in age from about 2.0 million to about 300,000 to 400,000 years old. The oldest specimens come from localities near Omo and Turkana in East Africa, from South Africa, and from the Djetis Beds in Java. Not surprisingly they resemble contemporary *H. habilis* specimens from Olduvai Gorge and Turkana, whereas the later ones resemble *H. sapiens*.

   The differences between *H. habilis* and *H. erectus* indicate that two interrelated sets of changes were taking place. The jaws and teeth of the hominids were becoming smaller, but their brains were becoming larger. The cranial capacities of the early *H. erectus* specimens average about 800 cubic centimeters, whereas those of some of the later specimens range from 850 to more than 1,400 cubic centimeters and average over 1,000 cubic centimeters. Their brains expanded differentially during this period. The parietal and temporal lobes—which are associated with motor skills and adaptive

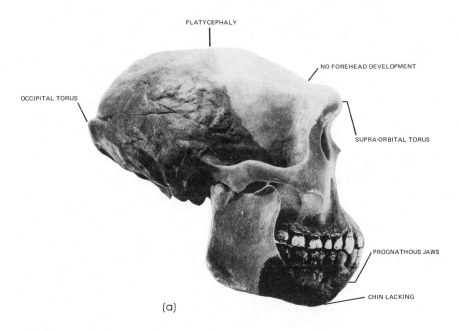

PLATYCEPHALY

NO FOREHEAD DEVELOPMENT

OCCIPITAL TORUS

SUPRA-ORBITAL TORUS

PROGNATHOUS JAWS

CHIN LACKING

(a)

Homo erectus was the first hominid to reside outside the tropics.

behavior—expanded more rapidly than the rest of the brain. As a result, the shape of the skull also changed, becoming higher and more rounded, and the frontal region became less flattened.

The remains of *H. erectus* in Europe and China show that hominids were beginning to live in temperate areas outside the African tropics. Fossils from Java indicate that humans inhabited Southeast Asia by 1.2 to 0.9 million years ago. Stone tools made more than 730,000 years ago have been found in central Italy, and stone implements found at Soleihac, France, may be 900,000 years old. These data indicate that our fossil ancestors had already begun to move into the temperate regions by a million years ago. One way they survived in temperate regions was by living in caves and building fires to provide heat and light. Cooking may also have originated during this period.

The major structural changes that have occurred in the human lineage during the past 300,000 years have been confined largely to the shape of the head. The cranial capacities of the archaic *H. sapiens*, that lived 300,000 years ago, averaged about 1,200 cubic centimeters. Those of modern *H. sapiens* average about 1,450 to 1,500 cubic centimeters. The older forms resembled *H. erectus* specimens, which is not surprising since there was evolutionary continuity between ourselves and the *H. erectus* populations that lived before us. In general, our faces have become flatter, our brow ridges less pronounced, and the backs of our skulls more rounded.

The archaic *H. sapiens* lived between 70,000 and 300,000 years ago. Their remains have been found in Indonesia, Europe, and Africa. Although all of the remains are quite fragmentary, it is clear that the major difference between the earlier and later specimens was the size of their brains. The archaic *H. sapiens*, taking both the earlier and the later forms, were remarkably similar in appearance in spite of the differences in their cranial volumes. This fact suggests that populations living in different parts of the world were subjected to the same selection pressures during this period.

The later archaic *H. sapiens* gave rise to a highly varied series of local populations. Anatomically modern *H. sapiens*, similar to contemporary human beings, are known to have existed in Africa and the Middle East about 100,000 years ago and in western Europe about 40,000 years ago. Between 70,000 and 45,000 years ago, the sheltered, well-watered valleys of western Europe were occupied by a relatively homogeneous series of fossils known as Neanderthals, who have provided us with the popular stereotype of the caveman: a short, brutish-looking fellow with a sloping forehead and a receding chin who stood at the entrance of his lair dressed in a bear skin with a wooden club resting on his shoulder. Neanderthals lived in regions just outside the borders of the frozen ground and tundra vegetation that covered much of northern and western Europe during the early part of the last glaciation. The individuals of the population had large cranial capacities—larger than those of modern humans—but their heads were shaped differently. Their skulls bulged along the sides and backs, and their foreheads sloped. They had prominent cheekbones, large brow ridges, and receding chins. They were short, with thick, barrel-like chests and short, stubby extremities. Many of their physical characteristics are also found among modern populations that live in cold environments; these features are usually interpreted as adaptations to cold conditions. The early part of the last glacial

Side view of an archaic *Homo sapiens* skull found near Steinheim, Germany, in deposits that are 150–200,000 years old.

cycle was the first time human beings lived continuously in exceptionally cold areas.

Three theories were proposed in the 1980s to account for the origins of modern human beings. The first, which has been called the African sapiens model, argues that modern humans evolved from late archaic *Homo sapiens* populations in Africa and were already present in southern and eastern Africa by 100,000 years ago. Some of the populations moved out of Africa as a result of environmental changes and hybridized with contemporary human groups in Eurasia. The second theory, labeled the recent African evolution model, argues that the transition to modern *Homo sapiens* occurred only in Africa, that the transition involved speciation, and that some modern human populations replaced local archaic *H. sapiens* populations in Eurasia; as a result, there was little or no continuity across the archaic-modern transition outside of Africa. The third theory, called the multiregional evolution model, claims that there is significant evidence for regional continuities between archaic and modern *H. sapiens* fossils in different parts of the world; this model implies that there were transitional forms, that the transition involved gene recombination rather than replacment or speciation, and that human populations in different parts of the world were being subjected to some of the same selection pressures.

These models were originally formulated on the basis of fossil evidence. However, since 1987, some paleoanthropologists have attempted to buttress their arguments with data derived from genetic and molecular studies, including those of mitochrondial DNA, which is inherited exclusively through women. Such appropriations are fraught with a variety of problems and have yielded contradictory and controversial results, which have typically been reported in overly simplistic terms by the mass media.

Fully modern human beings appeared in the fossil record about 40,000 years ago in Borneo and at various localities in the Near East. The first fully modern human skeletons in western Europe are about 35,000 years old— roughly the same age as a Neanderthal skeleton from St. Césaire in France. During the last 30,000 to 40,000 years, human beings also moved across the narrow water barriers that separated Australia and North America from the Eurasian landmass. With these movements, human beings occupied the last major uninhabited portions of the world.

FURTHER READINGS: A BRIEF GUIDE

The ideas of evolutionary biology and the social contexts in which they emerged are discussed by Peter J. Bowler, *Evolution: The History of an Idea* (Berkeley: University of California Press, 1984), and *The Mendelian Revolution: The Emergence of Hereditarian Concepts in Modern Science and Society* (Baltimore: Johns Hopkins University Press, 1989); and Marjorie Grene, ed., *Dimensions of Darwinism: Themes and Counterthemes in Twentieth-Century Evolutionary Theory* (Cambridge: Cambridge University Press, 1983).

G. Evelyn Hutchinson, *The Ecological Theater and the Evolutionary Play* (New Haven, CT: Yale University Press, 1965); and Richard Levins and Richard Lewontin, *The Dialectical Biologist* (Cambridge, MA: Harvard University Press, 1985), discuss the interconnections of ecology and evolutionary biology. Richard Levins, *Evolution in Changing Environments: Some Theoretical Explorations* (Princeton, NJ: Princeton University Press, 1968), presents an advanced analysis of diversity and development in changing environments.

Recent surveys of primate and human evolution are Russell L. Ciochon and Robert S. Corruccini, eds., *New Interpretations of Ape and Human Ancestry* (New York: Plenum Press, 1983); Eric Delson, ed., *Ancestors: The Hard Evidence* (New York: Alan R. Liss, 1984); and John G. Fleagle, *Primate Adaptation and Evolution* (San Diego: University of California Press, 1988). David Pilbeam spells out his scenario of Late Miocene hominoid evolution in "Distinguished Lecture: Hominoid Evolution and Hominoid Origins," *American Anthropologist*, vol. 88, no. 2 (1986), 295–312.

The early hominids are discussed by F. E. Grine, ed., *Evolutionary History of the Robust Australopithecines* (Hawthorne, NY: Aldine, 1988); and B. A. Wood, L. Martin, and P. Andrews, eds., *Major Topics in Primate and Human Evolution* (Cambridge: Cambridge University Press, 1986). Aspects of early hominid evolution are examined by Robert J. Blumenshine, "Characteristics of an Early Hominid Scavenging Niche," *Current Anthropology*, vol. 28, no. 3 (1987), 383–406; D. Falk, "Hominid Paleoneurology," *Annual Review of Anthropology*, vol. 16 (1987), 13–30; Tim D. White and Gen Suwa, "Hominids' Footprints at Laetoli: Facts and Interpretations," *American Journal of Physical Anthropology*, vol. 72, no. 4 (1987), 485–515; and Adrienne L. Zihlman, "A Behavioral Reconstruction of Australopithecus," in *Hominid Origins: Inquiries Past and Present*, ed. Kathleen J. Reichs (Lanham: University Presses of America, 1983), pp. 207–238.

Current thought about *Homo erectus* is examined by G. Philip Rightmire, *The Evolution of Homo Erectus*: Comparative Anatomical Studies of an Extinct Human Species (Cambridge: Cambridge University Press, 1990); and Geoffrey G. Pope, "Recent Advances in Far Eastern Paleoanthropology," *Annual Review of Anthropology*, vol. 17 (1988), 43–77.

Fred H. Smith, Anthony B. Falsetti, and Steven M. Donnelly, "Modern Human Origins," *Yearbook of Physical Anthropology*, vol. 32 (1989), 35–68, survey recent theories and relevant data concerning the origins of modern human beings. Günter Braüer, "A Craniological Approach to the Origin of Anatomically Modern *Homo sapiens* in Africa and Implications for the Appearance of Modern Europeans," in *The Origins of Modern Humans: A World Survey of the Fossil Evidence*, ed. Fred Smith and Frank Spencer (New York: Alan R. Liss, 1984), formulates the Afro-European sapiens hypothesis; Chris B. Stringer and P. Andrews, "Genetic and Fossil Evidence for the Origin of Modern Humans," *Science*, vol. 239 (1988), 1263–1268, discuss the recent African evolution and replacement hypothesis; Milford Wolpoff, "Multiregional Evolution: The Fossil Alternative to Eden," in *The Human Revolution: Behavioural and Biological Perspectives in the Origins of Modern Humans*, ed. Paul

Mellars and Chris Stringer (Princeton, NJ: Princeton University Press, 1989), pp. 62–108, and "The Place of Neanderthals in Human Evolution," in *The Emergence of Modern Humans: Biocultural Adaptations in the Later Pleistocene*, ed. Eric Trinkaus (Cambridge: Cambridge University Press, 1989), pp. 97–141, discusses the multiregional model and the role of gene exchange. The molecular and genetic evidence used to support the migration, displacement, and discontinuity models is examined by Shahin Rouhani, "Molecular Genetics and the Pattern of Human Evolution: Plausible and Implausible Models," in *The Human Revolution: Behavioural and Biological Perspectives in the Origins of Modern Humans*, ed. Paul Mellars and Chris Stringer (Princeton, NJ: Princeton University Press, 1989), pp. 47–61.

appendix C

The Changing Environments
of the Pleistocene World

Our immediate fossil ancestors appeared and lived during the later part of the Cenozoic era—the age of the mammals—which began about 65 million years ago. The Cenozoic has been characterized by rapidly changing climatic conditions, culminating in the dramatic fluctuations of the Pleistocene epoch—when intensely cold ice ages, each lasting tens of millennia, alternated with interglacial periods, lasting about 10,000 years each, which had climates resembling those of the present time. The Holocene epoch, which began about 10 millennia ago, is the most recent interglacial period.

The first thing that comes to mind about the Pleistocene epoch is the periodic formation of ice sheets, which grew to continental proportions in the upper latitudes of the northern hemisphere, and mountain glaciers, which grew to varying sizes at higher elevations in the temperate and tropical regions of the world. Other important changes also occurred during the glacial periods. Global climates were different, sea levels were lower, drainage systems consisting of lakes and rivers were different, and major natural environments—like tundra, tropical forests, savannas, and deserts—had very different configurations and were often far removed from their current locations.

THE CAUSES OF THE ICE AGES

The changing environments of the Pleistocene epoch formed the stage on which human beings evolved and enriched their culture-laden capacities. The environmental changes that occurred were complex, the product of numerous historically constituted processes and contingent events. The interplay of two factors was especially important in the changes that occurred during the

Pleistocene. One involved variations in the amounts and kinds of solar energy reaching the earth. The other involved ocean-floor spreading, continental drift, and the appearance of new physical features on the earth's surface.

The meteorologist H. H. Lamb (1961:124) described the relationship between solar radiation and climate in the following manner:

> Solar radiation supplies the energy, and the terrestrial atmospheric circulation is the mechanism of climate. . . . It is atmospheric circulation that produces weather and explains the distribution of such events as orographic rainfall, snow and snowfields, thermal instability, thunderstorms and tropical hurricanes, the extent of oceanic, continental, and arid climates.

Thus, changes in the kinds of solar radiation and their intensity produce changes in the world's climatic conditions by altering the patterns of atmospheric circulation. Over a period of time, these can produce changes in the size, shape, and location of major biogeographic regions—for example, deserts, grasslands, or forests.

Paleobotanical, paleontological, and sedimentary evidence indicate that the patterns of atmospheric circulation at the height of the last glacial period differed in at least one important way from those that prevail today. There was an equatorward displacement and compression of all zonal wind systems resulting from the enormous expansion of polar circulation. This difference had numerous consequences.

Daily or seasonal weather patterns that are now typical in a particular place may have been unusual or absent during the last glacial maximum. For example, the climate of the Chilean coast immediately south of Santiago is now dominated by a dry, cool air mass during the summer and by a moist, maritime air mass associated with westerly winds during the winter; consequently, summers are dry and winters are rainy in this area at the present time. However, during the last glacial cycle, the dry, cool air mass, which is associated with a high-pressure cell over the eastern Pacific Ocean, was displaced northward toward the equator, and the dominant air mass throughout the year was the moist maritime one; as a result, precipitation was abundant throughout the year instead of being seasonal, as it is now. The differences between the modern and glacial climatic regimes affect the biogeographic habitats that can exist in this area. The present climatic regime favors the development of scrub steppe—a community of plant species particularly well adapted to warm, dry summers and cool, wet winters. The climatic regime that existed during the last glacial cycle led to the northward spread of the temperate rain forest—a plant community that requires cool, wet conditions throughout the year—and its establishment in an area covered with scrub steppe when interglacial climatic conditions prevail.

In the mid-1960s, earth scientists began to recognize that the earth's surface was not a rigid body with fixed continents and ocean basins. They became aware, instead, that it is a brittle crust, made up of a number of larger and smaller plates that are in constant motion and interaction with one another; the plates collide, get stuck together, break apart, and disappear.

The theory of plate tectonics, as the new view is called, provides a framework for understanding the underlying mechanism and relationship of the earth's physical features—its continents, ocean basins, ocean trenches, mountain systems, earthquake zones, and volcanoes. The motion of the plates and their interaction mean that the shapes of the continents as well as their locations relative to one another and to the equator and poles of rotation have shifted through time; they also mean that the various physical features of the Earth's surface—for example, mountain ranges—are transient.

Let us briefly consider how plate tectonics and changes in solar radiation and atmospheric circulation interacted during the Cenozoic. The earth was much warmer 65 million years ago than it is today. Mean annual temperatures were about 10° to 15° C higher, and the temperature differences between the equator and the poles were about half of today's gradient. Consequently, tropical conditions extended to the 45th parallel, and even the polar regions had mild climates, which permitted the growth of temperate rain forests resembling those currently found in coastal British Columbia. This condition suggests that more and/or different kinds of solar radiation reached the Earth's surface. The positions, spatial relations, and surface features of the various landmasses indicate that the patterns of atmospheric circulation were also profoundly different from those today.

The earth's climate began to cool about 65 million years ago, as the continental landmasses were slowly beginning to assume their present positions and spatial relations and as heat transfer between equatorial and polar regions became less efficient. However, there still were no ice sheets anywhere on the earth's surface 50 million years ago. There were at least two reasons for this. First, a belt of warm tropical oceans extended completely around the earth's equatorial region: The waters of the tropical Pacific merged with those of the Panamanian Sea, which separated North and South America, and the Tethys Sea, the forerunner of the Mediterranean, which separated Africa and Eurasia. Second, high mountain ranges—like the Alps, Atlas, Himalayas, Andes, and Rockies—which block and effectively modify atmospheric circulation either had not yet formed or had only limited elevations. Thus heat transfer from the tropical to polar regions was still relatively efficient.

As the global temperatures declined, the contrast between polar and equatorial temperatures became increasingly marked, particularly after the Drake Passage, which separates South America and Antarctica, opened about 30 million years ago, permitting the formation of a circumpolar ocean current around Antarctica. This current, coupled with the closure of the tropical Panamanian and Tethys seas, restricted the southward transfer of heat. As a result, the Antarctic landmass became increasingly cold, and permanent ice sheets began to accumulate in the interior and slowly inched their way toward the ocean through valleys that dissected the temperate forests covering some of the low-lying coastal regions.

Cold water, resulting from large quantities of meltwater and sea ice, began to accumulate around 15 million years ago in the ocean deeps around

Antarctica. Portions of this cold, ocean-bottom water were deflected northward and upwelled along the west coasts of Africa, South America, and Australia. These cold, upwelling currents brought dry conditions to the west coastal regions of the southern continents; as a result, the Namibian Desert of Southwest Africa, the Atacama and coastal Peruvian deserts of South America, and the western desert of Australia came into existence about 10 million years ago.

About 14 million years ago, the collision of the African and Eurasian plates uplifted the Atlas Mountains and closed the Straits of Gibraltar. The Mediterranean, which was deprived and eventually cut off from Atlantic Ocean water and runoff from North Africa and the Black Sea drainage, became an enormous inland evaporating basin, resembling the Great Salt Lake. Six million years ago, the sea floor of the Mediterranean was salt-covered desert dotted with brine-filled holes. Atlantic waters breached Gibraltar about 3 million years ago, and the enormous waterfall, which dwarfed Niagara, slowly refilled the Mediterranean Basin over the next million years. These tectonic events were coupled with shifts in the patterns of atmospheric circulation, which resulted in more rainfall over central Africa and the Guinea coast and increased aridity over the northern portion of the continent.

The last 10 million years also witnessed other episodes of mountain building. The Himalayas formed rapidly after the Indian subcontinent, long an island fragment of the old southern supercontinent, collided with Eurasia. The Rockies, Andes, and Alps mountains, as well as the Tibetan Plateau and the Great Basin, were all thrust upward during this period and gradually transformed the existing patterns of atmospheric circulation. Glaciers slowly began to accumulate in the upland areas, first in Alaska about 9 to 10 million years ago and then, a few million years later, in central Asia, northern North America, and the cordillera of southern South America. The Antarctic ice sheet reached its maximum extent about 6 million years ago. Mountain glaciers and small continental ice sheets were beginning to accumulate about 2.5 to 3.0 million years ago in the higher latitudes and at higher elevations throughout the northern and southern hemispheres. By this time, cooling had already progressed to the point at which icebergs were dropping debris scraped up by the glaciers into marine sediments located far from the polar regions. Although the temperatures in the middle latitudes of the northern hemisphere were significantly cooler than they had been 60 million years earlier, they were still somewhat warmer than those of the present day.

THE PLEISTOCENE WORLD

By international agreement, geologists date the beginning of the Pleistocene to the time when cooling conditions were first recorded in marine sediments in southern Italy, which have been raised above sea level by tectonic movement. Geologists believe that these sediments were formed about 1.8 million years ago, which is approximately the same time that the earth's polarity shifted from normal to reversed—that is, compass needles began to point toward the south magnetic pole. The earth's polarity returned to normal about 730,000 years ago. Although the mechanisms underlying changes in the earth's polarity are not clear, the changes themselves are events that occur on a worldwide scale; they are also recorded in deep-sea cores and in iron-bearing, volcanic rocks, which can be dated with isotopic dating methods, like uranium or potassium argon.

Studies of the cores of marine sediments taken from various ocean floors preserve the earth's magnetic record and provide two kinds of information about climate change: (1) shifts in the ratio of oxygen isotopes absorbed in the skeletons (calcium carbonate) of small marine organisms called foraminifera and (2) changes in the composition of these fossil plankton assemblages. During periods of glacial climate, the lighter oxygen 16 isotope evaporates more rapidly from ocean water than the heavier oxygen 18 isotope and becomes concentrated in ice sheets. Therefore seawater and the skeletons of marine organisms become enriched with oxygen 18 during cooler periods: the colder the water, the greater the proportion of oxygen 18. Thus, when cores are taken from marine sediments or from glaciers, the relative abundance of oxygen 18 can be used as an indicator of the temperature that prevailed at that place at a given time in the past.

A sea core, V28–239, from the Solomon Rise in the South Pacific is 21 meters long, and the fossil assemblages contained in its sediments record climate changes over the past 2.1 million years. The oscillations of warm and cold climates preserved in this core are similar to the pattern preserved in the composite record yielded by cores from the Caribbean. Core V28–239 indicates that there were seven glacial periods during the last 700,000 years, each of which was separated by a much shorter interglacial period with an average duration of about 10,000 years. The glacial periods that occurred before 800,000 years ago had much shorter durations than those that occurred later, and the accompanying falls in sea level were not as great as those produced by the later glaciations.

Studies of loess sediments, layers of windblown dust, that were deposited under dry, cold conditions along the banks of the Danube River in Czechoslovakia and Austria yielded a climatic record comparable to the one found in the sea cores. This lowland area of central Europe was situated between the Scandinavian ice sheet and the glacier system of the Alps. During glacial periods, when the climate was cold and vegetation was sparse, enormous quantities of loess were deposited in the Danube and other river valleys of central Europe. When the glaciers retreated and the climate warmed, grass and trees covered the top of the loess deposits, and rich organic soils formed. As a result, the deep deposits at Brno, Czechoslovakia, are composed of layers of soils derived from organic materials exposed to different conditions, alternating with layers of unweathered loess. In some instances, these layers contain pollen, plant remains, and snails, which can be dated by paleomagnetic techniques. The number of layers and their pattern of alternation correspond to those exhibited by the sea cores during the past 950,000 years.

One difficulty in studying the development of the various glacial periods on land is that each glaciation has successively destroyed much of the evidence left by each of its predecessors. Consequently, we know much more about the last glacial period and its effects than we do about the earlier ones. This cycle began with the last interglacial period, which lasted from 128,000 to 118,000 years ago. The global temperatures were 1° to 3° C warmer than now, and the seas stood at least 20 feet higher than their present level. The climate then cooled rapidly. By 115,000 years ago, ice sheets had already expanded rapidly in higher latitudes and sea level had declined by more than 250 feet. The cold conditions would intensify over long periods of time, recede for a few thousand years, and then intensify once again. The glaciation reached its maximum extent about 18,000 years ago, when sea level was 430 feet below the present shorelines and exposed vast areas of continental shelf. The North American and Scandinavian ice sheets began to retreat and break up about 14,000 years ago, and the seas rose rapidly, reaching or even slightly surpassing their current levels around 5,000 years ago.

The rapid falls in sea level imply that the ice sheets formed rapidly and locked up millions of cubic miles of water. Some of the ice sheets, such as the more than 15,000-feet-thick dome centered over the Laurentian highlands of eastern Canada, formed on and swept over land surfaces. These coalesced with thick ice sheets that formed over water and were held in place by islands and sections of sea ice that had grounded on the continental shelves exposed by lower sea levels. The marine-based portions of these ice masses were unstable because of iceberg calving, the action of waves, and the formation of drainage streams along their southern margins. Disintegration occurred rapidly following the onset of higher sea levels and warmer climatic conditions induced by increased amounts of solar radiation. The maritime portions broke up first; their disintegration was followed by the retreat of the continental ice sheets and mountain glaciers outside the polar regions. By 7,000 years ago, only remnants of the once massive continental ice sheets remained in the northern hemisphere: in the mountains of Scandinavia, on Labrador, in a small area west of Hudson Bay, and on Greenland.

Globally averaged, sea-surface temperatures differed by about 2.3° C between full glacial and modern conditions; however, the differences were not uniformly distributed. The largest change, a drop of more than 17° C, occurred in the Atlantic Ocean north of the 40th parallel. Land temperature differences between glacial maximum and modern conditions averaged about 4° to 9° C, and these, too, were unevenly distributed. Air temperatures over much of South America, Africa, India, Southeast Asia, and Australia were roughly 4° to 6° C lower than today; the greatest differences, more than 10° C, occurred in central Asia north of Tibet and in central North America. Judging by the kinds of tundra vegetation found around Boston about 12,000 years ago, the area had average January temperatures of about −31° C and

July temperatures of 10° C. Today, these months average −3° C and 22° C, respectively.

Lower sea and land temperatures in the tropical and subtropical regions imply lower evaporation rates and less rainfall in those parts of the world. Sand dunes were more widespread and active in these regions during glacial maxima, as were the subtropical trade winds. One effect of these changes was that the rain forests of Amazonia and Africa shrunk significantly during the last glacial maximum, retreating to isolated refugia in some instances, whereas the Southeast rain forests spread and survived on the exposed areas of the continental shelf.

The advance and retreat of glaciers transformed many of the world's drainage systems. Thousands of lakes were formed by water melting from the glaciers themselves or by increased precipitation, ice dams, or the migration of subterranean water. Extensive systems of glacial and postglacial lakes existed in the Great Lakes region of North America and in the Great Basin of the western United States. An enormous glacial lake stretched from the Black to the Aral seas, and two other glacial lake systems, both larger than the modern Mediterranean, formed south of the ice sheet in Russia and Siberia. The predecessor of Lake Chad, which formed in the southern Sahara in early postglacial times, was several times larger than its modern descendant.

Large areas of continental shelf were exposed because of the lower sea levels. The most extensive of these were the east coast of South America, the Caribbean, Australia and New Guinea, Indonesia, and Beringia—the region between Alaska, Siberia, the Aleutian Islands, and the Arctic Ocean. The lower sea levels had other consequences as well. Habitable coastal areas were much larger than they are now. River gradients increased, so that some inland and coastal regions, like the Nile or the Atrato River Basin between Colombia and Panama, were probably better drained than they are now. And the flow patterns of ocean currents—such as the Falkland Current, which moves off the southeast coast of South America—may have changed significantly because of the different shapes of the continents. Such shifts would have had important consequences for local environments.

Thus, the environmental conditions of the Pleistocene, the world of our fossil ancestors, were often very different from those of today.

FURTHER READINGS: A BRIEF GUIDE

The theory of plate tectonics and continental drift is discussed by J. M. Bird, *Plate Tectonics* (Washington, DC: American Geophysical Union, 1980); and J. Tuzo Wilson, ed., *Continents Adrift and Continents Aground: Readings from Scientific American* (San Francisco: W. H. Freeman, 1976). M. J. Selby, *Earth's Changing Surface: An Introduction to Geomorphology* (Oxford: Clarendon Press, 1985), integrates plate tectonic, climatic, and environmental information.

The patterns of atmospheric circulation are examined by H. H. Lamb, "Climatic Changes within Historical Times as Seen in the Circulation Maps and Diagrams," *Annals of the New York Academy of Sciences*, vol. 95, art. 1 (New York, 1961); Hurd Willett, "The General Circulation at the Last (Würm) *Glacial Maximum*," *Geografiska Annaler*, Band 32, Nos. 3–4 (1950), 179–187; and CLIMAP Project Members, "The Surface of the Ice-Age Earth," *Science*, vol. 191 (1976), 1131–1137.

The analyses of deep-sea cores are discussed by N. J. Shackleton and N. D. Opdyke, "Oxygen-Isotope and Paleomagnetic Stratigraphy of Pacific Core V28–239, Late Pliocene to Latest Pleistocene," *Geological Society of America Memoir*, no. 145 (Washington, 1976), pp. 449–464. G. J. Kukla, "The Loess Stratigraphy of Central Europe," in *After the Australopithecines*, ed. Karl W. Butzer and Glynn L. Isaac (The Hague: Mouton Publishers, 1975), pp. 99–188, presents his analysis of the loess deposits in central Europe.

More detailed introductions to the Pleistocene and its environments can be found in Andrew Goudie, *Environmental Change* (Oxford: Clarendon Press, 1983); Björn Kurtén, *Pleistocene Mammals in Europe* (Chicago: Aldine, 1968); Björn Kurtén and E. Anderson, *Pleistocene Mammals of North America* (New York: Columbia University Press, 1980); Paul S. Martin and Richard Klein, eds., *A Pleistocene Revolution* (Tucson: University of Arizona Press, 1984); Neil Roberts, "Pleistocene Environments in Time and Space," in *Hominid Evolution and Community Ecology: Prehistoric Human Adaptation in Biological Perspective*, ed. Robert Foley (Orlando, FL: Academic Press, 1984), pp. 25–53.

Acknowledgments

Photo p. 1: AP/Wide World Photos. **Epigram 1, p. 2:** *The Two Jakes*, written by Robert Towne. Copyright © 1990 by Paramount Pictures. All rights reserved. **Figures p. 11:** Reproduced by permission of the Trustees of the British Museum. **Photo p. 16:** The British Museum. **Photo p. 18:** AP/Wide World Photos. **Figure p. 20:** Max Uhle, *Pachacamac, p. 19.* **Photo p. 23:** © Richard Dibon-Smith, Photo Researchers. **Epigram 1, p. 24:** Ruth Bleier, *Feminist Approaches to Science* (New York: Pergamon Press), quote from p. 79. © 1986 by Pergamon Press. Reprinted by permission of the publisher. All rights reserved. **Photo p. 25:** Copyright 1975 Academic Press. **Figure p. 25:** *American Antiquity*, vol. 30, no. 2, 1964. Reproduced by permission of the Society for American Archaeology. **Figure p. 46:** *Nature*, 226, 1970. **Figure p. 48:** Jeffrey T. Laitman, "The Anatomy of Human Speech." *Natural History*, vol. 93, no. 8, 1984. **Figure p. 58:** Karl Butzer, *Archaeology as Human Ecology.* Copyright © 1982 Cambridge University Press. **Photo p. 63:** Prehistoric de l'Art Occidental. **Epigram 1, p. 64:** *American Anthropologist* 80:4, December 1978. Reproduced by permission of the Anthropological Association. Not for sale or further reproduction. **Epigram 2, p. 64:** Copyright © 1982 by Cambridge University Press. **Photo p. 76:** The American Museum of Natural History. **Figure p. 78:** Courtesy of Thomas Kehoe. Milwaukee Public Museum. **Figure p. 81, top:** Brian M. Fagan, *People of the Earth: An Anthropology of World Prehistory, 6/e.* Copyright © 1989 by the Lindbriar Corporation. Reprinted by permission of HarperCollins Publishers. **Figure p. 81, middle:** Brian M. Fagan, *People of the Earth.* **Figure p. 81, bottom:** Colin Renfrew and Paul Bahn, *Archaeology: Theories, Methods, and Practice* (New York: Thames and Hudson Ltd, 1991). **Photo p. 82:** Chester S. Chard, *Man in Prehistory, 2/e.* (New York: McGraw-Hill, 1974). **Photo p. 88:** AP/Wide World Photos. **Photo p. 107:** AP/Wide World Photos. **Epigram 3, p. 108:** Copyright © 1974 by Transaction, Inc. **Epigram 4, p. 108:** Copyright © 1974 by Academic Press. **Figure p. 110:** James Mellaart, *Earliest Civilizations of the Near East* (London: Thames and Hudson Ltd., 1975). **Photo p. 111:** Brian Fagan, People of the Earth. **Figure p. 113:** Copyright ©1975 by Thames and Hudson, Ltd. Used by permission of Charles Scribner's Sons. **Photo pp. 118–119:** M. E. L. Mallowan, *Early Mesopotamia and Iran* (London: Thames and Hudson Ltd., 1965). **Figure p. 120:** Hans J. Nissen, *The Early History of the Ancient Near East 9000–2000 B.C.* (Chicago: University of Chicago Press): 1988. **Photo p. 132:** Scala, Art Resource. **Epigram 2, p. 133:** Janet L. Abu-Lughod. Copyright © 1989 by Oxford University Press, Inc. Reprinted by permission. **Figures p. 144–146:** Mortimor Wheeler, *Civilizations of the Indus Valley and beyond* (London: Thames and Hudson Ltd., 1966). **Photo p. 154:** Courtesy of the Cultural Relics Bureau, Peking, and the Metropolitan Museum of Art. **Photo p. 158:** Copyright 1977 by the Archaeological Institute of America. **Photo p. 169:** © Michal Heron, 1982. **Photo p. 182:** Bill Cella, Photo Researchers. **Photo p. 186:** The Museum of Primitive Art. **Epigram 1, p. 187:** Copyright © 1989 by Transaction, Inc. **Epigram 2, p. 187:** Copyright©1983 by Cambridge University Press. **Epigram 3, p. 187:** English translation copyright by Lawrence Hill Books, 1974. Reprinted by permission of the publisher, Lawrence Hill Books (Brooklyn, NY). **Epigram 4, p. 187:** Copyright © 1989 by Monthly Review Press. Reprinted by permission of Monthly Review Foundation. **Photo p. 197:** Courtesy of the Museum of Science, Boston. **Figure p. 202:** S.K. & R.J. McIntosh, "Stone to Metal: New Perspectives on the Later Prehistory of West Africa," Journal of World Prehistory, vol. 2, no. 1. Copyright 1988 by Plenum Publishing Corporation. **Photo p. 204:** Blair Seitz, Art Resource. **Photo p. 208:** © Eugene Gordon 1985. **Photo p. 227:** © Archivi Alinari 1992, Art Resource. **Epigram 3, p. 228:** Copyright 1971 by Chatto & Windus. **Epigram 4, p. 228:** Reprinted by permission of Duckworth. **Figure p. 233:** Reproduced by permission of Williams & James, London, England. **Epigram 1, p. 252:** Copyright © 1985 by Sir Moses Finley. All rights reserved. Used by permission of Viking Penguin, a division of Penguin Books USA Inc. **Epigram 2, p. 252:** Excerpt from *Arthur Rimbaud: Complete Works*, Paul Schmidt, ed., trans. Copyright © 1967, 1970, 1972, 1975 by Paul Schmidt. Reprinted by permission of HarperCollins Publishers. **Epigram 3, p. 252:** Reprinted by permission of Duckworth. **Figure p. 255:** Ruth Tringham, *Hunters, Fishers, and Farmers of Eastern Europe, 6000–3000 BC* (London: Hutchinson University Library, 1971). **Photo p. 258:** Department of the Environment. **Figures pp. 265–266:** Copyright © 1984 by Academic Press. **Figure p. 268:** T.G.E. Powell, *The Celts* (London: Thames and Hudson Ltd. 1980). **Photo p. 274:** Smithsonian Institution, National Anthropological Archives. **Epigram 1, p. 275:** Copyright © 1968 by Grove Weidenfeld. **Epigram 2, p. 275:** Copyright © 1960 by Columbia University Press, New York. Used by permission of the publisher. **Photo p. 279:** Reproduced by permission of the Society for American Archaeology from *Memoirs of the Society for American Archaeology, no. 26,* 1972. **Figure p. 289:** Painting by William R. Iseminger. **Figures p. 292:** Copyright © 1974 McGraw-Hill Book Company. Used by permission. **Photo p. 299:** George Holton, Photo Researchers. **Photo p. 304:** Copyright© 1968 by the National Geographic Society. **Figure p. 305:** Copyright © 1968 by the American Heritage Publishing Company. **Photo p. 307:** Courtesy of Richard E. Blanton, Purdue University. **Figure p. 310 & Photo p. 311:** Copyright © 1973 by Rene Millon. **Photo p. 314:** Giraudon, Art Resource. **Figure p. 318:** Courtesy of the American Museum of Natural History. **Photo p. 327:** Braniff International. **Figure p. 333:** *Early Ceremonial Architecture in the Andes*, Christopher B. Donnan, ed. Dumbarton Oaks. Trustees for Harvard University, Washington, D.C., 1985. **Figure p. 339:** Yale University Publications in Anthropology, copyright © 1953. **Figure p. 341:** Copyright © 1877 by Harper & Row. **Figure p. 349:** Smithsonian Institution. **Epigram 3, p. 350:** Copyright © 1986 by Cambridge University Press. **Figure p. 351:** Copper engraving published by Olfert Dapper. General Research Division. The New York Public Library. Astor, Lenox and Tilden Foundations. **Figure p. 352:** Copper engraving by Theodor de Bry. Rare Books and Manuscripts Division. The New York Public Library. Astor, Lenox and Tilden Foundations. **Photo p. 357:** London News Picture Library. **Photo p. 359, top:** Library of Congress. **Photo p. 359, bottom:** AP/Wide World Photos. **Figure p. 370:** Copyright © 1974 by McGraw-Hill Book Company. Used by permission. **Photo p. 386:** Courtesy of Robert Harding Picture Library. **Photo p. 387:** Courtesy of the American Museum of Natural History. **Photo p. 388:** Courtesy of S.I. Rosen.

Index

6904